John Fante's *Ask the Dust*

Critical Studies in Italian America

Nancy C. Carnevale and Laura E. Ruberto, *series editors*

This series publishes works on the history and culture of Italian Americans by emerging as well as established scholars in fields such as anthropology, cultural studies, folklore, history, and media studies. While focusing on the United States, it also includes comparative studies with other areas of the Italian diaspora. The books in this series engage with broader questions of identity pertinent to the fields of ethnic studies, gender studies, and migration studies, among others.

Series Board:
Marcella Bencivenni
Simone Cinotto
Thomas J. Ferraro
Edvige Giunta
Joseph Sciorra
Pasquale Verdicchio

John Fante's *Ask the Dust*

A Joining of Voices and Views

Stephen Cooper and
Clorinda Donato, Editors

FORDHAM UNIVERSITY PRESS
NEW YORK 2020

Copyright © 2020 Fordham University Press

All rights reserved. No part of this publication may be reproduced, stored in a retrieval system, or transmitted in any form or by any means—electronic, mechanical, photocopy, recording, or any other—except for brief quotations in printed reviews, without the prior permission of the publisher.

Fordham University Press has no responsibility for the persistence or accuracy of URLs for external or third-party Internet websites referred to in this publication and does not guarantee that any content on such websites is, or will remain, accurate or appropriate.

Fordham University Press also publishes its books in a variety of electronic formats. Some content that appears in print may not be available in electronic books.

Visit us online at www.fordhampress.com.

Library of Congress Cataloging-in-Publication Data available online at https://catalog.loc.gov.

Printed in the United States of America
22 21 20   5 4 3 2 1
First edition

I dedicate this work to my parents, Jennie and Franco Donato, who came west from Chicago to the San Fernando Valley to make their two daughters, Nina and me, Italian Americans for whom the cultural landscape of John Fante's Ask the Dust *resonates profoundly. I also dedicate it to my husband, Sergio Guarro, who came from Italy, and to our children, Marcello, Adriana, and Gianluca.* —C.D.

For Janet, Daniel, Lizzy, and the whole family. —S.C.

CONTENTS

Introduction — 1

1. New Approaches to John Fante's *Ask the Dust*

From the Particular to the Universal: Vittorini's Italian Adaptation of *Ask the Dust* — 15
  Valerio Ferme

When Spirituality Ebbs and Flows: Religion and Diasporic Alienation in *Ask the Dust* — 43
  Suzanne Manizza Roszak

"Sad Flower in the Sand": Camilla Lopez and the Erasure of Memory in *Ask the Dust* — 58
  Meagan Meylor

"A *Ramona* in Reverse": Writing the Madness of the Spanish Past in *Ask the Dust* — 83
  Daniel Gardner

2. Sibling Arts: *Ask the Dust* in Dance, Music, the Graphic Novel, and French

Dancing with the Dust: Translating *Ask the Dust* to the Stage — 111
  J'aime Morrison

Ask the Lyrics: John Fante in Music — 127
  Chiara Mazzucchelli

Watch Out or You'll End up in My Novel: The Lost World
of *Ask the Dust* — 145
   Robert Guffey

Don't Ask the French — 157
   Philippe Garnier

3. *Ask the Dust* and Its Effects: Readers and Writers Respond

Amid the Dust — 167
   Miriam Amico

The Passion That Became a Festival — 177
   Giovanna DiLello

I Had Bandini: Reading *Ask the Dust* in Prison — 193
   Joel Williams

Writing in the Dust — 201
   Alan Rifkin

How Hitler Nearly Destroyed the Great American Novel — 213
   Ryan Holiday

4. *Ask the Dust* and Its Due: Two Filmmakers and Bukowski Pay Tribute

Interview with Robert Towne — 237
   Nathan Rabin

Letters from Los Angeles — 245
   Jan Louter

"My Dear Bukowski," "Hello John Fante": Preface to *Ask the Dust* — 261
   John Fante and Charles Bukowski

5. The Attic, the Archive, and Beyond

From Family to Institutional Memory: A Conversation
with Stephen Cooper — 273
   Teresa Fiore

Prelude to "Prologue to *Ask the Dust*" — 281
   Stephen Cooper

Goodbye, Bunker Hill *John Fante*	290
The Road to John Fante's Los Angeles *Stephen Cooper*	296
Acknowledgments	315
List of Contributors	319
Bibliography	325
Index	331

Introduction

When John Fante's *Ask the Dust* appeared in November 1939, it did not seem destined for great things. The enthusiasm that had greeted his debut novel *Wait Until Spring, Bandini* one year earlier was now missing from the major reviews, which ran from grudging acknowledgment to condescension. The *New York Times* conceded the book was "a novel experience." But on the whole, novels about novelists, particularly young novelists, make a tour de force rather than a naturally interesting story."[1] The *Saturday Review of Literature* paid a similar backhanded compliment. "It is charming, it is fantasy, and it isn't real. In our own way of thinking, Mr. Fante has done enough of this. It is past spring now and time for Bandini to feel the really great pangs of mortality."[2]

Such faint praise did little to ameliorate the effects of the bruising legal battle waged by Fante's publisher, the small Pennsylvania-based firm of Stackpole Sons, in its campaign to expose the vilest schemes of Adolf Hitler by bringing out an unauthorized, unexpurgated version of his *Mein Kampf* in the same year as *Ask the Dust*. "These days I have not time nor thought nor energy for anything but communion with Adolf of Munich," harried Stackpole editor William Soskin wrote Fante in early 1939, even as Fante, far away in Los Angeles, was diving into the dreamwork of writing *Ask the Dust*. "If we can ever get clear of the lawyers and sheriffs," Soskin went on, "that Kampf of his will be a sensation."[3]

In the end, Stackpole lost the lawsuit, a fortune in attorney fees, and most of the focus that might have been trained on a properly funded publicity campaign, and *Ask the Dust* entered the world with little fanfare. Soon the horrors of World War II were displacing those of the Great Depression, and *Ask the Dust*, with its poetic evocation of that era and its casualties, plummeted into out-of-print oblivion.

Except for a twenty-five-cent Bantam paperback edition of *Ask the Dust* that came and went in 1954, that oblivion would last for the next forty years. For his part Fante bore the indignity with a characteristic mix of cynicism and bravado even as he endeavored to save the novel from vanishing. Both before and after its publication, he and Bill Soskin tried to interest various Hollywood producers in a movie version, with no success. In 1941 Fante teamed up with B-film director Norman Foster to write a screenplay based on *Ask the Dust* that enticed no takers, while on his own Fante worked up a radio adaptation for the *Lady Esther* variety hour that the show's host, Orson Welles, never got around to broadcasting. Years later, in the sixties, the wish for a film version resurfaced and Fante dug in again, this time with frequent collaborator Harry Essex (whose fervid imagination lay behind such Cold War chillers as *It Came from Outer Space* and *Creature from the Black Lagoon*) on another *Ask the Dust* screenplay that never got off the ground. In the early seventies Fante optioned the novel's film rights to up-and-coming screenwriter Robert Towne but the gambit would come to nothing in Fante's lifetime. As late as 1974 John was begging lifelong friend Carey McWilliams, the former Los Angeles activist who was by then in New York editing *The Nation*, to help court the interest of small-press publishers in bringing out a new edition of the novel. "I would give both testicles," Fante pledged in a desperate letter to McWilliams, "if the editors could be persuaded to do my *Ask the Dust*."[4]

The net result of all these efforts was so much wasted time, and yet the record could not be clearer: Fante believed in *Ask the Dust*, knew that in the tragic romance of Arturo and Camilla he had achieved something extraordinary, and strived, struggled, and repeatedly failed to save it from being forgotten.

Enter Charles Bukowski. By now the story is well known of how in 1978 the street-poet laureate of Los Angeles convinced his publisher, John Martin, that Fante was no figment of Bukowski's wine-soaked imagination but rather one of the greats. When at last *Ask the Dust* reappeared in 1980 from California's Black Sparrow Press with a preface by Bukowski, Fante was slowly dying from the ravages of diabetes. The book's rebirth, however, together with the fervent local response that welcomed it, worked upon him a miracle of revival. Although now blind, legless, and intermittently raving mad with pain, he sprang back from a terrible period of depression to write the ebullient *Dreams from Bunker Hill*, dictating to his wife Joyce the final installment in the saga of Arturo Bandini even as a ground-shifting French *Ask the Dust* was being prepared along with, most fittingly, a new Italian edition.

When in the 1980s Italian readers caught on to Fante, it was as if the prodigal Italian American son had finally found his long way home. Like a certain concentrated but knowing segment of American readers, above all in Fante's adopted state of California, the ancestral land of his emigrant father embraced John through his works with a passion that lives on to this day. Indeed, Italians take second place to no one in their enthusiasm for Fante's works, his emblematic life story, and his American iteration of *Italianità*. And so we find ourselves introducing this volume with its featured American and Italian perspectives, among others we are happy to say, all of which together demonstrate the breadth of interest and depth of appeal that, inauspicious beginnings aside, *Ask the Dust* continues to command. Those beginnings, both critical and biographical, should be instructive to anyone drawn to explore the novel's thematic depths, which are finally coming into focus.

In 1934 the twenty-five-year-old Fante was amazed to find himself a salaried scenarist with an office and a secretary on the studio lot of Warner Bros., surrounded by "a lot of people [who] bow low when I pass, hating my Dago guts."[5] He marveled as much at all the money he was making as at the obtuseness of his employers for the kind of work they were paying him to do. Go to the Doheny Library at the University of Southern California and you will find in the Warner Bros. archives a fifty-five-page film treatment concocted by Fante entitled simply "Bandini." Typecast as Italian, which in the industrialized mentality of Hollywood could mean only East Coast Italian, Fante dutifully set this earliest extant trace of the Bandini family not in his home state of Colorado much less in Los Angeles but rather in New York's Little Italy, where gravestone carver Svevo Bandini and his ten-year-old son, Gino, get entangled in so much movie hokum including a gangland slaying, hidden treasure, and a jail sequence with Svevo behind bars.

This episode is instructive precisely for the way it reveals the blinding power of received notions. In 1934 Fante had never ventured farther east than Nebraska and yet here he was, charged with fleshing out stereotypes about what "Italian" must mean and, in so doing, laying it on thick and then thicker. Is it too great a leap from this example to a possible explanation for why it took so long for Fante and his works to be rightly recognized for who he was and what they are, namely, something other than the conventionally expected? For his great Italian American novel—this great *American* novel, *Ask the Dust*—takes place not on the Lower East Side, as in the works of Pietro di Donato or Mario Puzo, but in the Los Angeles of, yes, certainly, mean downtown streets but also of smog-stained palm trees and sun-warmed beaches where you can nearly drown skinny-dipping at midnight, of rural San Fernando Valley farmland and Central Avenue jazz joints, and always, beyond the mountains, the eternal desert. And this great Italian American love story involves at its center, of course, an Italian American protagonist, Arturo Bandini, but also and just as essential to the fullness of Fante's vision, a Mexican, Camilla Lopez, by turns Arturo's idolized Mayan princess and loathed, reviled foil on their dizzying, torturous way to becoming Americans.

In this light we feel a slight confession is in order, for neither of us can be called properly an Italian Americanist. Rather, one of us is a creative writer-cum-biographer and the other is a specialist in eighteenth-century Europe. In making our mea culpa though we wonder if it might bespeak a more important fact, namely, that *Ask the Dust* presents an object example of how such a quintessentially Italian American work of literature can succeed in bringing together such a wide spectrum of experts and enthusiasts as the contributors joined here. Perhaps *Ask the Dust* has had to wait for its moment because the novel itself has defied canonical novelistic criteria. As the diversity of materials comprising this book suggests, *Ask the Dust* requires a wider than normal berth, one that can fully accommodate the work's heretofore opaque interdisciplinarity, not to mention its newfound life as a text of intersectionalities that may be addressed in any number of ways in today's broadening practice of scholarship. Perhaps it has taken this long for *Ask the Dust* to receive its critical due because many of us have had to wait for the right critical tools to understand it. Those tools are now at hand in today's rich variety of available approaches, and so our design in discovering, recruiting, and arranging this volume's variety of voices and views has been as inclusive as it is untraditional. Both in content and form, this book embodies at once the need for a new paradigm in Fante scholarship and the developing landscape of Fante studies.

Accordingly, we have gathered not only a number of theoretically informed scholarly essays but also a range of other texts addressing thematic, biographical, and archival aspects relevant to the work, its author, and their continuing reverberations. In bearing witness as a whole to *Ask the Dust*'s mythopoeic power and productivity, the assemblage serves our goal of contributing something decisive to the literature that so far has left the novel suspended in minor-classic limbo, a sort of niche or cult-favorite kind of orbit.[6] Through the interplay of these many different modes of reading and methods of critical reassessment we aim to meet the needs and concerns of a diverse readership, both academic and general. In fact, we are convinced that Fante's crossover appeal requires just such an approach. Taken together, that appeal and this approach effectively demonstrate not just the relevance of but also the need for current and future theoretical orientations in grappling with the *Ask the Dust* of our own advancing era. At the same time, the enduring thematic currency of the novel some eighty years after its publication is vividly underscored.

If anything, *Ask the Dust* offers an embarrassment of critical riches. The new insights presented here showcase but a small part of the novel's significance in terms of an array of approaches enabled by manifold intersectional concerns: Italian American identity and the Italian diaspora; migration and the Latinx, specifically Chicanx immigrant experience; ethnicity and interethnic relations; whiteness; gender and masculinity; religion; class; the literary representation of urban and geographical space; the literary history of Los Angeles; the West and pulp western literature; translation studies; Italian studies; American studies; and the artist and the *Künstlerroman*, among others.

And it's easy to think of more. What about the ongoing history of the novel's reception in the many countries and cultures where it appears in translation? Or the archeological exploration of Fante's core influences in such foundational Russian and Scandinavian modernists as Dostoevsky and Hamsun? And surely there are essays in the fertile field of ecocriticism waiting to be written on the novel's ecological aspects, all that dust permeating the orange blossom- and gasoline-drenched air, not to mention the ocean, the earthquake, or the "supreme indifference" metamorphosing into "silent consoling wonder" of the unmapped Mojave Desert.

Whether this abundance of critical opportunity should help propel at last Fante's signature work into the evolving canon of American letters—indeed, of world literature—will be for others to judge. For now, we are pleased to offer the following selection of critical analyses, historical reconstructions, investigative and creative literary journalism, public talks, personal responses, archival gems, typewritten letters sent off in despair and gratitude and awe, recorded interviews, considered reflections, and reminiscences both bitter and sweet as so much evidence on which to help build just such a judgment.

This book is organized into five parts and twenty chapters, each looking at Fante's work and legacy through different academic, cultural, or artistic lenses.

Part 1 introduces new approaches to the study of *Ask the Dusk*. It opens with Valerio Ferme's fascinating account of the first Italian rendering of Fante's novel in 1940s Fascist Italy, "From the Particular to the Universal." Until now largely neglected, this crucial moment in the internationalizing of American literature helps illuminate the anti-Fascist "myth of America" deployed by intellectual opponents of Mussolini. Detailing the pressures exerted by government censors on Fante's work, Ferme shows how, having denied permission for an Italian translation of *Wait Until Spring, Bandini*, they said yes to *Ask the Dust*—but only on certain conditions. Ferme's analysis of the way Vittorini responded to these conditions makes this record of his translation an adventure at the crossroads of world politics and literature.

In her illuminating "When Spirituality Ebbs and Flows," Suzanne Manizza Roszak draws out the intersectional linkage between the novel's investment in the sacred and its depiction of the Italian diasporic experience in the United States. Despite Arturo's self-professed Americanism, and outright fits of atheism at that, we come to see how his vehement bursts of pride in Catholic doctrine and tradition show forth the depth of his estrangement from the majority society of 1930s Los Angeles.

Meagan Meylor's "Sad Flower in the Sand" opens a fresh interpretive path into the novel. By framing the fraught figure of Camilla against the implied backdrop of the Repatriation Program, the vigilante action of forced deportation whereby for much of the 1930s Mexicans and Mexican Americans throughout the West were herded into trains and buses and dumped south of the border, Meylor unearths the novel's political unconscious and by extension its relevance to today's global immigration crisis and the consequences especially for women.

Owing to their shared engagement with the significance of Camilla, the character who is attracting more and more of today's critical attention, the essays by Meylor and Daniel Gardner provide a useful counterpoint in their overlapping concerns and frames of focus. Gardner's "A *Ramona* in Reverse" reveals how Fante used one of the founding works of southern California literature, Helen Hunt Jackson's late nineteenth-century romance *Ramona*, as an ironic template for his vision of twentieth-century realities, in particular the racist underpinnings of so much popular Western culture.

Part 2 surveys the multimedia afterlives of Fante's novel. First in the grouping comes J'aime Morrison's "Dancing with the Dust," a behind-the-scenes report on how Morrison, a professor of theatre, transformed *Ask the Dust* into a live performance featuring original songs, Apache dance, and electrifying performances by a troupe of student actors. Taking her cue from Roland Barthes's concept of the pleasure of the text, Morrison delineates the process of choreographing the novel as an act of bodily writing that by final curtain transforms Camilla into the story's protagonist.

From Chiara Mazzucchelli's "Ask the Lyrics" we learn of Fante's impact on pop culture and music both in Italy and the United States. Exploring the interrelationships among literature, music, and such abidingly current issues as immigration and ethnic identity, Mazzucchelli reviews a playlist of songs from both sides of the Atlantic that draw on *Ask the Dust* and other Fante works for narrative references, lyrical imagery and, above all, inspiration.

In "Watch Out or You'll End up in My Novel," Robert Guffey reports on the ongoing significance of the connection between John Fante and Charles Bukowski as evinced by Noah Van Sciver's 2015 graphic novel *Fante*

Bukowski. Guffey channels Ruskin's idea of the importance of sincerity as he analyzes the influence of *Ask the Dust* on the oneiric tendencies of so much Southern California fiction in its quest to recapture the magic of lost time.

Louche, knowing, and offhandedly amusing, "Don't Ask the French" by Philippe Garnier, longtime West Coast cultural correspondent for the Paris daily newspaper *Libération*, recounts the inside story of how he came to translate *Ask the Dust* and why the novel's appearance in French helped spark a mania across France for all things Fante.

Part 3 offers a set of personal accounts detailing the contributors' respective reactions to *Ask the Dust* and other works by Fante. Anecdotal and often openly emotional, these texts multiply the angles from which the novel can be viewed even as their cumulative impact heightens our sense of its significance.

In her remembrances "Amid the Dust," Miriam Amico pays homage to the two luminous months she spent helping to archive the John Fante papers at UCLA Special Collections. During daily encounters with manuscripts containing the writer's most intimate visions and reflections, Amico comes to see how two journeys, hers from Sicily in 2010 and Fante's from Colorado some eight decades earlier, brought them both not only to Los Angeles but also to the realization of their inner selves.

In "The Passion That Became a Festival," Giovanna DiLello traces the history of the three-day celebration of John Fante's life and works that is held every August in the village of Torricella Peligna, high in the Abruzzi mountains. As founding director of the festival, DiLello has overseen the growth of the event from its early experimental days to an international gathering of readers, writers, filmmakers, academics, and others who share in her dedication to Fante's legacy.

Joel Williams, a descendant of the Shoshone-Paiute tribes, offers a powerful addition to the genre of the-book-that-changed-my-life in "I Had Bandini." The story of how Williams discovered the novel while serving a twenty-seven-year-to-life sentence in a California maximum-security penitentiary grows only more dramatic as he traces his development as a man who, through a self-disciplined program of reading and writing, finds a way to overcome the existential bonds of his confinement.

In "Writing in the Dust" novelist and literary journalist Alan Rifkin mounts a sweeping case for *Ask the Dust*'s seminal influence on the literature of southern California dreaming. As insightful as it is elegant, the essay holds back nothing in making Rifkin's learned yet very personal case: "Every Los Angeles writer at the outskirts of vision feels a connection to *Ask the Dust*, the 1939 novel that, more than any other, seems to weep over this city's corpse in the ecstasy of possessing it."

Personally engaged and deeply researched, investigative journalist Ryan Holiday's "How Hitler Nearly Destroyed the Great American Novel" scrutinizes the archival record to clarify the collision of historical forces that long haunted the trajectory of *Ask the Dust*. Before Mussolini's censors drew a bead on the writings of John Fante, agents of Adolf Hitler were hijacking the attention of his editor and draining the assets of his publisher in a legal case that went all the way to the United States Supreme Court. The issues involved in that case and their effects upon *Ask the Dust* tell us as much about Fante's day and age as about our own era of alt-right provocateurship and #noplatform.

Part 4 is a tribute to *Ask the Dust* by two filmmakers and an author. Screenwriter Robert Towne avows the influence of *Ask the Dust* on his work, not least his Academy Award–winning script for the classic Los Angeles detective noir *Chinatown*, in an interview with Nathan Rabin. Decades after optioning the rights to *Ask the Dust* and earning, not easily, John Fante's friendship, Towne goes on to discuss how he finally realized his ambition to direct a film adaptation of the novel.

Rotterdam-based filmmaker Jan Louter traveled to Los Angeles in 2000 to make *A Sad Flower in the Sand*, his poetic feature documentary about *Ask the Dust* that aired nationally in 2006 on the PBS series *Independent Lens*. "Letters from Los Angeles" gives us Louter's half of his diary-like correspondence with a friend in Holland, editor of the Fante-inspired Dutch literary journal *Bunker Hill*.

"'My Dear Bukowski,' 'Hello John Fante'" gives us a first-person glimpse into the friendship between Fante and Charles Bukowski. As the poet is preparing to compose his preface to the 1980 Black Sparrow Press reissue of *Ask the Dust*, Fante writes to express his profound gratitude and respect, which Bukowski returns in kind. Bukowski's "Preface to *Ask the Dust*" is presented as he typed it. The manuscripts reproduced here of Bukowski's text and the two preceding letters can be found in the John Fante Papers at UCLA Library Special Collections.

Part 5 considers the importance of archives in light of two newly discovered pieces of writing by John Fante before closing on the reflections of his biographer. This part begins with "From Family to Institutional Memory," Teresa Fiore's interview of volume coeditor and Fante biographer Stephen Cooper. Circling around the idea of the archive and its multifarious importance, Cooper uses his experience in researching Fante's life and career to show the value in cultivating family sources of archival materials for the advancement of knowledge and the benefit of posterity.

In "Prelude to 'Prologue to *Ask the Dust*'" Cooper recounts the discovery of a remarkable letter from John Fante to his friend and fellow Italian American writer Jo Pagano. Written in 1933 and published here for the first time, the letter reveals the confused depths of Fante's doubts about his ability to write—a confusion that prefigures the visionary clarity of another remarkable letter written five years later, the one now known as the "Prologue" to *Ask the Dust*.

The year after *Ask the Dust* came out John Fante wrote "Goodbye, Bunker Hill," a wistful look back on his early days in Los Angeles when he was young and broke, prowling the heart of the city on an empty stomach, soaking up atmosphere and observing real-life characters so he could make good on his desire to write. "Gala days those. Old Bunker Hill, I loved you then!"

Our collection concludes with "The Road to John Fante's Los Angeles." Originally presented as the 2011 Bonnie Cashin Endowed Lecture at UCLA Library Special Collections on the opening of an exhibit from the newly archived Fante Papers, the essay reflects on the journey that started when Stephen Cooper first read *Ask the Dust* as a young man—a journey that continues to this day.

The views assembled here come from a mixed chorus of voices, each moved to respond in its special way to *Ask the Dust*. As coeditors working together over the past several years, we are pleased to offer this book as our way.

S. C. and C. D., February 14, 2019

Notes

1. Jack, "A Brash Young Man," 7.
2. N. L. R., "Review of *Ask the Dust*," 20.
3. William Soskin to John Fante, February 1, 1939. John Fante Papers, UCLA Library Special Collections, box 27, folder 7.
4. Cooney, *Selected Letters*, 295.
5. Moreau and Fante, *Fante/Mencken*, 86.
6. The literature includes Cooper and Fine, *John Fante*; Cooper, *Full of Life*; Collins, *John Fante*; and Kordich, *John Fante*. Italian approaches to Fante can be found in Vichi, *John Fante*, and Caltabellota, *John Fante*; Vichi, *Fuori dalla polvere*; and Margaretto, *Non chiarmarmi bastardo*.

Works Cited

Caltabellota, Simone, and Marco Vichi, eds. *John Fante*. Rome: Fazi Editore, 2003.
Collins, Richard. *John Fante: A Literary Portrait*. Toronto: Guernica, 2000.
Cooper, Stephen. *Full of Life: A Biography of John Fante*. New York: North Point Press, 2000.
Cooney, Seamus, ed. *John Fante: Selected Letters 1932–1981*. Santa Rosa, CA: Black Sparrow Press, 1991.
Cooper, Stephen, and David Fine, eds. *John Fante: A Critical Gathering*. Madison, New Jersey: Fairleigh Dickinson University Press, 1999.
Jack, Peter Monro. "A Brash Young Man in Love with Fame." *New York Times*, November 19, 1939.
Kordich, Catherine J. *John Fante: His Novels and Novellas*. New York: Twayne Publishers, 2000.
Margaretto, Eduardo. *Non chiarmarmi bastardo, io sono John Fante*. Soveria Mannelli: Rubbettino Editore, 2017.
Moreau, Michael and Joyce Fante, *Fante/Mencken: John Fante and H. L. Mencken, a Personal Correspondence 1930–1952*. Santa Rosa, CA: Black Sparrow Press, 1989.
N. L. R. "Review of *Ask the Dust*, by John Fante." *Saturday Review of Literature*, November 25, 1939.
Vichi, Marco. *Fuori dalla polvere*. Florence: Edizioni Clichy, 2015.
———. *John Fante: Fuori dalla polvere*. Florence: Edizioni Clichy, 2005.

1. New Approaches to John Fante's *Ask the Dust*

From the Particular to the Universal: Vittorini's Italian Adaptation of *Ask the Dust*

Valerio Ferme

In 1939 Elio Vittorini, who was establishing himself as one of Italy's foremost writers of his generation, wrote to Luigi Rusca, editor at the Mondadori publishing company and director of its "Medusa" series, which specialized in translation of foreign authors into Italian:

> The two novels by John Fante, *Wait until Spring, Bandini* and *Ask the Dust*, are both highly recommendable. The first, which achieved great success, is truly a masterpiece. One could have some artistic reservations about the second, simply because the first was so great. But the true interest in both novels lies in their curious representation (alternately brilliant and gloomy) of human life. There are only a few sentences that are censurable, but those are easy to eliminate.[1]

Thus began the editorial process that would lead, two years later, to *Il cammino nella polvere*, Vittorini's highly redacted version of John Fante's *Ask the Dust*.

The translation of Fante's most famous work comes toward the end of Vittorini's trajectory as a translator during the era of Fascism. It stands out and complements *Americana*,[2] the 1941 editorial project Vittorini undertook with the editor Valentino Bompiani. *Americana* highlights the interest of Italian writers and publishers in American authors during the Fascist years, at a time when the United States had become a source of cultural interest for many European intellectuals.[3] Much has been written about this interest and the translation work that accompanied it in Italy, especially through the work of Cesare Pavese and Elio Vittorini himself.[4] By the time Vittorini proposed Fante's work to Rusca, the Italian market had already absorbed numerous translations of major American authors, especially those who, between 1925 and 1940, had become household names not only in the United States but worldwide.[5] Indeed, given the relatively lesser stature of Fante in the panorama of American literature (though, in the years 1938 to 1939, when *Wait until Spring, Bandini* and *Ask the Dust* were published, the Italian American author achieved a noticeable degree of critical success in the United States),[6] Vittorini's decision to translate *Ask the Dust* raises two questions that I will answer in this essay. Why did Vittorini decide to translate *Ask the Dust* for Mondadori's "Medusa" series, despite judging it inferior to *Wait until Spring, Bandini*, which Mondadori would only publish in the same series in 1948 (translated by Giorgio Monicelli as *Aspettiamo primavera, Bandini*)? Excerpts of *Wait until Spring, Bandini* had been published in the journals *Oggi* and *Omnibus* between 1938 and 1940, the appearances of which, as Raffaella Rodondi observes, might be attributed with one exception to Vittorini himself, since his translations of American authors often appeared in these journals.[7] In addition, Vittorini translated the opening chapter of *Wait until Spring, Bandini* for *Americana* in 1941, in a redacted version that complied with the regime's request to censor blasphemous cuss words and to eliminate negative depictions of Italian citizens such as the one relating to Svevo Bandini in the novel.[8] Given his initial recommendation to Rusca, his belief that the books might easily avoid censorship, and the substantial translated portion of *Wait until Spring, Bandini* already published in *Oggi* and *Omnibus*, one wonders what convinced Vittorini and Rusca to translate *Ask the Dust* rather than the earlier, more popular novel.

Also, what is the relationship between Vittorini's translation of *Ask the Dust* and the critical pronouncements he made about Fante and other American writers in the years preceding and following its publication? In particular, my analysis contextualizes Vittorini's interest in the work of American writers such as Fante within the broader framework of Vittorini's intellectual and cultural stances in the late 1930s and early 1940s. This was a time when the Sicilian author rejected both the cultural premises of Fascism and the oppressive stylization of Italy's mainstream literary currents. The former would lead to his arrest in 1942 and to the subsequent participation in the armed resistance; the latter resulted in a stylistic transformation that found its full expression in Vittorini's masterpiece, *Conversazione in Sicilia*, published in installments in the journal *Letteratura* from 1938 to 1939, around the same time that Fante published his two novels. Although it is not always fruitful to establish cause-and-effect relationships between a writer's critical pronouncements and fictional developments, the parallels between the two are particularly intriguing in the case of Vittorini. This essay concludes with a close reading of passages from Fante's original and Vittorini's translation to explore the ways in which the Italian author transforms and makes Fante's work his own.

Vittorini: Translator or Coauthor?

In a previous essay on Vittorini's translation of Saroyan's writings, I explored the relationship between Vittorini's work as a translator and the aesthetic practices that he employed in his own writing between 1933 and 1936, following the publication of *Il garofano rosso*.[9] As is now well accepted, Vittorini began his work as a translator after the publisher Mondadori hired him as its chief editor and translator of English-language books in 1933. Initially, he translated English writers such as Daniel Defoe, D. H. Lawrence and William Galsworthy before extending his translation practices to American authors. Vittorini claimed in a number of recollections to have been a self-starter who received some help from the famous Italian critic Mario Praz. However, letters from Vittorini and statements by his wife Rosa, as well as subsequent commentaries and publications, have uncovered the significant contributions provided to Vittorini's activities as a translator by Lucia Rodocanachi, a Jewish friend of Eugenio Montale. Rodocanachi worked as a shadow translator not only for Vittorini but also for Carlo Emilio Gadda, Camillo Sbarbaro, and Eugenio Montale himself.[10] Although Rodocanachi was never acknowledged as Vittorini's collaborator in the final published translations, and although she often remained uncompensated for her efforts, she no doubt continued to play a significant role in Vittorini's career as a translator, since her shadow-collaboration with Vittorini is still noticed and discussed by friends of hers and by Vittorini himself as late as 1941.[11]

With respect to the question of originality as it pertains to the passage from source to target language texts in Vittorini's translations, it is crucial to understand how Rodocanachi and Vittorini collaborated. In this sense, Rosa Vittorini's explanation of their give-and-take process is extremely helpful:

> Mrs. Rodocanachi gave Elio a literal word-by-word translation, which was impossible to read. Then, he would shape those words. The construction and the inventiveness were his; he did not feel bound by those cold words. He always reminded her to translate literally, precisely, word by word, article by article, phrase by phrase. And then he transformed it into a novel. The novels he translated became his own.[12]

If what Rosa Vittorini says is accurate,[13] one has to acknowledge that a significant transformation of the original text occurred as it was translated into Italian. Since his own understanding of English was limited—resulting at times in egregious mistakes[14]—Vittorini relied on a word-by-word target language literal translation. In doing so, he was dealing with a stripped-down copy that had lost what one might call the essential poetic element of the source text. Indeed, if someone else, whether Rodocanachi or another shadow-translator, provided him with a "literal" translation, such translation would disperse the rhythms and musicality of the original American text, as well as the symbolic meanings emanating from the combination of words and sentences in the original. Thus, the bare-boned, literal translation would lose those elements that contribute substantially to the poetic nuances of a text. In their stead remains the plot, its overarching message as presented through the narrative development, and the narrative perspective; in short, its narrative superstructure. At the same time, this distancing from the original allows Vittorini to add a new poetic substratum to the text as the final, target-language translator. Freed from a faithful obligation to the symbols and prosodic rhythms of the original, but nevertheless intrigued by another author's ability to create lyrical representations of the modern world, Vittorini uses his knowledge of Italian linguistic rhythms and allusive metaphors to create analogue poetic moods in the target language texts. The distinction lends credit to Vittorini's rebuttals to those critics who claimed that his writing had been heavily influenced, linguistically and stylistically, by his discovery and translation of American authors.[15] My point is that a Bloomian "anxiety of influence" is less felt in the linguistic components of Vittorini's translations, precisely because a previous translation by Rodocanachi (or other ghost translator) already would have lost some of the rhythms of the original. Instead, and understandably so, the content of the novels as it pertains to the lyrical expression of new symbols would exhibit the most parallels with Vittorini's own work.

Vittorini's Critical Appraisal of Fante

Vittorini first mentions Fante in a brief article on another Italian American author, Pietro Di Donato, under the rubric "Letture Americane" in the weekly *Oggi*. In reviewing Di Donato vis-à-vis other contemporary Italian American authors, Vittorini lists "Jo Pagano . . . Jerre Mangione and Atanasio" before naming "John Fante, the best and most gifted of the small group who, with the novel *Wait until Spring, Bandini*, has put himself as far as the freshness of his work alongside Saroyan, Caldwell, and the other Americans who are all the rage."[16] Vittorini's early comparison between Fante and Saroyan and Caldwell (but not Faulkner, Hemingway, and Steinbeck, who are grouped among the "others" who are all the rage) requires an explanation. Saroyan and Caldwell were two of the most important authors in Vittorini's literary pantheon, as his early review essays on American authors, with one exception, had discussed Saroyan and Caldwell in *Omnibus* and *Letteratura* in 1938.[17] They were also two authors whose work Vittorini proposed for translation, as he himself made clear in letters, first to Valentino Bompiani—"There would be wonderful books to translate on these two. But unfortunately they are all subject to censorship" (May 21, 1938)—and later to Sebastiano Alianò: "Among my translations, I should differentiate between those commissioned to me and those that I myself have suggested to the editor . . . 1939 W. Saroyan: *Che ve ne sembra dell'America?*, selected short stories" (February 11, 1940).[18] Endorsing Fante side by side with Caldwell and Saroyan reveals a strong appreciation that might lead, as evidenced by the letter to Rusca that opens this essay, to a desire to translate Fante's novels into Italian.

This initial assessment of Fante's worthiness as an author returns in Vittorini's review of the best books of 1939 in *Almanacco Letterario Bompiani* ("America"). The enthusiasm for Fante's *Wait until Spring, Bandini* here provides the lead-in to the article.[19] Once more, Vittorini compares him to Saroyan and Caldwell, but now adds Hemingway to the list:

> Among the best fiction books published this year in the United States are two novels by Italian-Americans. They are both *first books*, both by young writers. One is John Fante, author born in 1908 [*sic*], and known in Italy for a number of short stories. The title is *Wait until Spring, Bandini* and was published by Stackpole. Like the short stories, the novel follows an autobiographical plot, but is of a lyrical, rather than psychological, nature. Close to the narrative genre of William Saroyan, especially in the dialogue, it should be considered, with the works of Saroyan, Caldwell, Hemingway, et cetera, as fundamental in the area of new experiences.[20]

The short stories referenced by Vittorini are, according to Raffaella Rodondi, the ones that Vittorini and Maria Martone translated for *Omnibus* and *Oggi*.[21] That said, what matters is Vittorini's recognition of the "lyrical" nature of Fante's work and the comparison he makes between that style and Saroyan's, which shared many similarities with the style adopted by Vittorini between 1938 and 1939 in writing his most famous book, *Conversazione in Sicilia*.[22] Indeed, two years later, Vittorini himself would admit to this literary cross-pollination, even as he defended his own originality:

> About the Americans, let's be clear. . . . I do not deny at all their influence: I know that, translating them, I gained much help in creating my own language. At the same time, I know that I translated them in a language *of my own*. . . . Again: the Americans I translated have a language of their own in the original, and in my translations, they have, at least as far as the sentence structure, only one, mine.[23]

This suggests that one of the reasons Vittorini found an affinity with Fante's work was the lyrical, at times oneiric quality of the Italian American writer's prose.

Only in January 1940, however, did Vittorini finally focus his critical attention on *Ask the Dust*, which had been published the previous year in the

United States. In a review titled "Un nuovo romanzo di Fante," Vittorini reiterates that Fante is the best among the small group of Italian American authors publishing at that time in the United States. Comparing him again to Caldwell and Saroyan, Vittorini clarifies that what he likes about Fante's work is the originality of his fantasy, not the psychological dramas, which in fact detract from the overall quality of the novel:

> He shares especially with Saroyan a number of qualities: the freshness of the language, the youthful elasticity of his means of expression . . . However, the world he depicts is completely different from Saroyan's. . . . This world is in part willed, constructed, registered through the mechanical aids of memory and psychology: a calculated world. And because it is willed, constructed, calculated, this world has blemishes that diminish its poetical quality, and blur and obfuscate it, and relate it to outcomes of an obsolete literature. In the single episodes he is fresh, pervaded by the youthful power of pain and joy. But in the succession of episodes, in their interlocking, in their appearance as a whole, he is subject to the influences of literary conventions: the realistic conventions of gloomy hues.[24]

On the heels of his positive endorsement of *Wait until Spring, Bandini*, Vittorini's muted and lukewarm assessment of *Ask the Dust* is surprising. The reason, as he explains it, is that in the second novel, Fante has concentrated on these "gloomy hues," which have been the focus of too much past literature, without innovating the "means of expression" through which to present them: "John Fante has chosen to present this gloom as gloom, believes in it, and has wanted to summarize it in a tragic symbol by giving us the lovers' conflict between Bandini and the poor Mexican Camilla, as well as the maniacal Vera."[25]

Vittorini's critique of *Ask the Dust* becomes clearer in a subsequent article in the weekly *Il Tempo* (August 1940). After briefly introducing Fante as a "neo-American" author, Vittorini clarifies that he is one of a cadre of writers who have emigrated to the United States more recently and, therefore, do not "accept the old *Yankee* tradition" but bring to the country "a new legend." What this means, in Vittorini's highly lyrical and rhetorical language, is that, because as immigrants they have conquered a new land and a new language, they are "incapable of believing . . . in every alleged a priori law pertaining to reality, psychology, or syntax"; they believe instead "in life as a sequence of wonders, and in man as the protagonist of creation, man with a capital M, lyrical I, despoiled of *deep seated* (thus mediated) distinctive traits as character."[26] As such, it would be improper to call them by their hyphenated ethnic origin (e.g., Armenian-American, Italian-American), since they embody a move beyond the particularity of specific ethnic and racial groupings toward a new, "universalizing" idea of America. In this appraisal, Vittorini expanded on a thought that emerged with more clarity in an earlier article he had devoted to William Saroyan. There, Vittorini had claimed that Saroyan is the "most American" writer because, as the son of immigrants, his cultural and historical background is not tied to a particular American past but opens onto the "common civilization of humankind" exemplified by modern America's cultural melting pot. This independence from America's previous history allows Saroyan not only to integrate a "personal, hereditary memory of Armenia" with his modern surroundings but also to see all immigrants who, "like him have arrived from some part of the old world," as participating in the construction of the new world, each contributing in a unique way to the creation of a new culture that embodies humanity as a whole: "Saroyan can see beyond the geographical limits of America, he sees the whole earth, so that Man, this Armenian or this Filipino, or even this Assyrian, becomes, even while maintaining his special flavor, . . . a symbol for the whole human race."[27]

Vittorini then argues that, precisely because these authors have abandoned the need to embed their work in reality and its psychological, mediated interpretation, they have generally eschewed writing novels in the old sense of "a narrative form that establishes, develops, and solves a realistic context." Instead, and again Saroyan is the prime example, they write stories that focus on the lyrical appraisal of the world by their protagonists, who become symbolic vessels of a new way to conceive the relation between man and land that is devoid of the ideological weight of past human experiences. This leads Vittorini to differentiate explicitly between the success he attributes to *Wait until Spring, Bandini*, and the failures he sees implicit in *Ask the Dust*:

> [In *Wait until Spring, Bandini*,] having unsuccessfully attempted to tie himself to a specific situation, [Fante] provided a number of images of human life that correspond to the qualities I mentioned earlier [the lyrical I, devoid of mediated, psychological traits]. But in [*Ask the Dust*] he has established a situation (that is extremely realistic, if not naturalistic) and he develops and brings it to resolu-

tion. So we have an absurdity, a misunderstanding: on the one hand, the page where Fante reveals himself, with joint exaltation and irony, as lyrical I, as symbolic man, Man itself; and on the other, an absurd thematic lead, a tragic plot that is reminiscent of *Of human bondage* [sic] by Maugham and similar books.[28]

The comparison that Vittorini makes between Fante's two books and the translated collection of Saroyan's short stories titled *Che ve ne sembra dell'America* goes to the heart of the Italian author's evolution as a writer. Having started his career following the formalist approach that dominated Italian literary circles in the 1920s, Vittorini eventually wrote two books: *Piccola borghesia*, a collection of short stories, and the novel *Il garofano rosso*, in which he had experimented first with psychological realism and then with an even less satisfying naturalism imbued with ideological pragmatism. His rejection of both approaches, as he would say years later, came from his need to write in more "universal" terms about the shared essence of the human experience, even as it originates from the individual experience of the writer.[29] Significantly, this switch in literary perspectives occurred as Vittorini began reading the works of American authors who, he believed, had been more successful in addressing the changed relationship between human beings and their surrounding world following the dramatic changes that modernity had wrought on contemporary society. In Vittorini's view, *Wait until Spring, Bandini* is still a book in which episodes dominate the narration, and the plot is secondary to the development of the conflicted yet generally universalizing emotions of human beings attempting to negotiate a new world to which they are not attached by long-held psychological or cultural beliefs. This is what Vittorini calls the "new legend" of American literature, which through linguistic innovation and lyrical adaptation discovers new relationships between modern man and his world.[30] Conversely, *Ask the Dust* develops many of the same effects through the lyrical I of Arturo Bandini as representative of the struggles of modern man, but then reverts (in Vittorini's opinion) to the worn-out psychological realism of an earlier generation and to a plot based on clichés of failed relationships and to the biological and economic naturalism found in the novels of Emile Zola, Frank Norris, Theodore Dreiser, and Sinclair Lewis.[31] In the end, although Vittorini still groups Fante with Saroyan and Caldwell in the famous notes he wrote for the collection *Americana*, there is a sense that in his second novel, Fante fails to continue the successful elaboration of the "new legend" so prominently embodied in *Wait until Spring, Bandini*.[32]

Il cammino nella polvere: *Translation as Adaptation*

Having explored Vittorini's critical appraisal of Fante, one wonders why Vittorini would translate a book that he had panned in his reviews, especially at a time when, as the evidence suggests, he had been able to impose his choices on the publishers more frequently than in earlier years.

In his proposal to Luigi Rusca that he consider translating Fante's two published novels, Vittorini concludes his remarks by claiming that there is little in either novel that is "censurable" and that the little there is "is easy to eliminate." The year was 1939, when Italy and the United States were not yet at war with each other, and the censorship of the Ministry of Popular Culture had not started to target translations of American writers more directly as would happen by 1940, due to the official enmity of the two countries.[33] If, in fact, up to the late 1930s the ministry had been more concerned with censoring sexually explicit and other such improper content, by the early 1940s the ministry had turned its attention to alternative cultural representations of the world and critical depictions of Italy and Italians in popular fiction, whether foreign or indigenous. Vittorini had experienced this transition firsthand in the censorship that had befallen first *Il garofano rosso*—whose sexually explicit content had forced cuts and revisions to its serialized publication in *Solaria* and its complete banning as a book two years later—and then with *Conversazione in Sicilia*, where Silvestro's reflections on the corrupt nature of the establishment and the loss of innocence caused by his brother's death in battle forced Vittorini into densely allegorical representations designed to avoid the cuts of the censors. Finally, with regard to the ministry's scrutiny of translations, one might remember that the ministry forbade the translation of any novel by Hemingway because his *A Farewell to Arms* (made into a film by Frank Borzage in 1932) had portrayed the retreat of Italian troops after the debacle of Caporetto during World War I in a manner perceived as to highlight their lack of courage.[34]

By 1941, *Wait until Spring, Bandini* had thus become a difficult text to translate because, contrary to Vittorini's initial opinion, it contained more than a "few sentences that were censurable." Indeed, the book as a whole had become highly problematic. For one, in *Wait until Spring, Bandini*, the father-and-son pair of Svevo and Arturo Bandini display characteristics that would incur the wrath of the censors. Svevo, born in Italy but maladapted to the world in which he lives, the fictional Rocklin (Boulder) of the 1920s, is a drunkard, a church-dodger, and a womanizer who spends his money on alcohol and cards when he is not otherwise ignoring or abusing his family. Given how central the concept of traditional family values was to Fascism, the novel's representation of Svevo was extremely negative, for instead of promoting stereotypical "good" Italian values he subverts them throughout. Indeed, the second half of the novel, centering on Svevo's extramarital affair with the rich widow Hildegarde, would have made the novel censurable both on moral and patriotic grounds, as it presents an Italian citizen (Svevo was born in Italy) defying his obligations to family and giving a bad name to Italians through his infidelity and blasphemous swearing. Fante's depiction of his alter ego, Arturo, is equally controversial. As Paola Montefoschi has shown, Vittorini was aware that Arturo's embarrassment at being Italian American would not pass muster with the censors. Indeed, the Sicilian author deleted almost every reference to Arturo's lack of identification with his father's country from the texts he published in journals and in *Americana*: "Vittorini omitted all references that could be understood to be offensive to the nationalistic spirit of the time, sentences that revealed a refusal of one's roots and contemptuous emotions toward the motherland by the young offspring of immigrants."[35] Thus, what in 1939 had seemed easy fixes to the novel, by 1941, when the United States and Italy were on opposite sides of a global conflict, had become insurmountable thematic and linguistic obstacles to the translation of *Wait until Spring, Bandini*.

Conversely, *Ask the Dust* did not present similar obstacles to a translation into Italian. Removed from his Italian family in Colorado and now living in Los Angeles where he is pursuing a career as a writer, Arturo Bandini, the speaking I of the new narrative, focuses on the struggle to make it on his own, and on his coming of age as a man, especially through the relationships he develops with the two women, Camilla and Vera, who initiate him into sexual adulthood. While Arturo's origins as an Italian American inflect the narrative, they do not dominate it; nor does Arturo express the rejection of his origins that pervades *Wait until Spring, Bandini*. Instead, Arturo displays a certain pride in his origins as an Italian American through the realization that "Smith and Parker and Jones, I had never been one of them,"[36] while displaying a slightly contemptuous attitude toward the mythology of America as the land of plenty (obviously affected by the country's bankruptcy following the Great Depression). The Fascist censors could endorse such a critical attitude because it would help paint the United States in a negative light. Arturo's ambivalence toward the United States, side by side with his emerging pride at assimilating ("I was an American, and goddamn proud of it"[37]), allows Vittorini to effect in his translation certain correctives that render the Italian version less problematic for the censors. As a result, and due to Vittorini's propensity as a translator for appropriating original texts both stylistically and ideologically, *Ask the Dust* was a much easier text to maneuver past the government's censorship (fig. 1).

Within this context and on a number of levels, an analysis of *Ask the Dust* and Vittorini's translation evinces the translator's intervention. The first and most obvious one occurs at the level of the title, which Fante borrowed from Knut Hamsun's novel *Pan*. (Although the words "ask the dust" never occur in Fante's novel, the line from *Pan* is referenced in "Prologue to *Ask the Dust*.") Vittorini's translation transforms the quotation into *Il cammino nella polvere*, which loosely translates into "the walk [or journey] in the dust." In the original, the title reflects Arturo Bandini's rhetorical questioning of his environment as he seeks to understand the circumstances he is experiencing in Depression-era Los Angeles. These circumstances are both professional and personal, and they are tied to Camilla Lopez's descent into drug addiction and madness.[38] Vittorini's reworking creates the expectation of a broader yet equally symbolic "journey" of self-discovery in the protagonist, for while "the walk in the dust" suggests both physical and mental desolation, it also indicates a less uncertain, even more directed outcome. Unlike the question embedded in the imperative of Fante's original title—a question that is never answered—the journey implied in Vittorini's translation finds its fulfillment in the publication of Arturo's first novel and in his final, tragic gesture of dedicating the book to Camilla, his muse, and throwing it in the direction where she has disappeared into the Mojave desert. In short, the journey arrives at its destination.

Vittorini operates even more obvious interventions on the original novel at the textual level. Montefoschi notes that, while not as prevalent as in *Wait*

CASA EDITRICE A. MONDADORI
VIA CORRIDONI 39
MILAN, ITALY

NEW YORK OFFICE:
425 FIFTH AVENUE
CALEDONIA 5-8125

January 22nd, 1941

John Fante
211 Pleasant Street
Roseville, California.

Dear John Fante,

      I must apologize for not having answered your letter of December 26th sooner but the delay is not due to any fault of mine; unfortunately your letter, for some mysterious reason, was not forwarded to me, together with my other mail, during my absence of three weeks from New York. I found it waiting for me upon my return here three days ago.

      First of all, I thank you a lot, also on behalf of Mondadori, for your biographical notes and for the photograph which I received from Viking Press.

      Viking Press, some time ago, offered me your DAGO RED for Mondadori. I read it and I can't tell you how enthusiastic I am about it. I have sent it to Mondadori and hope they will accept it.

      From your letter I gather that you were not advised of Mondadori's impossibility to publish WAIT UNTIL SPRING, BANDINI. The Ministero per la Cultura Popolare, to whom they have to submit every book before publication, did not give them permission to publish it in Italy. They have, however, given the O.K. on ASK THE DUST which will be published shortly.

      You are entitled, by contract, to three copies of the Italian edition, gratis. But as I have sent a full copy of your letter to Mondadori, I am sure they will send you five copies. I only hope they will eventually get here, what with the present conditions of the mails from abroad.

      Your words of praise for our Italian Genius certainly sounded good.

      Thanks again and greetings.

Yours sincerely
Carla Castaldi

FIGURE 1. 1941 letter to John Fante from Milan publisher Mondadori citing censorship by the Fascist Ministry for Popular Culture. (Courtesy of John Fante Literary Group LLC and UCLA Library Special Collections.)

until Spring, Bandini, references to religion that might have been considered blasphemous were omitted in the translation:[39] for example, "Hya Hackmuth. I used to say, *Jesus how you can write*! Then the lean days came" becomes simply, ". . . Poi erano venuti i giorni di magra" in the translation;[40] and, soon thereafter, "I am twenty, I have reached the age of reason, I am about to wander the streets below, seeking a woman. Is my soul already smirched, should I turn back, does an angel watch over me, do the prayers of my mother allay my fears, do the prayers of my mother annoy me?" is succinctly reduced to "Venti anni ho io, ho raggiunto l'età della ragione e cammino per le strade cercando una donna" (*AD*, 19/*IC*, 15).[41] Elsewhere, when Arturo admits, "I have not read Lenin, but I have heard him quoted, religion is the opium of the people. . . . Myself, I am an atheist: I have read *The Anti-Christ* and I regard it as a capital piece of work. . . . The Church must go, it is the haven of the booboisie, of boobs, and bounders and all brummagem mountebanks" (*AD* 22), the passage is completely omitted in translation. Moreover, as might be expected, references in the original to morally offensive situations are glossed over by Vittorini, such as the abusive beating that Arturo's friend Carl inflicted on his wife because she did not want to abort the baby they had conceived, a passage that also is eliminated in the translation

Similarly, Vittorini omits or changes numerous culturally specific details present in the original.[42] These alterations homogenize the text for Italian readers, who might find the original references difficult to understand without being fully immersed in their context; they also allow the narration to move from the particular to the general, from local references to less culturally specific ones, a move that, conveniently for Vittorini, allows him to "universalize" the narration in a way that aligns with his aesthetic and cultural pronouncements. For example, in the opening page of *Ask the Dust*, Fante, a lifelong baseball fan, inserts a moment wherein Arturo reflects on the sporting news:

> Sitting there I smoked a couple of cigarets [*sic*], read the box scores of the American League games, scrupulously avoided the box scores of National League games, and noted with satisfaction that Joe DiMaggio was still a credit to the Italian people, because he was leading the league in batting.
>
> A great hitter, that DiMaggio. I walked out of the restaurant, stood before an imaginary pitcher, and swatted a home run over the fence. (*AD*, 11)

Vittorini translates as follows:

> E fumai due sigarette, lessi il notiziario sportivo della Lega Americana, notai con soddisfazione che Joe Di Maggio era ancora in testa alla classifica e così onorava gli italiani.
> Un uomo valente, quel Joe Di Maggio. Tornato fuori tirai un calcio a un immaginario pallone e lo feci volare al di sopra di un'immaginaria palizzata. (*IC*, 3–4)[43]

In moving from the original into Italian, Vittorini avoids the specific references to the American and National Leagues, which might have been too complex for an Italian audience to understand, but leaves intact the mention of Joe DiMaggio, partly because DiMaggio's fame had crossed the ocean and his name would be immediately recognizable even by an Italian audience; partly because, precisely because DiMaggio was the son of Italian emigrants to the United States and had succeeded at the highest levels of the American athletic pantheon, he represented a positive depiction of Italians worldwide that could readily be embraced by the regime. Vittorini also changes the protagonist's imaginary baseball home run into a soccer reference, which would allow his Italian audience to sympathize more readily with Arturo's dreamy ambition to emulate a sports hero. It is not surprising, therefore, to find smatterings of these changes and omissions throughout the text, as when "Coke" and "Root beer" become "Un piccolo dolce" and "Birra," the latter possibly the result of Vittorini's own misunderstanding; or when the names of famous American journals (*The Atlantic Monthly*, *Saturday Evening Post*) or personalities (Bing Crosby, Theodore Dreiser) are removed *in toto* from the text (*AD*, 53/*IC*, 61).

More controversial are the changes that Vittorini effects in the texts around the issues of race and national origin. Although these are an integral part of Arturo Bandini's development and coming-of-age trajectory in *Ask the Dust*, Vittorini's adaptation skirts around them for a number of reasons. The most obvious one concerns the representation of Vera Rivken, the older woman who first seduces Arturo. As the original makes clear, Vera is Jewish: "Solomon was watching her sternly . . . I could sense the consanguinity, and I knew then that she was Jewish too. Solomon went back for the drinks" (*AD*, 82); "She was a housekeeper for a rich Jewish family in Long Beach" (85); and, "Oh great Italian Lover Bandini, reciprocate! Oh Jewish girl, if you would be so kind, if you would approach these matters more slowly!" (91). The Italian, however, omits all three references to her religious and ethnic background: "Solomon la studiò attentamente, poi andò a prenderci da bere" (*IC*, 98); "Abitava a Long Beach dove faceva la governante per una ricca famiglia" (102); "Oh Bandini, grande amante italiano, ricambia! Voi, però date tempo al tempo, signora!" (109).[44] While such excisions would be controversial for the modern reader, they were expected in 1941 Italy. In fact, following the 1938 publication of "Razzismo italiano" (Italian racism) by a number of Italian scientists aligned with the regime, Mussolini had officially established that Jews did not belong to the Italian race, and Italians should not in any way mingle, marry, or procreate with Jews.[45] Although in Arturo Bandini's coming-of-age, Vera's Jewishness and thus her outcast status are essential for his development, helping him move beyond his initial rejection of others who, like him, are immigrants in 'white' America, Vittorini erases the detail in compliance with censorship norms emanating from the regime.

The confluence of censorship and racial directives emerges more virulently in Vittorini's translation of the many instances in which Arturo attacks and insults Mexican Americans, first and foremost Camilla Lopez.[46] Indeed, seemingly on purpose, Vittorini exacerbates the verbal assaults that Arturo launches on Mexicans early in the novel. Although the Italian author avoids translating the terms "Spick" and "Greaser," he establishes a relationship of superiority between Arturo and Mexican Americans, in particular after watching a Mexican-looking man hook up with a prostitute who had initially propositioned Arturo himself (*AD*, 23). In the original, Arturo sneers, "You stinking Greaser—what have you got to smile about? You come from a bashed and a busted race, and just because you went to the room with one of our white girls, you smile. Do you think you would have had a chance, had I accepted on the church steps?" (*AD*, 24). The translation is much more forceful in establishing a distance between Arturo and the Mexican, suggesting Arturo's agency in the Mexican's success and registering the latter's racial inferiority: "Il diavolo ti porti, messicano, di che hai da sorridere? Tu vieni *da una razza inferiore*, e sol perché sei stato con una bianca, sorridi. Credi che saresti andato con lei se io avessi accettato il suo invito dianzi? *A me questa fortuna devi*" (*IC*, 20; emphasis added).[47] Whereas in the original Arturo's comment that the Mexican comes from a "bashed and busted race" denotes a certain understanding of the suffering Mexicans have had to endure in the

United States, in the translation Vittorini has Arturo speak an even more aggressively racist message that separates him and those he is insulting ("You come from *an inferior race*. . . *You owe it to me* [that you were able to sleep with a white woman]"). We can imagine the censors nodding in agreement as they read this passage.

Yet, precisely because Vittorini could lay it on thick for the censors, the changes he effects in the text a few pages later allow him to transform Fante's novel into the kind of subversive work for which the Italian author had a strong affinity. Nowhere is this more evident than in the paragraphs that conclude chapters 5 and 6 in the original. The first pertains to the infamous exchange between Arturo and Camilla where he harangues her for wearing *huaraches*:

> "Those huaraches—do you have to wear them, Camilla? Do you have to emphasize the fact that you always were and always will be a filthy little Greaser?"
>
> She looked at me in horror, her lips open. . . . I heard her moaning. "Oh, oh, oh."
>
> I tossed my shoulders and swaggered away, whistling with pleasure. . . . I was an American, and goddamn proud of it. This great city, these mighty pavements and proud buildings, they were the voice of my America. From sand and cactus we Americans had carved an empire. Camilla's people had had their chance. They had failed. We Americans had turned the trick. Thank God for my country. Thank God I had been born an American. (*AD*, 44)

Vittorini's translation reduces the passage to Camilla's reaction:

> "Queste *huaraches*—dissi—devi proprio portarle, Camilla? Hai proprio bisogno di mostrare che non sei una bianca?"
>
> Essa mi guardava inorridita. Poi si portò le mani alla bocca. . . . Scappando mugolava: "Oh! Oh! Oh!"[48] (*IC*, 49)

On its own, the omission of the chapter's concluding paragraph suggests that Vittorini was playing to the Ministry of Popular Culture's request to play down the celebration of the United States on which the ministry had based its refusal to authorize the publication of *Americana* in 1940. By eliminating Arturo's bombastic pride in gloating over his "Americanness" and the "empire" that had been created on the immigrant shoulders of people like him, Vittorini cleverly erases a passage where Arturo affirms his wishful desire to be fully assimilated and integrated in American society.

This erasure, however, assumes a subtly different meaning when it is juxtaposed with the concluding paragraphs of chapter 6. Here, Arturo describes the discrimination he too felt growing up the son of Italian immigrants in Colorado, comparing it to the desolation he sees in those same Anglo-Americans who had poured scorn on him:

> When I was a kid back home in Colorado *it was Smith and Parker and Jones who hurt me with their hideous names*, called me Wop and Dago and Greaser, and their children hurt me, just as I hurt you tonight. They hurt me so much I could never become one of them. . . . Camilla, when I see their faces I feel the hurt all over again . . . and sometimes I am glad they are here, dying in the sun, uprooted. . . .
>
> . . . I have vomited at their newspapers, read their literature . . . desired their women. . . . But I am poor, and my name ends with a soft vowel, and they hate me and my father, and my father's father . . . , but they are old now, dying in the sun and in the hot dust of the road, and I am young and full of hope and love for my country and my times, and when I say Greaser to you it is not my heart that speaks, but the quivering of an old wound, and I am ashamed of the terrible thing I have done. (*AD*, 46–47; emphasis added)

Vittorini's translation is subtly different:

> Quand'ero ragazzo, nel Colorado, *detestavo gli Smith, i Parker, i Jones. Li detestavo, non ero uno di loro*! Essi mi chiamavano "wop", mi chiamavano "dago", i loro figli m'insultavano come io, Camilla, ho insultato te stasera. Mi offendevano, mi umiliavano, e tanto mi hanno offeso, tanto mi hanno umiliato che non ho potuto diventare uno come loro. . . . Così, Camilla! E quando ora vedo le loro facce, sento, alle volte, tornare in me tutto l'antico affanno, e altre volte goisco che siano qui, sradicati, morendo al sole. . . .
>
> . . . Io ho vomitato sui loro giornali, ho letto la loro letteratura, . . . desiderato le loro donne, ma sono povero, e il mio nome finisce con una vocale, e così essi mi odiano, odiano me, mio padre, il padre di mio padre . . . , però sono vecchi, ora, muoiono al sole, e io invece sono giovane e pieno di speranza, e amo il mio paese, amo la mia epoca, e se ti dico che non sei una bianca non è col cuore che parlo, parlo con la mia vecchia ferita, per via della mia vecchia ferita, ed ho vergogna di me stesso che lo faccio.[49] (*IC*, 52–53; emphasis added)

In Fante's original, the emotional contrast between the respective endings of chapters 5 and 6 stands out. Whereas chapter 5 concludes with Arturo boastfully affirming his Americanness and thus his superiority to the Mexicans who preceded the recent waves of immigrants, chapter 6 ends on the admission of his own marginalized status: insulted and rejected by Anglo-Americans and therefore as much an outsider as Camilla and her people, Arturo confesses shame for his attacks on her, consequences of the "quivering of an old wound" that still pains him.

Vittorini's translation, however, exerts a further distinction. In the original passage at the end of chapter 6, the Anglos are the agents of the conflict and of the rejection ("it was Smith and Parker and Jones who hurt me with their hideous names"). In the Italian version, Arturo speaks of his agency in rejecting them, even repeating himself to emphasize it ("I detested the Smiths, the Parkers, the Joneses. I detested them, I was not one of them"). Absent the passage at the end of chapter 5 where Arturo affirms his sense of belonging as an American, the translation effects a noticeable subversion of the original. One of the recurring themes of *Ask the Dust* is the ambivalence that Arturo Bandini experiences toward his own Americanness and that of his fellow ethnic minorities, an ambivalence that is vividly displayed in the endings of these two chapters. If the end of chapter 5 reveals Arturo's wistful desire to be considered a full-fledged American, over and above Camilla and her race, the end of chapter 6 exposes the exact opposite: rejected by the Smiths, Parkers, and Joneses of his youth, Arturo admits not being able to become one of them and what they stand for—to the point of rejoicing at their shriveling existence—and reveals that his own hurt at being discriminated against is what pushes him to discriminate against Camilla. Without the ending to chapter 5 in the translated version, Arturo's outpouring at the end of chapter 6 makes it harder for the reader to comprehend this ambivalence. This difficulty is compounded by the fact that Vittorini makes Arturo the agent of the rejection of the Smiths, Parkers, and Joneses in this chapter, thus attributing to Arturo the intent of *not* wanting to be included in the America represented by the Americans of his youth. Thus, whereas in Fante's original Arturo is frequently suspended in the ambivalence that comes from wanting and not wanting to be a member of the dominant group, in Vittorini's translation he sides more decisively with the people who inhabit the margins of this society, and thus seems to refuse the ideology that subtends mainstream white America.

This textual subversion contributes to the alignment of *Il cammino nella polvere* with other cultural and political projects undertaken by Vittorini from the late 1930s to the early 1940s. In my earlier analysis of the importance of

Saroyan in the development of Vittorini's aesthetics, I showed that authors such as Saroyan had helped Vittorini develop a civic conception of literature, whereby writers could deploy their works to represent and fight for the *mondo offeso* (injured world) of the common man. Literature could thus be a tool of protest against the humiliating conditions to which many human beings in the West were being subjected as a result of modernity's implosion through the Great Depression, and the rise of totalitarian regimes in numerous countries. Fante's *Ask the Dust* is an expression of this injured world, but its deeply ambiguous relationship with members of "injured people" from other races, especially Mexicans, made it less "universalizing" in the embrace of their common suffering. As discussed earlier in this essay, Vittorini's admiration for Saroyan, Caldwell, and even Fante rested in his belief that they were "neo-Americans" in whom one no longer felt the particularity of different ethnicities so much as the universalizing tendency toward a poetry of modern Man (capital M emphasized). But the open ambiguity of *Ask the Dust* about its characters' sense of belonging made the novel less suitable for projecting this message.

Vittorini's adaptations, omissions, reworkings, and overall subversion of the original thus have a double function. Not only do they help the book pass the scrutiny of the censors, they also present the protagonist and the other characters as exemplary of the *mondo offeso* and the *astratti furori* (abstract rage) that were central to Vittorini's ideological position vis-à-vis society and to his literary aesthetics.[50] Even as the omissions from and changes to Fante's novel domesticate the text for an Italian readership, they also "universalize" story particulars (e.g., by omitting culturally specific references to baseball, etc.), so that the plot loses much of its Californian flavor and assumes an expanding symbolic scope capable of transcending geographic boundaries. Vittorini further enhances this universalization of the human experience through his textual manipulations of Fante's novel. By mitigating Arturo Bandini's ambivalence toward his own sense of belonging in America—in so many words, "Yes, I am proud to be American; no, I am not, because the Anglos have excluded me"—and by highlighting instead the common displacement and suffering experienced by the marginalized ethnic populations of the United States, Vittorini pushes the text toward a critique of American society that would have been welcomed by the censors. In doing so, however, he is also criticizing any society, including the one in which he was living, that would set out to homogenize and acculturate people to one way of belonging. *Il cammino nella polvere* moves the experiences of Arturo closer to those of the people that, in the original novel, he struggles to accept as his equals, and toward the experience of any human being oppressed by social or racial inequalities. As a result, the book that on first impression had not persuaded Vittorini about its ability to tell a poetics of humanity as a whole, because it was too particular and individualistic in its plot and concerns, becomes in translation a much deeper reflection on the human condition and its frailty. Not surprisingly, whereas the original concludes with a deeply internalized reflection on the power of the desert to erase one's existence— "You could die, but the desert would hide the secret of your death, it would remain after you, to cover your memory with ageless wind and heat and cold" (*AD*, 164)—Vittorini's adaptation moves this reflection to a universal reflection on the human condition: "Si moriva, ma il deserto nascondeva il segreto di ciò, seppelliva sotto il vento, e il caldo, il freddo la memoria degli esseri umani" (*IC*, 195).[51] In the transposition from the original "your memory" to the "memory of human beings" in the Italian version is rooted Vittorini's own ambivalence toward Fante: a great new American writer, yes, but one in need of a creative translator to make him truly universal.

Notes

1. Albonetti, *Non c'è tutto nei romanzi*, 466–467. Unless otherwise noted, all translations are mine.
2. Although Vittorini completed *Americana* in 1941, the volume was only published in 1943, after numerous delays caused by the interference of the Minister of Culture, Alessandro Pavolini. Significantly, many of Vittorini's notes were eviscerated from the published volume but circulated in literary circles in copy-edited form. For a history of the publication vicissitudes of *Americana*, see the detailed accounts provided by Rodondi, *Elio Vittorini*, 162–170, and Manacorda, "Come fu pubblicata *Americana*."
3. The French philosopher Jean-Paul Sartre, for one, attributed the rejuvenation of the French novel in the late 1930s and under German occupation to the translation of American novelists into French. Sartre, "American Novelists in French Eyes," 114.
4. On the translations from American literature during the fascist years, see, among others, Fernandez, *Il mito dell'America negli intellettuali italiani dal 1930*

al 1950, which ascribes the birth of the myth to the translation work of Pavese, Vittorini, and a few others. See also my corrective to Fernandez's analysis, *Tradurre è tradire*, in which I show that the interest in America (and therefore the myth) predates Fernandez's initial phase by at least ten years: it was more endemic, and was the result of the cross-pollination between pop-culture phenomena such as cinema and jazz and the appeal that such writers as Jack London and Zane Grey had on Italian readers. Since then, additional studies have provided further evidence of the complexity and pervasiveness of translation models throughout the cultural panorama of the *ventennio*. See Antonelli, *Pavese*, and Ferrari, *Myths and Counter-myths of America*.

5. Among the most translated, one need only mention Jack London, Sinclair Lewis (the first US-born Nobel Prize for Literature winner, in 1930), Pearl S. Buck (also awarded a Nobel Prize in 1938), Erskine Caldwell, William Faulkner, Ernest Hemingway, and William Saroyan.

6. Stephen Cooper details the critical acclaim that welcomed *Wait until Spring, Bandini* in 1938. The novel was included in several "best of the year" lists and chosen by at least two reviewers "as the finest novel of 1938," selling moderately well. See Cooper, *Full of Life*, 156–157. Interestingly enough, the critical appraisal of *Ask the Dust* in 1939 mimics Vittorini's evaluation, as readers found the book "lacking in warmth and simple human interest." As Cooper notices, however, "time has been kind to *Ask the Dust*, which today is widely regarded as Fante's masterpiece" (171).

7. See Vittorini, *Letteratura*, 78n1. Paola Montefoschi offers a corrective to Rodondi's observation that the translations in *Oggi* and *Omnibus* were simply excerpts from *Wait until Spring, Bandini*. Montefoschi believes that the first of these short stories, published in Italian with the title "Il conto del droghiere" in the December 10, 1938 issue of *Omnibus*, was in fact the translation of the short story "Charge It," which had appeared in the April 1937 issue of *Scribner's Magazine*. Indeed, given the publication of "Il conto del droghiere" in Italy in December 1938, it is likely to have been accessible to the translator before *Wait until Spring, Bandini*, since the latter, like the short story, was only released in December 1938. See Montefoschi, "La leggenda Americana," 155.

8. This should act as a slight corrective to Cooper's statement in *Full of Life* about the translation of the novel into Italian, following its successful publication in the United States (157). While redacted chapters appeared in some journals, the complete translation had to wait, as I have mentioned, until 1948. For the translation of chapters from the book, see my comments later in this essay.

9. See Ferme, *"Che ve ne sembra dell'America?"*

10. See Vittorini, *I libri*, 424. See also Marcenaro, *Genova*, as well as Andreini, "Il lavoro editorial di Vittorini per Bompiani," and De Nicola, *Introduzione a Vittorini*. In recent years, Rodocanachi's importance as a translator has

been acknowledged in an edited volume dedicated to her life's work. On the collaboration between Rodocanachi and Vittorini from 1933 all the way to the publication of *Americana*, see Aveto, "Traduzioni d'autore e no," 153–191.

11. See Marcenaro, *Una amica*, 135–136 and 175; and Aveto, "Traduzioni d'autore e no," 179.

12. De Nicola, *Introduzione a Vittorini*, 44.

13. The overall accuracy of Rosa Vittorini's statement is questionable, as comments made by Vittorini, Montale, and Rodocanachi in their correspondence suggest that often even the finished product was more the result of Rodocanachi's speed, discipline, and nuanced understanding of English than Vittorini's. See Marcenaro *Una amica*, 132–136. Flavio Cogo also notices that the translations from English officially attributed to Rodocanachi, independent of her work for Vittorini and other Italian writers, demonstrate much more than simple, literal, understanding of the language (*Elio Vittorini editore*, 137–138). That said, Vittorini's stylistic choices are often apparent in a number of the translations attributed to him that relied on Rodocanachi's help.

14. Andrea Muzzatti points out one such mistake in the chapter that Vittorini translated from *Wait until Spring, Bandini* for *Americana*: In the passage, "He jerked the curtain string; it shot up and rattled like a machine gun, and the white naked morning dove into the room, splashing brightly over him" (Fante, *Wait Until Spring*, 25), Vittorini's translation mistakenly assumes that "dove" is a noun rather than a verb, so he has to reinvent the passage to read "... e l'ignudo mattino bianco penetrò, colomba, nella stanza e si estese, vivido, intorno a lui" [... and the white naked morning, entered, like a dove, in the room, and expanded, alive, around him] (*Americana*, 1023), where "dove," now understood as denoting the bird, becomes an appositive for the "white naked morning." See Muzzatti, "Italiamerica," 108. Vittorini's command of English would always remain dubious, as confirmed by his reluctance to write in English when he corresponded with Hemingway and Caldwell later in life (see *Gli anni del Politecnico: 1945–1951*), or with the poet and editor James Laughlin (see Chirico, *Elio Vittorini epistolario Americano*).

15. This polemic is saved in a series of letters he exchanged with Enrico Falqui between March and May 1941, one of which pertains specifically to his translation of *Ask the Dust*. See Vittorini, *I libri*, 119–130.

16. Vittorini, "Pietro Di Donato," 9.

17. The first book by an American author that Vittorini reviewed was *Pylon* by William Faulkner in 1937. This was followed by a longer article he penned in November 1937 on the African American author Waters Edward Turpin (in "Terre Basse"). The next few articles he wrote on American authors were dedicated to Saroyan ("Saroyan l'armeno" and "Notizia su Saroyan") and Caldwell ("Cotone e tabacco" and "Caldwell").

18. See Vittorini, *I libri*, 91 and 99.

19. The book was published in the United States in 1938, but Vittorini would have been able to access it only after it had achieved a discreet success and its fame traveled outside the United States in 1939.

20. Vittorini, "America," 174.

21. See Vittorini, *Letteratura*, 78n1. Fante's short stories first appeared together in the 1940 collection *Dago Red*. Although many of them had been published previously, mostly in *The American Mercury* (Cooper, *Full of Life*, 185–186), it is unclear whether Vittorini would have had access to copies of the American magazine in Italy. With the exception noted in note 7 of this essay, I surmise with Rodondi that Vittorini's reference to short stories pertains to the excerpts that appeared in *Oggi* and *Omnibus* as condensed translations of chapters from *Wait until Spring, Bandini*.

22. See Ferme, "Che ve ne sembra dell'America?"

23. Vittorini, *I libri*, 121.

24. Vittorini, "Un nuovo romanzo di Fante," 20.

25. Vittorini, 20.

26. Vittorini, "America," 42.

27. Vittorini, "Notizia," 141.

28. Vittorini, "America," 42.

29. Vittorini, *Garofano rosso*, 195.

30. Vittorini, *Letteratura*, 160–161.

31. Vittorini, 145–146.

32. Interestingly, as we have seen, the highly redacted translation of the opening chapter of *Wait until Spring, Bandini* concludes the anthology *Americana*, a testament to the importance that this novel still held for Vittorini in his discussion of the "new legend" created by the new generation of American writers.

33. Although Mussolini at times railed against the United States during the early years of his dictatorship, and often advocated Italy's autarchy especially in the cultural sphere, the regime showed itself to be mostly benevolent toward the import of American cultural artifacts during those years. This was especially true of the film industry, as almost two-thirds of all films shown in Italy from 1922 to 1938 were American (see Ferme, "Americanization of Italian Culture"). Conversely, in 1940, the ministry explicitly stated its opposition to American culture, as demonstrated by the response of Minister Alessandro Pavolini to Valentino Bompiani's inquiry about the delay in the censor's approval for *Americana*: "I remain of the opinion that—at this time—the publication of the anthology is inappropriate. The United States is potentially our enemy: their president has displayed the well-publicized negative attitude toward the Italian people. [The reference is to the Enemy Alien Act of 1940, whereby communist, anarchist, and fascist sympathizers, especially of German and Italian nationality, were targeted, and all noncitizen, resident adults had to register with the

government.] It's not the time to show any courtesy toward the United States, not even of the literary kind" (D'Ina and Zaccaria, *Caro Bompiani*, 39).

34. Gulì, "La censura cinematografica in era fascista," 3.

35. Montefoschi, "La leggenda Americana," 162. Among the passages changed or omitted, as examples, are the following: "His name was Arturo, but he hated it and wanted to be called John. His last name was Bandini, and he wanted to it to be Jones. His mother and father were Italians, but he wanted to be an American. His father was a bricklayer, but he wanted to be a pitcher for the Chicago Cubs. They lived in Rocklin, Colorado." Vittorini translates: "Of the three, the one called Arturo wished he had a different name. It was not easy to be Arturo's mother. The house was in Rocklin, Colorado" (162). And: "What kind of people were these Wops? . . . Oh Sure, he was a Dago wop, so he had to have a mustache, but did he have to pour those eggs through his ears? Couldn't he find his mouth? Oh God, these Italians" translated as "What an impossible family! [. . .] Oh God, it wasn't enough that he had a moustache, he also had to smear his face, damned Neapolitan!" (163).

36. Fante, *Wait until Spring, Bandini*, 46.

37. Fante, 44.

38. In the "Prologue to *Ask the Dust*," the citations runs: "Ask the dust on the road! Ask the Joshua trees standing alone where the Mojave begins. Ask them about Camilla Lopez, and they will whisper her name" (*The Big Hunger* 143).

39. Montefoschi, "La leggenda Americana," 159–161.

40. Fante, *Ask the Dust*, 16; emphasis added; and Fante, *Il cammino*, 11. Hereafter cited in text as *AD* and *IC* and page number. Here, and elsewhere where I record Vittorini's Italian translation, I have found it useful to provide my own English translation to show the differences between the original and the target language text. Vittorini's translation reads: ". . . Then the lean days had arrived."

41. "I am twenty years old, I am now an adult and I walk the streets looking for a woman."

42. See Cogo, *Elio Vittorini editore*, 181–182.

43. "I smoked two cigarettes, read the sporting news about the American League, and noticed with some pleasure that Joe Di Maggio was still leading the league, making us Italians proud. / Such a gifted man that Joe Di Maggio. Having walked outside, I kicked an imaginary soccer ball and let it fly over an imaginary fence."

44. The three passages can be translated as follows, respectively: "Solomon scrutinized her carefully, then went to get us drinks"; "She lived in Long Beach where she worked as a governess for a rich family"; and "Oh Bandini, great Italian lover, reciprocate! Lady, however, you let things run their course."

45. The Manifesto, originally announced in July 1938, was published in the first issue of the journal "In difesa della razza" on August 5, 1938. Mussolini's first official law against Jews was promulgated on September 5, 1938, and

subsequently followed by ever more stringent rules against the participation of Jewish Italian citizens in the daily life and operation of the country (in particular the Royal Decree of November 17, 1938, n. 1728).

46. Arturo Bandini's treatment of minorities and ethnic groups in this novel as well as in *The Road to Los Angeles* is at times difficult to bear, as it espouses many of the stereotypically racist statements circulating in the 1930s about members of those groups, including Italian Americans. Although some of the character's outbursts might have been shared by John Fante himself, it is important not to confuse the emotions expressed by a fictional character and by the author himself. Stephen Cooper expertly draws these distinctions in the pages dedicated to *Road to Los Angeles* in *Full of Life*, 132–136.

47. "Go to hell, Mexican, what are you smiling about? You come from *an inferior race*, and you smile just because you have been with a white woman. Do you think you would have been able to sleep with her if, earlier, I had accepted her offer? *You owe me this stroke of luck*."

48. "I asked: 'Do you have to wear these *huaraches*, Camilla? Do you really have to show that you are not a white woman?' / She looked at me horrified; then put her hands over her mouth. . . . Running away, she mumbled: 'Oh! Oh! Oh!'"

49. "When I was a kid in Colorado, *I hated the Smiths, Parkers, Joneses. I hated them, I was not one of them!* They called me "wop", they called me "dago", their children insulted me like I insulted you, Camilla, this evening. They hurt my feelings, they humiliated me, and they hurt my feelings so much, they humiliated me so much that I could not become like them. . . . Just like that, Camilla! And now, when I see their faces, sometimes I feel rising in me the same ancient grief, sometimes instead I rejoice that they are now here, uprooted, dying in the sun. . . . / . . . I have vomited on their newspapers, read their literature, . . . desired their women; but I am poor and my name ends in a vowel. So they hate me: they hate me, my father, the father of my father. . . . But now they are old, they die in the sun, while I am young and full of hope, and I love my country, I love my times, and if I tell you, you are not white, I am not speaking from the heart, but from my old wound, because of my old wound, and I am ashamed of myself for doing it."

50. Vittorini, *Il garofano rosso*, 201.

51. "People died, but the desert concealed this secret: under the wind, the heat, and the cold it buried all traces of human beings."

Works Cited

Albonetti, Pietro, ed. *Non c'è tutto nei romanzi*. Milano: Fondazione Mondadori, 1994.

Andreini, Alba. "Il lavoro editorial di Vittorini per Bompiani." In *Vittorini vent'anni dopo*, edited by Paolo Mario Sipala and Elena Salibra, 163–177. Siracusa: Ediprint, 1988.
Antonelli, Claudio. *Pavese, Vittorini e gli americanisti: il mito dell'America*. Bagno a Ripoli: Edarc, 2008.
Aveto, Andrea. "Traduzioni d'autore e no. La 'segreta' collaborazione d'autore con Lucia Rodocanachi." In *Lucia Rodocanachi: Le carte la vita*, edited by Franco Contorbia, 153–191. Firenze: Società Editrice Fiorentina, 2006.
Bukowski, Charles. Preface to *Ask the Dust*, by John Fante, v–vii. Santa Rosa, CA: Black Sparrow Press, 1995.
Chirico, Gianpiero. *Elio Vittorini epistolario americano*. Siracusa: Arnaldo Lombardi Editore, 2002.
Cogo, Flavio. *Elio Vittorini editore 1926–1943*. Bologna: ArchetipoLibri, 2012.
Contorbia, Franco. *Lucia Rodocanachi. Le carte la vita*. Firenze: Società Editrice Fiorentina, 2006.
Cooper, Stephen. *Full of Life: A Biography of John Fante*. New York: North Point Press, 2000.
De Nicola, Francesco. *Introduzione a Vittorini*. Bari: Laterza, 1993.
D'Ina, Gabriella, and Giuseppe Zaccaria, eds. *Caro Bompiani. Lettere con l'editore*. Milano: Bompiani, 2007.
Fante, John. *Ask the Dust*. Santa Rosa, CA: Black Sparrow Press, 1995.
———. *The Big Hunger: Stories 1932–1959*. Edited by Stephen Cooper. New York: Harper Perennial, 2002.
———. *Il cammino nella polvere*. Translated by Elio Vittorini. Sancasciano di Val di Pesa: Club degli Editori, 1971.
———. *Wait until Spring, Bandini*. Santa Rosa, CA: Black Sparrow Press, 1983.
Ferme, Valerio. "The Americanization of Italian Culture Under Fascism." *Quaderni del 900* 2 (2002): 51–69.
———. "*Che ve ne sembra dell'America?* Notes on Elio Vittorini's Translation Work and William Saroyan." *Italica* 75, no. 3 (1998): 377–398.
———. *Tradurre è tradire: La traduzione come sovversione culturale sotto il Fascismo*. Ravenna: Longo, 2002.
Fernandez, Dominique. *Il mito dell'America negli intellettuali italiani dal 1930 al 1950*. Translated by A. Zaccaria. Caltanissetta: Salvatore Sciascia, 1969.
Ferrari, Fabio. *Myths and Counter-myths of America: New World Allegories in 20th century Italian Literature and Film*. Ravenna: Longo, 2008.
Gulì, Roberto. "La censura cinematografica in era fascista." *Cinecensura: 100 anni di revision cinematografica in Italia*. http://cinecensura.com/wp-content/uploads/2014/04/La-censura-cinematografica-in-epoca-fascista_Gul%C3%AC.pdf.
"Il Manifesto della razza." *In difesa della razza* 1, no. 1 (1938): 1.

Manacorda, Giuliano. "Come fu pubblicata *Americana*." In *Elio Vittorini: Atti del Convegno nazionale di studi (Siracusa-Noto, 12–13 febbraio 1976)*, edited by Paolo Maria Sipala and Ermano Scuderi, 63–68. Catania: Greco, 1978.

Marcenaro, Giuseppe. *Genova nella cultura italiana del <APOS>900*. Genova: Cassa di Risparmio di Genova e Imperia, 1983.

———. *Un'amica di Montale*. Firenze: Camunia, 1991.

Montefoschi, Paola. "La leggenda americana. Vittorini traduttore di John Fante." *L'Illuminista* 4, no. 12 (2004): 147–170.

Muzzatti, Andrea. "Italiamerica: La Fante-Vittorini Connection." In *Elio Vittorini: IL sogno di una nuova letteratura*, edited by Lisa Gasparotto, 104–111. Firenze: Casa Editrice Le Lettere, 2010.

Rodondi, Raffaella, ed. *Elio Vittorini: Letteratura arte società. Vol 2, Articoli e interventi, 1937–1965*. Torino: Einaudi Editore, 2008.

Sartre, Jean-Paul. "American Novelists in French Eyes." *Atlantic Monthly* 178, no. 2 (1946): 114–117.

Vittorini, Elio. "America." *Almanacco Letterario Bompiani*. Milano: Bompiani, 1940.

———. "America: IV." *Il Tempo* 4, no. 66 (1940): 42.

———. "Caldwell." *Omnibus* 2, no. 12 (1938): 7.

———. "Cotone e tabacco." *Omnibus* 2, no. 38 (1938): 7.

———. *Gli anni del Politecnico, 1945–1951*. Torino: Einaudi, 1977.

———. *I libri, la città, il mondo: Lettere 1933–1943*. Torino: Einaudi, 1985.

———. *Il garofano rosso*. Milano: Oscar Mondadori, 1991.

———. "Notizia su Saroyan." *Letteratura* 2, no. 1 (1938): 141–143.

———. "Pietro Di Donato." *Oggi* 1, no. 22 (1939): 9.

———. "Saroyan l'armeno." *Omnibus* 2, no. 2 (1938): 7.

———. "Terre basse." *Omnibus* 1, no. 35 (1937): 7.

———. "Un nuovo romanzo di Fante." *Oggi* 2, no. 1 (1940): 20.

Vittorini, Elio, ed. *Americana*. Milano: Bompiani, 1943.

Where Spirituality Ebbs and Flows: Religion and Diasporic Alienation in *Ask the Dust*

Suzanne Manizza Roszak

In recent scholarship on the work of John Fante, one of twentieth-century Los Angeles's most compelling literary voices, issues of spirituality and the sacred have not been a common emphasis. Fante's work is marginalized to some degree within the greater context of American modernism,[1] and when his novels are taught and studied, it is often for their depictions of Italian American cultural identity outside the realm of religion. Yet Fante's novels evoke a whole host of dimensions of Italian diasporic identity in the United States during the 1930s and later, and their exploration of concepts that are key to diaspora theory—including social alienation and selective accommodation—is indeed intrinsically tied to their examination of Italian spirituality in the American context.

William Safran's conception of social alienation within diasporic communities gives us a foundation for examining experiences in which diasporic individuals find themselves facing prejudice and resistance to their integration into the host society in which they have settled. Meanwhile, James Clifford's theory of selective accommodation provides a lens through which to view the peculiar combination of acquiescence and resistance to borrowed social norms that often characterizes the response of diasporic communities to a new host culture. Both of these aspects of the diasporic experience are at work in Fante's *Ask the Dust*, which examines the life of a second-generation Italian immigrant in Los Angeles, a young man named Arturo Bandini. Despite his self-professed Americanism, Bandini faces alienation by members of Los Angeles's more traditionally white "majority culture" and hesitates to adopt entirely the social mores of this culture into which he has thrust himself.

Interestingly, in *Ask the Dust*, the ebbing and flowing spirituality of Fante's narrator-protagonist becomes a kind of barometer of both his social alienation and his approach to selective accommodation. Bandini's skepticism about organized religion and even about the existence of God becomes a marker of his attempts to shake off his Italian cultural inheritance and accommodate the norms of the consumerist, secular America that provides the setting for Fante's novel.[2] At the same time, Fante's narrator exhibits almost violent bursts of investment and pride in Catholic doctrine and culture, and such moments come to indicate the depth of Bandini's alienation from the culture that surrounds him in 1930s Los Angeles. Ultimately, tracing this ebb and flow of investment in the sacred in *Ask the Dust* allows us to reach a more nuanced understanding of the Italian diasporic experience.

Arturo Bandini and Definitions of Diaspora

It may be helpful at the outset to contextualize this line of argument with a few observations about developments in our understanding of diaspora. In his 1991 article on diasporas in modern societies, William Safran argues that only the Jewish diaspora genuinely qualifies as "the ideal type," or fits the most traditional pattern of diasporic experience.[3] In Safran's attempts to widen the definition of the concept while still applying it somewhat selectively,[4] he asserted that only the "Armenian, Maghrebi, Turkish, Palestinian, Cuban, Greek, and perhaps Chinese diasporas" could be "legitimately" understood as diasporic based on a typology of six features of diasporic communities.[5] Had the development of the theory halted there, we might be hard pressed to legitimate the idea of an Italian diaspora. However, before more than a few years had passed, other theorists such as James Clifford actively asserted the need to preserve a more inclusive definition of the term, arguing that "we should be wary of constructing our working definition of a term like *diaspora* by recourse to an 'ideal type,' with the consequence that groups become identified as more or less diasporic, having only two, or three, or four of the six basic features. Even the 'pure' forms [e.g., the Jewish diaspora] . . . are ambivalent, even embattled, over basic features."[6] This broader vision of diaspora remains prevalent in the field today. In this theoretical context, it has become increasingly possible to conceptualize the history of Italian emigration as encompassing diasporic movement and experience—including several characteristics that Safran and Clifford have emphasized as essential to diaspora, and that become increasingly visible in Fante's novel when we consider questions of spirituality.

I have already mentioned social alienation and selective accommodation, both of which will be essential to this essay because of their centrality to *Ask the Dust* and because of how they connect with Bandini's ever-changing relationship to the spiritual. Nevertheless, there are other qualities of diaspora to consider as well: for instance, "collective histories of displacement and violent loss,"[7] or the existence of diasporic individuals who "continue to relate, personally or vicariously, to [their original] homeland in one way or another."[8] For such individuals, Safran claims, "their ethnocommunal consciousness and solidarity are importantly defined by the existence of such a relationship."[9] As I have noted elsewhere,[10] Bandini's references to how he was "born poor, son of miseried peasants" evoke the Southern Italian agricultural laborers who were driven from their homeland by what Jennifer Guglielmo calls "impoverishing policies brought about by the [Italian] government" in the wake of Italian unification.[11] Through Bandini's comments, Fante marks his protagonist's presence in Los Angeles as the legacy of socioeconomic persecution and his family's "displacement" as a legitimate form of "violent loss," thus deemphasizing Bandini's self-professed assimilationism and instead stressing the reality of his diasporic identity. Indeed, as Clifford writes,

> Diasporic populations do not come from elsewhere in the same way that "immigrants" do. In assimilationist national ideologies such as those of the United

States, immigrants may experience loss and nostalgia, but only en route to a whole new home in a new place. Such narratives are designed to integrate immigrants, not people in diasporas. . . . *People whose sense of identity is centrally defined by collective histories of displacement and violent loss cannot be "cured" by merging into a new national community.*[12]

Given Bandini's "miseried" heritage, even when he casts himself as an assimilationist, referring to the United States as "[his] country" (*AD*, 47) and exclaiming that he is "an American and goddamn proud of it" (44), we have reason to doubt the validity of his self-interpretation. By the same token, even the first chapter of *Ask the Dust* illustrates Bandini's strong sense of "ethnocommunal consciousness and solidarity" born of his vicarious ties to Italy. Although Bandini himself is an American-born US citizen, he continually identifies with other Italians who link him vicariously to his family's original homeland. Italian men are a particular focus for Bandini in this respect—from Joe DiMaggio, whom he describes as "still a credit to the Italian people" (11), to "Leonardo, a great Italian critic" (14), and finally to "a few other Italians, Casanova and Cellini" (90). That Bandini insistently labels each of these men as "Italian" demonstrates their significance to his "ethnocommunal consciousness." From the start of *Ask the Dust*, then, we can see fundamental elements of diasporic experience in the text—elements that will grow even stronger and more visible through Bandini's fraught relationship to the sacred.

Another cornerstone of Safran's theory is that members of diasporic communities "believe that they are not—and perhaps cannot be—fully accepted by their host society"; thus, he argues, they "feel partly alienated and insulated from it."[13] This hallmark of many diasporic communities, especially those that are targets of racial or cultural prejudice, is also easily visible in *Ask the Dust*, in which Fante's narrator grapples with precisely this experience of alienation within the context of Los Angeles society. In fact, while Italian Americans might enjoy nearly full acceptance in the contemporary United States, Bandini's narrative is embedded in a historical moment—the Great Depression of the 1930s—when Italians did indeed confront real and in some cases extreme prejudice within US borders. In fact, as Clive Webb has noted, the real-life counterparts of Bandini and his parents faced more than ethnic slurs, with lynchings occurring in the American South and in other US states into the early twentieth century. Despite the fact that *Ask the Dust* does not directly depict this sort of violence, it does provide examples of xenophobic condescension and mean-spiritedness on the part of other Americans, reactions that can foster quite understandable feelings of alienation among diasporic individuals. In one instance, the proprietor of Bandini's hotel misidentifies him as "a Mexican" (*AD*, 48) and then argues with him about Western geography, insisting that Bandini's hometown of Boulder "is not in Colorado" (49) and refusing to let him remain in the hotel until he bows to her ignorance and agrees with her. In another moment, Bandini confides that as a child in Colorado, he was called "Wop and Dago and Greaser" (46), proclaiming that his tormentors "hate me and my father, and my father's father, and they would have my blood and put me down" (47). Such moments clearly contribute to our impression of Bandini as an alienated figure—and, thus, a diasporic one.

Before we consider how Bandini's spirituality dovetails with his diasporic identity, there is one more aspect of his experience with diaspora that we should consider in broader strokes. Bandini's approach to living in Los Angeles "encode[s] practices of accommodation with, as well as resistance to,"[14] the culture of the country and the city in which he has found himself. It is this balance that Clifford refers to in discussing "selective accommodation."[15] On the one hand, a current of cultural assimilation is visible in Bandini's adoption of quintessentially American interests and values, from baseball to the myths of the American Dream and white American cultural superiority. From the first page of the novel, we watch Bandini immerse himself in the most stereotypical of US pastimes as he "read[s] the box scores of the American League games" and takes pleasure and pride in DiMaggio's "leading the league in batting" (*AD*, 11). More complexly, Bandini indulges in problematic fantasies of upward mobility that belie his intermittent anti-classist impulses, just as he participates in sadly typical racist discourses that expose him as a hypocrite. Continually dreaming of himself as "a great author with that natty Italian briar, and a cane, stepping out of a big black car," Bandini indulges in the rags-to-riches mentality, buying into a largely unrealistic yet ever-popular vision of American life (13). He also perpetuates popular modes of discrimination against the novel's Chicanx characters that—as he himself admits[16]—echo his own experiences of ethnic discrimination. Sadly, this racist tendency becomes an additional marker of Bandini's willingness to assimilate. On the other hand, in some moments, Bandini roundly rejects the influence of the "majority culture" in favor of his own brand of Americanness. When, for example, he describes "the forlorn street of poverty for the Negro and swank for the whites" (140), Bandini bears witness to the intersectionality of racial inequality and class hierarchy,[17] critiquing a prevalent aspect of American society's organization in the 1930s from what seems to be the detached perspective of an outsider, and adding a layer of complexity to earlier descriptions of black characters that highlight his tendency to Other and exoticize blackness. In other moments, Fante's narrator simply longs for his home and family, but in a way that is distinctly culturally inflected: he misses "spaghetti swimming in rich tomato sauce, smothered in Parmesan cheese" (28). Granted, in previous decades, spaghetti had become popular in the United States at large as "a good response to meat shortages and the national embrace of Italy as an ally" in World War I,[18] and Bandini's mother's "rich tomato sauce" may arguably be more Italian American than Italian. Yet here, in his own way, Bandini "encodes a practice of resistance" to the all-American meal. Such moments also enhance our sense of Bandini's social alienation, so that one aspect of diasporic experience functions to deepen the other.

Clearly, a pattern of diasporic ambivalence emerges in *Ask the Dust* as Bandini's character develops. The sense of "violent loss" and enduring cultural connection that Bandini exhibits combines with his experiences of accommodation and alienation to establish him as a diasporic character more than a true assimilationist. Even if in some moments Bandini seems to *aspire* to full assimilation, the reality of his identity remains more complex—and Bandini's spirituality will only serve to make this complexity more obvious.

Selective Accommodation, Social Alienation, and Spiritual Engagement

So, then, how does Bandini's religious identity—his own fraught relationship to the sacred—help to further shape and reflect these aspects of his diasporic identity? The same pattern of social alienation and selective accommodation that marks Bandini's overall experience as diasporic is also visible in his relationship to his spirituality and his frequently ambivalent participation in religious rituals. More specifically, the gaps in Bandini's accommodation of US norms surrounding religion become indicators of his social alienation, intensifying our sense of Bandini's estrangement from mainstream Los Angeles society and American culture more generally. As before, the selectivity of accommodation deepens social alienation for Fante's diasporic figure.

At first, one or two chapters into Fante's novel, early references to religion might seem just to show how tenuous Bandini's links to the Italian diasporic community are. Indeed, Bandini appears quite eager to accommodate US social norms that encouraged Italian Americans to assimilate by deemphasizing their Catholic roots.[19] This becomes obvious when Bandini prepares to write a letter to his mother reporting his attendance at Mass; he soon clarifies that, as "an atheist" (*AD*, 22), he has gone to church only "to look at ... [t]hose beautiful girls" (15) who attend the service. Here, Bandini shows his unwillingness to profess a commitment to organized religion—or even to acknowledge the existence of God. Although his atheism is partly a reflection of Nietzsche's influence rather than of US culture in specific (he mentions having read *The Antichrist*), we can also interpret such comments as Bandini's attempt to disassociate himself from his Italian cultural heritage, replacing it instead with a secular set of values that he perceives as more thoroughly American. These implications of Bandini's attitude toward religion are especially visible given the obvious importance of his faith to his mother, who is more strongly linked to both Catholicism and the diasporic community than Bandini is.[20] When he stresses his need to mislead his mother, Bandini's rejection of the sacred suggests the vexed nature of his relationship to Italian diasporic culture in the United States—a relationship that he partly deprioritizes by accommodating the expectations of those outside his diasporic community.

Our impression of Bandini's self-distancing from religious faith as a form of accommodation of the "host culture" deepens as we follow him inside the sacred space of the church that features prominently in the novel's second chapter (fig. 2).[21] Bandini tells us,

> I pulled the huge door open and it gave a little cry like weeping. Above the altar sputtered the blood-red eternal light, illuminating in crimson shadow the quiet of almost two thousand years. It was like death, but I could remember screaming infants at baptism too. I knelt. This was habit, this kneeling. I sat down. ... A prayer. Sure, one prayer: for sentimental reasons. Almighty God, I am sorry I am

FIGURE 2. Postcard image of the altar of Our Lady Queen of Angels mission chapel, where Arturo goes to argue with God, in the Los Angeles Historic Plaza District.

> now an atheist, but have You read Nietzsche? Ah, such a book! Almighty God, I will play fair in this. I will make you a proposition. Make a great writer out of me, and I will return to the church. (*AD*, 22)

Here, even when Bandini consents to pray for old times' sake, temporarily obeying a social convention of his diasporic community, he undercuts the gesture by describing it as sentimental rather than as genuine. Likewise, Bandini's particular brand of bargaining with God emphasizes the transactional rather than the sacred character of a religion from which Bandini otherwise seems eager to distance himself, emphasizing its morbid elements (the "weeping" and the "blood-red eternal light" that is "like death") with a critical eye. And again, because the novel encourages us to see Bandini's Catholic identity as a specific feature of the Italian diasporic community of which he is a part, this impulse to turn a prayer into a materialistic proposition also functions as a signal of Bandini's accommodation of the norms of the "majority culture" that surrounds him, not his involvement in the diasporic community that has produced him.

Yet in the end, the pull of spirituality as a diasporic tie is equally strong, and it emerges that Bandini is more linked to the Catholic faith of his ancestors than he might wish to admit. A closer reading of the passage above suggests that Bandini remains intellectually and emotionally linked to the church, even if that linkage is unpleasant. In commenting on "the quiet of almost two thousand years" and the "screaming infants at baptism," Bandini reveals his abiding attention to the fundamentals of Christian history and ritual. Moreover, in promising to "return to the church" if God transforms him into "a great writer," Bandini takes part in a tradition among "less affluent Catholics in Italy" of "bargaining with God, Mary, or a local saint, promising to perform certain acts of devotion in exchange for some requested blessing."[22] In this case, of course, the "act of devotion" is itself a signal of Bandini's nonbelief, since he rebels to the point of refusing to associate himself with the church at all unless the "requested blessing" materializes. Still, his mentality also functions as an indicator of the ways that Bandini's identity continues to be influenced by the religion of his family and his diasporic community, rather than the larger cultural milieu of Los Angeles or the United States.

Similar tendencies become especially visible in Bandini's sexual identity, as it is implied that Bandini cannot bring himself to have sex with women because he cannot stop "[thinking] about the Blessed Virgin" (*AD*, 19). In fact, when he encounters a prostitute on leaving the church in chapter 2, Bandini's desire to experience sex—and, notably, his willingness to turn sex into an economic transaction—is tempered by an incredibly strong wave of religious guilt. "Your whole life is doomed to celibacy," Bandini tells himself, "you should have been a priest, Father O'Leary talking that afternoon, telling us the joys of denial. . . . Oh Mary conceived without sin, pray for us who have recourse to thee" (25). In this moment, the stream of Bandini's consciousness is ultimately overtaken by a sacred text, that of the Miraculous Medal of the Immaculate Conception. Granted, this particular reference is to a tradition of French origin that, together with Bandini's mention of the Irish Father O'Leary, gestures toward a pan-European culture of Catholicism. Nevertheless, Bandini here is certainly more aligned with Italy—and the supposed "superstitions of religion" that led southern Italian Catholicism to be treated with suspicion and condescension by northern Italians and other Americans alike[23]—than he is aligned with the original, traditionally Protestant and increasingly secular culture of the United States.

Here, Bandini practices a decidedly selective and limited form of accommodation, thus marking himself as diasporic—and, in this respect, as alienated from his adopted homeland. In fact, in this instance, Bandini's religious fervor does not merely reflect his social alienation; it actually drives it, since the young man's religious cultural inheritance makes it impossible for him to connect with others through the experience of sex.

We see the same impulse to revert to religion when, in the aftermath of a cataclysmic earthquake, Bandini makes disparaging comments about his Protestant neighbors and, in the same breath, expresses his identification with Catholic culture: "Around the bonfire the people were singing hymns. . . . I turned away. Jesus, these Protestants! In *my church* we didn't sing cheap hymns. *With us* it was Handel and Palestrina" (*AD*, 99; emphasis added). Again, Bandini embodies the concept of selective accommodation, resisting identification with either the original Puritan heritage of the United States or its intermittently more secular ideals, practices, and expectations. He also gestures toward the alienation that he feels from the American culture that surrounds him by specifically identifying himself as part of a group that is separate from it. By using that simple pronoun "us" in referencing matters of religion, Bandini efficiently communicates the extent of his self-distancing from the dominant social structures of 1930s Los Angeles. In this way, again, religious faith becomes a measure not just of a diasporic character's commitment to the sacred but also of his commitment to the ethnic community of which he is a part.

Interestingly, the events of the novel seem to reward Bandini's renewed faith after the earthquake, pushing Fante's narrator to experience more insistent feelings of identification with his religious community. "The world was dust, and dust it would become. I began going to Mass in the mornings," he recalls. "I went to Confession. I received Holy Communion. ... I bought a new rosary. I poured nickels and dimes into the Poor Box. I pitied the world" (*AD*, 104). Soon afterward, Bandini reports that "like a dream it came. . . . [A]n idea, my first sound idea, the first in my entire life, full-bodied and clean and strong, line after line, page after page" (106). Readers who expect that Bandini will interpret this event as the culmination of his "bargaining" with God will not be disappointed, as indeed, in response to his good fortune, he exclaims, "Oh God do I love you" (106). Likewise, when he finally submits the completed novel born of this "first idea," Bandini engages in a flurry of religious rituals: "I prayed once more. I went to mass and Holy Communion. I made a novena. I lit candles at the Blessed Virgin's altar. I prayed for a miracle" (145). This is not to say that Bandini becomes genuinely more pious by the novel's end. On the contrary, inclined to delusions of grandeur, he compares himself with the divine in ways that suggest an understanding of theology that would be incomplete at best and sacrilegious at worst according to Catholic expectations, calling himself "indomitable" (129) and expressing "rapturous self-satisfaction" (124) at an act of sexual assault. Not only does Bandini assign qualities to himself that are traditionally assigned to God by calling himself invincible or "indomitable," but he also directs feelings of "rapture" toward himself when they are traditionally directed toward God or the church. Considered alongside the "masochistic form of Catholicism, partly southern Italian and partly American Irish, in which suffering and self-abnegation" are highly desirable of worshipers,[24] these views of Bandini's appear starkly nonconformist—even heretical. Yet the shift in Bandini's attitude does still emphasize the power of his continuing relationship to religious rituals and expectations of divine support, even as he oscillates between belief and disavowal.

Reflecting on the Italian Diaspora through Religious Ambivalence

Many have argued that the current of Italian emigration that occurred after the unification of Italy in 1871 was "an expression of rebellion against oppression . . . a conscious rejection by a segment of the peasantry of the new social order which condemned them to political and economic subordination."[25] At the same time, the ties of the Italian diasporic community to Italy have remained strong—a fact that is as visible in the high number of return migrants to Italy as in the persistence of Italian cultural traditions (even if in transmuted forms) in countries such as the United States.[26] While Arturo Bandini is far from being uniformly dedicated to or immersed in religious practices and beliefs, his bursts of commitment to Catholic doctrine and culture speak to the compelling and complex nature of the Italian diasporic experience. It is only by examining Bandini's voluntary disavowals of spirituality and religion that we can achieve a true sense of how fraught, inconsistent, and complex his diasporic sense of self truly is. Indeed, it is largely through Bandini's contradictory, fluctuating relationship to the sacred that *Ask the Dust* allows us to penetrate the reality of his diasporic experience in all its anxious, emotional patchiness. Perhaps most importantly, however, tracing how investment in the sacred ebbs and flows in *Ask the Dust* allows us to reach beyond the individual character of Bandini, recognizing this same complexity and contradiction more broadly in the Italian diasporic experience in the United States and elsewhere—all through the intensely specific lens of spiritual identity.

Notes

1. For example, *Ask the Dust* has received limited attention outside of forums devoted exclusively to Italian American fiction. As I note elsewhere, Catherine J. Kordich, Melissa Ryan, Charles Scruggs, and Matthew Elliott are among the few critics who have written about the novel for more general audiences. See Roszak, "Diaspora."

2. This is not to suggest that the United States was overwhelmingly secular by the 1930s, although of course the structures of the US national government had always been secular, at least in name. However, it is true that significant currents of secularization had swept through the United States by this time. For instance, Catholic immigration had ironically made the country's public schools "more secular in order to neutralize the charge that these schools were de facto Protestant institutions (which to a large extent they had been, as Catholics correctly discerned)" (Hollinger, *Cloven Tongues*, 9).

3. Safran, "Diasporas," 84.

4. Safran was attempting to combat what he perceived as the dilution of the term "diaspora" by its over-application to too wide a variety of cases, posing his own definition "lest the term lose all meaning" (83).

5. Safran, 84. Safran describes these features thus: "1) they, or their ancestors, have been dispersed from a specific original 'center' to two or more 'peripheral,' or foreign, regions; 2) they retain a collective memory, vision, or myth about their original homeland—its physical location, history and achievements; 3) they believe that they are not—and perhaps cannot be—fully accepted by their host society and therefore feel partly alienated and insulated from it; 4) they regard their ancestral homeland as their true, ideal home and as the place to which they or their descendants would (or should) eventually return—when the conditions are appropriate; 5) they believe that they should, collectively, be committed to the maintenance or restoration of their original homeland and to its safety and prosperity; and 6) they continue to relate,

personally or vicariously, to that homeland in one way or another, and their ethnocommunal consciousness and solidarity are importantly defined by the existence of such a relationship" (83–84).

6. Clifford, "Diasporas," 306.

7. Clifford, 307.

8. Saffran, "Diasporas," 84.

9. Safran, 84.

10. These policies appear to have been intended to "discipline" a southern Italian peasant class that was perceived as uncivilized and racially inferior to the "northern ruling class" (Guglielmo, *Are Italians White?*, 9).

11. Guglielmo, 20.

12. Clifford, "Diasporas," 307; emphasis added.

13. Safran, "Diasporas," 83.

14. Clifford, "Diasporas," 307.

15. Clifford, 308.

16. During one moment of clarity, Bandini admits, "When I say Greaser to you [i.e., to Camilla Lopez, his Chicana love interest] it is not my heart that speaks, but the quivering of an old wound, and I am ashamed of the terrible thing I have done" (*AD*, 47).

17. Kimberlé Crenshaw coined this term in the late 1980s, arguing that "the tendency to treat race and gender as mutually exclusive categories of experience and analysis" ignores the fact that "the intersectional experience [of race and gender discrimination] is greater than the sum of racism and sexism." Crenshaw, "Demarginalizing the Intersection of Race and Sex," 209. Since then, the term "intersectionality" has also become a useful tool for describing other intersecting categories of prejudice and injustice, including discrimination based on sexual orientation, disability, religious affiliation, and other aspects of identity.

18. Parkin, *Food Is Love*, 121.

19. David A. Hollinger reminds us that "[p]rior to 1960, if you were in charge of something big and had opportunities to influence the direction of society, chances are you grew up in a white Protestant milieu" (*Cloven Tongues*, ix). Interestingly, however, this pressure to conform came not just from the Anglo-Saxon majority in this period but even from other Catholics with a different orientation to their faith: as Peter R. D'Agostino notes, "Many historians have pointed out, and many Italian Americans themselves can recount, how their particular 'style' of religiosity met with harsh criticism from fellow Catholics in the United States" ("Utterly Faithless Specimens," 36).

20. This detail of the novel is quite realistic; one researcher reports having discovered that "first-generation [Italian American] respondents remained strict Catholics, those of the second were moderate, and those of the third generation were marginal Catholics" (Gallo, *Ethnic Alienation*, 131).

21. This term continues to be used with diasporic communities even when some members (like Bandini) are second-generation immigrants. This use of the term further highlights how even diasporic individuals born in the host country may remain estranged from it to some degree.

22. Jacobson, *World's Christians*, 348.

23. Donna Gabaccia, quoted in Guglielmo, *Are Italians White?*, 9.

24. Casillo, *Gangster Priest*, 393.

25. Vecoli, "Italian Diaspora," 120.

26. According to Rudolf J. Vecoli, "in the period 1905–76, more than 8.5 million [Italian emigrants] remigrated" to Italy. Vecoli, "Italian Diaspora," 114.

Works Cited

Casillo, Robert. *Gangster Priest: The Italian American Cinema of Martin Scorsese.* Toronto: University of Toronto Press, 2006.

Clifford, James. "Diasporas." *Cultural Anthropology* 9, no. 3 (1994): 302–338.

Collins, Richard. *John Fante: A Literary Portrait.* Toronto: Guernica, 2000.

Cooper, Stephen. *Full of Life: A Biography of John Fante.* New York: North Point Press, 2000.

Cooper, Stephen, and David Fine, eds. *John Fante: A Critical Gathering.* Madison, NJ: Fairleigh Dickinson University Press, 1999.

Crenshaw, Kimberlé. "Demarginalizing the Intersection of Race and Sex: A Black Feminist Critique of Antidiscrimination Doctrine, Feminist Theory, and Antiracist Politics." *University of Chicago Legal Forum* 1 (1989): 139–167.

D'Agostino, Peter R. "'Utterly Faithless Specimens': Italians in the Catholic Church in America." In *Anti-Italianism: Essays on a Prejudice.* edited by William J. Connell and Fred Gardaphé, 33–39. New York: Palgrave Macmillan, 2010.

Elliott, Matthew. "John Fante's *Ask the Dust* and Fictions of Whiteness." *Twentieth Century Literature* 56, no. 4 (2010): 530–544.

Fante, John. *Ask the Dust.* New York: HarperCollins, 2006.

———. Letter to Jo Campiglia. November 29, 1938. "P.S." In *Ask the Dust.* New York: Harper Perennial, 2006.

Gallo, Patrick J. *Ethnic Alienation: The Italian Americans.* Rutherford, NJ: Fairleigh Dickinson University Press, 1974.

Guglielmo, Jennifer, and Salvatore Salerno. *Are Italians White? How Race Is Made in America.* New York: Routledge, 2003.

Hollinger, David A. *After Cloven Tongues of Fire: Protestant Liberalism in Modern American History.* Princeton, NJ: Princeton University Press, 2013.

Jacobsen, Douglas. *The World's Christians: Who They Are, Where They Are, and How They Got There.* Chichester, West Sussex, UK: Wiley-Blackwell, 2011.

Kordich, Catherine J. "John Fante's Ask the Dust: A Border Reading." *MELUS* 20, no. 4 (1995): 17–27.
Parkin, Katherine J. *Food is Love: Food Advertising and Gender Roles in Modern America*. Philadelphia: University of Pennsylvania Press, 2006.
Roszak, Suzanne. "Diaspora, Social Protest, and the Unreliable Narrator: Challenging Hierarchies of Race and Class in John Fante's *Ask the Dust*." *Studies in the Novel* 48, no. 2 (2016): 186–204. *Project MUSE*, doi:10.1353/sdn.2016.0022.
Ryan, Melissa. "At Home in America: John Fante and the Imaginative American Self." *Studies in American Fiction* 32, no. 2 (2004): 185–212. *Project MUSE*, doi:10.1353/saf.2004.0005.
Safran, William. "Diasporas in Modern Societies: Myths of Homeland and Return." *Diaspora: A Journal of Transnational Studies* 1, no. 1 (1991): 83–99.
Scruggs, Charles. "'Oh for a Mexican Girl!': The Limits of Literature in John Fante's 'Ask the Dust.'" *Western American Literature* 38, no. 3 (2003): 228–245. *JSTOR*, www.jstor.org/stable/43022257.
Vecoli, Rudolph J. "The Italian Diaspora, 1876–1976." In *The Cambridge Survey of World Migration*, edited by Robin Cohen, 114–122. Cambridge: Cambridge University Press, 1995.
Webb, Clive. "The Lynching of Sicilian Immigrants in the American South, 1880–1910." In *Lynching Reconsidered: New Perspectives in the Study of Mob Violence*, edited by William D. Carrigan. 175–204. New York: Routledge, 2014.

"Sad Flower in the Sand": Camilla Lopez and the Erasure of Memory in *Ask the Dust*

Meagan Meylor

In the prologue to *Ask the Dust*, composed in 1938 as a letter to his editor at Stackpole Sons Publishers, John Fante offers a vividly impressionistic précis that suggests the mystery at the thematic core of the as yet unpublished novel: "Ask the dust on the road! Ask the Joshua trees standing alone where the Mojave begins. Ask them about Camilla Lopez, and they will whisper her name."[1] By *Ask the Dust*'s somber close, Camilla has vanished into the desert surrounding Los Angeles, her body presumably covered over by dust that erases the "secret of [her] death."[2] If Camilla does indeed return to dust, readers should consider the following question when trying to fully understand the novel: in what ways does Fante challenge dominant discourse about 1930s Los Angeles and Mexican identity by focusing his poetic prose on the disappearing figure of Camilla?

After decades of obscurity, Fante's 1939 novel *Ask the Dust* is now considered perhaps the most seminal work in the literary history of Los Angeles, appreciated by generations of readers for its treatment of desire and cul-

"Sad Flower in the Sand" 59

tural identity set against the backdrop of an ethnically diverse neighborhood, Bunker Hill, in Depression-era Los Angeles. While Fante scholars have given considerable attention to the novel's protagonist Arturo Bandini, his Mexican American love interest, Camilla Lopez, has not been adequately analyzed. Scholarship concerning Camilla has tended to limit itself to her role in Arturo's projection of his "own sense of ethnic alienation" onto her, even as she acquiesces to mainstream Anglo mythologies and values.[3] In this essay, I aim to help fill this gap in the critical literature by examining the importance of Camilla through the lens of Los Angeles's social history, most notably in the city's treatment of marginalized ethnic identities during the 1930s. I will argue that through the novel's motifs of absence and presence regarding the figure of Camilla, *Ask the Dust* offers a counter narrative about the Mexican past of Los Angeles, a historical moment that is often erased, both explicitly and implicitly, by the collective memory of the city.

Regarded as "Fante's most compelling creation" by David Wyatt, the figure of Camilla has received a significant amount of critical attention since Fante's literary revival in the 1990s.[4] Following Stephen Cooper, many scholars have recognized Camilla's importance as an ethnic mirror for Arturo, a "reflection of his own insecurity as an Italian American."[5] As a young woman of Mexican heritage living in Los Angeles during the year 1933, Camilla "represents the Other, the supposed foreigner upon whom [Arturo] projects his fantasies," a reading that other critics of the novel corroborate.[6] For these scholars, Camilla embodies the "alienated Eden" and "pre-conquest landscape" of the region itself, even as she represents "the New World in its pristine state, before the Spanish conquest and the racism of Anglo Americans."[7] Various readings highlight Camilla's "romanticized ethnicity," and scholars such as Catherine Kordich argue that her "adoption of Anglo [and Hollywood] preferences" reflects her "cultural resonance, identity, and pride" as a border character in Los Angeles.[8] A more recent interpretation counters the established view that Arturo rediscovers "his own status as an alien and an outsider" through his interactions with Camilla, asserting instead that Arturo "perceives her as the embodiment of a racial otherness that helps him to imagine his own whiteness."[9] While Wyatt, Kordich, and others have established a critical conversation about the meaning of Camilla, additional close readings and analyses are needed to address the complexity of Fante's character. In this essay, I will challenge these interpretations and expand on others by placing Fante's novel within the sociohistorical context of 1930s Los Angeles, thereby enriching our understanding of Camilla's motivations, the development of her identity, and the mystery of her poignant fate.

In chapter 1 of *Ask the Dust*, before the reader is introduced to Camilla, Arturo fantasizes about the Mexican women living in downtown Los Angeles, the "Aztec princesses and Mayan princesses" that he desires to possess to reinforce his grandiose illusions of literary prowess (15). Through his alter-ego protagonist, Fante presents a romanticized portrait of the Mexican women in the Grand Central Market and the Church of Our Lady, where Arturo "[goes] to Mass to look at them" and devises ways of speaking with these "beautiful girls" (15). Inextricably linked with religious guilt and sinful behavior in Arturo's consciousness, his longing to claim one of these women as his "Mexican girl" is dependent upon his financial success as a writer: "in my fashion they were mine, this one and that one, and some day when another check came it would be a fact" (15). The Mexican women in these gendered urban spaces become commodities, objects that Arturo can consume in his attempt to lay claim to a white American identity. Although subjugated as a non-Anglo member of society, Arturo accentuates the exotic "otherness" of the Mexican women to suppress his own ethnic insecurities and affirm his heteronormativity as he tries to storm his way into the mainstream literary canon. Nevertheless, Fante emphasizes that Arturo's vision of the Mexican "princesses" is one of "dream and reverie," grounded in a flawed perception of himself rather than the historical reality of their existence in Los Angeles during the 1930s (15).

Through the ironic distance between the author's implied view and that of his dreamy protagonist, Fante draws our attention to the collective romanticization of Mexicans and Mexican Americans that predominated during this period, in large part because of the Southern California tradition of the "Spanish fantasy past." Originally coined the "Spanish heritage past" by Carey McWilliams, the romanticized—and heavily fictionalized—myth surrounding California's Spanish period became ingrained in the social memory of California due to the cultivation of the "Mission legend" by real estate boosters and tourists themselves.[10] In this historical construction, the Spanish colonial history of California was celebrated, while the origins of Mexican culture were denigrated and dressed up to appear more European—metaphorically as well as literally, as illustrated not only by the extravagant Spanish costumes that Mexican workers on Olvera Street were forced to wear but also by the theatrical reenactments of Helen Hunt Jackson's sentimental novel *Ramona* throughout the twentieth century.[11] To call into question this fictionalized social memory, Fante excavates the inner workings of ethnic alienation and self-definition through Arturo's interior monologue, as he struggles to define himself in opposition to another marginalized group in Los Angeles during the Great Depression. To analyze the romanticization of Mexican Americans that Fante focalizes through the figure of Camilla, I will be invoking the concepts of "social imaginary" and the "erasure of memory" that Norman M. Klein locates at the core of Los Angeles's history and culture.[12] Citing historical models of erasure, Klein explores the "chronicle of evasions" that occurred in downtown Los Angeles as a response to the Anglo anxiety about the growing Mexican presence in the Bunker Hill and downtown districts of Los Angeles during the early twentieth century.[13] Klein's theories of collective forgetting and cultural distraction regarding the city's Mexican past will help us appreciate how the cultural matrix of the Great Depression shapes the social realities of Fante's characters in *Ask the Dust*.[14]

Arturo first encounters Camilla through her voice. As he sits at a table in the Columbia Buffet where Camilla works as a waitress, Fante writes that Arturo "heard her voice without looking up" (34). Arturo orders and receives a cup of coffee from Camilla, his perception of her yet untainted by the racial prejudices that he must negotiate throughout the rest of the novel. Before Arturo sees Camilla's face—emblematic of her personhood and ethnic identity—he describes her as strong and healthy: "Her back was to me, and I saw the tight smoothness of her shoulders under a white smock, the faint trace of muscle in her arms, and the black hair so thick and glossy, falling to her shoulders" (34). Significantly, Arturo's initial impression of Camilla does not include the racial codes that he employs after she turns around, therefore allowing him to interpret the "contour of her face." Through Arturo's conflicted perspective, Fante suggests that Camilla was "not beautiful," except for the shape of her face and "the brilliance of her teeth" (34). However, Arturo contradicts himself within the same gaze, noting that Camilla was a "racial type, and as such she was beautiful," describing her nose as "Mayan, flat, with large nostrils," and her lips as "heavily rouged, with the thickness of a negress' lips" (34). By transforming Camilla from a subject into an object,

Arturo subverts his first impression of her beauty by imagining that "she was too strange for me," thus distancing himself from his own racial otherness, which he transposes onto her body to assert the supposition of his own whiteness (34). His consciousness clouded by racist narratives about identity—narratives that Fante was painfully familiar with, having grown up as a child of Italian immigrants in Colorado—Arturo struggles to *see* Camilla, despite his initial attraction to her strength and beauty. Seen in this light, the first encounter between Arturo and Camilla in the Columbia Buffet foreshadows the unstable dynamic that will take form between them, an impassioned relationship in which Camilla traverses the line between subject and object, presence and absence (fig. 3).

Despite Arturo's attempts to denigrate Camilla's appearance by effacing her selfhood through a racialized—and patriarchal—gaze, Camilla challenges these attempts by responding with laugher. Fante writes, "Suddenly she opened her mouth to the ceiling and laughed in a most mysterious fashion, so that even the bartender wondered at her laughter" (35). Arturo and the bartender Sammy Wiggins become confused by her laughter, which functions as a symbol of her challenge to Arturo's male gaze. Arturo reflects on this startling release of affect, asserting that he "understood her laughter. It was for me. She was laughing at me" (35). Camilla's laughter provokes Arturo to turn his gaze onto himself, leading him to touch his own hair and ensure that his collar and tie are "clean and in place" (35). He then looks into the bar mirror at the Columbia Buffet—representative of the ethnic mirror that is Camilla—and comments on his reflection: "I saw what was certainly a worried and sallow face, but not a funny face, and I was very angry" (35). In this scene, Camilla's "black large eyes flashing their laughter" facilitate a moment of self-awareness in Arturo, thus exposing the cracks in his sexist and racist treatment of her (35). Feminist critic Hélène Cixous writes the following about the role of laughter in the "feminine text," in other words, a text that decenters our cultural discourse about the supposed "natural" hierarchy of men and women: "Laughter that breaks out, overflows, a humor no one would expect to find in women—which is nonetheless surely their greatest strength because it's a humor that sees man much further away than he has ever been seen."[15] Considered through this theoretical lens, Camilla's laughter serves as a source of disruption, shedding light on Arturo's flawed sense of reality that emerges as a result of his

FIGURE 3. Marie Baray, John Fante's Mexican American lover, model for the character of Camilla Lopez in *Ask the Dust*. (Courtesy of John Fante Literary Group LLC.)

assuming a heteronormative white identity through the erasure of Camilla's selfhood.

As Arturo continues to observe Camilla in the Columbia Buffet, Fante draws our attention to Camilla's huaraches, physical objects that Arturo uses to castigate Camilla's Mexican heritage. When Arturo first notices the huaraches, Fante writes that he was "very grateful, for it was a defect about her that deserved criticism" (35). Described as "ragged" and "tattered," the traditionally peasant sandals serve as a metonym for both her racial caste and her impoverished state; ultimately, as Matthew Elliott has suggested, Arturo uses the huaraches to perceive Camilla as "an image of racial difference as a romanticized ideal" (35).[16] At the same time, Arturo's fascination with her feet sets up a sexual motif, as Camilla's body becomes highly sexualized through his male gaze. In addition, there is a possible evocation of "zapato" and "Zapatista" in Fante's attention to the huaraches, thereby making a connection between Camilla and Mexican insurgence. Thus, the tattered shoes of *Ask the Dust* can signify an amalgam of erotic, political, and cultural emblems that Fante addresses through the figure of Camilla. Furthermore, Fante makes repeated references to Camilla's movement throughout the Columbia Buffet, presenting her as a dancer moving gracefully within the physical space: "The girl moved like a dancer, her strong silk legs gathering bits of sawdust as her tattered shoes glided over the marble floor" (35). Although Arturo perceives Camilla as dancing inside the theatricalized beer hall, revealing her sensuality and gracefulness, the movement also evokes images of a marionette doll, a female object that is controlled and confined to a specific space. To combat his feelings of insecurity as a response to Camilla's sarcastic laughter, Arturo centers his attention on Camilla's restricted movement "back and forth" (36). In this way, both Camilla's huaraches and her confinement within the physical limits of the restaurant serve as signifiers that Arturo uses to construct his imagined patriarchal whiteness.

As the scene progresses, Camilla becomes filled with "grimness" and "bitter hatred," which cause her to let out a "shriek, a mad laugh like the clatter of dishes" (36). Arturo wants to hurt her in hopes of restoring heteronormative power dynamics but Camilla repeatedly interrupts his performance of white masculinity as an effort to erase her sense of selfhood. Consequently, his failure to define Camilla through a racialized male discourse is what propels Arturo's self-examination: "every time I looked at her she smiled her wish, until it had a mysterious effect on me, and I became conscious of my inner organism, of the beat of my heart and the flutter of my stomach" (37). As Fante writes in the aforementioned prologue to *Ask the Dust*, Arturo recognizes Camilla's anger and pain because he "understands how it is with this business of social prejudice," and yet he continuously positions Camilla as an exoticized "Other" through his ethnic self-fashioning.[17] Nevertheless, the figure of Camilla functions as a source of disruption in the text, challenging Arturo's racial prejudices in person as well as haunting his thoughts in her absence.[18]

When Arturo returns the next morning to the Columbia Buffet only to find it closed, he comes up with an idea for a gift that he wants to give Camilla: he erases his autograph in a copy of *The Little Dog Laughed* and writes instead, "To a Mayan Princess, from a worthless Gringo" (38). In doing so, he situates Camilla within the mythology of the romanticized Spanish past and aligns himself within dominant Anglo society, while simultaneously denigrating himself. After questioning the impressiveness of his inscription, he erases it again and writes a condescending message about his literary status:

Dear Ragged Shoes,

You may not know it, but last night you insulted the author of this story. Can you read? If so, invest fifteen minutes of your time and treat yourself to a masterpiece. And next time, be careful. Not everyone who comes into this dive is a bum. (39)

This palimpsest of inscriptions highlights Arturo's conflicted negotiation of identity, precisely because racist narratives that marginalize other ethnic individuals complicate his own social relationships and his sense of self. When later that morning Arturo returns again to the Columbia Buffet, he reads Camilla's "widened" eyes as a sign that she is glad to see him (41). As the projection of an unreliable narrator, Arturo's fantasy of Camilla as a "Mayan princess" in her "castle" is clearly a romantic veil disguising the racial tensions and insecurities at play within their complex relationship (41). Although Arturo's internal monologue suggests that Camilla's heightened response emerges from her desire to see him, we can surmise that other social forces may be provoking her alert state.

Throughout this key scene, Arturo and Camilla take turns insulting each other: Arturo pours his beer into a spittoon, Camilla rips up the copy of *The*

Little Dog Laughed, Arturo asks her why she wears huaraches and calls her a "filthy little Greaser" (44). After Camilla runs away from him in horror, Arturo appropriates narratives of white conquest and colonial history, asserting that he "was an American, and goddamn proud of it" (44). He continues his diatribe while smoking a discarded cigarette butt and standing in the gutter: "From sand and cactus we Americans had carved an empire. Camilla's people had had their chance. They had failed" (44). Through this monologue, Fante is satirizing Arturo's investment of whiteness—popularized as the "wages of whiteness" by W. E. B. Du Bois—that operates in opposition to Camilla's Mexican female otherness, the category to which Camilla has been assigned. Furthermore, the novel is shedding light on the prevalent social attitude that the history of the Mexican people is one of failure. However, Fante critiques this collective narrative through the confessional passage in chapter 6, in which Arturo feels guilty about his treatment of Camilla and reflects on his personal experiences with prejudice and racism: "Ah, Camilla! When I was a kid back home in Colorado it was Smith and Parker and Jones who hurt me with their hideous names, called me Wop and Dago and Greaser, and their children hurt me, just as I hurt you tonight" (46). In this moment of painful self-awareness, Arturo is unable to maintain his imperialistic persona and recognizes that he has been projecting his fears, desires, and insecurities onto Camilla because of his internalized self-hatred fostered by white supremacy and racist victimization. Although Arturo fails to express these apologetic insights to Camilla in person, Fante is highlighting the pervasive racism and marginalization of ethnic individuals in Los Angeles during the 1930s. Through the figure of Camilla—whose feminine matrix disrupts Arturo's attempts to define her within traditionally masculine and racialized structures—the novel offers a counter narrative to the Mexican history of Los Angeles to which Camilla belongs.

Although *Ask the Dust* does not make explicit the historical context of marginalization and racialized violence against Mexicans and Mexican Americans during the early twentieth century, Fante sheds light on such issues taking place just beyond the narrative frame through his fictional treatment of Camilla as a person of Mexican heritage living in Los Angeles. A close friend of journalist and attorney Carey McWilliams—whose political writing centered on the plight of migrant workers, the threatening rise of fascism in the United States, and the treatment of marginalized ethnic communities in California—Fante was both well aware of and sympathetic to the plight of ethnic laborers and Mexican working-class communities. As Cooper makes clear, "Fante may have been personally uninvolved in the political fray of his time, but he was neither uninformed regarding the issues nor indifferent to their developments."[19] In fact, Fante credited McWilliams for inspiration to write a sociological novel about the experiences of Filipino migrant laborers in California; through the early 1940s Fante worked hard on this novel, which he called *The Little Brown Brothers*, exploring American racism and the shameless treatment of Filipino immigrants.[20] Although this project failed to be completed or published, it reemphasized Fante's interest, evident throughout *Ask the Dust*, in fictionalizing the legacy of racism in the United States. By contextualizing *Ask the Dust* within a wider social framework, including a vivid portrait of Mexicans and Mexican Americans in the downtown districts of Los Angeles, Fante suggests the fear and violence that affected individuals like Camilla during this period. In attending to that context, we will gain important insights into Camilla and her role at the center of Fante's novel.

Historicizing Ask the Dust: *Mexican Repatriation in the 1930s*

Following the passage of the Immigration Acts of 1921 and 1924, Mexicans were encouraged to immigrate to the American Southwest as a solution to the region's labor shortages. As McWilliams writes, "In the years from 1920 to 1930, Mexican immigrants constituted the dominant element in the great migratory labor pool in California," replacing the labor pool that was formerly recruited in parts of Southeastern Europe and China, prior to the Chinese Exclusion Act of 1882.[21] Although some observers and academic circles cautioned against the facilitation of large-scale Mexican immigration to parts of Texas, Arizona, and California—gesturing toward the social welfare provided during economic downturns such as the 1920-1921 depression—the Los Angeles Chamber of Commerce initially cheered the influx of Mexican laborers, deeming them "cheap, plentiful, and docile."[22] Recruiting Mexican labor for jobs in agriculture, railroads, and other industries, US employers even directly requested the president of Mexico to send workers across the border to fill the labor demand.[23] However, as Mexicans began to settle in large numbers in various Los Angeles barrios (by 1930, the estimated Mexican-born population of the city was 368,000), an anxiety arose about the growth of urban blight in such areas as Bunker Hill, eventually leading to the redevelopment of downtown and the forced removal of residents from neighborhoods perceived as predominantly Mexican. While Mexican labor continued to be imported into the greater Los Angeles area during the decade from 1919 to 1929, hostility toward these new residents became a central feature of the collective imaginary of Mexican space and culture at the time.

Tensions over the growing Mexican population in Los Angeles were amplified during the Great Depression, as the need for external labor decreased and Mexican immigrants were used as scapegoats to blame for the struggling economy. David G. Guitiérez writes that, "as nationwide unemployment reached six million by the end of 1930 and eleven million by the end of 1932, Mexican workers were singled out as scapegoats in virtually every locale in which they lived in substantial numbers."[24] Popular media outlets promulgated the idea that Mexicans were burdening federal welfare programs throughout the country, resulting in a popular perception of the Mexican people as "foreign usurpers of American jobs" and "unworthy burdens on relief rolls."[25] Government officials recognized that a significant proportion of public relief funds for the unemployed would have to be dispersed in communities that were home to large numbers of Mexican American citizens born in the United States to immigrant parents. According to George J. Sánchez, these officials "believed the hard times made it imperative that the scarce jobs and resources be reserved for American citizens," referring more to ethnic background than actual definitions of citizenship.[26] As a solution to this perceived problem, the County of Los Angeles supported a "repatriation campaign," the wide-scale deportation of Mexicans and Mexican Americans from the United States between 1929 and 1937.[27] Without due process, the Immigration and Naturalization Service forced the relocation of over 500,000 persons of Mexican descent at "a wholesale per capita rate of $14.70," a far smaller amount than it would have cost the government to provide relief aid to these communities.[28]

While some Mexicans and Mexican Americans were coerced into purchasing one-way tickets to Mexico on their own, others were violently rounded up during raids in urban spaces and workplaces, regardless of their citizen-

"Sad Flower in the Sand"   69

ship status. As historian Vicki L. Ruiz asserts, "Mexicans were either summarily deported by immigration agencies or persuaded to depart voluntarily by duplicitous social workers who greatly exaggerated the opportunities awaiting them south of the border."[29] Mexican immigrants, as well as lawful citizens of Mexican descent, were immediately confronted with this fear of mass raids and arbitrary deportation, "scare-head tactics" conducted by local welfare bureaus and committees to remove Mexicans from the United States.[30] As Sánchez explains, "almost every Mexican family in Southern California confronted in one way or another the decision of returning or staying."[31] In his examination of how repatriation caused demographic shifts within Los Angeles, Sánchez also explains that "the maltreatment of Chicanos on relief, particularly the pressure put on residents by county officials to repatriate, deeply affected those Mexicans who stayed in the city."[32] Though unmentioned in *Ask the Dust*, it stands to reason that Camilla, as a young Mexican American woman living and working in downtown Los Angeles day in and day out in the 1930s, would likewise have been confronted with this same circumstance. With this historical context in mind, Camilla's behavior becomes much more poignant as we begin to examine the non-text of the novel, the moments of insight just beyond the frame of Fante's narrative (fig. 4).[33]

FIGURE 4. *Los Angeles Times* front page of April 24, 1931. (Copyright © 1931. *Los Angeles Times*. Used with permission.)

Race, Sexuality, and the Body: A Feminist Analysis of Camilla Lopez

Fante alludes to these anti-Mexican policies of exclusion throughout *Ask the Dust*. For example, in the Alta Loma scene, Arturo tries to check in to the hotel, only to face a race-based interrogation by the white landlady Mrs. Hargraves, who exclaims, "We don't allow Mexicans in this hotel," a comment to which she adds, "Nor Jews" (49). After assuring her that he is of neither Mexican nor Jewish descent, Arturo erases his name and hometown on his magazine—a literary moment representative of Klein's theories of "simultaneous distraction"—in order to accommodate her declaration that Boulder is in Nebraska, not Colorado.[34] As the figurative Anglo gatekeeper of Los Angeles, Mrs. Hargraves mirrors the racist system of inclusion and exclusion in the city. In this scene, Arturo must again negate his identity and heritage in order to be accepted by dominant Anglo standards, much as he attempts to erase Camilla's selfhood in his moments of ethnic re-fashioning.

As another example, Fante makes a veiled reference to the fear induced by discriminatory policies of repatriation in chapter 9, when Arturo visits Camilla at the Columbia Buffet after receiving a check in the mail for his story *The Long Lost Hills*. Inside the beer hall, Arturo notices that Camilla has traded her worn huaraches for white pumps, which hurt her feet and cause her to wince in pain. While I agree with the scholarly interpretation that her purchasing of white pumps represents a consumer effort to trade a Mexican identity for an Anglo one, it is useful to imagine what outside forces may be pushing her to appear more "white." Far from least among these would be fear of racialized violence or even forced deportation. Moreover, when Arturo calls Camilla his "little Mexican princess," Camilla vehemently responds, "I'm *not* a Mexican!" and asserts, "I'm an American" (61). Immediately denying her Americanness, Arturo declares that she will always be "a sweet little peon," a "flower girl from old Mexico," thus attempting to isolate Camilla within the mythology of the Spanish past as a means of laying claim to her otherness (61). Camilla responds by furiously throwing ethnic slurs at Arturo, then removing her white pumps; however, she ultimately apologizes to Arturo and replaces her huaraches with the white pumps once again, unable to suppress her desire to conceal her Mexican ethnicity by making herself appear more "American."

"Sad Flower in the Sand" 71

Waiting for Camilla to arrive at the parking lot with Sammy, the white bartender who works with her at the Columbia Buffet, Arturo rummages through her 1929 Ford Roadster. He discovers that Camilla has changed her name on the owner's certificate from Camilla Lopez to Camilla Lombard, and he asks her about this once they are driving together toward the beach. As she careens through the streets of Los Angeles—a moment of temporary agency, albeit reckless, that allows her to transgress conventional boundaries—Camilla responds that she uses the name Lombard "for fun," to which she adds, "sometimes I use it professionally" (64).[35] After asking Arturo if he likes his name, she inquires, "Don't you wish it was Johnson, or Williams, or something?" (64). In this moment, Fante is emphasizing the attempts of ethnic individuals to Anglicize themselves, in order to access resources denied to them or to evade outright violence and possible deportation. As Camilla and Arturo follow the "white line" on the pavement toward the beach, where "white fists" of water crash along the "white sand," these racial implications echo throughout the rest of the scene, much like the recurring image of fog that hovers over so much of the novel, suggestive of white privilege and the dominant collective imaginary that erases or "whitewashes" the Mexican past of Los Angeles (64–65). In *Whitewashed Adobe*, William Deverell asserts, "Los Angeles became a self-conscious 'City of the Future' by whitewashing an adobe past, even an adobe present and an adobe future. That whitewashing was imperfectly, even crudely accomplished—adobe yet showed through—but it was nonetheless a way by which white Angelenos created distance (cultural or personal) between themselves and the Mexican past and the Mexican people in their midst."[36] It is this whitewashing that Fante gestures toward in the wake of Arturo's violent reaction to Camilla's "supreme joke" of pretending to drown as well as their failed sexual encounter on the beach, where Arturo racializes his defensiveness by asserting that, "In my hotel they don't allow Mexicans" (67, 69). Illustrating the ways in which relationships suffer in a society rooted in racism and white supremacy, Fante shows how the social context of Los Angeles during the 1930s shapes the fictional realities of Arturo and Camilla.[37]

As Arturo struggles to lay claim to Camilla by reducing her to a unified feminine "other," he continuously fails to embody the role of the masculine patriarchal white male. In a poem he writes and sends to Camilla by telegraph, he plagiarizes the following line from Ernest Dowson, a nineteenth-century English poet and novelist: "I have been faithful to thee, Camilla, in my fashion" (75). Once Camilla receives the poem from Arturo, she proceeds to rip it into pieces, again disrupting Arturo's efforts to assert normative notions of Anglo masculinity in opposition to Camilla's exoticness, as a result of his ethnic insecurities. Even as Arturo reduces her to physical objects, Camilla's presence seems to haunt him, lingering even in her displacement: "I lay down and even Camilla who was a pillow with a tam-o-shanter for a head seemed so far away and I could not bring her back" (89). In Camilla's absence, Arturo becomes aware of his inability to possess her through a phallocentric perspective of authority.[38]

If Camilla is the disruptive feminine force of the novel, despite Arturo's attempts to transform her body into an exoticized sexual object, the figure of Vera Rivken represents the other side of femininity: the passive, the silenced, the empty body. A Jewish woman from Long Beach, Vera's scarred body becomes a space of abjection, a vessel through which Arturo can indirectly "have" Camilla, his "Mayan princess" (92). Arturo fantasizes that he is a conqueror "like Cortez, only . . . Italian" in a pre-conquest arena where there is "no California, no Los Angeles, no dusty streets, no cheap hotels, no stinking newspapers, no broken, uprooted people from the East, no fancy boulevards" (94). In Vera's bedroom, a space in which the silenced feminine object is confined, Arturo imagines his erotic conquest through the erasure of Camilla's body. As Kordich argues, "By assigning himself to the role of conqueror, he can subjugate an absent Camilla by proxy."[39] Although Arturo asserts that he possesses a unified Camilla through Vera-as-surrogate, the guilt that accompanies this sexual encounter lends itself to a reading of Arturo as unable to demonstrate traditional patriarchal structures. Ultimately, through Arturo's struggle to differentiate between reality and mythology following his failed possession of Camilla through Vera's body, the text offers a counter narrative about the Mexican past of Los Angeles; instead of presenting Mexicans as picturesque entities that Arturo can subdue, Fante examines the ways in which complex racial narratives have been used to construct the region's self-image, narratives that Arturo fails to appropriate in his interactions with Camilla and Vera.

During one of the novel's most memorable scenes, Arturo interprets the 1933 Long Beach earthquake as "the wrath of God" caused by his "mortal sign against Vera Rivken" (98, 96). As buildings crumble and dead bodies pile up around him, Arturo imagines that Camilla is dead and reflects on their complicated relationship; however, as he sits in a lot with other survivors and members of the Red Cross, he soon discovers that Camilla's name is not included in the broadcasted names of the dead. Although the earthquake scene can be read as a catastrophic natural disaster from which Arturo derives religious and sexual meaning, it can also be interpreted as a symbolic representation of the subversive feminine force in Fante's novel. As Cixous writes,

> There have been poets who would go any lengths to slip something by at odds with tradition—men capable of loving love and hence capable of loving others and of wanting them, of imagining the woman who would hold out against oppression and constitute herself as a superb, equal, hence 'impossible' subject, untenable in a real social framework. Such a woman the poet could desire only by breaking the codes that negate her. Her appearance would necessarily bring on, if not revolution—for the bastion was supposed to be immutable—at least harrowing explosions. At times it is in the fissure caused by an earthquake, through that radical mutation of things brought on by a material upheaval when every structure is for a moment thrown off balance and an ephemeral wildness sweeps order away, that the poet slips something by, for a brief span, of woman.[40]

Cixous's metaphor of the female subject as the fissure of an earthquake—an apocalyptic motif familiar to writers of Los Angeles literature—is useful for my reading of Arturo's experience with the Long Beach earthquake, as well as for my interpretation of Camilla as a disrupter of tradition and social memory in the novel. As the earthquake decenters his internal monologue, Arturo focuses on the possibility of Camilla's death: "She was dead and I was alive. Good. I pictured her dead: she would lie still in this manner; her eyes closed like this, her hands clasped like that. She was dead and I was alive" (100). It is in this moment of disorder that Arturo acknowledges that Camilla can die, thus affirming her personhood and undermining his romanticization of her as a static Mexican object isolated in the past; although Camilla is not physically present in the earthquake scene, Fante emphasizes Camilla's identity through her perceived absence.

Despite this temporary moment of recognition, Arturo makes persistent attempts to fashion a white American identity in opposition to Camilla's romanticized Mexicanness. When Arturo visits Camilla at the Columbia Buffet in chapter 13, he calls her a "little insolent beerhall twirp" after she repeatedly denies his requests for a date (107). He continues to demean her later in the parking lot when he seizes her wrist and declares, "You're going with me, Mexican" (107). However, Camilla fights back against his violent attempts to assert dominance over her, and she ultimately leaves the beer hall arm in arm with Sammy. In the following chapter, Camilla mysteriously appears at Arturo's apartment for a scene in which they discuss Camilla's relationship with Sammy. As Fante demonstrates, Camilla's desire to be with Sammy underscores her motivation to appear more Anglo, to be accepted by the dominant white society. By marrying Sammy, she can receive the Anglicized name that would serve as a source of security, despite Sammy's racist view of her as a "Little Spick" who, because of her inferior ethnic status, does not deserve to be treated like a human being (121). Much like the owner's certificate for her car, Camilla's attachment to Sammy stems from her yearning to escape the racialized violence and repatriation programs taking place in Los Angeles during the 1930s, which we can imagine would have been of considerable concern for a young Mexican American woman like Camilla. After Camilla mentions Sammy's poor health, Fante writes that Arturo "thought of throwing her out . . . that would be delightful: order her out, she so wonderfully beautiful in her own way, and forced to leave because I ordered her out" (115). Borrowing the language of repatriation, Arturo places himself in an authoritarian position because of his jealousy over Camilla's love for Sammy. In other words, Arturo imagines kicking out Camilla in order to quell his uneasiness when faced with Camilla's choice of Sammy as her lover instead of him.

Furthermore, Fante describes Camilla as "looking toward the window and the door like a trapped animal," an image suggesting the kind of anxiety that plagued Mexicans and Mexican Americans at large throughout the Greater Los Angeles of her era (116). Moreover, the physical confines of the apartment reflect the ways in which Camilla's body is restricted to certain social spaces; although Camilla holds a sense of agency in her ability to move throughout Los Angeles, her movement is an arrested movement. As both Arturo and Sammy direct her and police her body, Fante is shedding light on the wider social forces that are restraining Camilla's mobility—as well as threatening her forcible removal—as a Mexican woman in downtown Los Angeles. Camilla's sense of personal entrapment also references the limited possibilities for women during this time period. Camilla feels "stuck" by economic limitations and patriarchal expectations of marriage and family during a historical moment in which women are working for wages, and in many cases, becoming the main breadwinner for their family. In this way, Fante draws our attention to the ways in which his characters respond to disrupted gender roles and gender dynamics, while still being marked by gendered restrictions and social constraints. Similarly, in his essay about Arturo's construction of whiteness in the novel, Elliott argues that Camilla is marked as inferior because of the location of her apartment: "Excluded from most sections of the city by segregation laws, Camilla lives near Central Avenue, in what Arturo refers to as 'the Los Angeles Black Belt.'"[41] Because of such widespread regulatory mechanisms as restrictive covenants and redlining, Camilla is restricted to living in this specific space, unlike Arturo who can "pass" as white, and thus be admitted into Mrs. Hargraves's hotel.[42] Although Fante does not explicitly address this social context, we must surmise that Camilla's anxious behavior may be developing in some significant way out of these wider social concerns, especially the pervasive fear of deportation caused and reinforced by the systematic relocation and removal of the Mexican presence from Los Angeles.

Within *Ask the Dust*, Arturo attempts to mirror these exclusionary acts in his effort to fashion a heteronormative white identity. As Arturo grapples with the Madonna-whore complex perpetuated by his family's peasant Italian mythologies and the popular social imaginary of the Mexican past, Fante makes repeated references to Arturo figuratively writing on Camilla's face, thus erasing her selfhood and reinscribing his conflicted feelings about their scarred relationship. For example, Arturo envisions "memories of that night at the beach written upon [her] scornful face," and later describes her face as a "manuscript of misery and exhaustion" (117, 139). Through Arturo's figurative effacement of Camilla, Fante alludes to the systematic erasure of the Mexican population whether through deportation or the more insidious process of collective displacement that leads to ultimate forgetting. As Klein states, "Virtually no ethnic community downtown was allowed to keep its original location. . . . The overall effect resembles what psychologists calls 'distraction,' where one false memory allows another memory to be removed in plain view, without complaint—forgotten."[43] As Camilla becomes increasingly elusive by the end of the novel—her disappearance is a gradual movement, first from the Laguna Beach house, then from her own apartment into the desert—Fante gestures toward the social erasure of the Mexican presence in Los Angeles, a city that was once a part of Mexico.

Throughout the novel, Camilla's surroundings become increasingly restrictive, with Fante describing her bedroom as a "little prison" and "curtained trap," where she develops a dependence on marijuana to temporarily escape from her feelings of confinement and fear (*AD*, 142, 148). After Arturo declares that she "had quit" and "wanted to die," Camilla has a hysterical fit in her apartment building, causing the police to pick her up and transport her to the County hospital (147). Arturo makes many failed attempts to find Camilla as she is repeatedly transferred to nearby hospitals, ultimately resulting in her admittance to the County Institute for the Insane at Del Maria. When Camilla returns to Los Angeles after escaping from the institute and traveling throughout northern California, Fante describes her as overcome by fear: "She had nothing to say with her lips, but the ghastly cast of her face, the teeth too white and too big now, the frightened smile, these spoke too loudly of the horror shrouding her days and nights" (155–156). Although Fante does not grant us access into the consciousness of Camilla—about whom we know precious little in proportion to the amount of attention she receives—we can infer that her fear develops in some substantial degree as a result of the threatening social forces around her. In response to her mental unraveling, Arturo attempts to create a domestic haven for her by moving her to a home in Laguna Beach and purchasing her a dog that they name Willie; however, as his inability to perform at the shooting range foreshadows, Arturo ultimately fails to solidify this "domestic fantasy," and Camilla disappears yet again.[44]

It is important to address the question, in what ways does Fante himself generate and imprison his female character within a male-inscribed literary text? In discussing the metaphor of literary paternity in their classic study of nineteenth-century female writers, Sandra M. Gilbert and Susan Gubar state, "As a creation 'penned' by man, moreover, woman has been 'penned up' or 'penned in.' As a sort of 'sentence' man has spoken, she has herself been 'sentenced': fated, jailed, for he has both 'indited' her and 'indicted' her. As a thought he has 'framed,' she has been both 'framed' (enclosed) in his texts, glyphs, graphics, and 'framed up' (found guilty, found wanting) in his cosmologies."[45] Although Camilla is a deeply engendered literary creation within Fante's text—echoing the "penning in" and "sentencing" of

Mexicans and Mexican Americans during Repatriation—the novel presents Camilla's story in a time when "women have remained invisible in standard accounts of the 1930s," as Paula Rabinowitz has declared.[46] By giving Camilla an autonomous voice, Fante centers the working-class female subjectivity, thereby recasting the political (and literary) history of Depression-era Los Angeles.

In the novel's final chapter, Arturo discovers that Sammy has kicked Camilla out of his house in the Mojave Desert, where she has wandered off into the "wasteland" with nothing but her dog and a bottle of milk (164). Presuming Camilla dead, Arturo laments that the infinite dust of the desert will "cover [her] memory with ageless wind and heat and cold," again reflecting the processes of collective erasure embedded in Los Angeles's historical landscape (164). By examining Fante's novel through a sociohistorical lens, we can read Camilla's final departure—her final exile—as a powerful response to the systems of racial rejection, exclusion, and expulsion in Los Angeles during the 1930s. In her erasure, Fante evokes the silenced voices of the countless Mexicans and Mexican Americans who were marginalized and deported during the years of the Great Depression. Shedding light on these harrowing social realities, Fante offers his readers a window into the often lost and silenced histories of Los Angeles and its Mexican past through the figure of Camilla. As Arturo hurls his novel into the desert in dedication to the memory of Camilla, Fante makes it clear that *Ask the Dust* is not only Arturo's story: it is also, unforgettably, Camilla's.

Notes

1. Fante, *Prologue to* Ask the Dust, 1.
2. Fante, *Ask the Dust*, 164. Unless otherwise noted, all excerpts are from the HarperCollins edition, hereafter cited in text by page number.
3. Cooper, *Full of Life*, 172.
4. Wyatt, "LA Fiction," 40.
5. Scruggs, "Oh For a Mexican Girl!," 235.
6. Laurila, "Los Angeles Booster Myth," 115.
7. Ryan, *Out of the Shadows*, 205; Guida, "Imagination of the Past," 136.
8. Kordich, *John Fante*, 80.
9. Collins, *John Fante*, 137; Elliott, "John Fante's *Ask the Dust*," 534.

10. The phrase "Spanish fantasy past" has been widely used by historians in their discussions of the treatment of Mexicans and Mexican Americans in California during the nineteenth and twentieth centuries.

11. For more on the "Spanish fantasy past," see McWilliams, *Southern California*, and Kropp, "Citizens of the Past?" For more on the popularity of Helen Hunt Jackson's *Ramona*, see Dydia DeLyser, "Ramona Memories." For more on the cultural politics of Los Angeles in the 1930s, see Schrank, *Art and the City* and "Public Art."

12. Klein, *History of Forgetting*, 9.

13. Klein, 131.

14. Klein describes the theory of "distraction" as the process in which "fictions are built into facts, while in turn erasing facts into fictions." Klein borrows the theoretical term from the field of cognitive psychology to examine the collective forgetting that, he argues, shapes mass culture and public policy in Los Angeles.

15. Cixous, "Castration or Decapitation?," 55.

16. Elliott, "John Fante's *Ask the Dust*," 538.

17. Fante, *Prologue to* Ask the Dust, 2.

18. Cooper, *Full of Life*, 163. For further discussion on feminine characters and the subversion of patriarchal discourses, specifically within the works of William Faulkner, see Gwin, *Feminine and Faulkner*. Through the vehicle of feminist theory and poststructuralism, Gwin usefully argues that the tension between male writing and feminine characters creates "bisexual spaces," in which conceptions of gender are disrupted and traditionally masculine modes of narration are challenged.

19. Cooper documents Fante's skepticism of leftist political writing and organized political movements, as well as his close relationship to Carey McWilliams.

20. In addition, Fante and McWilliams collaborated on a screenplay in 1948 entitled *St. Anthony's Forty Blondes*, based on the true incident in which a Catholic priest attempted to place forty blonde orphans into adoptive Mexican American homes. The script depicts the clear social division between the Mexican community and white community, epitomized by the white mob that forces the Mexican families to give up the white children for fear of miscegenation and the disruption of hegemonic social structures within the community.

21. McWilliams, *Southern California*, 316.

22. McWilliams, "Getting Rid of the Mexican," 322.

23. Aguila, "Mexican/US Immigration Policy."

24. Guitérez, *Walls and Mirrors*, 72.

25. Ruiz, *Out of the Shadows*, 29.

26. Sanchez, *Becoming Mexican American*, 210.

27. Scholars have provided conflicting studies on the number of Mexicans

and Mexican Americans who were repatriated during the Great Depression. Estimates range from five hundred thousand to two million. For further reading on this topic, see Balderrama and Rodríguez, *Decade of Betrayal*, and Hoffman, *Unwanted Mexican Americans*.

28. McWilliams, *Southern California*, 317. For an eyewitness report of this campaign in action, see "Horde Departs for Native Soil," *Los Angeles Times*, April 24, 1931, 1: "One of the largest single groups of Mexican repatriates ever to leave in the vast migration back to Mexico—eleven hundred and fifty men, women and children—departed yesterday on two sections of the Southern Pacific's Sunset Limited, bound for Nogales and El Paso, from which points they will be distributed inland in the southern republic. . . . Piteous scenes were enacted at the station as the members of the group prepared to leave. Tears flowed freely among the adults and small boys and girls who had been born in the United States [and] were bewildered by the sudden turn of events which uproot their lives here and transfer them to another soil. Possessions among the travelers were scant. One elderly man hugged to his breast his only material possession—a much-used guitar. Another solicitously carried a caged songbird, which chirped cheerlessly in the chill rainy morning. A little boy and girl grasping each other's chubby hand held firmly to their English school books, and many mothers held babes in their arms.... The Mexicans ... have become fear-ridden at renewed activity of immigration officials, which they have misinterpreted as a wholesale deportation campaign directed at their nationality. Immigration authorities, however, deny a campaign against any single nationality and assert they are interested only in those subject to deportation by the law."

29. Ruiz, *Out of the Shadows*, 29.

30. Balderrama and Rodríguez, *Decade of Betrayal*, 2.

31. Sancehz, "Rise of the Second Generation," 10.

32. Sanchez, *Becoming Mexican American*, 224.

33. Scholars Mark Laurila, Kevin McNamara, and David Wyatt have all alluded to the 1930s repatriation programs in their analyses of Camilla's behavior and disappearance.

34. Klein, *History of Forgetting*, 13.

35. Scholars have pointed out that the name Camilla Lombard is a riff on Carole Lombard, the 1930s movie actress.

36. Deverell, *Whitewashed Adobe*, 7–8.

37. The Chicano theater collective Teatro de Esperanza exposes this social context that Fante alludes to in the 1976 play *La Victima*, which dramatizes issues of Mexican immigration, the repatriation campaign of the 1930s, and the threat of deportations in both the past and present. See Huerta, *Necessary Theater*, 316–365.

38. See Cixous, "Laugh of Medusa," 876.

39. Kordich, "A Border Reading," 26.

40. Cixous, " Laugh of the Medusa," 879. Minrose C. Gwin also includes this passage in her book *The Feminine and Faulkner*, as she analyzes the disruptive feminine characters of Faulkner's novels.

41. Elliott, "John Fante's *Ask the Dust*," 536.

42. Following the creation of the Federal Housing Administration in 1934, services such as insurance and home loans were denied to prospective property owners in defined geographical areas, oftentimes neighborhoods of color. This practice of redlining was coupled with the creation of restrictive covenants, which forbade property sales to African Americans and other ethnic minorities.

43. Klein, *History of Forgetting*, 1–2.

44. Kordich, *John Fante*, 75.

45. Gilbert and Gubar, *Madwoman in the Attic*, 13.

46. Rabinowitz, *Labor and Desire*, 3. In her study of little-known female writers of the 1930s, Rabinowitz urges us to "understand how women's lives, however private, nevertheless construct political history, and how women's writings engage in debates that extend into the so-called public arena."

Works Cited

Aguila, Jamie R. "Mexican/US Immigration Policy Prior to the Great Depression." *Journal of the Society for Historians of American Foreign Relations Diplomatic History* 31, no. 2 (April 2007): 207–225.

Balderrama, Francisco, and Raymond Rodríguez. *Decade of Betrayal: Mexican Repatriation in the 1930s*. Albuquerque: New Mexico University, 1995.

Cixous, Hélène. "Castration or Decapitation?" *Signs* 7, no. 1 (October 1981): 41–55.

———. "The Laugh of the Medusa." *Signs* 1, no. 4 (July 1976): 875–893.

Collins, Richard. *John Fante: A Literary Portrait*. Toronto: Guernica, 2000.

Cooper, Stephen. *Full of Life: A Biography of John Fante*. New York: North Point Press, 2000.

DeLyser, Dydia. "Ramona Memories: Fiction, Tourist Practices, and Placing the Past in Southern California." *Annals of the Association of American Geographers* 93, no. 4 (December 2003): 886–908.

Deverell, William. *Whitewashed Adobe: The Rise of Los Angeles and the Remaking of Its Mexican Past*. Berkeley: University of California Press, 2005.

Elliott, Matthew. "John Fante's *Ask the Dust* and Fictions of Whiteness." *Twentieth Century Literature* 56, no. 4 (2010): 530–544.

Fante, John. *Ask the Dust*. New York: HarperCollins, 2006.

———. *Prologue to* Ask the Dust. Santa Rosa, CA: Black Sparrow, 1990.

Fine, David. *Imagining Los Angeles: A City in Fiction*. Reno: University of Nevada Press, 2000.

———. "John Fante and the Los Angeles Novel in the 1930s." *John Fante: A Critical Gathering*, edited by Stephen Cooper and David Fine, 122–130. Madison, NJ: Fairleigh Dickinson University Press, 1999.

Gilbert, Sandra M., and Susan Gubar. *The Madwoman in the Attic: The Woman Writer and the Nineteenth-Century Literary Imagination.* New Haven, CT: Yale University, 1979.

Guida, George. "In Imagination of the Past: Fante's *Ask the Dust* as Italian-American Modernism." *John Fante: A Critical Gathering*, edited by Stephen Cooper and David Fine, 131–144. Madison, NJ: Fairleigh Dickinson University Press, 1999.

Gutiérrez, David G. *Walls and Mirrors: Mexican Americans, Mexican Immigrants, and the Politics of Ethnicity.* Berkeley: University of California Press, 1995.

Gwin, Minrose. *The Feminine and Faulkner: Reading (Beyond) Sexual Difference.* Knoxville: University of Tennessee Press, 1990.

Hoffman, Abraham. *Unwanted Mexican Americans in the Great Depression: Repatriation Pressures, 1929–1939.* Tucson: University of Arizona Press, 1974.

Huerta, Jorge. *Necessary Theater: Six Plays about the Chicano Experience.* Houston: Arte Publico Press, 1989.

Kipen, David. *Los Angeles in the 1930s: The WPA Guide to the Golden State.* Berkeley: University of California Press, 2011.

Klein, Norman. *The History of Forgetting: Los Angeles and the Erasure of Memory.* New York: Verso, 1997.

Kordich, Catherine J. "John Fante's *Ask the Dust*: A Border Reading." *MELUS* 20, no. 4 (1995): 17–27.

———. *John Fante: His Novels and Novellas.* New York: Twayne Publishers, 2000.

Kropp, Phoebe. "Citizens of the Past? Olvera Street and the Construction of Race and Memory in 1930s Los Angeles." *Radical History Review* 81 (2001): 34–60.

Laurila, Mark. "The Los Angeles Booster Myth, the Anti-Myth and John Fante's *Ask the Dust*." In *John Fante: A Critical Gathering*, edited by Stephen Cooper and David Fine, 112–121. Madison, NJ: Fairleigh Dickinson University Press, 1999.

McNamara, Kevin R. *The Cambridge Companion to the Literature of Los Angeles.* Cambridge: Cambridge University Press, 2010.

McWilliams, Carey. "Getting Rid of the Mexican." *American Mercury* 28 (1933): 322–324.

———. *Southern California: An Island on the Land.* Layton, UT: Gibbs Smith, 2010.

Rabinowitz, Paula. *Labor and Desire: Women's Revolutionary Fiction in Depression America.* Chapel Hill: University of North Carolina Press, 1991.

Ruiz, Vicki L. *From Out of the Shadows: Mexican Women in Twentieth-Century America.* New York: Oxford University Press, 1998.

Ryan, Melissa. "At Home in America: John Fante and the Imaginative American Self." *Studies in American Fiction* 32, no. 2 (2004): 185–212.

Sánchez, George J. *Becoming Mexican American: Ethnicity, Culture and Identity in Chicano Los Angeles, 1900–1945*. New York: Oxford University Press, 1993.

———. "The Rise of the Second Generation: The Mexican American Movement." Unpublished paper. 1986.

Schrank, Sarah. *Art and the City: Civic Imagination and Cultural Authority in Los Angeles*. Philadelphia: University of Pennsylvania Press, 2009.

———. "Public Art at the Global Crossroads." *Journal of Social History* 44, no. 2 (2010): 435–457.

Scruggs, Charles. "'Oh For a Mexican Girl!': The Limits of Literature in John Fante's *Ask the Dust*." *Western American Literature* 38, no. 3 (2003): 228–245.

Villa, Raúl Homero. *Barrio-Logos: Space and Place in Urban Chicano Literature and Culture*. Austin: University of Texas Press, 2000.

Wyatt, David. "LA Fiction Through Mid-Century." In *The Cambridge Companion to the Literature of Los Angeles*, edited by Kevin R. McNamara, 35–47. Cambridge: Cambridge University Press, 2010.

"A *Ramona* in Reverse": Writing the Madness of the Spanish Past in *Ask the Dust*

Daniel Gardner

As reminders of the bygone days of Spanish colonialism, both Mexican nationals and Mexican American US citizens living in Depression-era California could be tolerated as members of a cheap migrant labor force supporting the state's massive agricultural industry, but as residents of Los Angeles they were often treated as outcasts. This ambivalence, provoked by Anglo notions of the imagined Spanish past, suffuses John Fante's *Ask the Dust* (1939).[1] Considered through the lens of this ambivalence, the novel can be seen as a socially conscious literary effort to counter and revise the cultural imaginary exemplified by Helen Hunt Jackson's 1884 romance *Ramona*. Fante saw the spirit of *Ramona* haunting 1930s Los Angeles in the fantasies of identification that plagued victims of the novel's mythical treatment of colonial Anglo-Mexican relations. Through the proliferation of popular stereotypes perpetuated by the novel's influence, the dominant Anglo culture reinforced those relations by splitting the Mexican signifier into two basic signifieds sliding between obedience and disruption.[2] On the one hand, the discourse signified Mexican subjects as tolerable when seen in the romanticized light of the Spanish colonial or postcolonial Californio periods, eras attributed some measure of dignity in the social imaginary owing to their perceived European ancestry. On the other hand, the simple descriptor "Mexican" could and frequently was deployed pejoratively to designate an unwanted immigrant element of the population. Of course, the term oversimplifies and obscures intracultural differences such as national affiliations, regional identities, and generational experiences, but to many Anglos, "Mexican" meant non-Anglo and thus non-American. While "Anglo" itself is far too reductive to represent accurately the variegated white population of Los Angeles, the term was likewise used in this broadly stereotyping way. Such a view of Anglo identity explains how in the Los Angeles of *Ask the Dust* Fante's thoroughly Italian American protagonist Arturo Bandini can claim, if only wishfully, a wholly assimilated American identity even though in his Colorado hometown he was labeled a "Wop."[3] Out of such an ethnically conflicted environment, *Ask the Dust* emerges as a creative attempt to protest the colonial discourse of the Spanish past that Fante indicts Helen Hunt Jackson's *Ramona* for popularizing.

In 1946 Fante's friend Carey McWilliams published *Southern California Country: An Island on the Land*, his now classic study of the social and political forces that shaped the region's culture. Reflecting on the very few novels "that suggest what Southern California is really like," McWilliams recommended *Ask the Dust*.[4] As lifelong fellow spirits and drinking cronies, McWilliams and Fante held a special place for each other but McWilliams was also a cleareyed critic who did not dole out support lightly. While endorsing Fante's novel McWilliams criticized the many fantasies about Southern California deployed by nineteenth- and early twentieth-century boosters attempting to draw in tourists and investors. One fantasy that McWilliams took particular issue with was what he called "the Spanish heritage past." This fantasy envisioned modern Los Angeles as inheritor of the Spanish colonial and postcolonial Californio periods, replete with images of gracious haciendas and seductive señoritas. For McWilliams, the Spanish past became a profitable fantasy as a result of the immense popularity of *Ramona*.[5] (In acknowledgment of *Ramona*'s influence on California historiography, McWilliams borrowed from Jackson the phrase "An Island on the Land" for the subtitle of his book.) Beyond praising Fante for an exceptional literary work that portrays

Depression-era Los Angeles authentically, McWilliams draws pointed attention to the competition between booster fantasies and the truth. To claim that Fante rendered Los Angeles as "it really was" is to credit his literary deconstruction of the ersatz Spanish past. As post-Western scholars William Handley and Nathaniel Lewis explain, "authenticity . . . refers to the capacity of any author, whether novelist or historian, and any artifact, whether artistic or archeological, to bespeak originality. And originality has little authority or meaning without being copied."[6] In his subversive representation of the oft-copied Spanish past, Fante, in McWilliams's estimation, became an early and forceful debunker of booster fantasies, just as *Ask the Dust* has become an essential element of the "authentic" Los Angeles experience.

At the center of *Ask the Dust* is the struggle for an authentic claim to belonging in modern Los Angeles. As Fante shows through the tragic affair of Arturo and Camilla, this is a claim that the colonial discourse of the Spanish past complicates with its intentional confusion of fantasy and reality. For a text to project "reality," the modes of production that construct its "truth" must be obscured. So-called realist texts typically obscure their modes of production in order to project a seamless vision of "reality." By contrast, the modernist stream-of-consciousness narration of *Ask the Dust* calls attention to itself even as it immerses us in the disruptive and disorienting ambivalences of its characters' experiences, thus achieving its palpably realistic effects. In recognizing the fantasy of received racist truths and disclosing their mechanisms, *Ask the Dust* reveals the tenuous nature of the dominant culture's authority, providing us with an opportunity to construct new fantasies of identification based on the affirmation of difference.

Fante intimates his intention to deconstruct false notions of California when in *Prologue to "Ask the Dust"* he describes the projected novel as "*Ramona* in reverse."[7] By reversing the Spanish-past dynamics of *Ramona*, Fante intervenes in a misleading account of history by retelling it otherwise in the present. A regional manifestation of the national myth of the American West, the Spanish past entails a set of cultural beliefs and behaviors that treat with reverence the Spanish colonial history of California and, by extension, the cultural legacy that Southern California boosters later fabricated for consumption by their Anglo customers. In seeking to displace the stereotyping appeal of the Spanish past fantasy and, more broadly, popular notions of the West, *Ask the Dust* voices an alternate, non-Anglo narrative of the American experience. In effect, this alternate narrative resists the stereotype, a chief strategy of colonial discourse that upholds white supremacy as an idealized desire while forcing the subjugated Mexican "other" to mask its racial difference. Underlying this strategy, however, is an unspoken anxiety—another ambivalence—over the precariousness of that putative supremacy, an anxiety that surfaces in such works of popular literature as *Ramona* or in such artificially constructed public spaces as Olvera Street, adjacent to the historic city center of Los Angeles Plaza. At a time when it was typical to deny the legitimacy of Mexican communities in Los Angeles, *Ask the Dust* recognizes their presence as valid even as they were exploited as objects of manufactured desire, marginalized as social burdens, and subject to forcible removal. Furthermore, Fante's critique tracks the outcomes of systemic stereotypical representation by dramatizing how the imperialist nostalgia of the Spanish past results in what McWilliams would later call a form of "cultural schizophrenia" tormenting a vital part of the Los Angeles social body. Finally, in recognizing how the ambivalence of Mexican stereotypes disguises a crisis of colonial authority—the hegemony desires the other even as the hegemony opposes the other, insisting on imposing its own primacy—*Ask the Dust* counters the racial fetishism of *Ramona* by filling in the erasures so critical to the function of colonial discourse. Anticipating today's postcolonial studies by more than half a century, Fante's treatment of Arturo's quest to create an original work of literature reveals the revitalizing energy and productive power of stories marginalized or missing from the cultural archive.

Through narrative parallels, *Ask the Dust* criticizes *Ramona* for the romanticism of Jackson's effort at social protest, which, while well-intentioned, is undermined by her idealization of the desire for whiteness. Thematically, the two novels share much in common: both depict protagonists involved in interracial love affairs that lead to confrontations with Anglo villains. Caught between the Californio society that raised her without love and the Saboba Indian community that welcomes her, the "half-breed" Scots-Indian Ramona is the literary antecedent to Arturo Bandini, the aspiring Italian American writer who straddles the border of Los Angeles's dominant culture and its nonwhite margins. Yet the novels' respective plotlines differ significantly. Whereas Ramona finds mutual affection in her relationship with the Native American Alessandro, Arturo experiences unrequited love with Camilla Lopez. Frustrated desire turns to tragedy when at the end of *Ask the Dust*, after being spurned one last time by the white would-be pulp western writer Sammy, Camilla disappears into the Mojave Desert. By contrast, although tragedy strikes Ramona when Alessandro, driven mad by constant racist humiliations, steals a horse and is shot dead, romance triumphs in the end. True to its sentimentalism, *Ramona* concludes not with the death of Alessandro at the hands of an Anglo vigilante but with our heroine happily remarried to the doting landowner Felipe who has loved her all along. As Ramona's whiteness wins out over her half-Indian heritage, the contrast between her racial destiny and Alessandro's fate underlines the separateness of self and other that colonial authority requires. *Ask the Dust* disrupts the racial duality of *Ramona*'s colonial discourse through Fante's barbed mimicry of the love triangle. Arturo, Camilla, and Sammy all suffer, a point that Fante will reemphasize in the desert scene near the end of the novel where Arturo is moved by the recognition of humanity's common fate—a far cry from the strict delineation of difference upon which colonial authority stakes its claim to control. At the same time, the root resemblance of self and other that colonial authority disavows is represented in the doubling strategies of *Ask the Dust*.[8] However, the reversal of colonial authority that *Ask the Dust* executes as *Ramona*'s ironic double could not occur before the sensational reception of Jackson's romantic narrative was appropriated in the colonial discourse of Southern California's Spanish past fantasy.[9]

Immensely popular on publication and increasingly so in generations to come via Hollywood film adaptations and the annual Ramona pageant (known as America's Longest Running Drama), *Ramona* succeeded not as a novel of social protest but as a pretext for the Southern California boosters who appropriated Jackson's colonial nostalgia to serve their commercial designs.[10] These boosters capitalized on the continuing success of the novel by popularizing a set of discursive practices that would help entrench colonial attitudes and conditions well into twentieth-century Los Angeles. During the economic boom of the 1880s, real estate promoters made regular references to *Ramona* as an important part of the region's appeal. For decades publisher Colonel Harrison Gray Otis used his *Los Angeles Times* to exploit the romance of *Ramona* in order to lure investors and home buyers to Southern California with such headlines as "Ramona: The Greatest Attraction Yet Offered in the Way of Desirable Real Estate Investment" and "Camulos: The Real Home of Ramona."[11] Another significant figure in the booster movement, the prolific writer Charles Fletcher Lummis, published many articles in the *Times* and elsewhere linking the pastoral appeal of *Ramona* to the Southern California landscape, thereby playing a critical role in making the foreign heritage of the Spanish past a familiar part of local history (fig. 5).[12]

Spanish past boosters continued to exert their influence upon Los Angeles with the 1930 opening of Olvera Street and the revitalized interest in the surrounding plaza that followed. Both spaces exemplify how the Spanish past was constructed to market modern Los Angeles. Through the efforts of booster extraordinaire Christine Sterling, Olvera Street offered tourists a Spanish-themed retreat only months after the stock market crash that sent the nation into the Great Depression. More than a temporary escape, Olvera Street was touted as a local Los Angeles measure to mitigate the harsh realities of the national economic collapse. While lobbying for approval to develop the site, Sterling drew upon the logic of racial essentialism in citing labor skills supposedly peculiar to Mexican workers. These workers and their skills were needed to produce the sombreros, maracas and other kitschy crafts to be sold along the shaded promenade that Sterling envisioned as a commercially and socially productive remedy to the problem of unemployed Mexicans draining public relief programs, and thus a way to alleviate a chronic burden from the Los Angeles economy during the Depression.

In filtering his criticism of the Spanish past through the perspective of Arturo Bandini, Fante highlights the inherent ambivalence of the stereotype. As an Italian American, Arturo shares in the experience of an "in-between people," a group that while declared by the government "white on arrival" and thus presumably eligible for the benefits of first-class citizenship, by and large suffered the abuses of social marginalization from the dominant culture. World War II may have signaled a turning point in national perceptions of Italians and Italian Americans but before the war they embodied a conflicted image in the national psyche. Italian American experiences demonstrate the complicated identity politics at work in understanding whiteness as a process of becoming rather than being.[13] When at the beginning of *Ask the Dust* Arturo, buoyed by the thought that "Joe DiMaggio was still a credit to the Italian people," takes a playful swing with an imagined bat, he is identifying with a socially approved model of the Italian American, a celebrity who has earned widespread popular adulation by excelling in baseball,

FIGURE 5. Fan-magazine spread of publicity shots from the 1928 silent film adaptation of Helen Hunt Jackson's novel *Ramona*. (Photo courtesy of Ned Comstock, University of Southern California Cinematic Arts Library.)

the national pastime (11).[14] As a star of the celebrated New York Yankees, DiMaggio signifies a standard of American masculinity. Simultaneously, because he is of Italian descent, he functions as a signifier of a positive and thus desired Italian American identity.[15] He is, in Bhabha's terms, an example of the stereotype that makes the other palatable by delighting the dominant culture. Because he is socially acclaimed, moreover, he also appears to Italian Americans at large as a harbinger of the possibility that they too may become white. For Arturo, this passage of imaginative identification operates as a "mirror stage" wherein his current psychic state can be observed. At this early moment in the novel, Arturo expresses a narcissistic investment with the dominant culture as he recognizes a white reflection of his Italian American identity.

Coinciding with Arturo's recognition of a white self in his Italian ethnicity through identification with a popular Italian American celebrity is the allusion that Arturo's name implies to a historical figure whose memory is associated with strategic white identification. Despite Arturo's Italian heritage, his name is identical to that of a member of an elite landholding Californio family, Don Arturo Bandini, who as the husband of southern California historian Helen Elliott Bandini supported the United States in the Mexican-American War.[16] Tempting as it may be to imagine Don Arturo's pro-American stance as paralleling Arturo's own early anti-Mexicanism, the fact is that simple self-preservation motivated many Californios. Indeed, Californios used their reading of Anglo histories and romances by such historiographers and fiction writers as Hubert Howe Bancroft and Helen Hunt Jackson to lay claim to a white identity and so distinguish themselves racially from the Indian peons who worked their land.[17] As a referent to a prominent Californio family name then, "Arturo Bandini" recalls how Californios employed a rhetoric of self-identified whiteness as a strategy for resisting cultural obliteration by Anglo-American expansion.[18] Along with the Italian stereotype-in-demand as embodied by Joe DiMaggio, Arturo as white Californio forms another aspect of his identity, further evidence of the presiding contemporary belief that the Mexican presence in modern Los Angeles could be represented in a palatable manner only if tied to the past.

While Arturo seeks his white reflection in celebrity culture or historical fantasy, his racial difference remains the object of suspicion, whether from members of dominant Anglo society or others, like himself, on the margins. Such suspicion suggests the ambivalence underlying even the dominant claim to racial purity and cultural priority and the generalized wariness about others that results. For Arturo, specific memories of being called Wop, Dago, and Greaser recall the ethnic discrimination he suffered growing up in Boulder at the hands of "Smith and Parker and Jones," that is, the white, no doubt Protestant racists of his youth whose taunts provoked him to flee west to write a book (46). Standing out among these epithets is "Greaser," an indication that Arturo has incurred the derogatory stereotype hurled at Mexicans and Italians alike (46–47).[19] Less crude but just as direct, the landlady at the Alta Loma apartments pointedly asks Arturo, "Are you a Mexican?" (48–49), then announces the hotel's policy against Mexicans and Jews typical of the discriminatory racial politics of the Spanish Past and its Anglo gatekeepers. For her part, Camilla cites Arturo's dark skin and black eyes as evidence of his Italian identity, grounds enough for her to deny his claim of being a real American (122). Together with Arturo's own fantasized self-image, these external views, whether targeting his Italian background or a mistaken Mexican ethnicity, consolidate the stereotypes into an especially complex figure embodying both masks for the other—the palatable and the disruptive. Arturo thus constitutes a multivalent and unstable sign consisting of multiple signifiers and signifieds, Italian and Mexican, historical and modern, celebrated and suspected. The multiple and sliding significations mean that, as a subject, Arturo is always in the process of formation, confounding any fixed identification by either others or himself. Ambiguous and ambivalent both to himself and others, the doubling of Arturo positions him as a "mimic man," a subversive force capable of estranging colonial authority through Fante's ironic representation of its practices.[20]

The instability of Arturo's racial signification, both internal and external, creates understandable anxiety about his identity. Adding to this instability is the shift Arturo undergoes, from Boulder to Los Angeles, along the spectrum of discrimination. In Colorado the dominant culture categorically masked his racial difference with stereotypes of the disruptive Wop or Greaser. In Southern California the discrimination is less certain ("Are you a Mexican?") and more parochial (Mexicans are the target far more so than Italians). Taking advantage of his racial ambiguity, Arturo finds shelter in a Bunker Hill flophouse called the Alta Loma ("High Hill"), a name alluding to the Spanish past fantasy. Yet in order to secure a place in Southern California, Arturo must disavow his racial difference, as he does when he capitulates to the landlady, Mrs. Hargraves, in their dispute over his place of birth. To counter her suspicion that he is Mexican, Arturo states that he is from Boulder, Colorado, but Mrs. Hargraves objects that cannot be true since Boulder is in Nebraska. Surrendering to her ignorance, Arturo erases "Colorado" from the registry and writes "Nebraska" instead, at which Mrs. Hargraves exclaims, "So you're an author! . . . Welcome to California! . . . You'll love it here!" (49). Her know-nothing recognition of Arturo as a writer bespeaks the irony of his first fiction written in Los Angeles, namely, a petty lie of convenience committed to allay petty suspicion. And yet there is nothing petty about it, for in Arturo's mind Boulder is associated with his suffering acts of outright racial discrimination for being marked as the disruptive other. In order to have a place in Southern California, Arturo must deny his racial difference and thus reject a part of himself. Anxiety surfaces as the disruptive racial other jeopardizes his ability to have a place, that is, to belong in Southern California, so Arturo learns he must leverage the ambiguity of his racial difference by disavowing it to avoid detection. In this way, Arturo learns from past and present experiences of discrimination to reject himself, capitulate to dominant idealized desire, and regard racial difference as a threat to his fantasy of a stable white self and his need for a place in the world.

By staying at the Alta Loma, Arturo can be said to inhabit the Spanish past, a pervasive environment powerful enough to infiltrate his way of thinking with its imperialist nostalgia.[21] At one point, Arturo distills the racist discourse of the Spanish past when he declares, "I was an American, and goddamn proud of it. This great city, these mighty pavements and proud buildings, they were the voice of my America. From sand and cactus we Americans had carved an empire. Camilla's people had had their chance. They had failed" (44). Upon later reflection, Arturo realizes with remorse that his own racist stereotyping bespeaks "the quivering of an old wound," the wound of discrimination that he still bears. Thus emerges a causal sequence to explain the vicious circle of discrimination, as one wound suffered begets another wound inflicted in misguided efforts to quell the very anxieties that perpetuate the cycle.

In his own misguided efforts at securing an authentic American identity, Arturo fetishizes Mexicans both positively and negatively, revealing how the stereotype of the Spanish past functions through cultural commodification.

In a scene set at Los Angeles's Central Plaza, a space significant in the city's Spanish past fantasy, Arturo pins the "Spick" and "Greaser" stereotypes on a Mexican man for patronizing a blonde, ostensibly Anglo prostitute (23). Certainly Fante draws upon stereotypes of Mexican degeneracy here—the plaza was often associated in the *Los Angeles Times* with vice and health problems[22]—but Arturo's racism also suggests the ambivalence of the stereotype as a discursive mechanism, for even as the Spanish past stereotype is deployed to mask racial difference, it provokes in Arturo the anxiety of belonging.[23] Indeed, Arturo has gone to prostitutes in the past, takes pleasure in receiving attention from this same prostitute earlier in the scene, and then goes to meet with her soon after the Mexican man exits. The hypocrisy of Arturo's actions undermines the fantasy of cultural superiority inasmuch as the Mexican man more closely resembles Arturo than he is able to admit. In short, the threat posed by the Mexican man is a disruption to the definitive boundaries of race. By purchasing sex with the blonde prostitute, the man in the plaza consumes a fantasy of whiteness, no different from the fantasy Arturo pursues, and in this way, the man functions as Arturo's double. The white female body itself has become a commodity in circulation between the man and Arturo, a fetishized object of the desire for whiteness fundamental to the Spanish past fantasy. As the site of their encounter, the plaza and its environs function not only as a stereotyped staging area for Mexican degeneracy but also as a space developed by and for Anglos to indulge nostalgically in their cultural dominance through a commodification of imperial memory. Likewise, the blond, apparently Anglo prostitute of the plaza embodies the commodification of racial fantasies conceived and directed by Christine Sterling and her fellow boosters. As such, these and other racially objectifying fantasies demand to be seen as acts of cultural prostitution in the service of reinforcing Anglo dominance through the modern consumption of stereotypic reifications, be they human, architectural, or artifactual.[24]

Just as the Mexican man presents an ironic imitation of Arturo that threatens his sense of the racial order, the commodity fetishism exemplified in Arturo's perception of Mexican women mimics the colonial discourse of Sterling's 1930 "Mexican Market."[25] To solidify the authority of Anglo dominance in the present, the colonial discourse of the Spanish past must stereotype the anachronism of Mexican culture, rendering Mexicans into objects evocative of a romantic history. From the beginning of *Ask the Dust*,

Arturo sings his passion for the Mexican girls who haunt the plaza, the original center of Old Los Angeles: "Oh for a Mexican girl! . . . I didn't have one, but the streets were full of them, the Plaza and Chinatown were afire with them. . . . Aztec princesses and Mayan princesses, the peon girls in the Grand Central Market, in the Church of Our Lady, and I even went to Mass to look at them" (15). Arturo's attribution of historical identities onto Mexican women in the present—indigenous precolonial, Spanish colonial, and Mexican postcolonial—resonates with the booster demand for the commercial consumption of a fantasy evoking regionally anachronistic social orders that exhibit a range of cultural and class associations. The resultant mélange obscures differentiations by fixating on the other as an object of pleasure owing to the particular history of colonial dominance that is recalled. What emerges as significant is only that the Mexican girl exists in history; that is to say, she is palatable because she figures some history of conquest from a distant past that secures Anglo dominance in the present.

The gender politics of assimilation underpinning the commodification of racial identities makes Americanization a heteronormative masculine act and thus normalizes the disavowal of racial difference.[26] The significance of this point cannot be overstated given that the most frequently circulated representations of the Spanish past in 1930s Los Angeles involved images of a "dark señorita." Phoebe Kropp notes the pervasiveness of this castanet-playing dark lady: "In image after image, the city was personified by an alluring young Mexican woman, whose traditional dress included a lace mantilla and tall comb upon which was printed 'Los Angeles.' As one local writer explained the allusion, 'Los Angeles is symbolized by a dark señorita with a high comb, this is the second largest Mexican city in the world, [and] our advertising promises the prospective visitor Spanish atmosphere.'"[27] Arturo's search for a "Mexican girl" thus manifests the hegemonic masculinity at play in the colonial fantasy that feminized the Spanish past by coding racial difference as inferior and submissive and consequently masculinized the consuming Anglo present as superior and dominant.

Fante explores the gender politics of the stereotype through the relationship of his novel's lovers, as Arturo projects onto Camilla the "dark señorita" characteristics of this feminized figure of the Spanish past. This sense of the Mexican as an object from the past whose consumption reinforces the modernity and thus whiteness of the consumer emerges in Arturo's view of Camilla as a racial exotic to be conquered. In fact, Arturo encounters Camilla in explicitly colonial terms. Upon first seeing her Arturo observes, "Her nose was Mayan, flat, with large nostrils. Her lips were heavily rouged, with the thickness of a negress' lips. She was a racial type, and as such she was beautiful, but she was too strange for me" (35). As if performing the colonial gaze, Arturo attributes to Camilla specifically premodern ("Mayan"), marginalizing ("negress") characteristics that mark her as the racially differentiated object of colonial authority. And yet the other as presented here is also desirable, signaled by Arturo's use of the term "as such," which suggests that Camilla is beautiful only after her racial difference has been identified. As Bhabha explains, an important aspect of the stereotype's ambivalence is the presumption that its logic is apparent as a result of the "skin signifier."[28] No sooner does Arturo identify the source of Camilla's beauty, however, than he refuses it as "too strange." And yet it is to that strange beauty that he must return again and again throughout the novel in an anxious repetition of the ambivalence of colonial authority. Such repetition reflects a crisis of authority, evident in Arturo's fitful efforts to distance himself from the sensed threat of Camilla's difference. All of which takes on even greater point when we note that Arturo first discovers Camilla in all her racial exoticism inside the Columbia Buffet, the very name of which evokes the history of American Indian conquest. The site of Arturo's initial encounter with Camilla thus establishes the colonial dynamics informing their ill-starred relationship.

Arturo figuratively consummates the relations of colonial power evoked in the fantasy of the Spanish past when he imagines making love to Camilla Lopez as played by the mysteriously scarred Vera Rivken, another "dark lady" type. As director of this sexual fantasy, Arturo sets the scene for Vera: "'All of this land and this sea belongs to you. All of California . . . This is your beautiful land with the desert and the mountains and the sea . . . I'm a conqueror,' [Arturo] said. 'I'm like Cortez, only I'm an Italian' . . . There were no scars, and no desiccated place. She was Camilla, complete and lovely. She belonged to me, and so did the world. And I was glad for her tears, they thrilled me and lifted me, and I possessed her" (94). Although Vera is Jewish rather than Mexican, Arturo casts her as Camilla not as she is in the present, a poor waitress, but as "a Mayan princess." Arturo's description of this Camilla in such explicitly pre-Columbian terms, evocative of the imperialist nostalgia of *Ramona*, underwrites his assumption of whiteness. By identifying himself as "Cortez but Italian" Arturo grants himself the Spanish white identity he denies Camilla. As an Italian identifying himself as the white colonizer, Arturo effectively wishes away a large part of the reason for the degrading ethnic prejudice he experienced in Colorado as a boy. More to the point, the fantasy clarifies his attraction to Camilla because the prospect of sexual conquest reinforces his illusory sense of manliness and whiteness. Furthermore, the fantasy fulfills the process of assimilation he could not consummate with the plaza prostitute, securing, if only briefly, the dream of racial hegemony. Though the sexual conquest of Camilla is only a fantasy, Arturo does consummate the whiteness of his identity, if only temporarily, through the sexual objectification of his actual partner, Vera Rivken. As a Jewish woman who performs the conquest fantasy with and for Arturo, Vera demonstrates how the racial rules of the Spanish past for reinforcing Anglo supremacy extended to others—other others—beyond the Mexican population of Los Angeles.

Although Arturo's imitation of the colonial scenario would seem to reproduce and perpetuate its racist logic, his mimicry turns on him in the aftermath of the earthquake when he convinces himself that his encounter with Vera has called down on him "the wrath of God." The sexual performance of colonization typically romanticizes the colonial narrative and so figures what Yolanda Venegas refers to as the "erotics of racialization," a process whereby colonial narratives are rendered romantic, as in *Ramona*. Now, however, as Arturo wanders through the aftershock ruins of downtown Long Beach, the romantic trajectory of *Ask the Dust* reverses. In the first place, by casting Arturo as a racially differentiated object who performs the role of colonizer, Fante separates whiteness from its usual association with colonial authority. Second, the romance of the colonial narrative as performed by Arturo upon Vera is radically undermined when Arturo is stricken with guilt for having committed an act of adultery. If the ostensibly sacred mission of colonization is to bring civilization to savages through the extension of Christianity, Arturo's sin in indulging the erotic fantasy subverts the justification for the exercise of colonial power, as Fante's ironic representation of colonialism's malevolent effects makes clear.

Equally clear is Camilla's role as representative colonial subject. At the first point of contact she represents the palatable stereotype when Arturo notes her strange beauty. Obedience, the other aspect of the palatable stereotype, appears when Arturo observes her acting the meek equivalent of mere housekeeper to the white bartender Sammy despite her desire to be his lover. Later, in a letter to Arturo, Sammy confides his belief that Camilla, like all Mexican women, wants to be mistreated. Both instances suggest the degradation that belies colonial approval of the racially differentiated object as expressed through the palatable stereotype. After Sammy finally rejects her, Camilla comes to embody the disruptive stereotype as the drug-addled hophead beset by physical suffering, psychic trauma, and an escalating degree of social alienation. The self-destructive madness to which Camilla succumbs results from what McWilliams calls "a schizophrenic condition" of the Spanish past fantasy, an intolerable splitting of the subject into palatable and disruptive stereotypes—on the one hand a desirable figure of romance existing in the past and on the other a repellant personal and even public-health burden in the present. Camilla's desire for Sammy foreshadows this split as she recognizes and disavows her own racial difference by identifying with stereotypes that offer a fantasy of whiteness, as in her use of the Anglo pseudonym "Camille Lombard." Indeed, as a patient committed to a mental asylum, Camilla embodies the "schizophrenic condition" of the Mexican sign in a Southern California culture shaped by the paradoxical fantasy of the Spanish past and the inherent double-bind tensions of its racial logic. Elaborating this paradox, Kropp states, "Indian and Mexican residents became marginal citizens despite their central roles in Anglos' imagined regional past."[29] But Fante goes further, showing how the consequences of this split lead to nothing less than the effacement of racial difference through widespread disavowal achieved with the complicity of both dominant colonial subjects and their subordinate objects in the mutual idealization of whiteness.

By making Sammy primarily responsible for Camilla's madness and ultimate disappearance, Fante recalls the murder of Alessandro in *Ramona*. A would-be western pulp writer, Sammy parallels Jim Farrar, the drunkard cowboy who guns down Alessandro for stealing his horse. True, Alessandro does take Farrar's horse but only because, in a fit of madness, he mistakes it for his own. The madness afflicting Alessandro occurs because he can no longer cope with the sequence of tragedies that have befallen him and Ramona, tragedies recalling the history of forced removal, loss of ancestral lands, and genocide suffered by Native Americans at the hands of

Anglo-American expansionism. Like Alessandro, Camilla signifies the legacy of madness caused by the colonial discourse of the Spanish past romanticized in Jackson's novel and subsequently put into action through the booster efforts of the Los Angeles Times and the Chamber of Commerce to sell off Southern California as so much divisible real estate. Camilla's ultimate disappearance, like Alessandro's death, evokes the Vanishing Indian trope. On the one hand, by dramatizing the paradoxical bifurcation of the Mexican sign as tragedy in his reversal of the uplift at the end of Jackson's novel, Fante criticizes the racist ideology of the Spanish and the Western pasts. On the other hand, in recalling the "vanishing Indian" through Camilla's disappearance, Fante seems to present the Mexican people as passive victims of popular Anglo mythologies of the American West. In this light, the tragic portrait of Camilla is less an act of resistance to the racial politics of the Spanish past than it initially appears. While Fante is quick to fault *Ramona* as a failed social protest responsible in a significant way for the "ideological fallacy" of the Spanish past, he may be seen as capitulating, even if unconsciously, to the imperialist nostalgia of booster promotion by using, indeed, by concluding upon the "vanishing" other trope.[30]

In fact, to view Camilla's disappearance as simple victimization would be to ignore the so-called Mexican Repatriation Program to which her vanishing silently alludes. Indeed, the silencing of Camilla's voice as she walks away into the desert can be read as an ironic reference to a strategy aimed at dealing with an increasingly vocal Mexican community in 1930s Los Angeles. This strategy combined the actions of immigration agents and uniformed police officers to round up Mexicans and Mexican Americans alike and, with no pretense of due process, put them on trains to Mexico.[31] The belief that Mexicans were burdening social relief programs designed for Americans contributed to an anti-Mexican atmosphere sufficient to uphold these "repatriation" efforts. Yet while the city may have been motivated to unburden itself of Mexicans on public relief, it was more concerned with another problem—the threat of radicalism. Owing to record levels of unemployment, the 1930s saw more vocalized Mexican resistance to labor abuses and social mistreatment than in any previous decade. Mexicans organized strikes against conditions at the agricultural "factories in the fields" where they toiled as migrant pickers; importing such radical labor tactics to Los Angeles would have threatened the city's longstanding open-shop practices.

In McWilliams's view, repatriation was thus at its core an effort to deradicalize Mexicans who, left to their own devices, might organize to improve labor conditions and wages.[32] And this effort operated by making Mexicans disappear—or by instilling in those who remained in Los Angeles the constant fear of being caught and deported.

As a Los Angeles resident attuned to issues of social justice thanks to his friendship with the activist McWilliams, Fante was acutely aware of the anti-Mexican program of repatriation. In fact, in the early 1940s the two friends included this program as a plot element in "Home Is the Hunter," an unproduced film treatment they cowrote about the conflict between the forces of modernity in Los Angeles and a resistant Mexican population.[33] In this treatment—a comedy, sad to say, which perhaps explains its commercial failure—the marginalized Mexican community overcomes all adversity by demonstrating their utility not only to the city but also the war effort. Despite his sympathy with the working class, Fante himself foreswore open allegiance to any political cause; his early novel *The Road to Los Angeles*, a satirical jab at proletarian aesthetics among many other targets, attests to his avoidance of explicitly political writing. However, his sensitivity to the appalling labor conditions endured by Mexican workers may well explain *Ask the Dust*'s veiled reference to repatriation and, in Camilla, its individual human costs. If we listen closely, the echo of her disappearance can be heard to express the resistance that the city tried to silence, and thereby at least to question the claim that in *Ask the Dust* Fante was perpetuating racial stereotypes of Mexican dependence and passive victimization.

Through the twin disappearances of Camilla and Vera, *Ask the Dust* dramatizes how the violence of absence can catalyze the articulation of the marginalized subject's presence. As presented by Fante, Camilla and Vera acknowledge the open wounds and traumatic aftermath of being stereotyped. As with Camilla's vanishing, the absence of Vera, lost amidst the rubble and chaos following the earthquake, is precipitated by the performance of her role as other within the objectifying confines of colonial discourse. The tearful pain of that performance in the erotics of colonization, enacted out of her desire to be recognized even to the extent that she willingly participates in her own subordination, vanishes along with her body, a text of violation bearing a wound of such unspeakable horror that Arturo can barely bring himself to look at it (87–89). The presence of this wound recalls an unknown history of violation wherein past trauma still bears upon present experience. Indeed, such a wound leads Arturo to hateful acts of racism when in the grip of his fantasy of whiteness. At other moments, however, when confronted with the Real—the transient materiality of human existence that he faces in the aftermath of the earthquake, for example, or the mortality that he shares with the tubercular Sammy, recognized under the starry indifference of the night sky—Arturo sees the idealization of whiteness as a socially constructed fantasy, an act of narcissistic identification in the Imaginary. This realization comes at fleeting moments of clarity that expose the slippage between signifier and signified, as when he observes the complexion of the white racist Sammy, who has lived in a black neighborhood, darken "almost to blackness" out in the desert (62–63, 137). The novel anticipates this revelation early on when Arturo notices that the blond hair of the plaza prostitute, who has established the desirability of whiteness in her dealings with both the Mexican man and Arturo, is in fact dark at the roots (25). In the second half of the novel Arturo is gradually moved to acts of compassion that recognize the suffering and humanity of others, thereby exchanging his old identity of rejection and disavowal—"neither fish, fowl, nor good red herring" (75)—for one expressing the recognition and acceptance of difference—a "lover of all things, men and beast alike" (120).

Wounds record histories that can be read on textual bodies. Indeed, bodies marked by ethnic difference in *Ask the Dust* often amount to legible texts in which histories of violation can be read, as with the Swedish American girl at the King Edward Cellar, a skid row dive bar, with "old child's eyes [that] swim in blood written like mad sonnets" (77). When Arturo thinks of Vera's mysterious wound, he imagines "the page of a manuscript" and how he might fill it with words (90). Later he can "see [Camilla's] memories of that night at the beach written upon [her] scornful face" (117), he observes how "her hair spill[s] over the pillow like a bottle of overturned ink" (122), and he reads the signs of abuse on her body: Sammy is "a great writer, alright," he tells her. "That story he wrote over your left eye is a masterpiece" (132). Even to himself Arturo feels strangely textual, for "my heart is full of black ink" (86). Conversely, writing is described in corporeal terms where ideas come "full-bodied" and "[spurt] out like blood" (106). As Vera's body disappears, so does her story until Arturo recognizes not the sin of adultery but the trauma of the erotics of colonization. Once he moves past the egocentrism of his paranoia, a delusive product of seeing himself as a colonizer and thus as a member of the dominant group, Arturo can see the effects of discrimination beyond himself in the suffering of others across the landscape of Los Angeles.

Amidst the aftermath of his exploitative sex fantasy with Vera, still struggling through his earthquake-induced paranoia, Arturo dreams of a black-haired woman knocking at his window (102–106). The dark lady of this nightmare functions as an imaginative juncture wherein the absence of the colonial past as figured forth in his two vanished dark ladies, Vera and Camilla, exerts its presence in Arturo's psyche, leading to the aesthetic breakthrough that he has longed for since the early lean days of his arrival at the Alta Loma. With the "dark lady" as his muse, Arturo conceives an idea for his first book. It will be a "story about Vera Rivken" in which we can dare imagine him revising the colonial discourse of the Spanish past so that those on the margins of its vision are at last afforded their rightful place at the novel's center (106). In thus coming to terms with Vera's disappearance, as we can hope he will come to terms with Camilla's, Arturo will act on his newly earned knowledge that the violated experience of otherness, like the absence of all subject peoples from forms of inclusion and belonging, is a truth he must articulate, for, indeed, "vera" means that which is true, or real.

Furthermore, we can imagine the ethnic novel in the hands of Arturo revealing the hitherto unspoken truth of the absence, or perhaps the delegitimation, of a body of ethnic texts. Arturo's aesthetic endeavor appears an insurgent act to narrate the presence of histories of wounds that emerge out of absence. In this sense, it is a lack that motivates Arturo, an experience of negation that operates as his aesthetic muse, what Homi Bhabha would call a "desire for recognition" that restores agency to a subject who has been objectified by forces of colonial power.[34] Agency can be restored through desire, for desire signals a refusal to accept the present condition as fulfilling. Desire compels the subject to search for something to fill the void, the experience of lack, and, in doing so, the subject that has been acted upon regains the power to act. It is this desire for recognition that leads Arturo to transform the experience of Vera's wound of subjugation, marginalization, and disavowal as manifest in her absence into a new story meant as an alternative and corrective to the dominant discourse that Fante sees in Southern California, and American culture at large, as characterized by the Spanish

Past. Given that the disappearance of Vera precipitates the production of Arturo's first novel, it is reasonable to conclude that Camilla's disappearance will lead him into another productive period of insurgent writing.

Whereas the Western hailed the triumphant emergence of Anglo-American identity through romances of imperial conquest, ethnic narratives recount the emergence of a culturally hybrid American experience out of the tragedy of that Anglo-American conquest and its popular romantic accounts. Fante's *Ask the Dust* uses *Ramona* as a cultural resource to reverse the romantic stereotyping of Mexican identity perpetuated in Los Angeles through contemporary deployments of the Spanish past that denied the social legitimacy of the city's Mexican and Mexican American communities. Moreover, *Ramona* itself was in large part a response to popular Western representations of Indians and Mexicans as un-American savages. As a "*Ramona* in reverse," *Ask the Dust* would seem to imply that narratives of ethnic American experience are in some ways post-Western. As Arturo abandons the dying Sammy to his desert desolation, Fante suggests that modern ethnic literature, at least in its insurgent impulse to dramatize the desire for recognition through self-representation, emerges from the popular West and its moribund legacy of romances. Whether that legacy be the national tall tale of the Western or a regional variation, as in the Spanish past, modern ethnic literature refigures story elements and viewpoints to produce alternative narratives of multivalent experience. In this way, Arturo's telling of Vera's tragedy and Fante's rewriting of the Spanish past demonstrate that, as articulations of cultural hybridity rich with the transformative potential for revision, ethnic narratives can help us see American history and individual American experiences from other, untold perspectives.

Notes

1. This essay is part of a larger effort to investigate the relations of several early twentieth-century ethnic American novels and short stories to the western, its iterations, and variations circulating in popular culture as a means of making the broader argument that the power of the popular West bore and bears upon the literary articulation of ethnic American experience in the twentieth century. All references are to the HarperCollins edition of Fante's *Ask the Dust*, hereafter cited in text by page number.

2. Homi Bhabha's notion of the stereotype's ambivalence informs my reading of *Ask the Dust*. For more on how the stereotype functions within colonial discourse to both recognize and disavow racial difference, see Bhabha, *Location of Culture*, 99–107.

3. Phoebe Kropp elaborates such references to Anglo and Mexican as well as Indian identity in Southern California; for more information on the matter of racial terminology, identity, and region, see Kropp, *California Vieja*, 9.

4. McWilliams, *Southern California*, 364.

5. The pastoral Mediterranean landscape of *Ramona* derives from various mid-nineteenth century portraits of California as a garden. On the California garden mythologies that bear upon the Spanish past, see Starr, *Americans*, 365–414 and *Inventing*, 44–63; Sackman, *Orange Empire*, 47–49; and McClung, *Landscapes of Desire*, 54–56, 198–230.

6. Handley and Lewis, *True West*, 2.

7. Serving as a synopsis, the prologue outlines the story of *Ask the Dust*. I have consulted the original typescript held in the John Fante Papers at UCLA Special Collections

8. Like the "stereotype" that can delight and deride and waiver between fear and affirmation, mimicry is another ambivalent mode of colonial discourse with subversive potential; for more on mimicry's threatening imitation, see Bhabha, *Location of Culture*, 121–131.

9. This reception extended to the mass audiences drawn to a pair of popular Hollywood film adaptations of Jackson's novel. In 1936 Loretta Young played Ramona in a film of the same name. Eight years earlier, in 1928, Dolores Del Rio had starred in a silent version of *Ramona*. A letter from Fante to his mentor H. L. Mencken shows that as early as 1934 Fante, dazzled by his good luck in being employed as a contract scenarist at Warner Bros., was thinking of Del Rio (born Maria de los Dolores Asúnsolo López-Negrete) and her obviously fabricated stage name as raw materials for his imagination. Even though Fante considered Del Rio "the world's worst actress," he confided to Mencken, "all I do is write and laugh and think of Dolores Del Rio: the sorrows of the river. Sweet river. My river. I'm going swimming in that river. I'm going to navigate that river. I think maybe I shall buy that river. I am like Columbus. I stand at the water's edge and dream. And like my countryman, they shall bring me back in irons. But I love it." See Cooper, *Full of Life*, 117.

10. For information on the annual Ramona Pageant, see ramonabowl.com, accessed September 29, 2019. For critiques of the ways *Ramona*'s sentimental scheme undermines its social protest and romanticizes colonialism, see Harvard, "Sentimentalism," and Venegas, "Erotics of Racialization." By contrast, Luis-Brown, "White Slaves," is less dismissive of the novel's sentimentalism.

11. For a detailed account of the tourist boom *Ramona* caused in Southern California, see Delyser, *Ramona Memories*, 31–53.

12. Delyser, 46.

13. For a consideration of the bifurcated image of Italians in American culture, see Cosco, *Imagining Italians*. For an account of the social and political influences on the Italian American experience including discussion of white identification, see Mangione and Morreale, *La Storia*, and Guglielmo, *White on Arrival*. For more about how central race is to the history of European immigration, see Jacobsen, *Whiteness of a Different Color*.

14. For complementary readings of baseball and Americanization, see Kimmel, *Manhood in America*, and Baldassaro, *American Game*.

15. In Bhabha's conception, the stereotype ranges in its representation of the racially differentiated object from the disruptive to the delightful. To learn more about how stereotypical representations facilitate colonial relations and the disruptive potential of the other's palatability, see Bhabha, *Location of Culture*, chap. 3.

16. Baym, *Women Writers of the American West*, 267.

17. For an explanation of the strategic construction of Californio history by Californios, see Kropp, *California Vieja*, 30.

18. On the legacy and wealth of Californios, see Hubert Howe Bancroft's *California Pastoral*. Stephen Cooper first proposed that Arturo's name refers to Don Arturo Bandini, a retiring scholar. See Cooper, *Full of Life*, 77–78. The Bandini name can be directly linked to the production of *Ramona* and its tourist phenomenon. For details on Jackson's legendary stay at the Bandini-Couts family's Rancho Gaujome, the basis for the romantic descriptions that would appear in *Ramona*, see Kropp, *California Vieja*, 33 and 39.

19. Memories of prejudice provided inspiration for his writing and emerge in other stories too. Consider the title "The Odyssey of a Wop" (1933) where the speaker, a proto-Arturo Bandini, reflects on the meaning of the racial slur and how it contributed to his identity formation growing up in Boulder.

20. Bhabha, *Location of Culture*, 122–123.

21. For an insightful exploration of imperialist nostalgia, see Rosaldo, "Imperialist Nostalgia."

22. Kropp, *California Vieja*, 211.

23. On the racist portrayal of Mexicans as a public health concern, see Molina, *Fit to Be Citizens*.

24. Arturo passes and visits dancehalls on the way to the plaza. For an examination of the ambivalent perceptions of taxi dance halls as they relate to the assimilation of Filipinos, see I-Fen Cheng, "Identities." For more on the prostitute as a sign of American consumerism in the work of Fante's contemporary Nathanael West and writers on the Left, see Barnard, *Great Depression*, 147n34.

25. For more on how Spanish Past boosters continued to exert their influence upon Los Angeles well into the 1930s, especially with respect to the 1930

opening of Olvera Street and revitalized interest in the surrounding plaza, see Kropp, *California Vieja*, 227.

26. For a reading of how assimilation becomes a test of manhood in Fante's first published novel *Wait Until Spring, Bandini*, see Marinaccio, "Tea and Cookies."

27. Kropp, *California Vieja*, 207–208.

28. A concept derived from Frantz Fanon's seminal work *Black Skins, White Masks*, the "skin signifier" embodies a taken-for-granted logic of racial essentialism whereby skin complexion indicates certain inherent traits that are ostensibly self-evident, but, nonetheless, culturally constructed. Unlike the fetish, a private substitution, the "skin" is public. For a clarification, see Bhabha, *Location of Culture*, 112.

29. Kropp, *California Vieja*, 9.

30. Kropp, 7.

31. David Wyatt has hinted that the disappearance of Camilla may allude to the 1930s repatriation policy; while in accord with Wyatt's suggestive comparison, I elaborate the political implications of Camilla's allusion to repatriation. For his survey of Los Angeles literature and reading of Camilla, see Wyatt, "L.A. Fiction," 40. For a detailed record of repatriation policies and practices during the 1930s, see Balderrama and Rodriguez, *Decade of Betrayal*, and Kropp, *California Vieja*, 231.

32. For a developed investigation into the labor conditions of Mexican populations in Southern California during the first part of the twentieth century, see McWilliams, *Factories in the Field*.

33. For the complete typescript of "Home Is the Hunter," see the John Fante Papers at UCLA Library Special Collections.

34. Bhaba, *Location of Culture*, 12.

Works Cited

Baldassaro, Lawrence. "Dashing Dagoes and Walloping Wops." *NINE: Journal of Baseball History and Culture* 14, no.1 (Fall 2005): 98–106.

Baldassaro, Lawrence, ed. *The American Game: Baseball and Ethnicity*. Carbondale: Southern Illinois University Press, 2002.

Balderrama, Francisco, and Raymond Rodriguez. *Decade of Betrayal: Mexican Repatriation in the 1930s*. Albuquerque: University of New Mexico Press, 2006.

Barnard, Rita. *The Great Depression and the Culture of Abundance: Kenneth Fearing, Nathanael West, and Mass Culture in the 1930s*. Cambridge: Cambridge University Press, 1995.

Baym, Nina. *Women Writers of the American West, 1833–1927*. Urbana: University of Illinois Press, 2011.
Bhabha, Homi K. *The Location of Culture*. London: Routledge Classics, 2004.
Cooper, Stephen. *Full of Life: A Biography of John Fante*. New York: North Point Press, 2000.
Cosco, Joseph P. *Imagining Italians: The Clash of Romance and Race in American Perceptions, 1880–1910*. Albany: State University of New York Press, 2003.
Delyser, Dydia. *Ramona Memories*. Minneapolis: University of Minnesota Press, 2005.
Fanon, Frantz. *Black Skin, White Masks*. New York: Grove Press, 2008.
Fante, John, *Ask the Dust*. New York: HarperCollins 2006.
———. "Fish Cannery." Circa early 1930s, John Fante Papers, Library Special Collections, University of California, Los Angeles.
———. "Home Is the Hunter." Circa 1941–1942, John Fante Papers, Library Special Collections, University of California, Los Angeles.
———. "The Odyssey of a Wop." In *The Wine of Youth: Selected Stories*. 133–146. New York: Ecco, 2002.
———. "Prologue." Circa 1938. John Fante Papers, Library Special Collections, University of California, Los Angeles.
Guglielmo, Thomas A. *White on Arrival: Italians, Race, Color, and Power in Chicago, 1890-1945*. New York: Oxford University Press, 2003.
Handley, William R., and Nathaniel Lewis. *True West: Authenticity and the American West*. Lincoln: University of Nebraska Press, 2004.
Harvard, John C. "Sentimentalism, Interracial Romance, and Helen Hunt Jackson and Clorinda Matto de Turner's Attacks on Abuses of Native Americans in *Ramona* and *Aves sin nido*." *Intertexts* 11, no. 2 (2007): 101–121.
I-Fen Cheng, Cindy. "Identities and Places on Writing the History of Filipinotown, Los Angeles." *Journal of Asian American Studies* 12, no.1 (2009): 1–33. Project MUSE, doi:10.1353/jaas.0.0025.
Jackson, Helen Hunt. *Ramona*. 1888. New York: Signet, 1988.
Jacobsen, Matthew Frye. *Whiteness of a Different Color: European Immigrants and the Alchemy of Race*. Cambridge, MA: Harvard University Press, 1998.
Kimmel, Michael S. *Manhood in America: A Cultural History*. New York: Oxford University Press, 2006.
Kropp, Phoebe. *California Vieja: Culture and Memory in a Modern American Place*. Berkeley: University of California Press, 2006.
Luis-Brown, David. "'White Slaves' and the 'Arrogant Mestiza': Reconfiguring Whiteness in *The Squatter and the Don* and *Ramona*." *American Literature* 69, no. 4 (1997): 813–839. JSTOR, www.jstor.org/stable/2928344.
Mangione, Jerre, and Ben Morreale. *La Storia: Five Centuries of the Italian American Experience*. New York: HarperCollins, 1992.

Marinaccio, Rocco. "'Tea and Cookies. Diavolo!': Italian American Masculinity in John Fante's *Wait Until Spring, Bandini*." *MELUS: Multi-Ethnic Literature of the U.S.* 34, no. 3 (2009): 43–69. Project MUSE, doi:10.1353/mel.0.0040.
McClung, William A. *Landscapes of Desire: Anglo Mythologies of Los Angeles*. Berkeley: University of California Press, 2000.
McWilliams, Carey. *Factories in the Field*. Berkeley: University of California Press, 2000.
———. *Southern California: An Island on the Land*. Salt Lake City, UT: Peregrine Smith, 1994.
Molina, Natalia. *Fit to Be Citizens: Public Health and Race in Los Angeles, 1879–1939*. Berkeley: University of California Press, 2006.
Rosaldo, Renato. "Imperialist Nostalgia." *Representations*, no. 26 (1989): 107–122. JSTOR, www.jstor.org/stable/2928525.
Sackman, Douglas C. *Orange Empire: California and the Fruits of Eden*. Berkeley: University of California Press, 2005.
Starr, Kevin. *Americans and the California Dream 1850–1915*. New York: Oxford University Press, 1986.
———. *Inventing the Dream: California Through the Progressive Era*. New York: Oxford University Press, 1985.
Venegas, Y. "The Erotics of Racialization: Gender and Sexuality in the Making of California." *Frontiers: A Journal of Women Studies* 25, no. 3 (2004): 63–89. Project MUSE, doi:10.1353/fro.2004.0070.
Wyatt, David. "L.A. Fiction through Mid-Century." In *The Cambridge Companion to the Literature of Los Angeles*, edited by Kevin R. McNamara, 35–48. Cambridge: Cambridge University Press, 2010.

2. Sibling Arts: *Ask the Dust* in Dance, Music, the Graphic Novel, and French

Dancing with the Dust: Translating *Ask the Dust* to the Stage

J'aime Morrison

> The pleasure of the text is that moment when my body pursues its own ideas.
>
> —ROLAND BARTHES

As Camilla and Arturo tangle with one another against the backdrop of depression-era Los Angeles, the pair leave the memory of their encounters in the rooms of the Alta Loma, the streets of Bunker Hill, and finally on the dusty sands of the Mojave Desert. It is the pair's kinetic traces I have sought to embody in *DUST*, a dance theatre work, inspired by John Fante's *Ask the Dust*, which I created and directed in the spring of 2015 at California State University, Northridge (CSUN). The performance was developed during the year with a group of twelve theatre students and was performed in CSUN's new Experimental Theatre the following April. The production, which ran for eight performances, was warmly received by students, faculty, and others who attended, and I was particularly gratified by the positive reception I received from the author's family and friends in attendance.

When I first read *Ask the Dust*, I was moved by the rhythms of Fante's words across the page and I recognized immediately the musicality of the language and the potential for a translation of the text into choreographic form. If choreography is a kind of bodily writing, then what does the body write? What is lost or gained in translation when words become action, when the movements of the body generate the story? In this essay I reconstruct the process of creating this performance, including my work with student actors, designers, and my production team. I also explore the methods used in devising this adaptation, with an emphasis on the relationship between movement and language. When does dance become story, and how are movement and gesture freighted with narrative meaning when punctuated by the spoken word? My aim in writing this account will be to offer not merely an explanation of my process, but rather a discursive performance focused through a choreographic lens where I will dance with the dust of Fante's story.

As a dance-theatre artist I have always been drawn to language—to the word made flesh. In previous work I adapted Samuel Beckett's prose, the poetry of Portuguese poet Fernando Pessoa, and the letters and writings of Harry Houdini, Federico Garcia Lorca, and James Joyce. I am moved by words—language inspires gestures, floor patterns, falls, leaps, stillness, shifts, turns—dance. I mine the text for sound and sense, weight and rhythm. As I read *Ask the Dust* my body recognized the rhythm of the words as music, felt dramatic tension between the characters and sensed kinetic energy radiating from the desert landscape, the foggy city streets and the small dingy rooms where the novel takes place. The book became a kind of score, suggesting images and ideas beyond the narrative but yoked to it. I never wanted to "capture" Fante's story in a realistic or even a precise rendering; rather, I hoped to remain true to its spirit, as I saw it, as an evocation of the loss that attends the experience of displacement caused by emigration, exile, or other such dislocations. *Ask the Dust* is laced with departures: Arturo's journey from Colorado, Camilla's walk into the desert and her earlier passage from Mexico, Vera's flight west, and the peregrinations of those inhabitants of the streets, boarding houses and cafes who come from somewhere else, "to die in the sun" in Los Angeles.[1] French theorist Michel de Certeau contends, "Every story is a travel story" because narrative has the capacity to transport us.[2] Travel implies motion and reading Fante's novel led me to imagine a map of intersecting and overlapping movements: Arturo's night walks through the city, his trips to Long Beach, Santa Barbara, and the Mojave, Camilla's comings and goings from the diner, her drive to Santa Monica, her escape from the asylum back to Los Angeles and into the desert, and Vera's vigil in Long Beach—these are landscapes moved through but also transfigured by that movement—geography becomes choreography on stage.

Early in the process I knew I would begin at the end of the novel, with Camilla's departure. The last few lines of the novel seemed almost operatic to me and the tragedy of Camilla's loss and Arturo's search for her inherently theatrical. Initially I did not read the novel from beginning to end following a linear path. I read it in pieces, beginning at the end, and then jumping to the middle and back to the beginning. Immersing myself in the story this way was invigorating. Instead of accumulating information bit by bit, I experienced the various storylines simultaneously as a series of overlapping scenes that resonated with one another in my mind as what Roland Barthes termed, "discontinuous fragments."[3] The choreography of my gaze across the page, then back, then skipping ahead, meant that already in my mind I was experiencing the text as theatre: the interplay and rhythm of light and shadow—*fade up; blackout; crossfade; cue transition; slow fade to black.* As if I were switching on a spotlight each time I turned the page, reading *Ask the Dust* illuminated the performative nature of reading itself.

However, the act of writing is not as easily conceived in performative terms. As I sought to dramatize *Ask the Dust*, to spatialize and embody the narrative on stage, I grappled with how to create moments of dialogue and choral speaking out of Arturo's many interior monologues and Fante's paragraphs of exposition. Portraying an individual struggling to write a novel was not necessarily the story I wanted to tell, nor did it seem dramatically engaging enough for a full-length ensemble work. In some ways I felt I had to wrest the novel away from its narrative moorings to recompose and reshape it as dramatic material. Developing this project with CSUN theatre students greatly informed this process of experimentation. During class assignments students would storyboard ideas for specific scenes, invent characters, write backstories, and create prop lists, while I shaped a script from a novel that is told from the perspective of a single narrator. In the process of transforming the novel's prose into drama, sentences became lyrics, exposition was transformed into dialogue, and interior monologues were physicalized as gesture so that the singular experience of reading was transformed into the communal act of theatre. For example, I added the character of the Muse, who represents the spirit of 1930s Los Angeles and who serves alternately as Arturo's taskmaster and his inspiration as he struggles to complete his novel. In one scene the Muse leads him down Angels Flight to survey the city as they sing to one another: "Come to me the way I came to you, you pretty town. I love you so much, you sad flower in the sand!" At times she alights on his desk to distract Arturo and later she dances around him tapping out a rhythm with her feet in a flamenco style. Arturo matches her beats with the taps of his typewriter—she provides the rhythm and he gives her back the words in this playful duet.

As a creative exercise, students also wrote alongside the text, inserting their own writing, which was based on their personal experiences of immigration, violence, racial prejudice and the tensions inherent in the process of cultural assimilation—themes that are at the heart of *Ask the Dust*. I was drawn to the story because of its resonance with the lives of my students, many of whom expressed during rehearsal a profound understanding and recognition of the experiences of Camilla and Arturo. I wanted to highlight Fante's vision of Los Angeles as the destination for vast numbers of people looking for a new way of life in California—and the way this vision is repeated today with different migrant groups. In order to reflect this contemporary relevance, we added names and places connoting Hispanic or Latino histories whenever we could. In our script the Latino name is said first followed in sharp succession by the Anglo name. With their bodies and voices the actors emphasized the notion of silencing or covering up the first name. The ensemble sings:

> Ask the dust! Ask the dust on the road!
> Ask the sand along the Santa Monica Bay.
> Ask old Junipero Serra down on the Plaza.
> Ask the sawdust in the Liberty Buffet.
> Ask us for we are the uprooted ones.

> We are Sanchez/Smith and Jimenez/Jones and Perez/Parker. We have the dust of Chiapas, Chicago and Cleveland in our shoes. We come here by train and by car to the land of sunshine. To die in the sun. To find our place in the sun. We are the new Californians. We have found our paradise.

> *The Muse:*

> You have found your paradise!

The ensemble dances to Bing Crosby's *San Fernando Valley* as the Muse tosses oranges into the crowd shouting "Sunshine in the sky!"

In order to inform our sense of the city as Fante saw it, we examined the history of Los Angeles through archival research, museum visits, and walking tours of what was once the Bunker Hill neighborhood of Los Angeles where the novel is set. Reviewing the city in light of the novel we were prompted to ask: How is Los Angeles revised by each new generation? How do we account for what is lost as new histories, new buildings, and new neighborhoods inscribe themselves over these vanished geographies? And as individuals and as communities, how do we reinvent ourselves? Today there are few signs of what Bunker Hill was—but during class walking tours of the neighborhood we looked for traces, fragments, vestiges of the lost community of Bunker Hill. We walked alongside the steep steps of Angels Flight, ran our fingers across the wrought iron railings at the Bradbury Building, took in the grandeur of the Orpheum theater and marveled at the shimmering chandeliers at the Biltmore Hotel. By juxtaposing living memory against a historical archive of scripted, visual and urban records, we attempted to activate what theater historian Joseph Roach has termed the "kinesthetic imagination," where imagination and social memory converge.[4]

The history of Bunker Hill is particularly interesting in part because so little of the neighborhood remains. After Los Angeles became a city in 1850, affluent Angelenos began to build large homes on the hill and it soon became the most fashionable neighborhood in the city. In 1901 a funicular railway was built to carry passengers from the top of Bunker Hill to downtown. This railway, known as Angels Flight, figures prominently in *Ask the Dust* and influenced our set design. By the 1930s the neighborhood was quickly becoming overshadowed by more desirable areas such as Pasadena and Beverly Hills and many of the Victorian mansions were converted into boarding houses. Cheap hotels and apartments sprang up to accommodate an influx of Dust Bowl migrants, artists, and writers, including Fante himself. Scenic designer Efren Delgadillo Jr. came to rehearsal one day with a striking photograph of one of the Victorians being trucked off to Highland Park as a partially completed Dorothy Chandler Pavilion looms behind it. He incorporated the idea of the little house jacked up and ready to be transported into his design for Arturo's hotel room, which became a platform that could be moved and rotated around the stage. He also designed a long diagonal steel-deck ramp that bisected the performance space and rose to an elevation of over eight feet and echoed the steep angle of Angels Flight. This platform functioned as a sand dune, as Angels Flight, and as a dark alley behind the diner or a city street. The moving platform was positioned at times right up against the ramp so that, as in the novel, Arturo could step through his window into his hotel room. One of the other major design elements was what we called "the sail," an immense fabric backdrop that could be raised at different points in the show and which could be lit from behind and with front light to create shadows of the actors' bodies. At times the fabric functioned as a screen for video and still projections of Arturo's typewriter, Joshua trees, palm trees, Bunker Hill, ocean waves, a circus tent, an earthquake, flowers, close-ups of Camilla and the fluttering pages of Arturo's manuscript as he throws it into the desert (fig. 6).

In *Ask the Dust* the presence of the desert is palpable, felt in the continual force it exerts on the action and the characters alike. I considered the desert to be a thematic motif that would frame *DUST* in the beginning and at the end and recur throughout the piece. In "Prologue to *Ask the Dust*," written prior to the novel, Fante also began with desert imagery, with the dust

FIGURE 6. Arturo (Peter Vandehei) and Camilla (Lulu Mack) in *DUST*. (Courtesy of J'aime Morrison. Photo by Kenji Kang.)

on the roads of the Mojave and Camilla's footprints in the sand. I instinctively felt drawn to this structure of beginning at the end of the story, with Camilla's departure. Stephen Cooper explains in his biography of Fante that the author had originally opened the novel at the end, that is, with Camilla's disappearance into the desert. After hearing criticism of this strategy from a writing acquaintance, however, Fante decided on an alternate structure, beginning instead with Arturo in his hotel room.[5] If as Cooper suggests, Fante favored the "elemental power of a forward-moving narrative," I was drawn instinctively to Fante's initial impulse to begin at the end, to follow a circular, spiraling, and perhaps ultimately more "feminine" route through the narrative. I realized that for me the great arc of the story was not a young man's struggle to become a writer, but a divided woman's struggle to find, if not a unification of her various dimensions, an integration. What I sought to mine from *Ask the Dust* was the shadow story. I followed Camilla's trace, her narrative, which existed in the silences between the words and in the music of the language itself.

One of the most important ideas to emerge from our rehearsal process was the metaphorical concept of mirage as a place of wonder, an illusion or fantasy that appears real or possible but in fact is neither. As both a theatrical concept and visual motif, a mirage allowed me to play with shifting perspectives, inversions, reflections, and replications on stage. It was through the notion of a mirage that I arrived at the idea of dividing the character of Camilla into four separate women that would function, at times, as a chorus. One character would be Young Camilla, a version of Camilla as a child, before she had come to the United States from Mexico. Another character embodied the spirit of Los Angeles, muse to Arturo Bandini and also at times Camilla's guide. Another added figure was that of Our Lady of Guadalupe, and last was Vera, one of the broken women Arturo encounters on his late-night walks around the city. During the opening scene of *DUST*, the women are all dressed to resemble beautiful desert flora. As if summoned by Camilla's mirage hallucination, the women enter the space one by one and begin to chant ancient pronunciations for Mojave, "*Amohave, A-mochá-ves, Wah muk a-hah'-ve.*" They each take a turn dancing an expression of their part in Camilla's narrative, while Camilla, as if in a dream with her eyes closed, echoes each of their movements. I imagined that during this early scene Camilla is not yet capable of reconciling these various forces within her. Later, when she seeks refuge in the desert after escaping from the asylum, her dance with these women is one of incorporation. By the end, Camilla has found a way to embody her differences so that, instead of destroying her, these disparate parts of herself are integrated into a new identity. I have reimagined Camilla as a survivor, not wandering off into the desert to die as the novel suggests, but adapting to her surroundings and in this transformation, becoming the author of her own story. With the dust of Fante's words in her mouth, Camilla sings, "Here in this place, I have the space to write my own story, to write my own story."

The idea of Camilla becoming a writer was communicated through her final costume. During my research for the production, I came across an image of a straitjacket worn by Agnes Richter, a German seamstress held as a patient in an insane asylum during the 1890s. She embroidered her straitjacket with words, indecipherable phrases and drawings which documented her thoughts and feelings during her time in the asylum.[6] Probably not unlike Camilla's experience of incarceration in the asylum, Agnes Richter was not allowed to use conventional writing instruments, but she was allowed to sew. In effect, the straitjacket is covered with her "writing," her story stitched over every inch of fabric. Costume designer Garry Lennon transformed this idea into the exquisite final robe Camilla wears as she departs for the desert. The robe is inscribed with Camilla's words, the lyrics to her songs and her drawings of desert flowers: by its visual reference to her own writing, the garment signifies Camilla's release from the confines of someone else's narrative.

Two articles from the *New York Times* greatly informed my understanding of Camilla and helped me shape a point of view for her character. One was an op-ed article written by Charles Lyons about the alarming number of suicides among the Guaraní Indians of western Brazil. He describes the process by which the tribe was dispossessed of its lands and uprooted from its traditional way of life. As ranchers occupy land that once belonged to the tribe, the Indians come to inhabit a "nonplace," and as a result, they are committing suicide in alarming numbers. Lyons goes on to state, "Indigenous peoples suffer the greatest suicide risk among cultural or ethnic groups worldwide."[7] I could not help but wonder if Camilla, as a Mexican woman in the 1930s, perhaps occupied a similar kind of "nonplace" in the novel. She also does not fit into modern life; she is between identities as a Mexican and an American. She is neither of the desert nor of the city, and she is poor in a wealthy urban metropolis. Her story, her desire for a better life, and her lack of available options all resonate with the plight of the Guaraní Indians. Fante leaves the conclusion of *Ask the Dust* open to interpretation regarding Camilla's disappearance. Does she commit suicide by walking into the desert with only a bottle of milk for the dog? Does she die out in the dunes of thirst and hunger? Is she ambushed by human predators or consumed by wild animals? Certainly, one possible interpretation of the ending could be that because Camilla is not able to create a sustainable way of life for herself, she takes herself off to the desert to die. Yet because Fante leaves this aspect of the story intriguingly inconclusive, I was inspired to imagine an alternate route for Camilla. I saw her wandering the desert until she finds an old border road, one of a network of such roads built by California border patrol agents in the 1920s and 1930s, that would lead her out of the Mojave toward safety, freedom, and perhaps even a life as an artist herself.[8]

Freshman theater student Lulu Mack embodied Camilla Lopez with force and fury for our production and we spoke at length during rehearsals about how to represent Camilla's complicated character to the audience. We discussed heroines both fictional and real who offered darker portraits of the female psyche. We were having these conversations at the same time that several films were being discussed in the media for their portrayal of sexually or emotionally manipulative women. *Gone Girl* author Gillian Flynn, told columnist Maureen Dowd in an interview, "Dark sides are important. They should be nurtured like nasty black orchids."[9] I think these conversations helped free the actress playing Camilla to dig deep and to not be afraid of shocking the audience if need be. There are moments in *Ask the Dust* when Camilla *is* nasty, when she behaves aggressively and even becomes violent. These qualities are what make her a fascinating character, a character I felt necessitated greater exploration. When Lulu came to her audition she was dressed in a long flowing dress and she wore her hair down around her shoulders. I had selected the only narrative section of text spoken by Camilla, which I found in "Prologue to *Ask the Dust*," to use as the audition script. As I listened to this young woman speak the text, articulating her body for emphasis on certain words, I saw Camilla appear and I knew she was the star of my play: "I used to go to his room at the Alta Loma and toss pebbles at his window. He would pull me in and I'd stay, because I knew he wouldn't touch me. I hated him because he kept saying I should be proud I was a Mexican. And I dared him to touch me. I lifted my dress and threw it over his face and he who knew so much and was so clever with words, he blushed and he said, 'Please don't do things like that, Camilla'" (154). Camilla follows this speech with a violent, almost demented laugh, but it was Lulu's movement that communicated the full weight of her anger. She made a choice to drop her right hip and shoulder on the word "Mexican," in counterpoint to the text. As Camilla rejects Arturo's admonishments for her to be proud of her ethnicity as a Mexican woman, the student actress broke the continuity of her body's line in a gesture of dynamic force. In dance, the line of the body often refers to the profile of a moving figure in an extended shape, such as an *arabesque*. In ballet, such a linear shape signifies beauty and harmony, and by intentionally breaking this form the student seized on a fundamental facet of Camilla's character, which we developed further in rehearsals; she disrupts and denies such unity and instead embodies a forceful energy more connected to the movements of modern dance pioneer Martha Graham, which were weighted, angular, and thrusting. The lines of her body seem disjointed, broken, curving inward instead of radiating outward: Camilla as a danced implosion.

Fante refers to Camilla as a dancer several times in the novel starting with the first time Arturo sees her: "The girl moved like a dancer, her strong silk legs gathering bits of sawdust as her tattered shoes glided over the marble" (35). And yet as their relationship develops it might more accurately be characterized by the ferocity associated with the French Apache dance than the gliding movements of a waltz. Certainly, the verbal and physical assaults that Arturo and Camilla trade with one another lend the narrative a visceral kinetic impact. The Apache (pronounced a-POSH), named after early twentieth-century French street gangsters known as "Les Apaches" and the dance/fight pantomime they were known for, seemed the perfect form to express the friction between Camilla, her abusive boyfriend Sammy, and Arturo. Perhaps Fante was familiar with the comingling of dance and violence, because in one scene Arturo narrates what could be the choreography of an Apache dance, "I grabbed her arms and flung her like a dancer. She went spinning across the lot, but she did not fall. She screamed, charged at me. I caught her in my arms and pinned her elbows down. She kicked and tried to scratch my legs" (108). The Apache dance often involved such dramatic aggression, with women engaging in the battle with as much vehemence as the men. When I read the scene in the novel I wrote in the margins, "Apache!," excited by the text's implicit invitation for dance to take over some of the narrative conflict.

During a research trip to the Lincoln Center Library for the Performing Arts, I discovered a dance-theatre collaboration that deeply informed my overall vision for *DUST*. In 1933 the playwright Bertolt Brecht and the composer Kurt Weill collaborated on a work called *The Seven Deadly Sins*, which they referred to as a ballet-chanté or "sung ballet." The piece premiered in Paris at the Théatre des Champs-Elysées in a production that was produced, directed and choreographed by George Balanchine. I was immediately drawn to the idea of a "sung ballet" as a way to approach *Ask the Dust* because Fante's language, already resonant as music to my ear, seemed to call for some form of vocalization or song. Perhaps there was an austerity to his writing that I wanted to honor; I wanted to shape a theatrical language that included singing and dancing, but not as a recognizable work of musical theater. Using the ballet chanté as a structural idea I began to incorporate the voices of the performers as instruments to create landscapes of sound through chanting and singing. Our composer Dustin Rabi created beautiful orchestrations of the text, which when vocalized, unearthed deep reservoirs of emotion in the actors. Whether it was the rhythmic dissonance of Camilla's audible breath in the asylum scene, the waves of overlapping sounds in the opening scene which conjured the winds of the Mojave Desert, the fragmented speech of newly arrived immigrants, or the sensuous harmonies of the chorus as they sing, "Oh for a Mexican girl," the vocal arrangements added an unexpected sonic dimension to the performance.

Musically the world of the piece developed simultaneously with the choreography and the script—all aspects of the production moved forward together rather than one being inspired by the other. This kind of process is incredibly exciting and also rather daunting. I began listening to music before rehearsals started—I was drawn to music that sounded as if it came from the world of the novel. The first piece that really felt like "it" was a piece by Daniel Lanois called "JJ Leaves LA," from his album *Shine* (2003). The way he plays the pedal steel guitar sounded to me as if the instrument was speaking or telling a story—sometimes I heard the voice of the guitar as wailing. This sound led me to the soundtrack of the film *Paris, Texas* (2001) by Ry Cooder. When I played this music in rehearsal, I had the students drop to the floor and in slow motion roll toward the far end of the room. As they unfurled their bodies twisting and shivering with each reverberation of the guitar strings, shapes began to materialize and then disappear—a rattlesnake, a bird, a lone Joshua tree, a swirl of dust—the landscape of the story taking shape before my eyes. The film scores of Gustavo Santaolalla were also an early influence, particularly his music for the film *The Motorcycle Diaries* (2004). One of these tracks inspired me to stage a scene of Arturo dancing alone by red candlelight in the adobe church he visits in downtown LA. As the guitar rips, slides, and rocks, Arturo slides on his knees and beats his chest as he leans into a backward lunge, his heart to the sky. Our Lady of Guadalupe sings softly in Spanish behind him.

One of the most thrilling aspects of the process of developing *DUST* was hearing elements from Fante's novel echoed in the music. One particularly haunting passage was during the beach scene, in which Arturo swims out beyond the surf and almost drowns trying to save Camilla, who has led him to believe she cannot swim: "I lost the sound of her voice in the roar. 'I'm coming!' I yelled, and I yelled it again and again, until I had to stop to save my strength." He continues: "Her cries had stopped. I churned water with my hands, waiting for another cry. It did not come. I shouted. My voice was weak, like a voice underwater" (66). During this scene the actors run back and forth as if they are being pushed by the crashing tide while a larger-than-life video plays behind them of receding and then rushing water which threatens to envelop them. The above text is not spoken. Rather, the composer created music that communicated the rise and fall of the tumultuous ocean and expressed those submerged voices. Likewise, Camilla's screams and Arturo's struggle for breath were audible in the music, amplifying the danger and darkness in this pivotal scene. Rabi's shimmering instrumentations throughout *DUST* conjured character, landscape and drama just as his original score pushed the actors and me to pursue ever-greater registers of feeling.

After one evening's performance of *DUST* a woman approached me from the audience with tears in her eyes. She told me that Camilla's story was her story too, that she recognized in Camilla's struggle her own experience of assimilation and the trauma of trying to reconcile two cultures. As she spoke she folded her arms into her chest, each hand cupped as if clasping an invisible object. I knew immediately which scene she was referring to and what her gesture signified. In a scene called *Mirage Reprise* Arturo lies back in his bed—it is as if in his daydream he has returned to the desert. His bed slowly tracks in a large arc across the stage as we hear his thoughts on a voiceover:

> Sand from the Mojave had blown across the city, tiny brown grains of sand clung to my fingertips, my typewriter glutted with sand. It was even between the sheets of my bed.
> The heat rose out of the haze and my nostrils breathed it. Here was the desert beneath the streets, waiting for the city to die, to cover it with timeless sand—the desert was always there, a patient white animal waiting for civilization to flicker and pass into the darkness. (40)

These words bring Camilla to the stage clasping two white pumps in her hands. She sets them down and slowly unhooks her beloved huaraches from her feet. With difficulty she steps into the pumps she feels she must wear even though they are ill fitting and uncomfortable. She holds the huaraches and embraces them as if saying goodbye one last time to her past. She dances awkwardly in the pumps while projected on the screen behind her a slow-motion close-up video plays of her striding in bare feet. Camilla shouts out with defiance, "This is what the desert has done to my dreams. This is what the desert has done to my dreams." Her words silence Arturo and wake him from his reverie. This triptych juxtaposes Arturo's recurring thoughts of the desert with the image of Camilla's bare feet walking toward or perhaps past him. Her dance with the shoes becomes a layered mise-en-scène that demonstrates the power of theatre as an expression and formulation for "discontinuous fragments" (fig. 7).

I would love to go on writing out each scene and describing it in words, but ultimately *DUST* lives on the stage in the bodies of the performers. I hope the production will have another life in downtown Los Angeles, perhaps not far from Angels Flight. For now, I will close with the opening moments of the show, with Camilla in the desert.

DUST—a ballet chanté
Scene: 1—The Maternal Darkness
Place: The Mojave Desert
Time: 1939

FIGURE 7. Camilla's robe of many words. (Courtesy of J'aime Morrison. Photo by Kenji Kang.)

Sound of distant singers offstage. Camilla half starving, exhausted, wanders the Mojave Desert. She lies down in the sand. As she begins to lose consciousness Young Camilla appears beside her and begins to dance the story of her childhood. This vision of her younger self is joined by other aspects of Camilla's psyche: The Muse, *a spirit of Los Angeles;* the figure of Our Lady of Guadalupe; *and* Vera, *in some ways Camilla's cypher, another soul ravaged by broken dreams. This chorus of women encircle Camilla, and through dance, ritual and chant comfort her in her despair and loneliness. The women lead her onward . . .*

Notes

1. Fante, *Ask the Dust*, 14. Hereafter cited in text by page number.
2. de Certeau, *Practice of Everyday Life*, 115.
3. Barthes, *Grain of the Voice*, 209.
4. Roach, *Cities of the Dead*, 26.
5. Cooper, *Full of Life*, 168.
6. See Hornstein, *Agnes's Jacket*.
7. Lyons, "Suicides Spread Through a Brazilian Tribe," SR6.
8. For images and description of these border roads see Misrach, "Border Signs," 24–39.
9. Dowd, "Lady Psychopaths, Welcome," 11.

Works Cited

Barthes, Roland. *The Grain of the Voice, Interviews 1962–1980*. Evanston, IL: Northwestern University Press, 2009.
Cooper, Stephen. *Full of Life: A Biography of John Fante*. Santa Monica, CA: Angel City Press, 2005.
De Certeau, Michel. *The Practice of Everyday Life*. Berkeley: University of California Press, 1984.
Dowd, Maureen, "Lady Psychopaths, Welcome," *New York Times*, October 12, 2014.
Fante, John. *Ask the Dust*. New York: HarperCollins, 2006.
———. "Prologue to *Ask the Dust.*" In *The Big Hunger, Stories 1932–1959*, edited by Stephen Cooper, 143–161. Boston, MA: Black Sparrow Press, 2000.
Hornstein, Gail A. *Agnes's Jacket: A Psychologist's Search for the Meanings of Madness*. New York: Rodale Books, 2009.

Lyons, Charles, "Suicides Spread Through a Brazilian Tribe," *New York Times*, January 4, 2015.
Misrach, Richard, "Border Signs," *California Sunday Magazine*, November 2, 2014.
Roach, Joseph. *Cities of the Dead: Circum-Atlantic Performance*. Ithaca, NY: Columbia University Press, 1996.

Ask the Lyrics: John Fante in Music

Chiara Mazzucchelli

I was barely a toddler when English singer Kate Bush hit the European music charts with her debut single "Wuthering Heights" in 1978.[1] But my older sisters used to sing it all the time, so I learned to recognize the tunes well before my English was finally decent enough to read Emily Brontë's novel by the same title. Around the same time, Dire Straits, a British rock band that was very popular in Italy throughout the 1980s and early 1990s, released "Romeo and Juliet," thus turning Shakespeare's classic play into a classic track.[2] Now and again, I have stumbled across pages of classic literary works while listening to music. Some of these works are made explicit in the songs' titles, for instance Dire Straits' "Romeo and Juliet" and Guns N' Roses' "Catcher in the Rye."[3] In other songs, the inspiration is more or less hidden in the lyrics. Jefferson Airplane's "White Rabbit,"[4] for example, is one and the same as Lewis Carroll's and the nymphet teasing the young teacher in the 1980 song by the Police, "Don't Stand so Close to Me,"[5] is reminiscent of Nabokov's Dolores in *Lolita*, a novel I devoured during one of my boring summers as a teenager in Sicily. The crosspollination of literature and music is not a new phenomenon and classics of world literature inspire songwriters who incorporate them in their art in different ways and forms. Interestingly enough, even a not-yet-canonically classic author such as the Italian American John Fante has had an impact on popular culture and music both in Italy and in the United States. Grossly neglected by the American literary mainstream, John Fante has only recently become widely read in Italy and he has already developed unusual ties with music in both countries. In this essay, I will first survey the reception of John Fante's works and the factors that brought about the "Fantemania" of the late 1980s and 1990s. Next, I will present a review of some Italian and American songs that draw inspiration from Arturo Bandini, the protagonist of Fante's saga. Sheryl Crow, Red Hot Chili Peppers, The Good Life in the United States, and Vinicio Capossela, Raiz, and Marracash in Italy are some of the singers and groups who have paid tribute, in different ways and through different music genres, to Fante in their songs. Finally, I focus on Fante's legacy as an ethnic writer in certain musical texts that echo but also transcend Arturo Bandini's experience, thus allowing for a reading that is as relevant as it is appealing to today's world migrants. This essay testifies to and invites reflection on the influence of certain noncanonical writers on popular culture and how their experience often reverberates in larger society regardless of their canonization by mainstream literary critics.

The Reception of Fante's Works in the United States and Italy

In his seminal book *Italian Signs, American Streets*, critic Fred Gardaphé laments the fact that despite the support of H. L. Mencken and James Farrell, two leading critics at the time Fante was writing, the Italian American writer received little critical attention and was left out of most studies of the 1930s.[6] Contemporary American scholarship, too, has neglected to pay due attention to Fante's stories of the joys and pains of the struggling young ethnic person. Granted, Fante's novels are not your feel-good books about the difficult yet ultimately successful path to the American Dream. Nor will the aspiring artist find in Arturo Bandini's parable of the budding writer much reassurance that talent creates its own opportunities. Finally, to make things more complicated,

FIGURE 8. An ad for *Ask the Dust* in the *San Francisco Chronicle*, November 19, 1939: "A love story of the racially homeless." (*San Francisco Chronicle* / Polaris Images.)

while Fante is considered first and foremost an ethnic writer, the interethnic relations depicted in his novels, short stories, and novellas are tense and rarely cooperative. During the 1930s and 1940s, his semi-autobiographical novels must have appeared rough and raw in both content and style and, as such, difficult to appreciate for the average American reader (fig. 8).

Not surprisingly, as a beginning writer Fante received support and validation from Mencken, who was scouting for alternative voices in the American literary panorama. Mencken published Fante's first stories in *The American Mercury*, the important magazine of which Mencken was founder and editor. Fante, in his turn, immortalized Mencken in *Ask the Dust* as the "great" and "mighty" editor J. C. Hackmuth.[7] By 1940 Fante had already published a respectable number of short stories, a collection entitled *Dago Red*, and two novels, *Wait until Spring, Bandini* and his most acclaimed one, *Ask the Dust*. And yet, his career as a professional writer was not taking off.

In pre–World War II Italy Fante received a similar reception. His greatest admirer there, Elio Vittorini, included him in his 1941 *Americana*, an anthology of American narrative prose from its origins to the then-present and the first of its kind to be published in Italy. That same year, Vittorini also translated and published *Ask the Dust* under the title *Cammino nella polvere* for Mondadori, one of Italy's largest publishing houses. Nevertheless, Fante's reputation remained far from that of a great American writer on either side of the Atlantic.[8]

In fact, for most of his life, Fante eked out a living thanks to his work as a screenwriter for Hollywood until, in the late 1970s and early 1980s, his name finally reappeared in literary circles nationwide and abroad. Fante's rediscovery was serendipitous. In his 1978 novel *Women*, Charles Bukowski made his alter ego Henry Chinaski name John Fante as his favorite writer. Thanks to a worshipping Bukowski, Fante's novels were immediately republished by Black Sparrow Press, which also released some of the writer's unpublished manuscripts. In his passionate preface to *Ask the Dust*, Bukowski explained how it all began: "One day I pulled a book down and opened it, and there it was. I stood for a moment, reading. . . . And here, at last, was a man who was not afraid of emotion. The humour and the pain were intermixed with a superb simplicity. The beginning of that book was a wild and enormous miracle to me. . . . The book was *Ask the Dust* and the author was John Fante. He was to be a lifetime influence on my writing. . . . Fante was my god."[9]

Blind and with both legs amputated, a very ill Fante must have reveled in his newfound fame before diabetes killed him in 1983. We can situate the beginning of the Fantemania, or in Martino Marazzi's words "Fantology" in Italy just a decade later,[10] in the late 1980s and 1990s. In the wake of the American and also French rediscovery, and thanks to the interest of Pier Vittorio Tondelli and Francesco Durante, a few small publishing houses like Leonardo, Marcos Y Marcos, and Fazi published all of Fante's novels. In 2003 Mondadori published a Fante *Meridiano*, a collection of all his works edited by Durante, which consecrated the Italian American writer in Italy as an officially influential author. Eventually, the prestigious Einaudi reprinted all of Fante's novels with introductions by the new generation of Italian writers, such as Alessandro Baricco (*Chiedi alla polvere*), Gianni Amelio (*Sogni di Bunker Hill*), Niccolò Ammaniti (*Aspetta primavera, Bandini!*), Sandro Veronesi (*La strada per Los Angeles*), and Melania Mazzucco (*La grande fame*), just to mention a few. Fante's success in Italy is so far-reaching that every summer, since 2006, the international literary festival "Il Dio di mio padre" ("My Father's God") is held in his honor in Torricella Peligna, John's father's birthplace in Abruzzo.[11] He and his works are now the topic of innumerable readings, conferences, plays, documentaries, theses, etc. Over a half century later, Fante has finally been recognized as an important voice in the world literary panorama.

Fante's success especially among young writers should not come as a surprise. As Sandro Veronesi explained in an interview with Alessio Romano about Fante's fortune in Italy, "It was especially easy for writers to identify with an eternally aspiring writer."[12] In *Ask the Dust*, arguably Fante's masterpiece, Arturo is a sensitive but rough-around-the-edges twenty-year-old whose bursts of passion translate into horrifying racist rants, grandiose romantic gestures, and steamy relationships with imaginary women. Most importantly, in what has been read by many critics as a *Künstlerroman*, Arturo Bandini wants to be a writer, or better yet *the* American writer of the twentieth century. With the highest aspirations he has moved from Colorado to Los Angeles to launch his career but ends up instead living off his mother's money in a sordid hotel room, behind on his rent, on a starvation diet of coffee and oranges, and eternally awaiting a letter from his editor J. C. Hackmuth.

At the beginning of the novel, the only thing Arturo has managed to publish is a short story, "The Little Dog Laughed," which he describes as "a story to make you die holding the page, and it wasn't about a dog, either: a clever story, screaming poetry" (14). To Arturo, the publication is proof that he has talent and that, eventually, he will overcome the early struggles of a budding writer and become a big shot in the American literary scene. His visits to the local library excite his fantasy:

> the library with the big boys in the shelves, old Dreiser, old Mencken, all the boys down there, and I went to see them, Hya Dreiser, Hya Mencken, Hya, hya: there's a place for me, too, and it begins with B, in the B shelf, Arturo Bandini, make way for Arturo Bandini, his slot for his book, and I sat at the table and just looked at the place where my book would be, right there close to Arnold Bennett; not much that Arnold Bennett, but I'd be there to sort of bolster up the B's, old Arturo Bandini, one of the boys. (13)

Like Arturo Bandini, all aspiring writers dream of seeing their books on the shelf among such essentials as the Bible and the *Divine Comedy*, so his literary ambitions make it easy for writers to identify with him. However, Fante's influence is now so pervasive that it includes other areas of Italian and American cultures as well, not least in music that celebrates the writer's legacy in several different ways.

Fante in the American and Italian Musical Panoramas

In fact, Fante has also become a favorite source of inspiration not only for writers but for many singers as well, both in the United States and in Italy. Of the four novels that make up Arturo Bandini's saga, *Ask the Dust* is the one that inspires most of the discussions in the literary and nonliterary circles on both sides of the Atlantic Ocean.[13] For the most part, this success can be explained by the larger-than-life personality of its protagonist. Depending on the singer and the song, Bandini is the romantic guy desperately in love with Camilla, the struggling wannabe writer, or the American-born son of working-class immigrant parents. The songwriters acknowledge their debt to Fante by slipping into their lyrics a subtle reference to the work to which they pay tribute. For instance, the famous Los Angeles–based band Red Hot Chili Peppers included in their 2002 album *By the Way* the song "Can't Stop," where a clear homage to their fellow Los Angeleno appears in the following lyrics: "Go ask the dust for any answers/Come back strong with fifty belly dancers."[14] Again in the American rock scene, in 1996 Sheryl Crow included in her second album *Sheryl Crow* the track "Superstar," where the song's narrator "beat[s] around the streets like Bandini looking for Camilla."[15] As it turns out, Arturo's infatuation with Camilla Lopez, the Mexican waitress he loves in his own impossible way, has proven especially inspiring to writers and singers alike.

Arturo and Camilla have a special kind of relationship. After the first stormy encounter between the two at the Columbia Buffet, when insults fly back and forth for no particular reason other than a mutual attraction-repulsion, Arturo can't stop thinking and fantasizing about his "Mayan princess" (41). The morning after, he resolves to go look for her and brings with him a copy of his first and only published story in hopes of impressing her: "Eight o'clock and I was down on Spring Street. I had a copy of *The Little Dog Laughed* in my pocket. She would think differently about me if she read that story. I had it autographed, right there in my back pocket, ready to present at the slightest notice" (38). In the lyrics of "Album of the Year," a song that American indie rock band the Good Life released in 2005, the turbulent love story between a reticent woman and a songwriter is reminiscent of Arturo and Camilla's stormy relationship:

> The first time that I met her
> I was convinced that I had finally found the one.
> She was convinced I was under the influence of all those drunken romantics.
> I was reading Fante at the time.
> I had Bukowski on my mind.

The song's narrator feels like he needs to prove his worth to his beloved woman and in order to impress her he swears, "I'll write the album of the year," replicating Arturo's desire to sweep Camilla off her feet with his publication.[16]

In both cases, the love story ends with the young woman leaving her wannabe famous artist. When Arturo walks back to the beach house that the two have just rented, Camilla is gone. A heart-broken Arturo remembers: "There was no sign of her, or of [their dog] Willie. I unloaded my things. Perhaps she had taken the dog for another walk. But I was deceiving myself. She was gone.... I looked again for some note, some message. There was no trace of her. It was as though she had not so much as set foot in that house" (160). The relationship between the songwriter and his woman results in a similar abandonment. When the young man walks into the shared apartment, he finds her "picking through which records were hers/Her clothes were packed in boxes/with some pots and pans/and a toaster." In the end, the young men's narcissism feeds their ambition, but it also makes them incapable of having a functional romantic relationship.

Fante and his literary alter ego Arturo have also inspired music in Italy. In fact, some of the greatest interpreters of contemporary Italian music are hardcore *fantiani*, such as Francesco De Gregori, one of Italy's most-beloved *cantautori*, or singer-songwriters from the 1970s, and Vinicio Capossela, one of the most original and finest protagonists of today's Italian musical panorama. Capossela most famously included in his 1996 album *Il ballo di San Vito* the song "L'accolita dei rancorosi," openly inspired by Fante's *The Brotherhood of the Grape*.[17] *Cantautori* such as De Gregori and

Capossela and also rock singers Piero Pelú and Luciano Ligabue are some of Fante's earliest and most vocal supporters. These singers are not alone in their militant appreciation of Fante and his works in their songs. A score of lesser known artists and bands have paid tribute to Fante. For instance, in 2004 the Rome-based indie rock band Citizen Kane released their first self-produced album, *Tutte le parole che ogni giorno perdo*.[18] Among the seven tracks is "Chiedi alla polvere."[19] One year later, in 2005, the Turin-based pop-rock group Perturbazione, which recently gained national notoriety thanks to their participation in the 2014 edition of the Sanremo Festival, released their fifth album, *Canzoni allo specchio*, which includes "Chiedo alla polvere" ("I Ask the Dust").[20] However, John Fante's novels certainly offer much more in terms of inspiration than the romantic relationship between Arturo Bandini and Camilla and the multilayered meanings to which the title *Ask the Dust* lends itself. In his works, Fante repeatedly tackled topics such as family relations, religion, artistic aspirations, difficult relationships, and especially social issues relating to economic and ethnic status.[21] These latter aspects inform the music of individual Italian artists and musical groups of different genres who celebrate in their lyrics the struggles of hard-working people and the difficulties faced by immigrants in today's multicultural Italy.

The Italian American Ethnic Experience in Italian Music

As the American-born son of a first-generation Italian immigrant in the 1930s, John Fante had witnessed first-hand the impact of injustices, inequities, and discrimination on an immigrant's family life. The author was keenly and painfully aware of the sense of uprootedness that his father Nick experienced in America and its consequences on the family.[22] In fact, most of Fante's literary production has an autobiographical streak and revolves around the themes of heritage, ethnic identity, and social conflicts. In his fiction, the Fantes became the Bandinis, the Toscanas, and the Molises, but their last name always ended in a vowel and thus betrayed the family's immigrant roots. The Italian American writer felt an extreme ambivalence toward his ethnic heritage and this constant fluctuation between pride and shame is exemplified in Arturo Bandini's schizophrenic ethnic identity.

When we first meet Arturo in *Ask the Dust*, he is a struggling writer in Bunker Hill whose indigence is matched only by his ambition. On page one we read that Arturo "noted with satisfaction that Joe DiMaggio was still a credit to the Italian people," thus showing that he nurtures a sense of belonging to the Italian community in the United States (11). However, this sense of pride is short-lived. Early enough in the novel, Arturo identifies instead with the Anglo-Saxon majority, even pitting himself, somewhat desperately, against other immigrant groups in the United States. For instance, when he first arrives at the Alta Loma Hotel we are told that the landlady, Mrs. Hargraves, informs him of the hotel's segregationist policy: no Mexicans or Jews allowed. "I'm an American," Arturo proudly announces (49).[23] In his article "John Fante's *Ask the Dust* and Fictions of Whiteness," Matthew Elliott suggests reading this scene as a rewriting of the immigrant's arrival at Ellis Island, where the Italian-American migrant Arturo from Colorado has to convince a skeptical gatekeeper (read, immigration officer) that he deserves to be admitted and, eventually, to realize his Californian (read, American) Dream (531–532). The self-styled "Gringo" (38) further elaborates on his vaunted Americanness: "I was an American, and goddam proud of it. This great city, these mighty pavements and proud buildings, they were the voice of my America. From sand and cactus we Americans had carved an empire. Camilla's people had had their chance. They had failed. We Americans had turned the trick. Thank God for my country. Thank God I had been born an American!" (44). But just like everything else about Arturo, his Americanness, too, is more than anything else, a grandiose fantasy. Arturo is the immigrants' son who is not equipped to resolve the ethnic dilemma. Torn between the pulls of filial devotion and cultural identity and the tugs of assimilation to mainstream America, Arturo oscillates from one extreme to the other.

His irresolution is equaled only by his narcissism, which makes him incapable of empathy, let alone ethnic solidarity. In fact, his self-centeredness leads him on the path to shallow relationships and social and ethnic isolation.

In *Ask the Dust*, the young Italian American builds his self-esteem on the ruins of others' self-esteem, especially Camilla's. His sense of self-worth and Americanness seems to grow with the growing distance that he puts between himself and his adored Mexican waitress. To be sure, Arturo's reprehensible behavior is a projection of his own ethnic insecurities. In fact, back in his room from the Columbia Buffet where he has once again insulted Camilla by calling her a "Greaser," he finally admits, if only to himself, that his own ethnic status is at the root of his contempt for hers:

> Smith and Parker and Jones, I had never been one of them. Ah, Camilla! When I was a kid back home in Colorado it was Smith and Parker and Jones who hurt me with their hideous names, called me Wop and Dago and Greaser, and their children hurt me, just as I hurt you tonight. They hurt me so much I could never become one of them, drove me to books, drove me within myself, drove me to run away from that Colorado town.... I have vomited at their newspapers, read their literature, observed their customs, eaten their food, desired their women, gaped at their art. But I am poor, and my name ends with a soft vowel, and they hate me and my father, and my father's father, and they would have my blood and put me down ... and when I say Greaser to you it is not my heart that speaks, but the quivering of an old wound, and I am ashamed of the terrible thing I have done. (46–47)

But his confession remains a private one. Arturo will never have the courage, nor perhaps the willingness, to come to terms with his ethnic identity by sharing his experience with Camilla. He thus fails to build any kind of connection with his own or any other ethnic community of 1930s America.

The experience of minority groups, in a broader sense, and the feelings of rejection and acceptance tied to the immigrant experience with which Fante dealt so extensively in his novels have inspired the music of at least a couple of singers of national renown in Italy, namely, rapper Marracash and dub artist Raiz. A discussion of this specific aspect of Fante's work and its reflections on Italian music is particularly significant in light of Italy's experience with immigration, a theme on which Raiz elaborates in his lyrics. Marracash, on the other hand, brings to the forefront a discussion on the multidimensional aspects of Italy's long history of emigration by dealing with issues related to internal migration. In fact, movement to the north of Italy, caused mainly by staggering unemployment rates in the south, is a phenomenon that has exacerbated the already tense relations between the regions and created social tensions and conflicts in the Italian population that are comparable to the ethnic problem at the center of Fante's American novels.[24]

Despite the most obvious differences in terms of time and place, Fabio Rizzo, better known by his stage name Marracash, has a lot in common with John Fante—and, by extension, Fante's alter ego Arturo Bandini—starting with the migratory experience of their respective families. Born in the bellybutton of Sicily in the late 1970s, the rapper grew up on the outskirts of Milan, where his family moved to look for better opportunities. Marracash grew up a poor Sicilian immigrant in the projects of Barona, an outsider in his own country because of his southern origins. Through their art, both Fante and Marracash try to earn the respect of those around them, Fante as a writer in Los Angeles, Marracash as a rapper in Milan. Both use their words to explore the sting of being marginalized because of their minority status.

Backed by artist J-Ax, an early member of the Dogo Gang of Club Dogo and ex-frontman of Articolo 31, arguably Italy's most popular hip-hop group to this day, Marracash released a self-titled debut album in 2008. The single "Badabum cha cha" became the most played track in Italian clubs that summer and most of the songs on *Marracash* took up the serious theme of migration. As Marracash explains in "Popolare," the self-styled "prince of Barona" owes his name to his Sicilian heritage: "When I went to school as a child, as a child / the kids in my class used to call me Moroccan, Moroccan."[25] Just as the terms *dago* or *wop* identified Italians in the United States in a derogatory way, the adjective *Moroccan* is intended as an insult to Sicilians in that it implies their non-Italianness as well as a racial association with their African neighbors. Marracash remembers his difficult childhood as the son of Sicilian immigrants growing up with other immigrant and working-class families in a section of Milan where violence, drugs, and crime were common ways to deal with social issues, and where books were his only exit. In an interview with Andrea Laffranchi for the national Italian newspaper *Corriere della Sera*, the "intelligangsta" talked about his love of reading and singled out his favorite three "deviant" authors: Bukowski, Fante, and William Saroyan.[26]

Fante most explicitly inspired the fourth track in *Marracash*, tellingly titled "Chiedi alla polvere." The song is the MC's "gift" to the pariahs, the families who live in the projects cramped all in one room, in conditions that call to mind the immigrants' tenements of Fante's times. "I'm in the middle of it and I didn't choose it," the rapper sings, "it's hell / ask the dust, it's different here."[27] Although the lived experience of both Marracash and Fante is marked by an acute sense of social injustice, the Sicilian-Milanese rapper is able—unlike the writer—to situate his personal experience in the larger historical and cultural frame that pushed his family—and most other immigrant families, for that matter—to leave everything behind in Sicily to look for better opportunities in northern Italy. This is how the hip-hop artist conveys his message in rap language:

and to my grandpa who, in Sicily, still squeezes grapes in his garden while my
    father's life has been squeezed out of his body
and to my dirty dirty filthy south
and to those who have suffered and now want everything right away
mine is a progeny of defeated ones
the fucking cycle of vanquished and fake myths our hunger is atavistic
and if you're hungry you don't chew, you swallow
if you chewed you'd know how much the world hurts you.[28]

From the personal to the historical through the sociological, with a literary reference to Verga and his "ciclo dei vinti,"[29] in his version of "Ask the Dust" Marracash takes Fante's lesson on the immigrants' experience a step further. The rapper brings out the richness of Fante's work by providing a new focus on a less explored migratory phenomenon, namely, internal migration, the remarkable proportions of which have affected Italian society, culture, and economy. Thus he succeeds, where Arturo falls short, in placing his personal experience within the larger and multi-dimensional Italian diaspora.

Whereas Marracash's association with Fante is through commonalities in their lived experience, Gennaro Della Volpe, aka Raiz, the ex-singer of the popular dub group Almamegretta, traces some apropos parallelisms between the historical experience of Italians abroad and the recent phenomenon of immigration in Italy. With lyrics mostly in Neapolitan as well as standard Italian and English and a sound that is a mix of reggae and folk rhythms with Eastern and Arab influences, the group Almamegretta—whose name translates, significantly, as Migrant Soul—often advocates solidarity and respect for immigrants in their music. Their first album established the group's identity in terms of both style and themes. One of their first tracks was "Figli di Annibale," in which "the dark complexion, the dark hair, and the dark eyes" of Italians are attributed to the "great general Hannibal." From the Carthaginian leader, the Almamegretta continue, Italians have inherited the "color of the blood that flows in their veins."[30] The lyrics specifically focus on issues of cultural cross-encounters and multiculturalism, the Mediterranean, and the southern population of Italy. In their lyrics, Almamegretta mix subalternity and pride with respect to their southern Italian background.

After more than a decade of collaboration, Raiz left the group to pursue a solo career as a reggae dub artist. The *fantiano* singer paid musical homage to the Italian American writer in his first solo album, tellingly titled *WOP*.[31]

To an Italian American ear, the album's title and title track both evoke a history of discrimination and powerlessness that for a long time characterized Italian immigration in the United States. Whether the term is really an acronym for Without Papers or a distortion of *guappo*, Neapolitan slang for thug or pimp, it is a derogatory slur that was commonly addressed to Italians especially during the years of mass emigration to the United States, and it still has the power to arouse rightful resentment in the Italian American community. In Raiz's hands, the use of historically harmful hate speech has a twofold purpose: first, it reminds Italians of their not-so-distant past of discrimination abroad and, second, on account of that past it elicits understanding of and solidarity with Italy's own swelling wave of immigrants today.

Raiz is able to turn Fante's immigrant story into a parable of the struggles of migrants everywhere, regardless of their ethnic origins or country of destination. In order to do so, he draws from his Neapolitan roots and, especially, the history and role of Naples and the Mediterranean as centers of ancient trade routes as well as of today's immigrant encounters.[32] Raiz's questioning of any blind claim to an exclusionary national identity starts with challenging the notion of a "pure" Italian race. Because of its geographical location, embedded as it is between Europe and Africa, and on the east-west axis between Western Europe and western Asia, the Mediterranean Sea has historically been the strategic epicenter of cross-cultural exchange. As a crossroad of civilizations, Raiz reminds us, the Mediterranean has witnessed the interaction of different cultures, languages, customs, and religions. "Wop" thus pays homage to the "mix of races" of which Italians are a very good example. In fact, as a Neapolitan Raiz adds in his dialect, "I'm French, I'm Spanish / I'm a bit American too" ("so' francese, I' so spagnolo / songo pure mericano") and he concludes in English, "I'm the meeting point of every culture on the earth . . . one blood, one blood."[33]

The self-disparaging term *wop* punctuates the song's refrain. With its use, Raiz intends to reclaim hate speech and deprive it of its disparaging potential. "Wop wop / yes this is my name," he sings, thus turning the ethnic slur into an expression of pride. The parallels between the history of Italian emigration abroad, so central to Fante's writings, and the integration of the over five million immigrants in Italy today, are drawn most strongly toward the end of the song, when the singer praises his "new Italy" made up of South Americans, North Africans, Albanians, and Indians, amongst others.

Raiz challenges his listeners to interrogate the selective memory of a country that until recently has evaded discussion of the diasporic proportions of its past and present emigration. He reminds all Italians that many—actually, too many—of our relatives had to leave the country to look for happiness elsewhere. The inevitability of the related phenomena of emigration, immigration, and the movement of people strikes us with stark simplicity as Raiz concludes: "You can't stop those who want [happiness] and don't have it!" In the end, like Marracash, Raiz draws from Fante's works to illustrate in his songs the strengths and vulnerabilities common to all migrants. Arturo Bandini's experience as an Italian American—read *wop*—in 1930s America has much in common with the experience of Southern Italians—read, *terroni* (rednecks)—looking for better opportunities in northern Italy, just as the past social, economic, and political disenfranchisement of Italians in the United States parallels that of Romanians, Moroccans, Albanians, and others in Italy today.

Conclusion

Despite his ever-growing popularity, Fante has not yet broken into the ranks of mainstream American literature. However, I suspect that Arturo Bandini will continue to charm and provoke readers and listeners alike with his passion, ambition, egomania, and childlike volatility. But Fante's legacy also lies in what he has to teach us about the hardships of immigrant life, a lesson we can apply to a segment of the world's population that, given the intensity of current global interconnectedness, is destined only to grow. In fact, the ethnic factor, once an exquisitely and quintessentially American condition, is now more widespread than ever. Inspired by John Fante and his works, the texts discussed here testify to the mutual influence between literature and music. More importantly, the artists who have taken up Fante's ethnic themes in engaged musical conversation are attempting to build bridges based on a common understanding of the challenges of the migrant experience. Through their music they are directing our attention toward the global rewards we can all reap once we accept and embrace the migration phenomenon in its inevitability and the opportunities it offers to migrants and their host countries alike.

Notes

A slightly different version of this essay appeared in *Forum Italicum* 49, no. 2 (2015): 596–610.

1. Kate Bush, *The Kick Inside*, EMI, 1978.
2. Dire Straits, *Making Movies*, Vertigo, 1980.
3. Guns N' Roses, *Chinese Democracy*, Geffen, 2008.
4. Jefferson Airplane, *Surrealistic Pillow*, RCA, 1967.
5. The Police, *Zenyatta Mondatta*, A&M, 1980.
6. Gardaphé, *Italian Signs*, 58.
7. Richard Collins points out how Hackmuth's initials, J. C., "suggest that he's Bandini's savior" (135) because he, just like the real Mencken with Fante, will bolster Arturo's ego and save him from anonymity by publishing his stories. The almost twenty-year-long correspondence between Fante and Mencken is collected in Moreau and Fante, *Fante/Mencken*. For the relationship between mentor and mentee, see also Scruggs, "Oh for a Mexican Girl." Overall, Fante published eight short stories in the *American Mercury*. His stories also appeared in various magazines such as the *Atlantic Monthly*, *Harper's Bazaar*, and *Scribner's*.
8. For a detailed history of the publication and reception of Fante's works in Italy, see Amoroso, "John Fante."
9. Fante, *Ask the Dust*, 6. Hereafter cited in text by page number.
10. Marazzi, *Voices of Italian America*, 181–183.
11. "My Father's God" is the title of a short story Fante first published in 1975 in the journal *Italian Americana*. The story was later republished in the 1985 collection *The Wine of Youth*.
12. Romano, "La fortuna di Fante," 45. "Specificamente per gli scrittori era anche abbastanza ovvio che ci si immedesimasse in un eterno aspirante scrittore." Unless otherwise noted, all translations are my own.
13. Chronologically, *The Road to Los Angeles* was the first novel Fante wrote but the last to be published, appearing posthumously in 1985. The first to be published, in 1938, was *Wait until Spring, Bandini*, while *Dreams from Bunker Hill*, which was dictated to his wife Joyce, appeared in 1982. In Stephen Cooper's words, "Taken together, these four novels trace Arturo's development from his impoverished Colorado boyhood to his ordeals as a possessed young writer in the lower depths of Los Angeles, and later as a scriptwriter in the gilded confines of Hollywood" ("Eternal City," 85).
14. Red Hot Chili Peppers, *By the Way*, Warner Bros., 2002.
15. Sheryl Crow, *Sheryl Crow*, A&M, 1996.
16. The Good Life, *Album of the Year*, Saddle Creek, 2005.
17. Vinicio Capossela. *Il ballo di San Vito*. CGD East West, 1996. The lyrics of the song and a translation by Teresa Fiore can be found in the special

volume of *Quaderni del '900* dedicated to Fante and edited by Fiore herself. When in 2004 Einaudi republished the novel with the title *La confraternita dell'uva*, they invited Vinicio Capossela to write the introduction.

18. "All the words that I lose every day."

19. Citizen Kane. *Tutte le parole che ogni giorno perdo*. EP Autoprodotto, 2004.

20. Laffranchi, "Canto la droga pensando a Dost."

21. It is worth noting here that despite his preoccupation with issues of social equity and justice, Fante was never really a committed political writer. Catherine Kordich writes: "Politics were always of minimal concern to Fante; though he wrote about socioeconomic circumstances similar to those that preoccupied Henry Roth, Steinbeck, and Farrell, Fante was no revolutionary and his works did not overtly challenge the socioeconomic system" (*John Fante*, 10).

22. Both the working-class and immigrant themes are subsumed in the person of Nicola Fante, John's father, who was fictionalized under several names in many of Fante's short stories and novels, most notably in the 1938 *Wait until Spring, Bandini*. Nick Fante was a bricklayer who had emigrated from the rocky mountains of Abruzzo to pursue the American Dream in Colorado. According to several biographers, John's father was a very good bricklayer and a charming man, but he was unfortunately also characterized by a horrible temper and was prone to heavy drinking, bar fighting, gambling, and cheating, often venting his fury on his wife and children. It is difficult to determine how much Nick's problems were inherited from his childhood in Abruzzo, but the generally anti-immigrant and especially anti-Italian and anti-Catholic sentiments of turn-of-the-twentieth-century America certainly did not help his mood and condition. See Collins, *John Fante*; Kordich, *John Fante*; and Cooper, *Full of Life*.

23. Collins points out, "this early acquiescence and the injustice around him take on new meaning later, when he falls in love with a Mexican and loses his virginity to a Jew, literally embracing the outsiders that his landlady excludes from her topsy-turvy hotel, and thus learning how to embrace his own status as an alien and an outsider" (*John Fante*, 137).

24. The Italian Unification was supported by an imperial ideology that resorted to the disturbingly familiar rhetoric of the so-called civilizing enterprise. Cultural and social sophistication were deemed to be lacking in the rural south, while the north, eager to embrace the industrial model set up by the most powerful European countries, was considered superior. In Italy, the Manichean polarization characterizing any imperialist project and based on such dichotomies as rationality versus irrationality, modernity versus backwardness, and progress versus obsolescence, followed territorial criteria: the category "good Italians" was occupied by northerners, while southerners were "bad Italians."

25. "Io quando andavo a scuola da bambino, da bambino / La gente nella classe mi chiamava marocchino, marocchino." *Marracash*, Universal Music Group, 2008.

26. Laffranchi, "Canto la droga pensando a Dostoevskij."

27. "Ci sto in mezzo e non l'ho scelto no, è l'inferno / Chiedi alla polvere qua è diverso." *Marracash*, Universal Music Group, 2008.

28. "E a mio nonno che in Sicilia ancora spreme la vite nell'orto / ed a mio padre hanno spremuto la vita dal corpo / ed al mio sporco-sporco sud-sudicio / e chi ha su-subìto e vuole tutto su-subito / la mia è una genia di sconfitti / il fottuto ciclo dei vinti e finti miti / la fame è atavica / chi ha fame ingoia non mastica / se masticasse saprebbe il mondo quanto male gli fa."

29. In late nineteenth-century Italy, Sicilian realist (Verismo) writer Giovanni Verga planned to write a narrative cycle, entitled I Vinti (The Vanquished), which was inspired by French Naturalism and, especially, the works of French writer Emile Zola. In his novels, Verga meant to illustrate humanity's struggle with progress and, particularly, its consequences on those who occupy the lowest echelons of the social order. Of the five novels Verga had originally planned to write, only two were published, *I Malavoglia* and *Mastro-Don Gesualdo*; a third one, *La Duchessa di Leyra*, was never completed and *L'onorevole Scipioni* and *L'uomo di lusso* were never even begun.

30. Almamegretta, *Animamigrante*, CNI, 1993.

31. An early *fantiano*, along with Capossela, Raiz has performed musical readings of Fante and has participated in the literary festival held in Torricella every year since 2006.

32. A similar take in the realm of critical and cultural studies comes from Franco Cassano. His 1996 book *Il pensiero meridiano* is a manifesto of sorts of the Global South, in which the Italian sociologist-turned-politician attempts to restore some balance between the North and the South by appealing to the "crucial role" that the Mediterranean plays in Southern thought. Cassano writes, "Certainly, the Mediterranean has always been crossed by conflicts, but it is also the sea where, from the beginning, people have mixed their languages, histories, and genetic patrimonies. The Mediterranean 'we' is a 'we' full of others, where the dream of every purity and ethnic cleansing is a criminal delirium that, as we have already seen, leads to a spiral of slaughter" (*Southern Thought*, xxix).

33. Raiz, *Wop*, Phoenix, 2004.

Works Cited

Amoroso, French. "John Fante: L'odissea "italiana" di un 'wop.'" *Quaderni del '900* 6 (2006): 19–30.

Bukowski, Charles. *Women*. Santa Rosa, CA: Black Sparrow, 1978.

Cassano, Franco. *Southern Thought and Other Essays on the Mediterranean*. Edited and translated by Norma Bouchard and Valerio Ferme. New York: Fordham University Press, 2012.

Collins, Richard. *John Fante: A Literary Portrait.* Toronto: Guernica, 2000.
Cooper, Stephen. *Full of Life: A Biography of John Fante.* New York: North Point Press, 2000.
———. "John Fante's Eternal City." In *Los Angeles in Fiction: A Collection of Essays,* edited by David Fine, 83– 99. Albuquerque: University of New Mexico Press, 1995.
Cooper, Stephen, and David Fine, eds. *John Fante: A Critical Gathering.* Madison, NJ: Fairleigh Dickinson University Press, 1999.
Elliott, Matthew. "John Fante's *Ask the Dust* and Fictions of Whiteness." *Twentieth Century Literature* 56, no. 4 (2010): 530–544.
Fante, John. *Ask the Dust.* Santa Barbara, CA: Black Sparrow, 1980.
———. *The Brotherhood of the Grape.* Santa Rosa, CA: Black Sparrow, 1988.
———. *Dreams from Bunker Hill.* Santa Rosa, CA: Black Sparrow, 1982.
———. *The Road to Los Angeles.* Santa Rosa, CA: Black Sparrow, 1985.
———. *Wait until Spring, Bandini.* Santa Rosa, CA: Black Sparrow, 1983.
———. *The Wine of Youth: Selected Stories.* Santa Rosa, CA: Black Sparrow, 1985.
Gardaphé, Fred L. *Italian Signs, American Streets: The Evolution of Italian American Narrative.* Durham, NC: Duke University Press, 1996.
Kordich, Catherine J. *John Fante: His Novels and Novellas.* New York: Twayne Publishers, 2000.
Laffranchi, Andrea. "Canto la droga pensando a Dostoevskij." *Corriere della Sera,* July 31, 2008. http://www.corriere.it/spettacoli/08_luglio_31/marracash_successo_rap_07bc4da2-5ec3-11dd-89c2-00144f02aabc.shtml.
Marazzi, Martino. "Swearing in: Il senso della cittadinanza nella letteratura di Fante." *Quaderni del '900* 6 (2006): 31–40.
———. *Voices of Italian America: A History of Early Italian American Literature with a Critical Anthology.* New York: Fordham University Press, 2012.
Moreau, Michael, and Joyce Fante, eds. *Fante/Mencken: John Fante and H. L. Mencken: A Personal Correspondence 1930–1952.* Santa Rosa, CA: Black Sparrow Press, 1989.
Romano, Alessio. "La fortuna di Fante in Italia in tre interviste." *Quaderni del '900* 6 (2006): pp. 43–55.
Scruggs, Charles. "'Oh for a Mexican Girl!': The Limits of Literature in John Fante's *Ask the Dust.*" *Western American Literature* 38, no. 3 (2003): 228–245.
Vittorini, Elio, ed. *Americana: Raccolta di narratori dalle origini ai nostri giorni.* Milano: Bompiani, 1941.

Watch Out or You'll Wind Up in My Novel:
The Lost World of *Ask the Dust*

Robert Guffey

In his introduction to the 1980 Black Sparrow Press edition of John Fante's *Ask the Dust*, Charles Bukowski refers lovingly to the "magic" of Fante's 1939 Los Angeles novel. This is not the only time I've heard aficionados of *Ask the Dust* use the words *magic* and *magical* when describing the emotions they experienced upon discovering the book. Significantly, these are not words I've heard attributed to Fante's other novels, short stories, or screenplays—only to *Ask the Dust*.

What do people mean when they say *Ask the Dust* is a "magical" book? In part, they're no doubt referring to the world Fante portrays in the novel. The Los Angeles in which *Ask the Dust* takes place is paradoxically realistic while also tinged with a subtle undercurrent of borderline dream logic. The recurring imagery of sand and dust seems to suggest a near-mythical metropolis half-buried in the desert, somewhat like the surreal Los Angeles Steve Erickson creates in his impressive 1985 debut novel, *Days Between Stations*, where blinding sandstorms are a permanent fixture of the Southern California landscape. Early in Erickson's novel we find this passage:

Then, the first of the sandstorms came. She watched it from her window—a mild one, compared to the ones that would blow through the city later. It left a fine silt on the buildings, and took some of the paint off the cars. All the windows were left like round portholes, the sand filling the corners; and there was the slight rattle of sand on the roof. Sand fell with the opening and closing of doors, and in the dark people wore sunglasses to keep the sand out of their eyes. Since their apartment, and the window she watched from, faced the west toward the ocean, she could never see the storms approaching, coming from the deserts in the southeast as they did; but people began watching for them from their moonbridges in the day, sighting the black cloud far away on the edge of the Santa Ana Freeway, and from the bridges at night as the storms cast a gauze across the moon itself.[1]

In the first chapter of *Ask the Dust*, Fante writes: "Through that [hotel] window I saw my first palm tree, not six feet away, and sure enough I thought of Palm Sunday and Egypt and Cleopatra, but the palm was blackish at its branches, stained by carbon monoxide coming out of the Third Street Tunnel, its crusted trunk choked with dust and sand that blew in from the Mojave and Santa Ana deserts."[2] In this sentence Fante juxtaposes the religious and the exotic ("Palm Sunday and Egypt and Cleopatra") with the gritty, unseemly details of everyday life in a metropolis polluted by industry gone awry (that palm tree stained "blackish" by carbon monoxide). It's this melding of the beautifully exotic and the tragically mundane that helps create the near-surreal, off-kilter feel of Fante's Los Angeles.

The sand imagery returns, exaggerated to almost phantasmagoric degrees, in chapter five: "Sand from the Mojave had blown across the city. Tiny brown grains of sand clung to my fingertips whenever I touched anything, and when I got back to my room I found the mechanism of my new typewriter glutted with sand. It was in my ears and in my hair. When I took off my clothes it fell like powder to the floor. It was even between the sheets of my bed" (40). This sand-choked Los Angeles feels very much like Erickson's, a mirage that exists only in someone's fever dream—a dream that nonetheless seems intensely real while one is trapped in the throes of the fever. Of course, the association between sand and sleep and dreams extends far back into antiquity, much further back than even E. T. A. Hoffmann's classic 1816 short story "The Sandman," which Sigmund Freud considered to be the quintessential tale of "the uncanny"—a dream-like occurrence at once strange and familiar, a description that could just as easily apply to Bandini's experiences in Fante's Los Angeles.[3] In chapter five, as if to underscore this dream imagery, protagonist Arturo Bandini addresses his beloved Camilla Lopez in the private citadel of his own mind: "leave me alone while my mind travels the infinite loveliness of your splendid glory; just leave awhile to myself, to hunger and *dream with eyes awake*" (41; emphasis added).

In chapter fourteen, the sand is now threatening to swallow the entire city, rising to a significance that seems almost apocalyptic:

> Here was the endlessly mute placidity of nature, indifferent to the great city; here was the desert beneath these streets, around these streets, waiting for the city to die, to cover it with timeless sand once more. There came over me a terrifying sense of understanding about the meaning and the pathetic destiny of men. The desert was always there, a patient white animal, waiting for men to die, for civilizations to flicker and pass into the darkness. Then men seemed brave to me, and I was proud to be numbered among them. All the evil of the world seemed not evil at all, but inevitable and good and part of that endless struggle to keep the desert down. (120)

Of course, keeping "the desert down" is impossible, but it's made clear early on in the book that Fante's Los Angeles is a realm where the impossible is a common occurrence. After all, Los Angeles is a city carved out of a blazing desert; by all rights, it shouldn't even exist.

In chapter one of *Ask the Dust* Fante's description of the Alta Loma, the cheap hotel in which Bandini lives, establishes the dream-tinged realism of the novel: "It was built on a hillside in reverse, there on the crest of Bunker Hill, built against the decline of the hill, so that the main floor was on the level with the street but the tenth floor was downstairs ten levels. If you had room 862, you got in the elevator and went down eight floors, and if you wanted to go down in the truck room, you didn't go down but up to the attic, one floor above the main floor" (15). Bandini's daily existence is literally upside-down, a subtle indication that life in Los Angeles can reverse the everyday laws of reality. True, the Alta Loma is based on a hotel that did indeed exist in Bunker Hill at one time, but Fante's choice to emphasize such counterintuitive details makes them come across as fragments of a waking dream.

In many ways, the setting of *Ask the Dust* is a lost world filled with the artifacts and ruins of a time so removed from our lives today that we approach the book almost like an anthropologist granted the ability to travel temporarily into the past and ride around inside the heads of people who inhabit a geography we wish to know with deeper intimacy. The glimpses we get of LA's Bunker Hill, where Bandini attempts to carve out a future for himself, might as well be fragments of Mars photographed through a telescope ages before we were born. Some elements of Bandini's odyssey do indeed remain in today's Los Angeles, available for us to experience firsthand, but for the most part Bandini's oneiric desert world is as distant as L. Frank Baum's Land of Oz. One can still detect faint echoes of Bandini's world among such leftovers of the past as the Angels Flight funicular railway near the appropriately named "John Fante Square" (located at Fifth Street and Grand, the center of Bunker Hill) and the oceanside streets of downtown Long Beach where Bandini manages to survive the catastrophic 1933 earthquake, but such key *Ask the Dust* locations as the Victorian mansions of Bunker Hill and the sprawling Pike amusement park of Long Beach, now all long gone, are as inaccessible as the Emerald City itself.

It's worth noting, by the way, that Oz—with its magical "Shifting Sands" featured so prominently in the series—is yet another construct of the Southern Californian imagination, for Baum was well ensconced in the heart of Hollywood, in a large two-story home he called "Ozcot" on Cherokee Avenue, when he wrote the last eight volumes of his Oz epic. In fact, many aspects of the later Oz books were influenced by the Southern California landscape in which Baum spent the final decade of his life. Even before moving permanently to California, he wintered often at the Hotel del Coronado, an important inspiration for the Emerald City.[4] The Deadly Desert, the Impassable Desert, the Great Sandy Waste, and the aforementioned Shifting Sands—the four quadrants of a vast wasteland isolating Oz from the rest of the world—were no doubt inspired by much the same Los Angeles landscape that gave birth to Fante's *Ask the Dust*.

This ineffable connection to a destroyed, borderline-mythical world explains some of the plaintive sadness we feel when reading Fante's evocation of 1930s Southern California. Informing this sadness is the inherent romanticism of a story about a young artist attempting to find his way in a strange land far from home. For the most part, a story about a twenty-year-old writer trying to finish his first novel might seem a surefire recipe for disaster, a clichéd exercise in literary self-indulgence. But Fante's tale defies the odds, never feeling pretentious even though Bandini comes off that way himself.

What enables Fante to pull off this delicate tightrope act is the fearless openness with which he approaches his readers. All the shameful, embarrassing, politically incorrect thoughts that course through any normal human's brain—and which we're expected to scour from our consciousness in this antiseptic Brave New World of ours—is laid out on the page for all to see. Like William Burroughs twenty years later (especially in his first three novels, *Junky*, *Queer*, and *Naked Lunch*), Fante is not afraid to reveal the potentially incriminating details of his inner life and display them like exhibits in a dubious art gallery composed of missteps, fits of rage, failure, self-hatred, racism, and misogyny. These are the emotions, banned from polite discussions in today's overly modulated world, that help animate and deepen the novel's magic.

The romanticism of Bandini's odyssey, the struggle of a young man finding his way into the impenetrable world of publishing from three thousand miles away, clearly influenced Charles Bukowski and many other LA writers who followed in Fante's footsteps. What sometimes mars these later attempts at emulating Fante's style is a lack of that aforementioned, ineffable *magic*; perhaps more importantly, such works are often marked by a total absence of sincerity.

The perfect parody of this absence of sincerity is portrayed in Noah Van Sciver's 2015 graphic novel entitled *Fante Bukowski*, which revolves around the mundane exploits of a struggling young writer named Kelly Perkins who's so obsessed with John Fante and Charles Bukowski that he legally changes his name to "Fante Bukowski." The entire book is a scathing satire, holding up to criticism the type of frustrated artist who attempts to honor the memory of his heroes by plagiarizing them. Clearly, the best way to honor one's heroes is to forge a new path on one's own, to find one's *own* magic, to evolve instead of imitate (fig. 9).

Fante is a classic example of a writer who understood the importance of originality over mimicry. It's obvious from his early 1930s short story, "To Be a Monstrous Clever Fellow," that Fante was a great admirer of the works of James Branch Cabell, a brilliant fantasist whose works were quite popular during the first few decades of the twentieth century, but who is rarely

FIGURE 9. Parody of the struggling young writer. (Courtesy of Noah Van Sciver. Photo by Charles Hood.)

mentioned these days. Though Cabell has been influential on such popular novelists as Neil Gaiman, Robert Heinlein, Fritz Leiber, and Tim Powers, one would be hard-pressed to find any respectable literary salon in which Cabell's name is now invoked. But when Fante was just beginning his career, Cabell was still considered one of the preeminent names in American literature. Fante's "To Be a Monstrous Clever Fellow," though without a doubt influenced by Cabell's works such as the 1919 novel *Jurgen: A Comedy of Justice*, bears no trace of Cabell's signature style. The anonymous narrator—who reveals more than just a passing resemblance to the Arturo Bandini of *The Road to Los Angeles* (written in 1936, but not published until 1985), *Wait Until Spring, Bandini* (1938), *Ask the Dust*, and *Dreams from Bunker Hill* (1982)—muses to himself sadly at one point in the story: "I'll never be able to write like Cabell. Wistful, shy, sweet writer."[5]

Wistful, shy, sweet. These are adjectives no reasonable person would ever apply to Fante's writing. The narrator is, of course, correct; he's self-aware enough to know he will never be able to mimic another writer's style. To do so would be redundant and pointless. Though Cabell is referenced numerous times in this story—not only in the title and the opening epigraph, but also in the inner thoughts and dialogue of the narrator—the style of Fante's tale couldn't be more removed from Cabell's rococo, satirical fantasy worlds. Fante had absorbed whatever inspiration he needed from Cabell, then launched out on his own in order to forge his own unique style that would eventually produce the four-volume Saga of Arturo Bandini and numerous other works.

The irony of Van Sciver's *Fante Bukowski* is that the main character, though obsessed with Fante's writing, is in truth Fante's mirror opposite. Perkins doesn't understand that the best way to emulate one's heroes is to acknowledge their greatness, then shed their influence and leave them in the dust as soon as possible. As Bukowski writes in his introduction to *Ask the Dust*, "Fante was my god and I knew that the gods should be left alone, one didn't bang at their door" (6). Bukowski carved his own path through the world of American letters, an approach that was as different from Fante's as Fante's was different from Cabell's. Case in point, the cockeyed Los Angeles cityscape of Bukowski's last novel, *Pulp*, is as unlike Fante's Los Angeles as one could imagine.

Though the protagonist of *Fante Bukowski* would no doubt hate to admit it, he far more resembles Sammy Wiggins, the hopeful but talentless writer of amateur pulp fiction in *Ask the Dust*, than Arturo Bandini. From what we see of Sammy's writing, it's clear he aspires to be the next Zane Grey, author of *Riders of the Purple Sage* (1912) and other bestselling pulp westerns:

> Coldwater Gatling wasn't looking for trouble but you never can tell about those Arizona rustlers. Pack your cannon high on the hip and lay low when you seen one of them babies. The trouble with trouble was that trouble was looking for Coldwater Gatling. They don't like Texas Rangers down in Arizona, consequently Coldwater Gatling figured shoot first and find out who you killed afterwards. That's how they did it in the Lone Star State where men were men and the women didn't mind cooking for hard-riding straight-shooting people like Coldwater Gatling, the toughest man in leather they had down there. (116)

It's obvious from this sample that Sammy's writing is based on fiction he has previously read, not on his own life experiences much less on any imaginative originality. The same is true of Perkins in *Fante Bukowski*. His art is based on his own skewed misreadings of Fante and Bukowski's work. He has absorbed the surfaces of Fante and Bukowski, but not the core identities that make both writers stand out from their peers. In *Ask the Dust*, Bandini hopes to be a successful writer, just like Perkins; Bandini, however, doesn't sell his second story to his hero, the New York magazine editor J. C. Hackmuth (based on the writer-editor H. L. Mencken), until he at last shuts off his mind and stops trying. There's a good reason why the epitaph on Bukowski's gravestone reads "DON'T TRY." In *Ask the Dust*, Bandini succeeds only when he stops trying. He forgets about churning out an immortal work of literature and instead pecks out a simple, straightforward letter to Hackmuth. Convinced that he's dashing off a mere piece of transient correspondence, his intense self-consciousness dissipates, allowing his creativity and sincerity to pour onto the page. The result of this letting-go is that Hackmuth offers to purchase the letter and publish it as a short story under the title "The Long Lost Hills."

Though Bandini and Perkins are both plagued by crippling fears, the two characters couldn't be more different. Like Perkins, Bandini is often paralyzed by indecision and anxiety, but his prose must be fearless, as we gather when Hackmuth accepts that forty-page outpouring as a piece of fiction worthy of inclusion in a prominent New York magazine. Perkins, on the other hand, is frightened to reveal his true self to others, constantly hiding behind his appropriated name. On the first page of Van Sciver's graphic novel, we see Perkins wearing a T-shirt that reads, "CAREFUL OR YOU'LL WIND UP IN MY NOVEL," a motto that's both hilarious and pathetic for its gross overstatement of Perkins's nonexistent status as a writer. But Perkins doesn't understand this. More obsessed with the image he's projecting than with the actual act of writing, he's trapped himself in a posturing mode of perpetual imitation, so much so that his first attempt at a novel is an unconsciously plagiarized version of Milan Kundera's *The Unbearable Lightness of Being* (1984). No matter how much Perkins attempts to emulate his literary icons, he can't seem to get out of his own way. If you've ever spent time in even a single creative writing workshop, you know this fellow ... and you know him well. Perhaps he's your boyfriend or your roommate or your best friend. Perhaps he was you in the past. Perhaps he's you *now*. In any event, in any incarnation, he's the writer you *don't* want to be.

Reading *Ask the Dust* and *Fante Bukowski* back to back is a fascinating and instructive experience. They're the twin forks in the road of a struggling artist's future. One road leads to creativity and enlightenment, the other to the middle of a dark forest with no way out. The last panel of *Fante Bukowski* finds Perkins lying on the grass, staring up at the moon, lost in the woods at night on the outskirts of town. Due to the telltale presence of a powerline peeking up out of the trees not far away, the reader can see that Perkins is almost out of the forest. Perkins, however, doesn't know that. He thinks he's lost. The implication is clear: If only Perkins could shift his perspective, he too might find his way out of the forest and onto the alternate path of *Ask the Dust*.

Van Sciver's *Fante Bukowski* is an insightful satire about the vast gap between art and artifice, craftsmanship and pretentiousness, individuality and idolatry. At first Van Sciver seems to set up his protagonist as little more than the butt of an ongoing joke, running the risk of presenting Perkins as the shallowest stereotype possible, but as the episodic tale progresses the reader begins to sympathize more and more with Perkins's naive and confused arrogance. Ultimately, Van Sciver's indeterminate ending leaves behind some wisp of hope that maybe—just maybe—"Fante Bukowski" will finally figure out how to shed his cocoon of influences and affectations and become who he's meant to become: *himself.*

The shadow of *Ask the Dust* looms over Van Sciver's entire narrative. Ask yourself: How many novels of the 1930s are so influential that they become the core of another artist's work seventy-six years after their publication? In fact, are there any such novels by the dozen or so other 1930s writers whose work has persisted—James M. Cain, Raymond Chandler, Isak Dinesen, William Faulkner, F. Scott Fitzgerald, Ernest Hemingway, Zora Neal Hurston, Aldous Huxley, H. P. Lovecraft, John Steinbeck, Nathanael West? That *Ask the Dust* continues to exert a powerful influence on practitioners of such a relatively young art form as the graphic novel is a significant sign of its enduring influence on younger generations. (Van Sciver was thirty-one when *Fante Bukowski* was released.)

The importance of *Ask the Dust* to Van Sciver's work is evidenced by the fact that the artist has drawn a simulacrum of Fante's most famous book as the back endpaper of *Fante Bukowski*. The front endpaper, appropriately, depicts the cover of Bukowski's *Pulp*. The choice to spotlight *Pulp* is, I think, not random. The word *pulp* recurs throughout *Ask the Dust* almost as often as do images of sand and dust. For example, the first appearance of a pulp magazine in Fante's novel occurs in the fifth paragraph of chapter one: "Then there was the elevator man, a broken man from Milwaukee, who seemed to sneer every time you called your floor, as though you were such a fool for choosing that particular floor, the elevator man who always had a tray of sandwiches in the elevator, and a pulp magazine" (12). "Pulp western magazines" crop up near the beginning of chapter three when Bandini equates these magazines to the "madness" of clutter spread out on the floor of his neighbor's apartment: "His room was madness, pulp western magazines over the floor, a bed with sheets blackened, clothes strewn everywhere, and clothes-hooks on the wall conspicuously naked, like broken teeth in a skull" (29). In this one sentence Fante explicitly links the pulps with uncleanliness, insanity, and death. The significance of the pulps reemerges when it's revealed that Camilla's boyfriend (and Bandini's far less talented rival), Sammy, has aspirations of being a successful pulp writer (116). The pulps are also referenced during a crucial scene in the final chapter when Bandini finds Sammy calmly reading a "pulp western magazine" in his isolated shack despite the fact that Camilla, who is hopelessly in love with Sammy, has disappeared into the desert and at that moment could very well be dying (162).

Throughout *Ask the Dust* pulp magazines are signifiers of spiritual emptiness, the desolation lurking just beneath the pavement of Los Angeles. In Fante's world the desert sands and the pulps are intertwined; they represent the death of originality, risk-taking, and personal involvement in one's art. Perkins, by stealing the names of two previous writers, chooses to place himself firmly within that wasteland of unoriginality, the desert that leads nowhere at all.

Van Sciver's graphic novel is a humorous warning about the dangers of losing oneself in another's identity and the importance of finding your own way through the dark forest of the mind, an odyssey that Bandini manages to make despite all the roadblocks in his path: crazy girlfriends, Catholic guilt, devastating earthquakes, demanding landlords, extreme poverty, virulent racism, and most importantly the fear of shutting off one's mind and allowing one's true identity and potential to rise to the surface for all to see.

Bandini's ability to overcome this fear is perhaps the core "magic" to which readers of *Ask the Dust* have always been attracted, the enlightening sorcery of discovering one's true self in a dark world that so often demands the exact opposite from its docile citizens—the arbitrary shutting down of one's creativity and individuality. This intense belief in one's own individuality remains, perhaps, the one true road back to that "magical" lost world of self-discovery represented by Fante's fictionalized Los Angeles.

Notes

1. Erikson, *Days Between Stations*, 46.
2. Fante, *Ask the Dust*, 16. Hereafter cited in text by page number.
3. Freud, *Complete Psychological*, 17:241.
4. See Arends, "Follow the Yellow Brick Road."
5. Fante, *Big Hunger*, 100.

Works Cited

Arends, Robert. "Follow the Yellow Brick Road... *The Wizard of Oz* and Coronado!" San Diego Blog, March 8, 2013. http://blog.sandiego.org/2013/03/wizard-of-oz-coronado/. Accessed March 20, 2018.

Erickson, Steve. *Days Between Stations*. New York: Poseidon Press, 1985.
Fante, John. *Ask the Dust*. Santa Barbara, CA: Black Sparrow Press, 1980.
———. *The Big Hunger: Stories 1932–1959*. Edited by Stephen Cooper. Santa Rosa, CA: Black Sparrow Press, 2000.
Freud, Sigmund. *The Complete Psychological Works of Sigmund Freud*. Vol. 17. London: Hogarth Press, 1955.
Sciver, Noah Van. *Fante Bukowski*. Seattle: Fantagraphics Books, 2015.

Don't Ask the French

Philippe Garnier

The first time I came across the name John Fante on a printed page I thought it was a joke. Or at least an invention. The best I can recall it was a throwaway line in one of Bukowski's lesser "Dirty Old Man" columns then running in the LA underground weekly, *Open City*. Or maybe it was in *South of No North*, I'm not sure. I am sure of the year, though. It was 1978. I'd just moved from Paris to Los Angeles, where I had translated *Notes of a Dirty Old Man* for a fledgling (most extremely fledgling) French publisher. Bukowski and I sometimes exchanged notes—and his answers to my questions often sounded embarrassed. "How the hell should I know what I meant by that?" he'd write. "You know what time of night I was whipping those things off?" He sometimes even questioned the validity of publishing the book in France at all: "Very uneven stuff. Ephemeral. *Post Office* much better." So I translated *Post Office* as well (much better). But I never asked him about Fante. The very existence of an author who had supposedly written a novel with the improbable title *Wait Until Spring, Bandini* seemed about as likely as a second baseman with wings rescuing the LA Angels, as in one of Bukowski's more fanciful tales. It didn't help that Bandini was the name of a company from way back in the city's past that as late as 1978 was still advertising around Southern California, since what they advertised was fertilizer—literal horse shit.

Then one day, on a hunch that still makes me wonder, I went to the downtown Los Angeles Public Library and looked up Fante in one of the musty index card drawers they still had at the time, and sure enough they had the man, and a thing by him called *Ask the Dust*. Before I could see the book though I had to come back because not only was it a reference copy restricted to reading only on the premises, but on top of that it wasn't even in the stacks: the library staff had to fetch it out of storage in some other part of town where they kept titles that were rarely called for.

But soon they had the book for me and I read it in the big fiction reading room of the Fifth Street Central Public Library. In those days the fiction room was still on the second floor and smelled of floor wax and the bums who dozed under the sunlight streaming in from the high windows, and I sat there reading, stunned by the immediacy of Fante's voice. Much later, after I read the preface that Bukowski wrote for the 1980 Black Sparrow Press reissue of *Ask the Dust*, I often fantasized that I'd read the same copy of the novel that had been such a breakthrough for him, except that Bukowski got to take the book with him to his room in East Hollywood instead of reading it over two afternoons in the library at the foot of Bunker Hill, site of so much of the novel's action. At the time, developers in all their wisdom had already leveled the hill by half, the same types who later made a mockery of the Angels Flight cable car by trying to revive it like some theme-park ride for tourists. And instead of looking up the Alta Vista Hotel (the original of the novel's Alta Loma) as Bukowski had done in the 1950s, I had to do my detective work through a wonderful volume of photographs of Bunker Hill just published by a local bookseller.[1]

After I had read as many Fante books as I could lay my hands on, I wrote a four-page feature on Bunker Hill and Fante for my newspaper in Paris, *Libération*, which employed me as some sort of cultural correspondent. The photographs of the Third Street Tunnel and the Angels Flight funicular that were used to illustrate the piece came from a leaflet I'd kept of a photo exhibit held at the Los Angeles Public Library just before the 1986 arson fire that burned through much of the building, destroying whole collections. The 1939 Stackpole Sons first edition of *Ask the Dust* that I had read disappeared from the library around that time, but something tells me it was more likely stolen.

Two things happened very quickly after my article appeared in France. First, a letter came, forwarded by John Martin, publisher of Black Sparrow Press. (Like me, Martin had also originally thought Fante was an invention, if you want to believe the article Bukowski wrote for *Oui* magazine in December 1984.)[2] The letter was from Joyce Fante, widow of John, thanking me for the *Libération* article and asking if I'd like to meet her. Then a second letter arrived, this one from the French independent publisher Christian Bourgois. In a leap of faith prompted by my piece, Bourgois was writing to tell me he had bought the French rights to three or four Fante books: would I be interested in translating one, and if so, which one? I remember feeling sorry for the guy. He'd bought *Bandini* and *Dago Red*, both fine books, to be sure, but also *Dreams of Bunker Hill*, which I have never much cared for. Bourgois had built his reputation by publishing the American Beat writers and poets and he was known for trusting both his instincts and his collaborators' taste. But still. Four books. It all seemed fantastic to me. I liked Fante, sure, but I very much doubted the appeal his writings might have for the wider French reading public.

Still, I wanted in, and I knew which book I would choose to translate. In fact, there was only one I'd ever want to be mixed up with, the one that had sung to me in that wax-smelling reading room at the foot of Bunker Hill. My translation of *Ask the Dust* was not the first Fante book Bourgois published. In June 1986 he had put out *Wait Until Spring, Bandini*, then in September *Ask the Dust*, and in early 1987 the short stories of *Dago Red*. It was not until later that year, with *My Dog Stupid*, that Fante became a French publishing story, a real phenomenon. By then, piles of his books could be found in railroad stations and airports across the country, an astonishing feat for a novelist who for decades in his own country had remained unpublished and unread.

Of course, in France there had been a build-up—the reviews were increasingly good until they grew almost fanatical. As for me, I was mostly pleased that Bourgois had agreed to use the illustration I suggested for the cover of *Ask the Dust*. A black-and-white close-up of a pair of ragged huaraches worn by a Mexican lettuce picker, taken by Dorothea Lange in the 1930s for the Farm Security Administration program, had caught my eye, making me think of the novel's Camilla and the terrible scene between her and Bandini in the Columbia Buffet. Diligently I sent Bourgois a page from a catalogue with a thumbnail image of the photo, and I included the Library of Congress number so that for a few bucks he could order an archival-quality print. Barely two weeks later I was shocked to receive in the mail a preview copy of *Demande à la poussière* along with an exultant note from its publisher: "Isn't my *photograveur* [photo engraver] a genius?" Bourgois had fashioned the book's cover from a reproduction no bigger than a postage stamp (fig. 10).

By then I had started to understand the French infatuation with Fante. I should have spotted it earlier, as I had written a biography of David Goodis, an American hardboiled crime writer then still very obscure in his own country, but for whom the French had demonstrated an incredibly durable affection. In 1984, when my book was published, twelve of Goodis's seventeen novels were in print in France, whereas none was available in the United States—not even his two best-known ones, *Dark Passage* and *Shoot the Piano Player*. One of the answers to this mystery (besides the too obvious ones, generally involving Jerry Lewis) was that Goodis seemed to be a virtual composite of the *artiste maudit* that the French love to latch on to. Even though his novels had been reprinted year after year in France, so little was known about him that the French had conveniently conflated his life with that of the piano-playing protagonist played by Charles Aznavour in the Truffaut film adaptation. Their assumption was that Goodis had lived like his guttersnipe antiheroes, a chain-smoking alcoholic writer who died destitute. Even after I proved in the biography that Goodis, while indeed a smoker, had lived with his parents in Philadelphia most of his adult life and had a quarter of a million dollars in the bank when he died in 1968, the French preferred to stick to the romantically tragic image of their projection.

Fante was none of that, of course, but his alter ego in *Ask the Dust* was. The image of Arturo Bandini was irresistible to the French largely because the character was based as much on Fante's own experience in Depression-era downtown Los Angeles as on the more general literary cliché, the one of the struggling artist you find in Balzac, Maupassant, Zola, and, most pertinently, Knut Hamsun's novel *Hunger*. The image of Arturo as the starving writer living on oranges in a flyblown hotel room was almost as irresistible

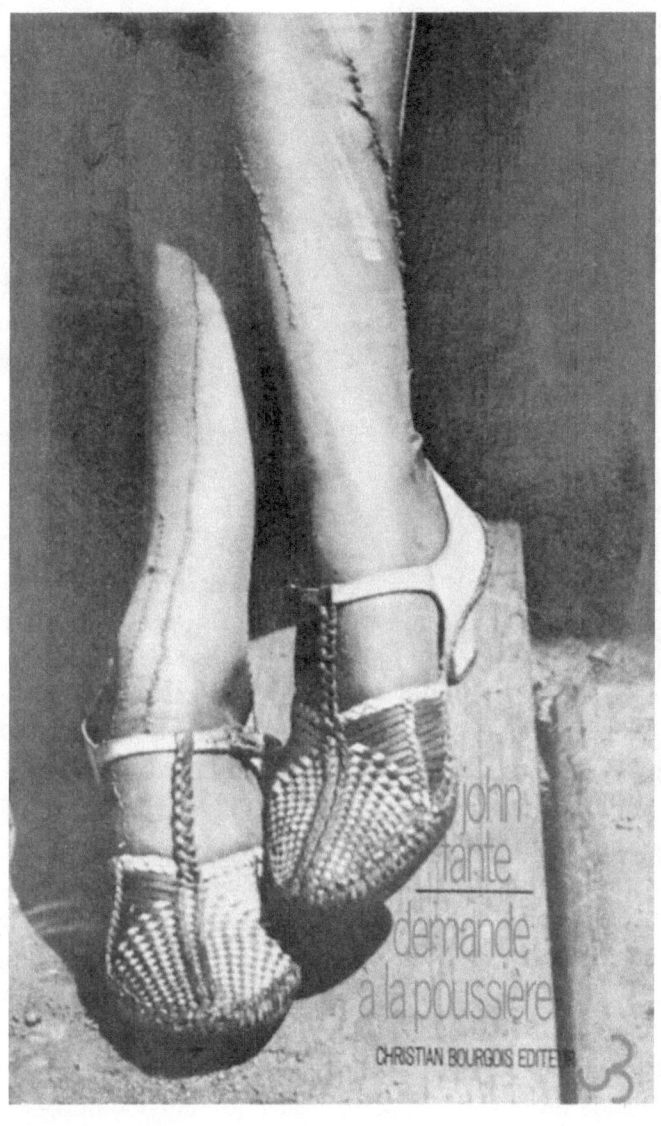

FIGURE 10. French cover of *Ask the Dust*. (Courtesy of John Fante Literary Group LLC. Photo by Charles Hood.)

to French readers as the fact that John Fante the author had been rejected in his own country—or at least appeared to have been. And the French truly fell in love with Fante's swaggering, groveling upstart creation, again happily mixing the biographical Fante with his fictional alter ego. He was short, he was an immigrant, he was Catholic, he was one of the swarthy hordes. Nothing, not even Fante's occasional bestseller success as with *Full of Life*, or later the big Hollywood money, could erase the image of Arturo Bandini, unknown author of "The Little Dog Laughed," struggling to survive in his cramped hillside room at the Alta Loma as he strove to write impossible masterpieces. Such was the force of Fante's second published novel. Such was the strength of the image.

Later, the French also took to Fante the scoundrel, Fante the golfing skirt-chasing screenwriter, even to Fante the reluctant family man—his long-suffering wife, his loathed children, his beloved savage dogs. *My Dog Stupid* soon became the second-favorite Fante book in France. By then Fante had become a cottage industry. Black Sparrow was putting out his unpublished manuscripts, his correspondence with H. L. Mencken, everything short of his grocery lists. Most of his novels were optioned by filmmakers, most of them French, although the only one to actually make one of these adaptations was Belgian, and one could say he poisoned the well.[3] I still recall a rather surreal lunch in the Shirley Temple Room at the Twentieth Century Fox studio commissary with Joyce Fante, French director Daniel Vigne (*The Return of Martin Guerre*), Joyce's Japanese-American agent Paul Yamamoto, and producer Mel Brooks. Joyce had called me to the rescue ("Please don't leave me alone with those people"). Apparently, the comedian's wife, actress Anne Bancroft, was crazy about *My Dog Stupid* and had engineered the meet. But it was quickly obvious that Brooks was only going through the motions—you could conclude nothing else from his moody, utterly humorless behavior at the table. The book was eventually optioned by producer-director Claude Berri, with the same ultimate result—no film—as so many other Fante options, that is, until Robert Towne came out with his long-awaited 2006 adaptation of *Ask the Dust* and its armature of good intentions. At least Towne had the gumption to flesh out the part of Camilla—he had the right star after all, Salma Hayek, by far the best thing in the movie—but Cape Town did not make the grade as a substitute for our visions of 1930s Bunker Hill. CGI or not, the very air did not feel the same.

By the millennium the Fante craze had subsided, at least in France. But Fante has remained a household name over the years and Bourgois has kept his works in print in various omnibus and pocket editions. His influence has been acknowledged by a few good French writers, of whom Philippe Djian (*Betty Blue*) was perhaps the most honest.[4] The only puzzling thing, perhaps, is why decades before going all in for *Ask the Dust* the French never took to Knut Hamsun's *Hunger*, the obvious model for this sort of struggling-artist-coming-of-age novel. But Hamsun was already celebrated in his own country, whereas John Fante had to wait until he was blind, legless, and nearly dead before being recognized for his past accomplishments. He had time to sign a few Black Sparrow reprints of *Ask the Dust*, and then no more. *This* sort of tragic, romantic biography the French could get behind.

Notes

1. Hylen, *Bunker Hill*.
2. Bukowski, "I Meet the Master."
3. Dominique Deruddere, director of *Wait Until Spring, Bandini* (1989).
4. "As a young writer I used to say, 'When I feel sick I don't go to the doctor, I go to my bookseller.' It wasn't a joke, it was true, and it happened often ... I'd fall upon John Fante and things would get better." Quoted in "Tout mon travail porte sur la langue," interview by Sébastien Dubos, LaDepêche.fr, December 10, 2014, accessed February 26, 2018, https://www.ladepeche.fr/article/2014/10/12/1970587-philippe-djian-tout-mon-travail-porte-sur-la-langue.html

Works Cited

Bukowski, Charles. "I Meet the Master." *OUI, For the Man of the Eighties* 13, no. 12 (December 1984): 75.

Hylen, Arnold. *Bunker Hill: A Los Angeles Landmark*. Los Angeles: Dawson's Book Shop, 1976.

3. *Ask the Dust* and Its Effects: Readers and Writers Respond

Amid the Dust

Miriam Amico

I was twenty-three the first time I heard of John Fante, drinking wine with an old friend in a bar in our hometown of Palermo. The author's name made me curious, for it sounded both Anglo Saxon and Italian. When my friend gave me a copy of *The Brotherhood of the Grape* and I went home and read it, however, my curiosity turned to fascination. Here was a novel like none I had ever read. Each page brimmed with so much love, death, passion, and faith, and with so many family dramas, all told with brutal honesty and a tragic sense of humor, it was clear to me that this writer, John Fante, was on a metaphorical journey seeking the roots of his Italian American identity.

Pushed by a desire to know more, I bought and read everything by Fante I could find. From *Wait Until Spring, Bandini* to *The Road to Los Angeles*, from *The Wine of Youth* to *Full of Life*, I was amazed by the way the protagonists of his novels and stories could be at once desperately dramatic and just as hilarious as they struggled with their connections to Italy, often in contradiction with the attempt to be accepted as American among other Americans.

My amazement was confirmed once and for all when I finally read *Ask the Dust*. In this novel the setting is neither the Colorado of *Wait Until Spring* nor the Northern California of *Brotherhood* but rather sun-drenched Los Angeles. Depicted as a "sad flower in the sand," the city plays a major role, representing both a land of opportunities and a harsh barrier to the protagonist, antihero par excellence Arturo Bandini, in his desire to be accepted in American society. Although Arturo embodied an unbridled and aggressive masculinity in his deplorable treatment of Camilla, I could identify with him. Even his most hateful behaviors proved his humanity, and as he traversed the city burning with desire to become a great writer, his constant stream of consciousness swept me up on a wheel of emotions, from manic depression to delusions of grandeur. What an epiphany that book was for me!

Summing up the importance of Los Angeles in Fante's works, Stephen Cooper suggests that "it was when writing about Arturo Bandini in three of the four Bandini novels that [Fante] wrote about Los Angeles with the deepest passion and to the most penetrating effect. In those novels the city plays host to one of the most powerful—and most problematic—literary achievements of our time."[1] Recognizing the importance of the city for Fante, a timid desire began to grow inside me. Perhaps the time had come to visit Los Angeles myself.

After devouring Fante's last novel *Dreams from Bunker Hill* and Cooper's biography, I was overwhelmed by feelings of melancholy and abandonment. I wanted to read more, to learn more, but there was nothing left. Then, in 2009, I heard that UCLA had acquired the writer's literary papers, his memorabilia, his personal notes and letters, and I knew there was only one thing to do: go to Los Angeles and see them with my own eyes.

By then I was twenty-six and yet I had never crossed any ocean. More importantly, I knew no one in the boundless city of Los Angeles. The thought of setting off alone on such a journey thrilled and terrified me, but my love for the Italian American writer and my desire to explore the city where his greatest works were set drew me on. Like Arturo Bandini, I too had something to ask the dust of the City of Angels. And so, aware of what I was leaving behind at home in Sicily but clueless as to what I would find in Los Angeles, I came with the hope that my journey would lead *somewhere*. Like a mantra, Arturo's words from *Ask the Dust* kept ringing in my head: "Los Angeles, give me some of you! Los Angeles come to me the way I came to you, my feet over your streets, you pretty town I loved you so much, you sad flower in the sand, you pretty town."[2]

I arrived in Los Angeles on October 1, 2010, dizzy with anticipation. On October 2 I was sitting in the stillness of the reading room at UCLA Special Collections. There at last I could fill out a request card, wait for the librarian to bring this or that numbered box, then spend hours leafing through the typed pages of John Fante's original short stories and novels, his handwritten letters and personal journals. For the next two months my visits to the library became a sweet and exciting daily habit. It felt like I was meeting the writer in person, getting to know him more intimately day by day. Those were silent encounters but full of intensity, and they helped me recreate both the writer and the man. The experience of not only seeing but actually touching the same papers that Fante had once held in his hands was a revelation, as was discovering so many unpublished letters, notes, short stories and personal objects. For an enthusiastic reader of Fante's books, the John Fante Collection—some fifty-odd boxes spanning seventy-five years—is a triumph of revelations and surprises.

I often found myself staring at one of those yellowed pages, its scent carrying me back to an earlier Los Angeles, warm and dusted by the Mojave Desert. I would lose myself imagining the passionate Fante pounding away at his typewriter, tireless, fervid, his stomach empty like Arturo's yet his mind full of dreams and desires. Those precious documents exuded the energy of a young man in his early twenties, hungry for life and literature, his eyes alive and restless as he wandered the streets looking to satisfy his appetites. For me, my eyes alive too, my heart beating, those days in the library grew to be filled with moments of magical satisfaction (fig. 11).

I remember the day when, in a box containing scrapbooks and diaries of the young Johnny, I happened upon a piece of cardboard wholly covered by signatures of his name, *John Fante* again and again and again. I smiled, reminded of Arturo's visionary obsessions in *Ask the Dust*, where he fantasizes himself a famous author, complete with an imaginary throng of fans, preferably female, forever demanding his autograph: "And the world was so wonderful, because every two minutes some gorgeous one gazed at me, the great author, and nothing would do but I had to autograph her menu" (13).

I also recall coming across another treasure, the original correspondence between Fante and Charles Bukowski. Like so many Italian teenagers, I

FIGURE 11. John Fante, handwritten note: "Now that I'm doing this book, shall do considerable prowling around Lower Spring and Main Sts." (Courtesy of John Fante Literary Group LLC and UCLA Library Special Collections.)

had been a fan of Bukowski during my adolescence. The fact that in the late 1970s he was the person to initiate the rediscovery of Fante's forgotten works, starting with *Ask the Dust*, had made me and I am sure all Italian readers of Fante eternally grateful to "Hank." Those letters bear proof of a warm, sincere friendship and a mutual esteem between two giants of American literature. In almost every letter, the small humorous sketches drawn by Bukowski—the "brotherhood bottle," the cartoonish dogs, the scraggly self-portraits—are a delight, as is the open admission of sheer respect for the Italian American writer.[3]

In a letter dated February 2, 1979, for example, Bukowski asks a series of questions regarding *Ask the Dust* in order to gather information for the soon-to-be famous preface he was preparing to write for the Black Sparrow Press reissue of the novel. As for Fante's answers, Bukowski does not expect the absolute truth: "To me, of course, it doesn't matter whether things are fiction or fact, or an admixture—as long as the writing is live, and Christ knows, it's plenty live in *Ask the Dust*." Bukowski then ends the letter with words of the highest admiration: "*Ask the Dust* reads better than ever. You can really put the line down, full of butter and sunlight and agony. This novel deserves a roaring rebirth." This letter is thrilling, no doubt, but it is Fante's response of February 22, 1979, that I particularly cherish, the one where he thanks Bukowski for writing the preface to *Ask the Dust*: "It is good to know that there is another voice in the world besides my own that will shout hurrah for what I consider my best effort. Believe me, I am awfully pleased and grateful."[4]

Yet another special letter I found in the papers was an invitation dated February 13, 1940, not quite three months after the publication of *Ask the Dust*. Demonstrating the early success Fante enjoyed among Italians, the invitation came from New York–based Italian literary critic and journalist Giuseppe Prezzolini, a leading figure in the promotion and diffusion of Italian culture and the Italian language in the United States: "I have read your books with interest and pleasure. The next time you are in New York, I should like very much to have you as a guest of honor at an informal tea at the Casa Italiana. I feel sure that the students as well as the teachers of Italian who frequent the Casa Italiana will be very happy to know you."[5]

One of the most unexpected discoveries I made in the collection is an unpublished manuscript of twenty typed pages, written in 1962, that surely deserves some attention.[6] Highlighting the writer's mischievous personality and what we might see as his predilection toward spite, the narrative introduces us to Justine and Juliette, two sisters living in nineteenth-century Paris, who, following the death of their father, decide to live lives of adventure. Juliette in particular—the naughtier of the two—abandons herself to the vortex of pleasure, releasing a flood of repressed sexual desires. While certainly no work of art, what a fun foray into erotic literature it is! Readers familiar with the genre will note a certain resemblance to the Marquis de Sade's infamous *Justine, or Good Conduct Well Chastised* (1791), a book that Cooper informs us had fascinated Fante.[7] It seems no coincidence that John's sister-in-law was named Justine, and it intrigues me to think that he must have had in mind the two sisters, Joyce and Justine Smart, as he was inventing this trifle. Could he have been indulging himself in an act of private revenge prompted by his perennial difficulties with the two Smart sisters, each in her way? Whatever the case, it is a unique piece, fruit of the writer's most secret fantasies.

It's no secret that Fante held only scorn for the profession of screenwriting but many documents in the collection help us understand and appreciate the decades of intense activity that he spent in the film industry. These documents include letters from important directors and producers, numerous studio contracts for his writing services, and Fante's own personal notes about how to write a screenplay.[8] Among the most interesting letters that I had the chance to see were from Francis Ford Coppola, writing to congratulate Fante on *The Brotherhood of the Grape*, and Fante's correspondence with flamboyant Italian producer Dino De Laurentiis, who hired Fante to write several screenplays. One of these letters is about Fante's signing on for a period of twelve consecutive weeks to pen the script of *Black City* (1961, directed by Duillio Coletti), with details about the writer's 1960 stay in Rome. It was in fact thanks to his screenwriting skills that Fante visited Italy for the first time and subsequently, visits that he vividly described to his family and friends in letters also held in the collection.

Reaching the end of the papers, when one might think to have seen everything, along come the writer's personal objects: grade reports, diaries, photos, prayer books and so forth that belonged to the young Johnny when he was going to school in Boulder and Denver. Opening the writer's diaries and high-school scrapbooks is like reading his earliest short stories and novels, especially the ones set in Colorado.[9] Two of Fante's passions, baseball and women, are reflected in his collection of photos of famous players and Hollywood starlets of the time, while his leather-bound copy of the *Regis School Manual* evinces his deeply Catholic education.[10]

As much as we all know that Fante's strength in telling a story derives from his raw honesty and spontaneity, I had never felt closer to the writer than while pondering the personal notes scrawled upon stray scraps of paper, dashed off no doubt between bouts of more literary writing. Such scribbled notes as "No golf today" or "No milk today" would cover an entire page, as if Fante were recording resolutions to control vices like those that overtake the protagonists of his works, or posting complaints to the gods of the kitchen who had failed him. Indeed, in the most moving of these notes Fante addresses God directly. Such fragments cast a new light on the writer's personality, illuminating lesser-known aspects of his inner world. Such was the case when I found this most delicate prayer: "Oh Lord, inside my heart, my blood. Come to me with the wonderful clarity of my boyhood. Bring to me the warmth I used to know in childhood." Would not such words soften even the hardest of Gods? Or then again, when Fante types, "I am alone now. More than ever. Each day and hour and year brings me deeper into the forest of loneliness, farther way from the day of light," he could be speaking for any of us.[11]

This, to me, feels like magic. Of all the thousands of items in the collection, this single page is perhaps my favorite, and not only because of this soulful confession but also because on the opposite side there is another fragment where Fante expresses a son's cautious affection for a volatile father: "I found Papa in the backyard, sitting under the magnolia tree. He had a jug of wine in his lap. It was a good time to talk to him. Wine made him gentle. On the other hand, it sometimes made him nasty. A light claret softened his heart. 'Hello, Papa,' I said. No answer. It was dago red."

Throughout his literary works, personal notes, and letters Fante sought to recover his Italian heritage, constantly telling stories of his family, of fights with his father, of the love he felt for his pious mother, even of his grandmother's vitriolic intolerance for everyone and everything American. With his autobiographical writings, Fante was raising fundamental questions about who he was and what he wanted to be. Those were the years when the contrast and the conflicts between old and new generations were complicating already vexed social dynamics, exacerbating the condition of alienation in which so many immigrants end up living. The inner tensions about his Italian origins as sketched in Fante's notes and unpublished short stories of the 1920s find their most eloquent expression in *Ask the Dust*, where Arturo feels radical, unstable feelings of love and hatred not only for himself and his own ethnic identity but also for Camilla, as well as for his adopted city. In so far as the xenophobia spreading over Los Angeles during the time of the so-called Booster Myth in the 1930s intensified this sense of immigrant otherness,[12] Los Angeles and its inhabitants play a fundamental role in Arturo's gradual realization of how his Italian family and their roots have made him different, and made him himself.

During my daily encounters with the writer's papers I developed a growing awareness of my own relationship with the city. I came to see my journey from Sicily as parallel to the journey from Colorado that John and, by fictional extension, Arturo too had made, the journey to Los Angeles. These journeys paralleled each other, helping us, albeit in different times and circumstances, to reach a stronger consciousness of our self-identities. What brought us to this city was our common passion for literature, and the chance to make something of ourselves. As hard as it can be to resist the downward spiral of alienation and loneliness in such a teeming metropolis as Los Angeles, especially for newcomers, somehow the city possesses a vibrant energy that allows you to find more than you even knew you were looking for, and to create a lasting bond. I came to understand that the outcome of my journey depended not only on the experiences Los Angeles was offering me, but also on what I was bringing with myself—the inherited awareness of my bond with Italy, which became stronger and more spiritual than ever.

Living far from the place where you were born and the people you grew up among teaches you what nostalgia for your land and your roots really is, as if your soul has split apart and you are constantly confronted with yourself from a more objective distance. The divided spirituality that informs our lives as foreigners living in a new country is beyond simple Catholic dogma. Author Tina DeRosa offers a beautiful definition of *Italianità* in relation to American writers of Italian descent: "On any level, Italianità is religious. When we look at our Italian American writers we get a different sense of religion." For DeRosa their works are "religious in the deep sensual or pagan sense . . . of family, of father, and of food; religion of the body."[13] Indeed, we express this religion through fluctuating manifestations of pure joy or total despair, no shades in between, in a constant, even comical melodrama. Fante journeyed to Italy only a couple of times, but through his family in Colorado he had absorbed enough *Italianità* to know the nature of those feelings so that in his writings he could forge new myths that "would bridge Italian and American cultures, creating a synthesis that can be called Italian Americana."[14]

My literary journey through the Fante papers at UCLA Special Collections gave me countless invaluable experiences. There was one mystery, however, that troubled me at first, a mystery that remains unsolved. You see, the original manuscript of *Ask the Dust*, that quintessential mirror of Los Angeles, is missing from the massive collection of the Fante papers. Its absence leaves an unbridgeable emptiness, to be sure, and yet my initial feelings of disappointment were slowly replaced by a sense of fascination, for although the absence is palpable, it also verges on the impish. As capricious and playful as the writer himself, it inspires me to lose myself in fantasies of all the improbable places where the manuscript could be. Avoiding merely realistic hypotheses, I abandon myself to the romantic illusion that *Ask the Dust* might have dissolved into the sands of the Mojave per its creator's wishes, becoming dust itself and giving the California desert a little more of its magical allure. In this scenario, the lost souls of Arturo, Camilla, Vera, Sammy, and all the novel's other unforgettable characters continue their journeys under the sun—and this is what really matters.

Notes

1. Cooper, "John Fante's Eternal City," 95–96.
2. Fante, *Ask the Dust*, 13. Hereafter cited in text by page number.
3. In a letter to Fante dated January 31, 1979, Bukowski writes: "Your writing helped my life, gave me real hope that a man could just put the words down and let the emotions ride out. Nobody has done this as well as you have. I am going to read the book slowly, enjoy it once again and hope that I can write a reasonable forward."
4. John Fante Papers, box 25, folder 1.
5. John Fante Papers, box 27, folder 5.
6. John Fante Papers, box 9, folder 5.
7. Cooper, *Full of Life*, 326–327.
8. Early manuscript drafts of the novel that would be published as *My Dog Stupid* are titled *How to Write a Screenplay*.
9. John Fante papers, boxes 49 and 51.
10. John Fante papers, box 49, folder 4.
11. John Fante papers, box 8, folder 4.
12. See Laurila, "Los Angeles Booster Myth," 112–119.
13. Gardaphé, *Italian Signs*, 140.
14. Gardaphé, 56–57.

Works Cited

Cooper, Stephen. *Full of Life: A Biography of John Fante*. New York: North Point Press, 2000.

———. "John Fante's Eternal City." *Los Angeles in Fiction: A Collection of Essays*, edited by David Fine, 83–99. Albuquerque: University of New Mexico Press, 1995.

Fante, John. *Ask the Dust*. New York: HarperCollins, 2006.
———. *The Big Hunger: Stories 1932–1959*. Edited by Stephen Cooper. New York: Ecco, 2002.
———. John Fante Papers (Collection Number 1832). Department of Special Collections, Charles E. Young Research Library, UCLA.
Gardaphé, Fred L. *Italian Signs, American Streets: The Evolution of Italian American Narrative*. Durham, NC: Duke University Press, 1996.
Laurila, Mark. "The Los Angeles Booster Myth, the Anti-Myth and John Fante's Ask the Dust." In *John Fante: A Critical Gathering*, edited by Stephen Cooper and David Fine, 112–119. Madison, NJ: Farleigh Dickinson University Press, 1999.

John Fante: The Passion That Became a Festival

Giovanna DiLello

The literary festival known as "My Father's God," dedicated to John Fante, is now in its twelfth year, a point of pride for a celebration occurring in such a remote mountain village as Torricella Peligna in the region of Abruzzo, Italy. Hosted by the hometown of Fante's father, Nicola Fante, the festival has grown into an international gathering of those who are passionate about the writer. It has been my good fortune to direct the festival from its inception.

I first came upon John Fante at the end of the 1990s in an article in *L'Espresso*. The name caught my eye for it was the same as my grandmother's, Dorina Fante. Curious, I studied the accompanying photograph to see if I could detect any resemblance, since Fante, like my own family, was described as being of Abruzzese origin. The black-and-white image depicted a defiant young man leaning over a chair, a look of bravado in his eyes.

Soon I discovered that Fante's father, like my grandmother's, had been a master bricklayer. Moreover, each family had a genealogy of difficult personalities and a history of immigration. Nick Fante was born in Torricella Peligna, whereas my grandmother's father, Antonio, hailed from Colledimezzo, two tiny villages dotting the Sangro-Aventino region of southern Abruzzi, where the name of Fante is still limited to families whose origins can be traced to one town or the other. It was thus through my grandmother that I approached the world of John Fante.

I began to read the Colorado-born writer, starting with his minor works. On a friend's advice I bought *1933 Was a Bad Year* because some scenes, he told me, were extremely funny and seemed to be set in Abruzzo. In fact, I found much of Italy in that book, the humble Italy that had been forced to emigrate. I was especially captivated by the family scenes presented by Fante with a sensitivity and candor I would have never expected from the tough guy pictured in *L'Espresso*. In addition to the spontaneity of his writing and a delicious sense of irony, the ease with which he turned his second-generation immigrant experience into literature struck a chord with me.

As the daughter of Italian emigrants, born in Canada and raised in Switzerland, I was attracted to Fante's vision. Here was an author who revealed the interior wounds that any immigrant might suffer from the ordeal of assimilation. Fante unpacked the mental processes that such second-generation migrants employ to establish themselves and their individualities in new cultures. Reading Fante, I couldn't help but think of myself as a child, how my black unruly hair, so different from the angelic locks of Swiss children, seemed the tangible sign of an unbridgeable distance generated by my belonging to that same working class that John Fante had described so well. Like the young boy in "The Odyssey of a Wop," I had conflicted feelings about my origins but, like him, I came to understand that all the frustrations and even shame over my Italian identity didn't have to be.[1] Through Fante I learned that I possessed an individuality that others should respect.

For this reason, in the year 2000, when offered the chance to write and direct my first documentary film, I immediately thought of John Fante. Work on *John Fante: Profilo di scrittore* began with a modest grant from the Region of Abruzzo. From the beginning a core feature of my concept was a storyteller from Torricela Peligna who would recount the deeds of his illustrious "compaesano" at different locations around the country, crosscut with interviews of Fante family members, friends, scholars, and fans in both Italy and the United States.

But the journey could commence in only one place, Torricella Peligna, the village that Nick Fante left for the United States in 1901. At an altitude of 900 meters, directly facing the Maiella Massif, Torricella Peligna is home today to 1,400 inhabitants, while in Nick's time some 5,000 people eked out a living there. Like all villages of the Sangro-Aventino region, however, Torricella was drained by three waves of migration, the first at the dawn of the twentieth century, the second in the bombed-out aftermath of World War II, and the third beginning in the 1960s.

It was in this town that I first met John Fante's son Dan during the 2000 presentation of his book *Chump Change*, an event organized by the earliest iteration of the John Fante Association. Dan was very receptive to the idea of my film. As we spoke, he touched on the great love he felt for his father, as well as the conflicted contours of their relationship. Dan urged me to contact his mother, Joyce, in California. I wrote immediately to Mrs. Smart-Fante, who replied that she had just undergone surgery and was thus in no condition to be interviewed but encouraging me to contact her husband's biographer, Stephen Cooper, as well as Tom Fante, John's youngest brother. I scheduled appointments with both and flew to Los Angeles, my low-budget crew in tow.

Stephen Cooper's contributions proved indispensable for the reconstruction of Fante's life, so much so that the content of our discussions became the narrative thread for the entire documentary. Tom Fante, for his part, helped me understand how his father Nick was nothing if not the classic southern Italian of former times, a hard-working father tyrant who left religion to his wife and children so he could commune with his paesanos in the saloon. This story parallels the story of my grandfather Giovanni, who gave my grandmother Giovanna ten children and a difficult life, as well as that of my other grandfather Federico who, like Nick Fante, sailed to Argentina for work leaving his wife a grass widow. In his fiction John Fante gives us a glimpse of this lost world without passing judgment, in the same way that the grandchildren in my family refrain from judging, blinded by the love we feel for our ancestors.

In California I interviewed John Fante's daughter, Victoria, who also embraced my project. Thanks to her I was able to meet her mother and film what would ultimately be Joyce's last interview. Seated on a sofa in her Malibu home, her face perfectly powdered, lipstick impeccably applied,

Joyce spoke to me about her husband—their first meeting, his hatred for her mother, John's internal war with himself, his paradoxical sense of inferiority and pride over being Italian, his willful difference from everyone else, his refusal to be compliant. From Joyce I also learned that she had played an important role in John's literary life, as his first editor at the start of his career and, after his death, with the dissemination of his works. Joyce was Fante's original fan and I was struck by the force of her persona. However, the depth of her love was revealed only later in the editing room as I watched her speak of her husband. In slow motion I saw how her eyes were transformed, and I realized I was witnessing the thrill of a passion still capable of enthralling her, even at the age of ninety.

My interviews continued in Italy where I met Naples-based literary journalist Francesco Durante. Editor of the monumental anthology *Italoamericana* and translator of many of Fante's novels, it is thanks to Durante that they were published for the first time in Italy, when he was the editorial director of the Leonardo Publishing House. He would become one of my most crucial supporters.

Later I met screenwriter Luciano Vincenzoni, who worked extensively with Dino De Laurentiis, for many years the most important Italian producer in Hollywood. Fante too received a number of assignments from De Laurentiis, among them the screenplay for Duilio Coletti's *Black City* (1961) starring another son of Italian immigrants, Ernest Borgnine. Vincenzoni had met Fante during this time and he shared with me several anecdotes that were included in the documentary, with the exception of one that I am happy to reveal here. According to Vincenzoni, he once heard writer Jack Kerouac confess that his two favorite authors were Louis-Ferdinand Céline and John Fante—a literary morsel that should whet our appetite to learn more about Fante's influence on the Beats.

With Vincenzoni's help I was able to interview Furio Scarpelli, a giant of Italian comedy who also shared a passion for John Fante. Scarpelli defined Fante's style with great insight, establishing an important distinction between the literary writer and the screenwriter. It is my pleasure to relate that distinction here for it shows how even among screenwriters Fante's writing had taken hold in Italy: "John Fante's writing is enchanting because it possesses a dimension that elevates it—the childlike quality of Mozart." Fante's ability to tap into the child's vulnerability and spontaneity has enabled readers to feel, as he himself had felt, those experiences that caused his personal suffering. Noting the absence of this dimension from Fante's film work, Scarpelli speculated that Fante must have thought it better to protect the inner workings of his creative genius rather than expose it to the industrial vagaries of cinema. Sad to say, neither Vincenzoni nor Scarpelli would live long enough to participate in the Fante festival.

As I sought out other people to interview in Italy, I began to realize that Fante was better known and appreciated by members of the cinema, music, and literary communities than by academics. In fact, it was artists who had most helped spread Fante's name and writings among young Italians. Such is certainly the case with Vinicio Capossela, Italy's most original contemporary folksinger and the most "Fantean" of them all. At the end of the 1990s he and poet Vincenzo Costantino Chinasky organized a small Italian tour of a musical reading dedicated to Fante. Capossela has also written a song, "The Acolyte of the Rancorous," several verses of which allude to Fante's novel *The Brotherhood of the Grape*.[2]

Musso, Musso	Knick knack, paddy whack
liscio e busso	Strong suit or pull back
passa appresso	High card, suit of sticks
carica a bastoni	Pass to the right
cala l'asso	Drop the ace in sight
piglia, strozzo	Take it, choke it
smazza il mazzo Cavallaro	Shuffle the Cavallaro deck
fuman trinciato forte	Smoking strong, blunt-cut cigarettes
Joe Zarlingo fa le carte	Joe Zarlingo dealing the cards
bestemmia in mezzo ai denti	Swears through clenched teeth
tira a fottere i compari	fucking over his cronies
bastardi si deridono tra loro	doctors' enemies
cirrotici, diabetici	cirrhotic, diabetic
nemici dei dottori	bastards mocking each other
sputan sulla terra	spitting on that same earth
dove andranno sottoterra	that will swallow them up some day
Accolita di rancorosi	A band of the contentious
settimini cuspidi e tignosi	Immature, biting, and stubborn plaintiffs
persi nelle vita	lost in life

come dentro una corrida	as if inside a bull ring
intrappolati tra melassa e baraonda	trapped between molasses and chaos
Accolita di rancorosi	A band of the contentious
camerati ruvidi e grinzosi	rough and wrinkled comrades
accaniti nel lavoro	stubbornly at work
sparagnini con la prole,	tight fisted with their offspring,
spendaccioni con le troie	lavish with their sluts
demoni rapaci	rapacious demons
sputan sulla terra	spitting on that same earth
dove andranno sottoterra!![3]	that will swallow them up some day!!

In order to interview Capossela I had to follow him around, concert after concert. The effort finally paid off as I was able to get into the film not only him but also his parents, representatives of "those roots from which we can never free ourselves," as Capossela puts it, echoing H. L. Mencken's advice to Fante.[4] I stayed in touch with Capossela and for a time he signed his e-mails "The Duke of the Abruzzi" while referring to me as Rosa Pinelli, Arturo's unrequited love in *Wait Until Spring, Bandini*. Caposella would become one of the most prominent participants in the Fante festival.

Another person I had to interview was Sandro Veronesi, one of the greatest living Italian writers and a man who held Fante in the highest esteem from the moment Fante's work was rediscovered in Europe. In 1997 Veronesi began to research Nick Fante's life for an episode of *Einstein's Warehouse—Food for Thought*, an RAI Tre television program written and narrated by Veronesi himself. Accompanied by Vinicio Capossela, Veronesi arrived incognito in Torricella Peligna to meet the last Fante living in Torricella Peligna, Vincenzo Fante, an elderly farmer who confirmed he was indeed Nick's nephew. The video is both entertaining and instructive, for no sooner does Vincenzo criticize Nick for being a litigious type than he immediately speaks up in his defense when asked about "the mystery" of Nick's relationship with wine. Vincenzo affirms that drinking has always been a way of life for the men of Torricella Peligna, especially during cold winter nights. As long as there was snow on the ground, he says, they would drink and drink until they were drunk, every night. So much for the mystery of Nick Fante's drinking!

Through my conversations with Capossela and Veronesi I learned that many Italian readers find their way to Fante through the hard-living California writer Charles Bukowski, who considered Fante his master and who, as we know, deserves credit for sparking the John Fante revival. Marco Vichi, author of the "Inspector Bordelli" series of crime novels and a serious Bukowski fan, has written an homage to Fante that Bukowski would no doubt appreciate. I offer it here as an example of the enthusiasm that Fante's work can generate:

> If John Fante's writing were a prescription medicine, the instruction sheet would read as follows: Ingredients: each book contains a pound of poison, an ounce of peace, a ton of rage and two tons of passion.
> Bulking agent: caustic truth.
> Use to treat all cases of literary boredom, disorders of the critical system, chronic apathy, introspective lethargy, heartburn.
> Dosage: administer massive amounts to adult patients as needed, several times a day. May be harmful to pregnant women and children; take only upon doctor's advice.
> Side effects: a verified hypersensitivity to good literature, an allergic reaction to literary "masterpieces," and an aversion to those who are lacking in courage.
> Warnings: Once the therapy has begun, be sure to have multiple refills of this prescription close at hand.
> Interaction with other literary works: Most patients taking this medication exhibit an irreversible alteration in judgment; it is therefore recommended that patients open no other book while ingesting Fante, unless they happen to be the works of other great writers.
> Special warning: Keep this medication away from the chicken-hearted and lily-livered.
> Expiration: This product has no expiration date.[5]

Among others I also interviewed Florentine novelist Varchi, the plot of whose second book, *Donne donne* (Women women), is halfway between Fante's *Ask the Dust* and Bukowski's *Women*. I continued with my research and interviews for two more years and in 2003 *John Fante: Profilo di scrittore* was released on VHS by the publishing house Fazi Editore with an accompanying booklet of essays edited by Marco Vichi and Simone Caltabellonta. My documentary adventure introduced me to many incredible people with whom I established a virtual confraternity dedicated to expanding John Fante's audience. Thus I continued to work on Fante between screenings of the film, festival to festival, including the 2003 Los Angeles Italian Film Awards where I accepted the prize for Best Documentary.

In August 2005 the Commune of Torricella Peligna named its library after John Fante. Marco Vichi and I were invited to participate in the event with a screening and presentation of my film. Afterward, Mayor Graziano Zacchigna asked me to develop a concept for honoring Torricella Peligna's most famous Italian American compatriot. My response was to propose a convivial literary festival where people who are passionate about Fante could meet every summer to celebrate his works and explore the Fante phenomenon. To designate this gathering, I wanted a name that would conjure up his father, old Nick, while at the same time making our Italian feeling for the writer clear. And so I came up with "My Father's God," the title of a raucous short story that Fante published in 1975 in a journal of Italian American writing.[6]

In this story a newly ordained priest spars with a rude Italian American bricklayer from Colorado, valiantly trying to convince him to return to Sunday mass following years of disinterest in the word of God. It has become the priest's personal quest to bring the young narrator's Papa back to the sacrament of confession, with scarce results. The title "My Father's God" thus expresses the multiple ways in which the father figure operates in Fante's works. Not only does it indicate how the father has become an icon of Fante's ancestry, it also highlights the writer's ironic view of family as well as the idolatrous exuberance of his characters. To underscore our intention in choosing this title, I proposed the cement mixer, basic tool of the bricklayer, as the festival's logo.

With support from the mayor, his cabinet, and cultural coordinator, the literary festival dedicated to John Fante, "My Father's God," was born at last. Following the wave of renewed attention to John Fante and his work in the 1980s and 1990s, the festival was the logical next step and a source of pride to the administration of Torricella Peligna, which had already sponsored a number of Fante events with the John Fante Association.

However, with the arrival of a new mayor who had been an opponent of Mayor Zachigna, the festival came into the world in a climate of tension. Such was the animosity between these two groups—whose warring advisors would provoke the fall of the Zachigna administration—that I found myself working in an atmosphere of political and administrative turmoil as I prepared the inaugural festival of July 2006. In a strange way it was all too reminiscent of Nick Fante's litigious character! And yet despite the difficulties of carrying out the first edition of the festival under such circumstances, I persevered. Ultimately there was a positive outcome in the person of Tiziano Teti, the current mayor of Torricella Peligna. A minority party advisor during that difficult first year, he has continued his commitment to the festival, carrying forward this extraordinary adventure with us over the past decade. For just one example, in 2009 he facilitated the inauguration of the Mediateca John Fante where books and documents about the writer from all over the world are archived.

Birth pangs notwithstanding, my network of fellow Fante enthusiasts from the documentary years has proven extremely useful to my ongoing work as the festival's artistic director. Numerous writers, musicians, artists, students, researchers, and scholars of every stripe have participated. Although mostly Italian, they have also come from the United States, Canada, the Netherlands, France, Spain, Eritrea, and Sweden. Among them have been experts and fresh faces, the famous and the unknown, all journeying to Torricella Peligna to render their personal respects to John Fante.

The greatest challenge from one year to the next has been to offer a program that is consistently faithful to the festival's mission by developing themes, topics, and ideas that are somehow related to John Fante. This means identifying motifs linking the various contexts, as well as trying to satisfy a heterogeneous audience with a wide range of activities including recent Italian publications on the topic, film screenings, literary readings and musical performances, a section on emigration and immigration, an awards category, and a spotlight on other writers whose work and inspiration connect to Fante (fig. 12).

Over these past dozen years, naturally, many events have focused on Fante's oeuvre. I still recall with great emotion the 2012 musical reading with Sandro Veronesi, Viniccio Capossella, Ray Abruzzo, and Dan Fante, whose collective passion captivated the audience for over two hours. Fifteen years after their incognito road trip, Capossela and Veronesi were together again in Torricella Peligna reading their favorite passages from Fante in Italian, interspersed with Ray Abruzzo reading in English, while Dan Fante recited his poems, many dedicated to his father, with actor Domenico Galasso repeating them in Italian. That same year Veronesi offered the keynote address, "John Fante and I," in which he highlighted the strength of Fante's characters and the compassion that transforms them into fully realized

186 *Giovanna DiLello*

FIGURE 12. Banner of the annual John Fante Festival, Torricella Peligna, Italy. (Courtesy of Giovanna DiLello.)

human beings. Fante's novels are made up of strong characters, he stressed, and these characters are full of energy, irony, and humanity. Veronesi spoke of learning this lesson from Fante's writing and applying it in his own.

Raiz, singer and frontman for the alternative rock group Almamegretta, has also demonstrated an interest in John Fante's characters. For the second festival he prepared a beautiful musical reading entitled "Bandini's Room," inspired by the important strand of Fante's oeuvre tied to families and emigration. In fact, in 2004 Raiz released a solo album, *Wop*, focusing on Italian American migrants, of whom Fante, in the eyes of many, represents the embodiment.

Torricella Peligna has also hosted one of the greatest artists ever to grace the Italian musical horizon, Francesco De Gregori, a singer-songwriter whose influence and reputation in Italy are on par with Bob Dylan's in America. De Gregori's passion for Fante has been well known since his 1994 appearance on *Pickwick*, the RAI television program about books. Invited to discuss *Ask the Dust*, he lauded the superiority of Fante's novel with respect to Bukowski. De Gregori is an extremely reserved artist and quite difficult to book but thanks to the efforts of Torricella Peligna's events committee, he performed memorably at the festival's 2009 centennial celebration of Fante's birth.

Less well known but equally passionate about Fante is the young folk singer from Molise, Luigi Farinaccio, who contacted me about a song he had written. Presented in his appearance at the 2010 festival, "Good Night, John" refers to Fante as a "guiding star," exclaiming, "Bandini is alive!" In celebration of Fante's Abruzzese roots and his effective role as domestic god, Farinaccio intertwined his experience at Torricella into the video he made of the song.

Although I had now seen the extent to which Fante appealed to musicians, I never thought I would find myself including one of the great stars of Italian jazz, Enrico Rava, on that list. I had discovered that one of his albums was called *Full of Life* and so I asked him if the title was a reference to John Fante. He answered that indeed the song paid homage to Fante, whose works he had loved since 1987, including the volume of letters Fante wrote home from Italy. Rava thus made a guest appearance at the 2011 festival with a moving jazz concert punctuated by his mythical trumpet and the accompanying verve of pianist Giovanni Guidi.

Over the course of the years several innovative features have been added to the festival, among them, in 2008, the John Fante First Book Prize, which has featured any number of talented finalists whose works have been published by some of the most prestigious publishing houses in Italy. The purpose of this national literary prize is to support and value the work of new authors of novels or collections of short stories. The prize was inspired by fictional events in the life of Arturo Bandini, the young aspiring writer-protagonist of Fante's best novels, who seeks to find his place in the world through his prose. Oversight of the prize has been entrusted to Francesco Durante, who presented a sneak preview of Fante's children's novel *Bravo Burro*, translated into Italian by Durante himself and published for the first time in 2010. Among those who have won the John Fante First Book Prize to date are Dunja Badnjevic, Cristian Frascella, Alberto Mossino, Federica Tuzi, Donatella Di Pietrantonio, Simona Baldelli, Luisa Brancaccio, and Enrico Ianniello. Durante presides over the jury of writers that awards the prize. They select three finalists in consultation with Professor Mario Cimini of the University Gabriele D'Annunzio (Chieti/Pescara), as well as with a popular jury of students from the university and readers from Torricella Peligna and surrounding towns in order to arrive at the selection of the winning work.

For the last several years there has also been a contest for "flash fiction," short stories of less than one thousand words featuring Fantean themes. The first contest winner, "The True Story of John Fante in Torricella" by Gianluca Di Renzo, plays with the uncertainty that persists to this day about whether or not Fante ever passed through Torricella Peligna during his Italian travels. Fante's biography has always played a central role in the festival program. It is evoked in the stories told by John Fante's children, Dan, Victoria, and Jim, who have attended every year since the festival's inception. These personal stories have enriched the celebration with the kind of insight and emotion our audience seeks and which only they, Fante's children, can provide. Dan Fante (who passed away while I was writing this essay and was greatly loved by our audience) generously shared with us a variety of his writings, including many about his father. For the tenth edition of the festival Victoria Fante read passages from her mother's unpublished diaries—one of the most memorable events in the entire run of the festival.

Stephen Cooper, Fante's biographer, has also addressed the private sphere of Fante's family life. He attended the festival in 2009 on the occasion of the centenary celebration of the writer's birth. We are in Cooper's debt for his magnificent biography, *Full of Life: A Biography of John Fante*, which has become an indispensable resource for any serious consideration of Fante and his writings. Other scholars who have attended the festival have likewise presented their work, including Gianni Paoletti (*John Fante: Histories/Stories of an Italian American*, 2005), Fabio Florio (*John Fante: History of an Italian in America*, 2014), and Spanish journalist Eduardo Margaretto (*John Fante: His Lives and Work—A Sonnet Unedited*, 2014).

By contrast, Luigi Rossi offered an alternate version of Fante's life in his novel *L'ultimo viaggio di Arturo Gabriel Bandini* (AGS Edizioni, 2012), a fictionalized biography told from Arturo's point of view. And in *The Dust of Via Bellini*, presented at the tenth edition, novelist Tonino Bozzi likewise took an imaginative approach, a sequel to *Ask the Dust* in which Arturo Bandini comes to Torricella Peligna.

As is evident from this "tracking shot" of festival highlights, "My Father's God" has opened its doors to many guests, among them great Italian and foreign writers. Some of these—Stephen Amidon, Nino Ricci and Andrea De Carlo—have come to present their novels, while others have talked about

Fante. Like Veronesi, Melania Mazzucco has underscored the theme of emigration while Stefano Benni performed an exquisite reading culled entirely from *Ask the Dust*. Another great representative of Italian literature took part in the tenth annual festival, writer-magistrate Giancarlo De Cataldo, known internationally for his *Criminal Novel*. As a judge of new writers on the RAI 3 program *Masterpiece*, De Cataldo discovered that Fante was among the most frequently cited authors by new, aspiring writers as a guiding spirit. More than ever, in fact, Fante has become a point of reference for many young Italian writers and artists. Case in point is the collection of short stories *E il cagnolino rise* (And the little dog laughed) (Editrice Tespi, 2009), in which an ensemble of writers pay homage to a story that does not exist, namely, the one in *Ask the Dust* that Arturo obsesses over having published but which we never get to read.

Twenty very young authors wrote short stories for a collection addressing the theme of the precariousness of young people's lives today and presented in Torricella Peligna in 2009. Among the generation of thirty-something Fanteans who have come through Torricella I'd like to add Abruzzese writer Alessio Romano, who in his novel *Solo sigari quando è festa* (Only cigars when it's a party) (Bompiani, 2015) names one of his key characters Fiona Fante in honor of his favorite author, as well as the actor and television host Francesco Mandelli, who had Fante's Los Angeles in mind when he wrote his first work *Osnangeles* (Baldini and Castoldi, 2014). And let us not forget the troupe of extremely young dancers, actors, and directors of "Ask the Dust . . . What Is Left of Them," presented in 2013 with theatrical direction by Monica Ciarcelluti and choreography by Elisabetta Di Terlizzi.

Fante has also been an inspiration for two very special Dutch writers, Henk Van Straten, who has gone so far as to tattoo a portrait of John Fante on his arm, and Jaap Scholten. At the 2014 festival their documentary *Against a Perfect Sky* confirmed the extent to which the Italian American writer has played a decisive role in their work. The film was shot in Torricella Peligna that same year during their quest for Fante's roots, under the direction of Jasper Henderson, himself a passionate reader of Fante and owner of the small Dutch publishing house Bandini.

Enthusiasm for Fante among young people has also spread through Italian universities. Over the last ten years many students have contacted me either to request material about Fante or to send copies of their theses. I discovered, however, that Fante is seldom read in university courses, and that the theses devoted to him and his work are the result of students' personal choice to work on Fante for their final thesis projects. In response to the high level of interest shown by students in recent years, the festival now has a section dedicated to theses that address any number of Fante topics, including but not limited to Fante's roots; the role of the father figure in his narrative; identity and autobiography in his works; the character of Arturo Bandini and the American dream; as well as Fante as a Los Angeles novelist. Thus the young people we welcome to Torricella every year range from college students to freshly minted high school graduates coming to present their senior projects on John Fante.

Despite the fact that Fante isn't much studied at the university in Italy, Italian academics have been intimately involved in the festival. I will always remember the roundtable discussion coordinated by Francesco Marroni, professor of English literature at the University Gabriele D'Annunzio (Chieti/Pescara) and a passionate reader of John Fante. In fact, a selection of festival roundtables was published in the university magazine *Merope* (May–September 2007). The festival has also had the privilege of hosting other important writers and scholars, among them French journalist Philippe Garnier, who discussed the dynamics of the Fante revival in 1980s France, and Fred Gardaphé, professor of Italian American literature at Queens College/CUNY, who spoke of Fante's film work and his relationship with Pietro Di Donato.

In addition to readings, concerts, and conferences over the years, there has also been a great deal of theater, monologues in particular, with "Prologo di *Chiedi alla polvere*" ("Prologue to *Ask the Dust*") featuring Giovanni Guidelli; "My Dog Stupid," with the television actor Andrea Brambilla, also known as Zuzzurro, directed by Giorgio Gallione; "Orgy" with Simon Gandolfo and directed by Federico Cruciani; and a recital by the Abruzzese cabaret artist Nduccio, "John Fante as Told by Me," about the relationship between Fante and Bukowski.

Over these first twelve years of the festival, John Fante's popularity has grown substantially in Italy. Though it may be true that we read little in Italy, within that little is a lot of Fante. It is no coincidence that today *Ask the Dust* is a "long seller," a cherished work that continues to sell over the years and decades. Considered an author with a cult following, Fante is also loved by less obvious readers, such as Maurizio Sarri, coach of the soccer team Napoli, and by restaurateurs who have dedicated their eating establishments to him. I'm thinking of the Bandini Restaurant in Portacomaro d'Asti and the pizzeria Dago Red in Sant'Arsenio, near Salerno—not to mention all the delectable, irresistible scenes that play out around the kitchen table in Fante's fiction.

"His strength lies in his ability to photograph things as they are at the precise moment in which they occur, without the complication of afterthought or the filter of modesty," writes Marco Vichi in the volume he conceived as a tribute to Fante. For Vichi, as for so many of us, Fante's writing is nothing more or less "than the adherence to sentiment, to human feeling."[7] In reality, his stories are shreds of shared existence that recount the precarious quality of life experienced by everyone at one time or another. And in all of this, Torricella Peligna ascends symbolically to the place where the soul resides, for as Vinicio Capossela reminds us at festival time: "Everyone has their own Torricella Peligna to define them, from which they can never break free."

Translated by Clorinda Donato

Notes

1. *Wop* is a derogatory term used to designate Italian immigrants in the United States, derived from the southern Italian dialectical term *guappo* meaning thug, pimp, swaggerer.

2. The song is taken from the 1996 album *Il ballo di San Vito* (St. Vitus's dance).

3. Vichi, "Due parole su John Fante," 23. Translated by Clorinda Donato.

4. In a letter dated August 31, 1932, H. L. Mencken wrote to Fante, "I have a feeling that you had better stop writing about your family. The subject seems to obsess you." Moreau and Fante, *Fante/Mencken*, 37.

5. Vichi, "Due parole su John Fante." In *John Fante*, edited by Simone Caltabellota and Marco Vichi, 23. Rome: Fazi Editore, 2003.

6. Fante, "My Father's God." The story later appeared in Fante's 1985 posthumous collection *The Wine of Youth*.

7. Vichi, *John Fante*, 30.

Works Cited

Fante, John. "My Father's God." *Italian Americana* 2, n. 1 (Autumn 1975): 18–31.

Moreau, Michael, and Joyce Fante, *Fante/Mencken: John Fante and H. L. Mencken, a Personal Correspondence 1930–1952*. Santa Rosa, CA: Black Sparrow Press, 1989.

Vichi, Marco. "Due parole su John Fante." In *John Fante*, edited by Simone Caltabellota and Marco Vichi. Rome: Fazi Editore, 2003

———. *John Fante: Fuori dalla polvere*. Firenze: Edizioni Clichy, 2005.

I Had Bandini: Reading *Ask the Dust* in Prison

Joel Williams

I remember exactly where I was and what I was doing when I first heard about the Los Angeles writer, John Fante. The year was 2008 and the place was Mule Creek State Prison, a maximum-security California penitentiary where I was dragging in my twenty-second year on a twenty-seven-to-life sentence, for murder.

I was on the yard, hanging out with a couple of other skins near the pull-up bars, when we heard the gunshot. Men everywhere dropped. It was the guard tower's mini-14, a totally different sound from the usual 40mm "Big Bertha" riot-control block gun. I had suspected something was about to go down ever since another skin—the term we Natives used for each other—had warned me to keep on my toes. Somebody was going to get moved on.

Stretched out prone in the dirt I lifted my head an inch to eyeball the yard. Guards with batons out and keys jangling on their utility belts ran past with medical staff trailing behind. Cordite filled the air as one man was hoisted onto a gurney and another was led off in handcuffs. Beside me Bear, a skin nicknamed for his size, rested his chin on a paperback.

"What book you got?" I asked.

"You don't wanna read this."

"Why's that?"

"'Cause you won't give it back!"

I smiled and he tossed it over, something to while away the next several days when the whole prison would be on lockdown. Hours later, when we were told to get up and go back to our cells, I stuffed the book in my back pocket.

My neighbor, Norm, later told me through the vent that the guy who got stabbed on the yard was my cellmate, a Maidu Indian named Lance. I was stunned. Sure, Lance had a gambling jones and was always in debt. Sure, he smoked too much herb. But hell, he was a nice enough guy and for me that counted, what with most everyone else out to pick your pocket and cut your throat. So sure, the news hit me hard.

To get my mind off things I picked up Bear's book. It didn't look like much—no flashy cover, no promise of action or sleaze. The title was an odd one, *Ask the Dust*, by a guy from my stomping grounds in Los Angeles. His name was John Fante and I'd never heard of him but as I flipped through the first few pages I saw Bukowski's name. I knew who *he* was so I read his introduction. And Bukowski revered John Fante. *My* literary hero, Bukowski, had a hero himself. I stirred up a cup of instant coffee, climbed into my bunk, and set off on a long night of reading.

And what a night it turned out to be. Fante's character Arturo Bandini pulled me into a Los Angeles I'd never experienced, an earlier world colored with subtle shades of poetry and streaks of vivid emotion. Bandini was exuberant, alive, searching. I reread sentences, whole passages, soaking in the beauty of Fante's words, wringing every nuance of meaning from his prose. And as always happened when I savored another writer's work, I felt the tug of jealousy. I too wanted to create beautiful works and move people, and once again I'd been beaten to the punch.

Still, as the evening hours thinned I found myself developing a great respect for the man and the writer John Fante. The way he danced in and out of first, second, and third person felt so natural I had to wonder why more writers didn't do the same. But more important, he wasn't shy about pulling back the curtains on the "intermittencies of the heart"—a phrase I seem to recall from the forward to a Knut Hamsun book whose title escapes me, *Mysteries*, maybe?—those incipient ups and downs when we teeter between surrendered desire and prideful reluctance, the moments when we are at our best and our worst.[1] Embarrassing, yes, but honest, truthful writing. Fante had more colors on his palette than any other writer I'd ever encountered. And believe me, I've done a lot of reading, because when you're doing a life term reading isn't an academic pursuit but a matter of mental and emotional survival.

That first night with *Ask the Dust* sparked my curiosity. After each scene I paused to scan the front and back of the book, searching for more about Fante, a photo, anything. I was trying to glean something about the man, some clue about what lay underneath. Maybe I hoped to see some wrinkle, some scar, so I could point and say, "Ah, there's his soul. There's the cause of his genius. There's his wisdom. His tragedy." But the photos I found gave no clues (fig. 13). I lay there on my bunk thinking, "Who is this guy?"

Ten years later the spine of that book is cracked, the pages smudged with cigarette ashes. Flipping through it I see underlined phrases—an elevator man "who seemed to sneer every time you called your floor," a cab driver

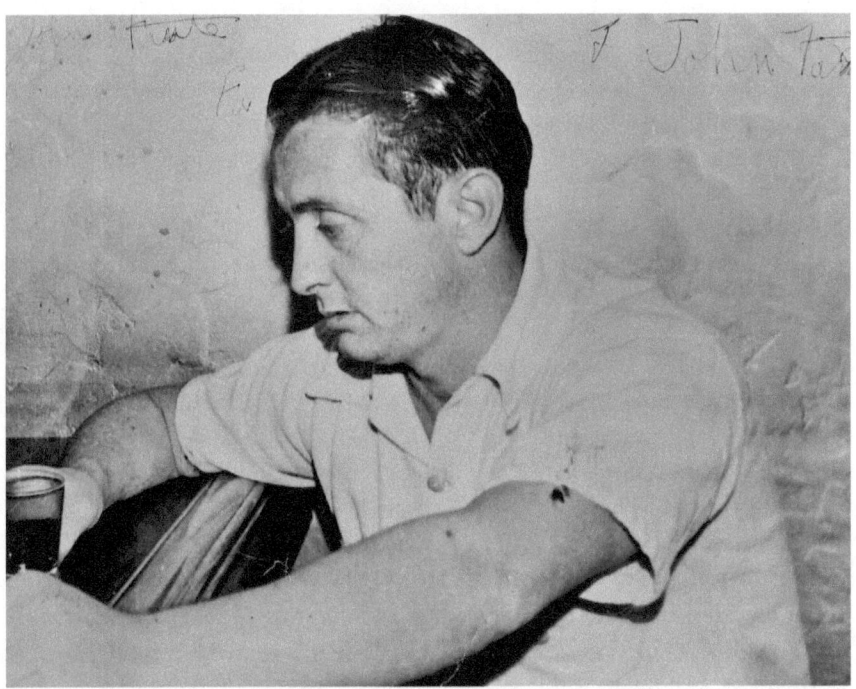

FIGURE 13. John Fante drinking. (Courtesy of John Fante Literary Group LLC.)

who "leered salaciously and then took us to Temple Street."[2] My thought: a writer land-marking his story's terrain with vagrant human feelings. I liked that, because any writer can *show* you but the greats make you *feel*.

And what's up with those huaraches? In the holy Columbia Buffet, heavy with desire, Bandini zeros in on Camilla's huaraches. The back-and-forth of their attack and counterattack is as hilarious as it is painful, right up to the end, when Camilla runs after Arturo to apologize:

"Young fellow!' she called. "Oh kid!"

I waited and she came out of breath, speaking quickly and softly. "I'm sorry," she said. "I didn't mean anything—honest."

"It's okay," I said. "I didn't mind."

She kept glancing toward the saloon. "I have to get back," she said. "They'll miss me. Come back tomorrow night, will you? Please! I can be nice. I'm awfully sorry about tonight. Please come, please!" She squeezed my arm. "Will you come?"

"Maybe."

She smiled. "Forgive me?"

"Sure."

I stood in the middle of the sidewalk and watched her hurry back. After a few steps she turned, blew a kiss and called, "Tomorrow night, don't forget!"

"Camilla!" I said. "Wait. Just a minute!"

We ran toward each other, meeting halfway. [This is where my gut tightened—J. W.]

"Hurry!" she said. "They'll fire me."

I glanced at her feet. She sensed it coming and I felt her recoiling from me. Now a good feeling rushed through me, a coolness, a newness like new skin. I spoke slowly.

"Those huaraches—do you have to wear them, Camilla? Do you have to emphasize the fact that you always were and always will be a filthy little Greaser?"

She looked at me in horror, her lips open. Clasping both hands against her mouth, she rushed inside the saloon. I heard her moaning. "Oh, oh, oh." (44)

Nostalgically, I look back on the streets of Los Angeles that Fante wrote about, because I walked those streets as a young man. I revel in their familiarity, even if *Ask the Dust* came out nearly half a century before my time. I walked up and down Bunker Hill where the Angel's Flight trolley used to run, I swam in the waves at Santa Monica beach. And that's why the novel means so much to me, because Fante transfigured Los Angeles. He took the same raw materials of concrete, steel, and desert dust and changed them into this strange, beautiful, wondrous thing called art.

Bandini was my outsider hero. His thwarted yearnings for love, success, and happiness mirrored my own. Like me, he too had relocated to Los Angeles. As he puts it, "It was five months ago, the day that I got to town by bus from Colorado with a hundred and fifty dollars in my pocket and big plans in my head" (15–16). My own road to Los Angeles at the age of seventeen, motivated by the fear and disgust of having an abusive father, involved heading to the nearest freeway onramp with a pack on my back and sticking out my thumb. But I could relate to Arturo, feel the bite of his frustrations just as sharply as he did. At home as a boy, on the streets of LA as a teen, in prison doing time as an adult, I always shouldered my outsider status in private, keeping it to myself, the feeling that something intrinsic separated me from others. I took it as truth and accepted as fact that my life and whatever I did with it were disconnected from everybody else in the world. A painted black line on the ground separated us. And in *Ask the Dust* I found company and reassurance in the character of Arturo Bandini. Other guys on the inside had actors and athletes and rock stars. I had Bandini. I felt a deep kinship with him over his peers' rejection because of his Italian American background, just as when the other kids called me "Beaner" because my mixed Indian skin got so dark in the summer.

Back in his room after the scene with Camilla, Arturo thinks back: "When I was a kid back home in Colorado it was Smith and Parker and Jones who hurt me with their hideous names, called me Wop and Dago and Greaser" (46). Then he admits, "their children hurt me, just as I hurt you tonight" (46). By "you" he means Camilla but thanks to Fante's finesse with the second person I felt Arturo's confession as deep as Camilla would feel it, if only he would say it to her.

And the hard-edged poetry of Arturo's words dug just as deep: "Eight dollars pouring out of my eyes, Oh Jesus kill me dead and ship my body home, kill me dead and make me die like a pagan fool with no priest to absolve me, no extreme unction, eight dollars, eight dollars" (26). I learned those lines by heart, the sound of them, their rhythm, their mystery. *Ask the Dust* became my textbook. I carried it with me on the yard, took it with me to the chow hall, gave it my own clumsy half-witted literary criticism. But I felt on intimate terms with everything in it. That book became my secret.

Later, when I began to write, I kept that to myself too. My writing became a private walled-off part of myself, like my emotions. When I read, it became my habit to keep the cover turned away from prying eyes. *TV Guide* was a common sight in prison, but Isaac Babel? Flannery O'Connor? Ernest Hemingway? Raymond Chandler? What the hell was all that? Behind bars you could be as dumb, tough, or cruel as you wanted to be, but they'd never forgive you for being intelligent or sensitive. That shit you had to hide. If not, you might as well have a *Kick me* sign pinned on your back.

So to learn how to write I had to do it on my own, by myself. There were no creative writing classes in prison, and for the fundamentals all I had to go on was a grammar book. By this time I had gotten ahold of a typewriter. I also had a new cellmate, a Pit River Indian named Sam. Sam had a job in the prison factory sewing boxer shorts for 30 cents an hour, minus the 55 percent restitution tax subtracted from every penny he made. Still, he liked getting out of the cell and I liked him gone because then I could pull out the typewriter and pound away. The stories I wanted to write were beautiful and complex stories about women and love and life, to showcase some fictitious wisdom I had about the opposite sex. But what did I know? As Arturo realizes, "That's your trouble: your ignorance of life. Why, my God, man, do you realize you've never had any experience with a woman?" (18). He goes on: "Ha, great writer this! How can he write about women, when he's never had a woman? Oh you lousy fake, you phony, no wonder you can't write!" (18). His words spoke my truth, and they cut me to ribbons. I hardly even had any visitors.

But in 2008, by way of a third party, I met a woman. She started coming to the prison on weekends to see me, and soon our meetings were filled with long discussions about books, films, music. She spoke five languages, was well traveled, had the life experiences and cultural interests that I had been thirsting for. At last I had someone who understood me. I felt at ease when we spoke.

The weekend after Lance got stabbed I couldn't wait to tell her about *Ask the Dust*. She probably wouldn't know who John Fante was so I would tell her what little I knew, the names of his other books, that he had died in obscurity, etc. But when I mentioned his name her reaction floored me.

"I know who he is," she said. "A friend of mine, Stephen Cooper, wrote his biography."

At that moment I recalled reading on the novel's copyright page grateful acknowledgment to Stephen Cooper for the kind use of his personal archives.

"If you'd like," she went on, "I can write to him and ask if he would care to correspond with you."

I sat there trying to take it all in. In my world things never happened that way. Mostly they never happened at all. It took a moment to process what she was saying. That black line on the ground—was it starting to fade?

Soon enough Steve Cooper and I were writing back and forth, actual letters in envelopes since another thing missing where I lived was computers. He sent books now and then and he became my mentor. He reached out and offered a fellow writer's hand: "Show what's happening in the external world—individualized perceptions of concrete realities via the protagonist's point of view, rendered as often as possible through the five senses—and trust that the inner world of emotion shines through." From Steve I discovered the literary thread that connected Dostoyevsky, Hamsun, Fante, and Bukowski. Through him my world became richer. Bigger. This went on for years.

Then, on August 6, 2014, I attended my fourth parole consideration hearing. After three denials, each spaced three years apart, and a total of twenty-eight years served, I thought I was finally prepared. Showing accountability, remorse, and rock-solid parole plans, I also presented other evidence weighing in my favor. I had three published books, more than ten literary magazine credits, and support letters from friends, editors, and publishers. But of all the letters I received for that hearing, the one that carried the most cachet was the one written by Stephen Cooper.

Today I no longer live in a six-by-ten-foot concrete cell. I am no longer exposed to daily cruelties and degradation. And I am not crushed under the weight of despair and loneliness. Today I feel normal, settled in, a happily married man—not to Steve's friend but to another amazing woman who also came to visit—working toward my college degree. Sometimes it all seems like a dream, like that feeling you get when you wake up knowing you've dreamt something, but you can't tell exactly what and you feel it slipping away. I know I have to write all of it down, before it's gone forever. That will be my task in the coming years.

Of my past, the memories and the wanted posters at the post office aside, there is one item that I brought out with me that is very important, a reminder of who I was, where I've been, and who I am today. It is what inspired me and gave me life, a reminder of the decision I made all those years ago to write. It is my dog-eared, underlined, highlighted copy of *Ask the Dust*. I see it now on the bookshelf across from me.

But the book also signifies something else. It represents another decision I made over thirty years ago, one that cost too many people too much. I was at a different crossroads then and when I made the wrong decision the world conspired to bury me, and I brought the shovel. When *Ask the Dust* appeared it was like a signpost in the road, pointing the way forward and out. A second chance at life, a window opening when doors were slamming shut all around me.

I still remember my throat getting tight and my eyeballs sweating the first time I read the opening chapters of *Ask the Dust*. Not because of any particular sentimental passage, but because I had stumbled across something remarkable: a writer who floated across the page on a river of emotions. And with it came an epiphany. Not only in my understanding of writing but in my life as well.

Notes

1. "The Intermittencies of the Heart" is the title of a chapter in *Sodom and Gomorrah*, the fourth volume of Proust's *In Search of Lost Time*. Joel has not yet read Proust and neither he nor his editors can figure out where he first encountered the phrase. We are letting his seeming recollection stand for what it's worth [editors' note].
2. Fante, *Ask the Dust*, 12. Hereafter cited in text with page number.

Works Cited

Fante, John. *Ask the Dust*. New York: HarperCollins, 2002.

Writing in the Dust

Alan Rifkin

I can still picture, if only barely, Evelyn Waugh arriving in Los Angeles back when not everything here had been named yet, and seeing the double meanings laid so bare—oasis and dust, paradise and exile—that he finished a novel in ten weeks (*The Loved One*, his sendup of an immortality-crazed mortuary) after it had taken him three years to write the one before.

Of course, the famous ironies of the Southern California landscape have gotten pretty gentrified since then. They've been coming true and getting commonplace at the same time—growing up.

It happened fast, because when I was growing up here and wanted to write, I could still detect at least the tail wind of Waugh's delirium—that hallucinatory, step-outside-time awareness of standing on our own graves. And I know this gets hazy. But in the California that I'm remembering, mostly Valley in my case, mostly seventies and eighties, I could tan and pretend there would never be cancers, or at least write about people who did. ("The goddess of the coast and the germ of a bag lady," as I once described a character.) I could make up histories out of place names, before the last figments vanished from the highway. I could wager everything on madness, like Pascal, because madness might be a latter-day prophecy. Or some kind of R. D. Laing exercise in going sane. There were outside rumors, of course, that madness wasn't really sane at all. But I wasn't sure of this yet in Los Angeles.

We were going to be ageless, find the Garden, reinvent brotherhood (or show where it had been lost).

At the same time I knew, like Waugh, that we were dreaming. And, as I was starting to realize, this reality disorder had been the starting point, the given, for an entire generation of local novelists. "In Los Angeles, it is always the first generation," the poet Kate Braverman once said—a group too quiet, too neglected, to consider itself a literary movement, except maybe in its secret fantasies. But that is where some neglect can begin to pay off.

The fact is, Los Angeles has always been pulling a certain type of writer away from realistic fiction toward something more permeable that no one ever bothered to name. Any aficionado can recite a short list of hallucinatory LA visions from the twentieth century, by people like Nathanael West and John Fante and Joan Didion and Carolyn See. They were a recurring dream that shook the bed once or twice each generation, like little earthquakes. Not that the writers themselves got too vocal about the subject, except in private. It could just seem so personal. The gorgeous estrangement. The flakiness, the longing. The possibly delusional proposition that the conflicts most central to the human condition—truth and illusion, spirit and flesh, heaven and earth, race and community—were reaching endgame mainly in Los Angeles.

In 2005, at the *Los Angeles Times* Festival of Books, I interviewed Francesca Lia Block, whose dozen-plus metamorphic novels since the mid-1980s, including the popular Weetzie Bat oeuvre, had been turning Hollywood's fallen angels into something like pagan myth. An hour's worth of fans had lined up for her autograph, but unless she was lying, the payoff was sitting down to answer questions, from someone similarly possessed, about the making of an LA fabulist—in her case, beginning with a childhood steeped in Greek mythology and Melrose Avenue. She talked about how orphaned she'd felt when punk monogamists John Doe and Exene split up, and how she didn't break through to her own brand of hallucinogenic fairy tale (I think her novels are Young Adult; they're also seriously horny) until she'd gone away to

Berkeley and her father was dying, and she yearned for a Hollywood lullaby. There seemed something almost stubbornly vulnerable about the proposition she'd kept staking her career on. ("How can I tell you this without sounding too crazy, too West Coast?" she'd once told the *New York Times*. "I believe life is infused with magic.") Yet all her success had streamed from this quintessential LA foolishness: writing as if no young generation elsewhere had really been young.

Then there's Steve Erickson, whom even those who love him struggle to get, but I get him, because he keeps writing the serial dreams of my Valley childhood: moon bridges, sand dunes, secret portals to Forever. Not that he trusted these visions right away. First he had to write five unpublished novels. "The whole activity," he told me once, "in the eyes of people I knew, and maybe even my own, began to seem a little insane"—a word that in Erickson's mouth has the hiss of someone spotting a nemesis across the room. He finally began *Days Between Stations* when he felt "there was nothing to lose, and therefore I could allow myself to bury LA under a sandstorm."

It's a literature that can seem like tag-team dreaming. After Didion's freeway dissociation in *Play It as It Lays* came Carolyn See's postapocalyptic *Golden Days*. Then Block gave us the Weetzie Bat series, about a teenager whose offspring—by two fathers, if anyone's counting—is named Cherokee: "a girl love-warrior who would grow up to wear feathers and run swift and silent through the LA canyons."

"Can we get past plot, already?" asks novelist Martha Sherrill, an LA native half-seriously complaining about her new East Coast–writer crowd[1]. She herself invented a starlet for an *Esquire* cover story—a magical-realist hoax—and then turned it into the novel *My Last Movie Star*.

Only in Los Angeles would so many novels, from West's *The Day of the Locust* to Robert Stone's *Dog Soldiers*, begin in realism and veer to something like biblical extra innings. ("Fuckin' L.A., man," says Stone's Nietzschean protagonist, "go out for a Sunday spin, you're a short hair from the dawn of creation.")

Indeed, when I moved south to be a family man in Long Beach, I started going to church—relieved to stop reinventing the language of religion from the desert floor up. But I knew I'd lost something, too. I wanted to be unmoored again—I wanted to give up God to resume the quest for Him. Like Block when she was exiled to Berkeley, I started a novella that grew out of LA memories—of bottle glass, tile chips, sagebrush in the hard mud of Malibu. After that came a novel I'm forever trying to finish, which arrived as the vision of a fasting man's pantry in 1940s Sherman Oaks. Carolyn See, riffing on what she says is a notion from Orthodox Judaism—and giving it a sort of Caltrans spin—told me once that she loosely believes Los Angeles to be one of the "twelve exits to heaven." I must have been thinking that, too. What I wanted was for my protagonist's pantry to have all these brand names that may never have existed, because if I could have named them, the secret off-ramp would have closed, the pantry would merely have been real. And then I couldn't have written.

All fiction is at some level dreamy, or it wouldn't be fiction. And novels from the bizarro LA may not be the most masterful fiction in the world. But they're the only American fiction that always looks beyond life's veil—to me the only fiction that's always worth reading.

Sometimes when I go to bookstores—where the first thing apparent is that our culture writes much too much and needs to shut up, needs some fundamentalist-futurist Ministry of Thought to cut us back to two or three nice books a year—I try works by Richard Russo or Vikram Seth or Annie Dillard, skilled outsiders, realists. The characters and manners are rendered deftly, the circle of life full and complete. But that's the problem. For all their storytelling, they only corroborate the veil of the senses. You feel reassured by them, or you should, but five minutes later, you smell a rat. Because who says the circle of life should be trusted?

And if you've surrendered, somewhere in the course of an LA childhood, to distrusting what the rest of the country deems familiar, the distrust becomes what's familiar, the local strangeness reassuring.

So I read Joy Nicholson's *The Road to Esmeralda*, in which an LA writer, haunted by his chicken-hawk dad from Yucca Valley, flees with his girlfriend into Mexican doom, post-9/11. While not actually bending the laws of physics—delirium in the jungle is so real it's practically ordinary—this book is prophetic: It chases the vanishing LA dream straight out of LA, finding no corner of the world unspoiled, no innocence left.

Or I read Erickson's *Our Ecstatic Days*, in which the portal to history, conscience, and maternal memory is a black LA lake that fills the lower floors of the Hotel of the Thirteen Losses, whose hallways are sailed by a doctor learning to specialize in buildings that are dying of grief.[2]

If you include writers with one foot in fantasy/sci-fi—if your LA vision leans toward time travelers and mermen with vestigial gills—the list becomes a catalog: Octavia Butler, Kem Nunn, James Blaylock, Scott Bradfield, Tim Powers, Kim Stanley Robinson, and all the descendants of Philip K. Dick.

Sometimes this LA literature jumps the ropes of literature itself. The urban theorist Norman Klein, who in another metropolis might set off a manhunt with nets, leads "anti-tours" of the city's "erasures" (lost pasts) and "social imaginaries"—things like trucked-in Victorian homes that create a "collective memory of an event or place that never occurred but is built anyway."

Even a *New York Times* op-ed by humorist Bruce Wagner—whose screenplays and novels of decadent Hollywood have drawn comparisons to both Charles Dickens and William Burroughs—began with mayoral politics and wound up staring at blackened hills:

> I am trying to remember who Antonio Villaraigosa is—I keep giving him the name "Vargas" in my mind, like the illustrator who used to do those pin-up paintings for Playboy, Alberto Vargas—but now I am remembering that he's the new mayor, I either dreamed that or it's true, and all any of us can do is hope that he will do something terrible or scandalous or flat-out crazy so we may always remember who he is and not think we are seeing his picture in a group photo in "The Shining" or starting to read about him in a newspaper that no longer exists and is crumbling in our hands before we can even finish.

The miracle being, perhaps, that an editor at the *New York Times* understood the sensibility behind those lines. Or pretended to, in the spirit of bicoastalism. Or caught on that a story was breaking out West that might not be understood until it was too late in the East Coast news day to report it. There's about that much connection left between Los Angeles and the commercially attentive outer world: They get that we're closer than they are to the vortex.

That isn't to say that visionary writing never happens back East. You hear sometimes of people in New York City who've dreamed. Colson Whitehead's *The Intuitionist* created a world of elevator maintenance that merged into the metaphysics of race and ascendance. Bernard Malamud concocted a talking Jewbird, and Paul Auster wrote about a vaudevillian runaway learning to levitate. I also think I see a parallel in Ben Katchor's "Julius Knipl,

Real Estate Photographer" cartoons: the dream-time back alleys, the almost plausible wholesale signage (Mortal Coil Mattresses), the vaguely theosophical insomnia clubs, with marathon lectures and fluorescent lights up bright.

But the origin of those dreams always turns out to be some fixed point in the definable past: the industrial age, the melting pot, the gothic South.[3] Those writers don't actually step outside time. They don't gaze into eternity for a living—although the Mojave wind may shift in their direction from time to time. "But what is the meaning of this?" John Cheever asked in his diary, freaking out while writing "The Swimmer" (a 1964 short story that some magical-realism fans claim as MR). "One does not grow old in the space of an afternoon. Oh, well, kick it around."

What's unique here is as near as Salvador Plascencia's mythic lettuce pickers in El Monte, and Ry Cooder's aural ghosts of Chávez Ravine. Playwright José Rivera, in *Cloud Tectonics*, posited a Mexican hitchhiker who'd been pregnant for two years. "The stories my grandparents told me," explains Plascencia, "were like Steinbeck, but with magic and witches."

Whether Latino or not, LA's literary visions always struck me as incestuously unique—a pidgin of images that simply couldn't have been composed anyplace else. Joy Nicholson says she hosted foreign guests at her Silver Lake apartment, first-time visitors who marveled from the picture window: "It's so ugly! It's so beautiful!" (They also refused bus directions to the Getty Museum—"We'll just walk"—a visual that could inspire a jungle novel all its own.) Ugly beauty is why LA's fabulist literature, even if better than the rest of the country's, will never *be* the country's, unless LA's strangeness fades out first. Here, when Francesca Lia Block confronts oleanders, they "look like cigarette cherries," and an anorexic character has "hip bones like part of an animal skull." Here, Kate Braverman's junkies accuse the surf with their tears, and the waves grow spines. Beauty and barrenness are inseparable, as every Angeleno instinctively knows them to be. Nicholson describes in an e-mail how she used to walk into the desert after dark, daring death: "I'd heard there were bikers and killers and freaks there, and I wondered if they would find me, and if I might come to a bad end with them. . . . I just wanted to know if I would snap out of my numbness. . . . (Obviously I wanted my father to rescue me—so I put myself in the "driest, worst desert" again and again—to see if he would come through. I guess maybe I was waiting for an Oasis to come to me.)"[4] For me, it was always man-made lakes—starting with the guitar-shaped pond in Encino behind the mystical Thriftimart "T." But I'm not alone there, either. Joan Didion invoked the same location in *Play It as It Lays*. Erickson's *Our Ecstatic Days* made LA's improbable lakes the very image of breaking through to the other side. And when my novel's protagonist swoons for lost paradise, he swoons lakeside. He swoons thinking about rounding a certain bend on Mulholland Drive, where time peels away, leaving in its place one of those fenced, forbidden vistas—a cobalt blue reservoir in the lap of a canyon a half-mile across. Wholeness, temptation, and loss, in a single glance. He swoons because alongside the Encino reservoir, the hills seem to stare directly into Utah, and because even when living in Los Angeles you long for it a little, as if it can never be your city altogether.

Of course, if you're a writer who depends on staring into Utah from Encino, you get used to some uneven results. What you don't expect is to keep bumping into other writers in their sleeping gowns. You don't expect to keep finishing each other's dreams. In the first short story I ever sold, a young heir to a swimming-pool business gets lost in Death Valley looking for a chapter president of the Lainie Kazan Fan Club. In Block's first book, from about the same time, a young guy stumbles upon a covenly chapter of the Jayne Mansfield Fan Club. In Sherrill's first novel, after a car crash in the desert, a reporter stumbles upon the ghosts of film stars at a hotel pool; in Plascencia's, a lettuce picker has his way with Rita Hayworth.

Stephen Cooper, who wrote the reissued biography of John Fante, *Full of Life*, was my graduate professor at Cal State Long Beach, and as I was writing this essay, he coined a name for this new school of writing: Southern California Dream Realism. I talked him into driving with me to the desert. I had two reasons: I wanted to chase the ghost of Fante's protagonist, Arturo Bandini, to the spot where he lost his Mayan Princess, and I wanted to talk about Fante's themes generally (fig. 14).

Every Los Angeles writer at the outskirts of vision feels a connection to *Ask the Dust*, the 1939 novel that, more than any other, seems to weep over this city's corpse in the ecstasy of possessing it. ("Los Angeles, give me some of you! Los Angeles come to me the way I came to you, my feet over your streets, you pretty town I loved you so much, you sad flower in the sand, you pretty town."[5]) We all are sufferers. We're not sure, exactly, if the intimacy of our suffering will survive the novel's journey to the big screen, to the masses, to the world. But on the page, it's strictly ours.

FIGURE 14. Original cover of the Stackpole Sons edition of *Ask the Dust* (1939): Arturo, Camilla, Joshua tree. (Courtesy of John Fante Literary Group LLC. Photo by Charles Hood)

Cooper's history with *Ask the Dust* is even more personal. "I was seeking to fill that absence that I didn't even consciously know defined me," he says. "And that was the loss of my father. So I would spend my days just mooning around, moving about, like most young writers, haunted by characters, trying to compose them and failing, failing, failing, failing, failing. . . . And then when I came upon *Ask the Dust*, it was a time in my life when I was living with every pore open to possibility."

Living, in other words, like Bandini himself, who finally writes his look-at-me novel, only to hurl it to the sands where his goddess went mad. "He's gotten what he wanted, in terms of having written the book . . . to be on the shelf next to the big guys. But desire is such that it outlives its fulfillment. And so he must desire something else. . . . It turns to dust, doesn't it, the fulfillment of desire. So getting what you want is, if you will, just a beginning of the eternal and unattainable story of desire."

The ethnic tension between Fante's lovers (an Italian and a Latina) was exquisite too, and Fante tried to turn up the heat under the LA melting pot in an unfinished novel titled *The Little Brown Brothers*, full of romantic impossibility in, among other places, a Wilmington cannery. But editors, Cooper says, misread the work as racist, and it was shelved.

"So we don't know how he would have worked this out. John knew how to cuss people out, but everything he wrote proves that he was doing his best to negotiate this core aspect of our culture. In fact, the only person I ever showed *The Little Brown Brothers* to—because I'm such a Boy Scout about all this—is Philippe Garnier, who translated *Ask the Dust* into French. And Philippe said, 'Oh, this must be published!'"

"Now I'm thinking," Cooper proposes, "what if X number of your visionary writers—I'm just riffing now—but what if Steve Erickson read these hundred pages? What if, name your 10 writers, they could respond however they wanted to? What if sixty years later, a group of writers read this and—not to finish it, but to take up the vision however they wanted to?"

I ask if the tensions in the book still read fresh today.

"Well, yeah. As fresh as they will remain until the republic is a cinder."

Joshua Tree, after we've parked, is disarmingly still. We climb over some boulders from the dawn of time, throw pebbles across a chasm, hear them strike. It's the kind of emptiness, behind the mirage, that makes you forget what you came for, or what people back in the city are writing for—not a bad place, all in all, to hurl a manuscript.

But minutes later, it happens—one of those desert-vision ruptures of reality. Outside a convenience store in Yucca Valley—graveyard to Robert Stone's dying soldier protagonist—beside the monster trucks and SUVs, a half-dozen marines in camouflage lounge atop an armored jeep, materialized but ghostly. They look a little like the plastic troops from *Toy Story*. You can see them with your mind's eye, and you can hit them with a stone; they move in slow motion through the liquor-deli traffic. It's like the scene in *The Day of the Locust* in which actors in period costumes improbably collide, or the back-lot earthquake in *The Last Tycoon*, with marooned extras, jungle backdrops and schooners interposed "like the torn storybooks of childhood," or the scene in . . . well, never mind. Robert Stone would have known what to say about it.

For now, though, I'm left, along with my protagonist, still peering into that Sherman Oaks pantry that started me writing. And I don't know if it's the future or the past that pulls me. I don't know if my real home is in the time capsule that LA's early hopes were stowed in or just outside the capsule's door, in the world that has vanished around it.

Maybe Southern California Dream Realism is just the ultimate extension of anybody else's literary mode—a way of seeing life stripped of time's pretense. It's a manner of always seeing the terminal desert from the depths of the paradise dream, or paradise from the stretches of life's dry march.

I do know that in our past, in the dark of that pantry, I see the East Coast. Some remnant of ancestry, a quaint hope of continuity, a proper burial gone wrong—Waugh's mortuary. I see how fooled my childhood was by every architectural simulation of history.

But I don't know what happens to a civilization, and a literature, that grows up alongside the constant vision of dust. Does the rest of the country even make sense to us here? Was all this aftermath built in from the start? Even the apocalypse, in Los Angeles, feels like history now, the erasures of paradise barely detectable, the age of visions five minutes from over.

That is one scenario for where LA literature is heading. Then there is Francesca Lia Block's view, which she offers in an unpunctuated e-mail: "life/death magic/reality young/old spirit/body masculine/feminine the walls seem to be dissolving and the worlds blending."[6] In other words, "Paradise Next."

I was stuck in traffic on Olympic Boulevard recently, at the last of sundown, heading east through Century City, and I had one of those feelings you get in a city that you now only visit—a city that is no longer the same place where you grew up. The people were strangers. They seemed wealthier and more cosmopolitan, and multinational, and they suffered and sighed separately in their mostly beautiful cars. The cheap apartments I'd once rented near UCLA now cost fortunes, and the sandlot meridians on Little Santa Monica Boulevard were landscaped, and everything porous and unfinished about this place—all the sweet neglect that once paid off in untold ways—had been finally built over. I wasn't sure if I would ever live in Los Angeles proper again, and my fear is that eventually no one here will think much about oasis and dust, paradise and exile.

Sherrill e-mails me in twenty-point type: "Sadly, postapocalyptic LA will just have to grow old like everywhere else."[7]

But it's always, somewhere, Los Angeles in the 1940s. That sunset in the rearview mirror, past the traffic jam: the cherry of a cigarette, an oleander red.

And think of the next, next generation. Think of Salvador Plascencia's El Monte—where the culture recedes and the lost things survive: the gangs and lettuce pickers, and the elements of milk and oranges and moths, cracked radiators, pollen and sunburns, and lovemaking and coil mattresses, and a ghost of Rita Hayworth. If you want dreams, go to the city's innermost edges. Go where the orphans and outcasts are.

Notes

1. A slightly different version of this essay appeared as the cover story in *Los Angeles Times Magazine,* November 13, 2005, and in Alan Rifkin, *Burdens by Water: An Unintended Memoir* (Long Beach: Brown Paper Press, 2015).

This and all other personal quotations are from recorded interviews excerpted in my "Soul Survivor," and "Writing in the Dust."

2. When a mom dives into the vortex to recover her lost son, her voice becomes a river of type that bisects each of the next 231 pages, then rejoins the text when she's back, sucking air—a typographical stunt so exacting that, rather than try to replicate it, Simon and Schuster opted to publish a JPEG image of Erickson's original manuscript.

3. "The only [other] place I can imagine it happening in this country is in the South," says Erickson. "Because in a way you could argue that the novels of Faulkner provided a basis for the fabulism that came out of South America. That whole idea of a mythical county, with mythical people. The stories aren't

fabulist, but there's certainly enough psychosis in them to push them into the realm of the surreal. . . . I just think that cities like New York or Chicago are too impenetrable to allow for the kind of breakdown that makes for fabulism. There's something about the porousness of LA's identity."

4. Nicholson, e-mail correspondence with author, September 2005 e-mail.

5. Claremont McKenna professor Jay Martin has pointed out that what W. H. Auden called "West's Disease"—an LA collision of foolishness, desire, and illusion named after Nathanael West—could just as well have been named after Fante.

6. Block, e-mail correspondence with author, September 2005.

7. Sherrill, e-mail correspondence with author, 2005.

Works Cited

Auden, W. H. "West's Disease." In *Nathanael West: A Collection of Critical Essays*, edited by Jay Martin, 147. Englewood Cliffs, NJ: Prentice-Hall, 1971.

Braverman, Kate, et al. "L.A. Lit (Does It Exist?): A Symposium." *Los Angeles Times*, April 25, 1999. http://articles.latimes.com/1999/apr/25/books/bk-30726.

Braverman, Kate. *Lithium for Medea*. New York: Seven Stories Press, 1979.

Cheever, John. "Journals: from the Sixties: A Writer's Notes on His Family, His Writing, and America." *New Yorker*, January 21, 1991. https://www.newyorker.com/magazine/1991/01/21/from-the-sixties-i.

Fante, John. *Ask the Dust*. New York: Ecco, 2006.

Fitzgerald, F. Scott. *The Last Tycoon*. 1941. New York: Scribner, 1988.

Klein, Norman M. *The History of Forgetting: Los Angeles and the Erasure of Memory*. 1997. New York: Verso, 2008.

Plascencia, Salvador. *The People of Paper*. San Francisco: McSweeney's, 2005.

Rifkin, Alan. "Soul Survivor," *Buzz Magazine*, April 1993. http://www.steveerickson.org/articles/soul.html.

———. "Writing in the Dust," *Los Angeles Times Magazine*, November 3, 2005. http://articles.latimes.com/2005/nov/13/magazine/tm-lit46

Smith, Dinitia. "Writing Frankly, Young-Adult Author Pushes Limits." *New York Times*, February 23, 2005. http://www.nytimes.com/2005/02/23/books/writing-frankly-youngadult-author-pushes-limits.html.

Stone, Robert. *Dog Soldiers*. New York: Houghton Mifflin Harcourt, 1973.

Wagner, Bruce. "L.A. Existential." *New York Times*, May 23, 2005. http://www.nytimes.com/2005/05/23/opinion/la-existential.html.

How Hitler Nearly Destroyed the Great American Novel

Ryan Holiday

There are horror stories about what can go wrong on release day, and then there is the story of John Fante. There has always been a rich genre of heartbreaking tales of *what could have been*—from albums released on September 11 to sculptures destroyed in transit—and then there is the novel *Ask the Dust*, a book whose tragic bad luck is spoken of in hushed tones—passed from writer to writer and repeated endlessly by critics and journalists—as the ultimate publishing nightmare.

The fact that a brilliant work would not be appreciated in its time is not, in and of itself, a remarkable event. But the nearly unbelievable (and up until now, largely unconfirmed) *how* of *Ask the Dust*—released in 1939 and now widely considered a sort of West Coast *Gatsby* though it did not begin to find its audience until the early 1980s as Fante, by then blind and a double amputee, lay dying of diabetes—was not some inexplicable, unavoidable force majeure. It was not ill-health or racism or hubris. It was something much more specific. It was something with a face and a name. Really just one name, in fact.

Hitler.

While the list of artists and writers victimized by the Nazis is long—from Stefan Zweig to Felix Nussbaum and a host of other "degenerates"—few of them were first-generation Italian immigrants living and writing books in sunny Southern California. Very few of those tragedies were rendered through a decision by a US Federal Court. And of course, none of them was ultimately redeemed by a chance encounter on the shelves of the Los Angeles Public Library nearly a half century later.

What follows, then, is one of strangest sagas in all of publishing—perhaps in all of art. It is a story of greed and stupidity, of bad timing and eventual vindication. Ultimately, it's the story of how some of the "finest fiction ever written in America" managed to triumph over undeniable evil.[1] And it's one that deserves the consideration of every creator, every publisher, every copyright attorney, and, as it looms ever larger, of anyone involved in the debate of what it means to #NoPlatform offensive and hateful speech.

The Truth Is Always Stranger Than Fiction

It does not seem that Houghton Mifflin—which had been a publishing powerhouse since the late 1800s—ever considered *not* publishing the dictated prison memoirs of the rising Austrian politician. Adolf Hitler had published *Mein Kampf*—a shortened version of its original title, *Viereinhalb Jahre (des Kampfes) gegen Lüge, Dummheit und Feigheit* ("A four-and-one-half year struggle against lies, stupidity and cowardice")—in 1925, in part to pay off his legal fees and fund his political ambitions. It was a steady seller in Germany as his political fortunes rose, increasingly becoming a book of international interest.

After seeking approval from its board, Houghton Mifflin's editors set out to acquire *Mein Kampf* just two months after the Reichstag fire gave Hitler the pretext for seizing dictatorial powers in Germany. The company, with its history of snagging lucrative exclusives on overseas political books, was the perfect partner for Eher-Verlag, the publishing house controlled by Hitler in Germany. The two houses, one in Boston, one in Munich, quickly reached an agreement for an exclusive license which, at the then-standard royalty rate of 15 percent, would have paid Hitler roughly 50 cents per copy. The publication announcement for *My Battle* (as Houghton Mifflin titled their first edition of *Mein Kampf*) on July 13, 1933, exhibits Houghton Mifflin director Roger Scaife's flair for hyperbolic publicity: "For the first time the German Dictator speaks to the American people. In the form of an autobiography, he tells the stirring story of the growth of an idea from the beginnings to the proportions of a great national movement and his own meteoric rise."

To publish an author who had already begun to push the world to the brink of war was controversial, even in the mid-1930s. So too was Houghton Mifflin's decision to publish a version of *Mein Kampf* that omitted some of Hitler's darkest rants about Jews, edits made by Nazi agents who hoped the abridged edition would make his views more palatable overseas.

What explains this? It's only slightly uncharitable to suggest there may have been ideological sympathies between Hitler and the leadership at Houghton Mifflin at the time. The advance copy Roger Scaife sent to President Franklin Delano Roosevelt included a note apprising him of recent objections to the use of Houghton Mifflin–published textbooks in New York City schools: "In confidence I may add that we have had no end of trouble over the book—protests from the Jews by the hundreds, and not all of them from the common run of shad . . . . although I am glad to say that a number of intellectual Jews have also written complimenting us upon the stand we have taken."[2]

This was important for FDR to know, Scaife concluded, due to the "number of . . . individuals from this race who hold important posts under your Administration." In a note that accompanied a complimentary copy of the book, Scaife explained to Hitler in October 1933 that, despite strong opposition, Houghton Mifflin had "nevertheless, persisted in our plans, and we believe that the actual publication of the book will result in wide discussion and, we hope, in satisfactory sale."[3] FDR, who had also read the book in its original German, took the time to write inside his prepublication copy of *My Battle*, "this translation is so expurgated as to give a wholly false view of what Hitler is or says."[4]

The truth was, most Americans had interests outside of German politics in 1933—not least the Great Depression, which was then in its fifth year. There would eventually be enough Nazis in New York City to fill Madison Square Garden—which they did, for the now infamous German American Bund Rally in 1939. But in 1933, *Mein Kampf* had sold just 4,633 copies in the United States (compared to worldwide sales of roughly 1 million copies, mostly in Germany, since publication). By 1937, sales had slowed to 1,723 copies in the United States. (Meanwhile, newlyweds and soldiers in Germany were given free copies at the expense of the state. The German government also forgave Hitler's tax debt on the copies he had sold before taking office.)

In the fall of 1938, as appeasement reigned in Europe and the Munich Agreement gave Hitler the concessions needed to annex Czechoslovakia, American interest in his book began to spike. Between September and October 1938, *Mein Kampf* sold more copies than it had in all of 1934. In the end, American sales in 1938 eclipsed all the previous years combined. Hitler had already sold millions of copies in Germany, but now he was a bestseller in the free world.

It wasn't simply his overseas exploits driving sales. Houghton Mifflin moved aggressively to promote the book, increasing accessibility with a lower-priced mass-market edition. The new edition included a blurb from Dorothy Thompson, an American journalist who had been expelled from Nazi Germany. "As a liberal and democrat I deprecate every idea in this book," she wrote. "The reading of this book is a duty for all who would understand the fantastic era in which we live, and particularly it is the duty of all who cherish freedom, democracy and the liberal spirit. Let us know what it is that challenges our civilization."[5]

Initially, Hitler's representatives were not pleased with the branding changes, and demanded an explanation and improvements. The managing editor for Houghton Mifflin attempted to placate their German business partners in a letter, explaining the publisher's logic. "The sales of the book in the original printing had not been up to our expectations, and we believed that a new promotion effort, of which this jacket is an important part, was desirable in order to secure for the book the distribution that its importance unquestionably deserved," Ira Rich Kent wrote to Arthur Teele, the lawyer for the German consulate in Boston, in March 1937.[6] Kent turned out to be right, and the increased sales—some 14,000 in 1938—flattered Hitler's vanity enough to satisfy him.

Perhaps by then the book had already served his purposes and was no longer a priority. Having earned millions from sales at home and across Europe, perhaps he was too busy and rich to keep track of the book's progress. But this was no longer simply a book by a charismatic international politician. In the years since Houghton Mifflin first published Hitler in the United States in 1933, he had gone from legitimately elected German chancellor to, after the Reichstag fire, dictator. A year later, the Night of the Long Knives purged the country of most of his political enemies. In 1935, the Nuremberg Laws excluded Jews from citizenship. By 1937 and 1938, Hitler's designs on Austria were in the air.

Likely in response to the rising criticism of their association with Hitler, and the poor optics of their highly sanitized first edition, Houghton Mifflin began negotiations with translators for the full manuscript of *Mein Kampf*, which would, for the first time, leave out nothing.

Wrong Place, Wrong Time

In 1938, John Fante, an ambitious twenty-nine-year-old son of an Italian immigrant—whose writing had kept him only a meal or two from starvation up until that point—published his first book, *Wait Until Spring, Bandini*, with the small firm Stackpole Sons. It is a beautiful novel that first introduced what would become a recurring character in most of Fante's books: Arturo Bandini. Based largely on Fante himself, Bandini had endured intense anti-Italian bigotry from his fellow Americans; he was egotistical and delusional and hilarious; and like his creator, he was an aspiring novelist. Fante's novels mix desperation and hubris, hope and pain; they are somehow uniquely American in their optimism. The same year *Bandini* was published, an optimistic Fante began floating the idea of a sequel to his editor at Stackpole, William Soskin. That idea would become *Ask the Dust*, an ode to love and Los Angeles.

As 1938 came to a close, Soskin wrote to let Fante know that he and General Edward Stackpole Jr., a World War I hero and owner of the publishing house, very much wanted to publish the book. "With the obstacles and difficulties of a first novel fairly successfully over," he wrote, "and with a considerable reputation established," expectations for the book were high. "The market will be receptive," he went on, "and they will believe everything we tell them. So it looks like fairly clear sailing." To Fante, who had lived in crippling poverty all his life, it was the closing words that would have landed most encouragingly: "The very best Christmas wishes to you, and may you be filthy rich next year."[7]

It appears that Soskin, like so many editors, was at least partly telling his author what he wanted to hear. Though *Wait Until Spring, Bandini* had been well-received by critics, it was not a smashing success. The idea that the market was clamoring for a second Fante novel was probably wishful thinking, and the advance Soskin offered for *Ask the Dust* reflected this, at some $800 (about $14,300 in today's dollars). It was, in the house's estimation, enough to cover Fante for the four months it should take to write the book.

It didn't take much for Soskin to convince Fante that he was destined for greatness. Arturo Bandini, his fictional alter ego, already knew it. This was a character who already saw himself on the shelves next to Dreiser and Mencken as he haunted the library fantasizing about his place in the literary pantheon. "Hya Dreiser, Hya Mencken," Bandini imagines saying in *Ask the Dust*, "Hya, hya: there's a place for me, too, and it begins with B, in the B shelf, Arturo Bandini, make way for Arturo Bandini . . . old Arturo Bandini, one of the boys."[8]

It happens that even as Soskin was writing to Fante, he was simultaneously in hot pursuit of another egotistical and often delusional author—the very same one Houghton Mifflin had been publishing since 1933. Because Adolf Hitler had renounced his Austrian citizenship in 1925, he listed himself as a "stateless German" when copyrighting *Mein Kampf* that same year. This technicality was one of Stackpole Sons' justifications for publishing an author already with another publishing house; under the US Copyright Act of 1909, the book was in the public domain. Better yet, an edition of *Mein Kampf* that did not enrich its despicable author the way the earlier Houghton Mifflin edition was doing would provide an attractive alternative at a time when Americans were attempting to understand the growing threat in Europe. Publishing it was basically a public service . . . and free money.

Approaching—perhaps attempting to poach—the very translators Houghton Mifflin was negotiating with for their new unabridged edition of *My Struggle*, Soskin and Stackpole revealed their plans to enter the market that Houghton Mifflin believed they legally controlled. In his fascinating and definitive paper on the publishing of *Mein Kampf* in the United States, Professor Donald Lankiewicz of Emerson College writes of Houghton Mifflin's quick moves to block intruders from interfering with their exclusive hold on the book. Hitler's agents were notified in Berlin and help was requested to curtail Stackpole's effort. Lankiewicz speaks of a heavy-handed call from Henry Laughlin, president of Houghton Mifflin, to General Stackpole to dissuade him from publishing his edition of *Mein Kampf*. It would be highly "unethical" to interfere with Houghton Mifflin's copyright, Laughlin said, and Stackpole would incur serious losses if Houghton Mifflin and Hitler's claims were upheld in court.[9]

Showing far more spine than most of Europe had shown toward Germany's gangster tactics, General Stackpole proceeded anyway. But the effect was almost immediately felt on the publisher's other titles, including *Ask the Dust*. "You must think me a complete louse," Stackpole publicist Katharine Theobald wrote to Fante in January 1939, explaining that the "MEIN KAMPF business" had delayed her response to a marketing inquiry from Fante.[10] After being uncharacteristically out of touch for over a month himself, Fante's editor Bill Soskin wrote, "You will forgive me, I know, because these days I have not time nor thought nor energy for anything but communion with Adolf of Munich" (fig. 15).[11]

Early 1939 found both houses, Houghton Mifflin and Stackpole, racing to get their competing unabridged editions to market and, on February 28, 1939, both did. According to *Cabinet Magazine*, Houghton Mifflin's edition sold 30,000 copies in the first month.[12] Stackpole's edition billed itself as unauthorized with the prominent tagline "This Edition Pays No Royalty to Adolf Hitler." (This practice led to a sharp rebuke from *The New Yorker*, which took issue with Stackpole "getting out of paying royalties to any author, even on the noblest grounds.")[13]

It too sold well. Houghton Mifflin, in partial response to the marketing of its new competition, promised to donate "profits" from the unabridged version to refugee charities—charities aiding those who'd been displaced by the author, who would continue collecting royalties.

Houghton Mifflin's threats against Stackpole had not been idle; their obligations to Hitler all but required them to pursue legal action to defend their copyright. In January 1939, just before the unabridged versions were released, Houghton Mifflin, splitting the legal costs with Hitler's publishing house, sued Stackpole Sons in a US Federal Court. It's a remarkable occurrence that rewrites the early history of World War II: Hitler's first real

STACKPOLE SONS
PUBLISHERS

WILLIAM SOSKIN

250 PARK AVENUE, NEW YORK CITY

February 1, 1939

My dear Fante:

    You will forgive me, I know, because these days I have not time nor thought nor energy for anything but communion with Adolf of Munich. If we can ever get clear of the lawyers and sheriffs, that Kampf of his will be a sensation.

    First, I must tell you that I thought Carey McWilliams' manuscript an elegant job and that I also thought there was no use in our publishing it because it is so definitely a sectional presentation. I realize that its implications are wide sociologically, but try to tell that to the bookstores. I was delighted about his appointment. For many years, ever since he contributed pieces regularly to my book pages on the EVENING POST, I have held him in high regard and he has seemed to me one of a few intact people, so that there is no lack of good will that decides us in this matter. I would hate to publish such a book and then encourage his displeasure because of its commercial failure.

    I talked about you at Columbia the other night. I gave a lecture to a lot of pathetically aspiring journalists and writers on the relationship among editors, publishers and authors. And you seemed to me a superbly horrible example. However, I seemed not to have concealed some fundamental liking or affection or something because all the talk after the lecture was express curiosity and interest in you. I gave them a taste of your new novel in a very vague outline, with the thought that they will all look forward to an important writer in the Fall. We are going to do that sort of thing systematically this year because I think the trade will be prepared to receive you handsomely then. I am hoping, too, that the new book will be successful enough to excite interest in BANDINI once more. I am rather pleased that it is still selling after the Christmas holidays. Damn few books are able to pick up that way, but the Chicago and San Francisco breaks helped considerably.

    Do shoot along some of the ASK THE DUST manuscript when you have about 10,000 words. I am most eager.

    I have written to Mervyn LeRoy and I will let you know if anything happens.

    Love and kisses.

    Bill Soskin

Mr. John Fante
3313 Temple Avenue
Los Angeles, California

FIGURE 15. Letter from William Soskin to John Fante, February 1, 1939. (Courtesy of John Fante Literary Group and UCLA Library Special Collections.)

FIGURE 16. The unexpurgated, unauthorized Stackpole Sons edition of *Mein Kampf*, 1939.

battle against an American veteran actually began a full two years before the United States declared war on Germany, and he was aided by the publishing house that had brought us Ralph Waldo Emerson and Henry David Thoreau (as well as providing, to this day, textbooks to millions of school children) (fig. 16).

Despite the brisk sales of both editions—11,500 copies for Stackpole in just a few months—the legal costs of this battle were significant. We can imagine the drain on an independent publisher like Stackpole Sons was far greater than it was on Houghton Mifflin. It was not a simple case, ultimately involving several appeals and higher courts. Houghton Mifflin's earliest attempt for an injunction against Stackpole's edition in February 1939 had been denied, with the judge finding that Stackpole "raised questions of title and validity as to plaintiff's copyrights which were not free from doubt, and that the issues could not properly be determined on affidavits."[14] But surviving summary judgment was hardly a victory for Stackpole, since it only delayed the inevitable.

In June 1939, Stackpole's number came up. Judge Charles Edward Clark handed down the first of the rulings in Hitler's favor, dismissing Stackpole's novel claim to *Mein Kampf* by asserting that a stateless person is in fact "entitled to the benefits of the American copyright laws." Nor was the court swayed by the public's right to read and understand Hitler's works without actively supporting his ambitions with their wallets. "Under the circumstances of entire absence of title or right in the defendants," Clark wrote in his decision, "their claim that the equities are in their favor—that they are engaged in a service of great social value in thus publishing this book—seems indeed bold."[15]

Twelve weeks before Hitler's tanks rolled into Poland, his propaganda offensive was winning its first legal victories under US Federal Law, aided by a publisher, Houghton Mifflin, who profited from every newspaper headline and radio denunciation of the German dictator. In late October 1939, as the Nazis began deporting Jews from newly captured territories, the US Supreme Court denied Stackpole's petition to hear the case.

In 1940, as British forces fought their way out of disaster at Dunkirk and as France surrendered to the Nazis, Stackpole continued to fight a desperate legal battle to prove that Houghton Mifflin's contract with Hitler might somehow be invalid and thus undermine their ability to enforce it. Like the armies of France, Denmark, Norway, and the Netherlands, this effort was doomed to failure. In 1941, as Operation Barbarossa was commencing—Germany's reckless invasion of Russia—Hitler took a moment to confirm through his publishing operation that in fact he had authorized Houghton Mifflin as his agents, thus validating the contract. On August 7, 1941, the court made its final ruling against Stackpole. In September, it announced damages.

Enjoined from selling any more copies of *Mein Kampf*, Stackpole was out not only their legal fees—Houghton Mifflin's fees were $23,000, and we can assume Stackpole's were similar—but also the cost of translating and printing the thousands of copies that already had been produced. The judgment later required the house to pay Houghton Mifflin—and indirectly, Hitler—some $15,250 in proceeds from the copies that had been sold.

Victory was complete. The bad guys had won.

Why Did Ask the Dust Fail?

The legend of John Fante has held that the legal battle with Hitler over *Mein Kampf* bankrupted his publisher and prevented the world from recognizing Fante's brilliance in his own time. In an otherwise brilliant essay appearing in the *Boston Review* in 1993, Neil Gordon helped establish that legend when he wrote, "Stackpole Sons was even sued out of existence by Adolf Hitler, for unauthorized publication of *Mein Kampf*."[16]

Like all legends, much of it is contradicted by basic fact.

Stackpole is still in business today as Stackpole Books, and since 1939 has published hundreds if not thousands of books. The legend also misses what's so truly incredible about what did in fact happen: Stackpole Sons wasn't killed by Hitler—*they were kneecapped by an American publisher on his behalf.*

But is this what prevented Fante's classic novel, heralded by William Saroyan at release as an heir to the tradition of Tom Sawyer, from reaching the audience it deserved?

It's less clear than one might suspect.

Stackpole's small print runs of Fante's books, particularly *Bandini*, which was released prior to the publisher's pursuit of *Mein Kampf*, indicates they had relatively low ambitions for the author in the first place. The print run for *Ask the Dust* was only 2,200 copies and was priced 50 cents lower than his previous book.

Judith Schnell, the current publisher of Stackpole Books, explains that this was quite typical for their house at the time: "Stackpole's model was to publish books and put them out there. I don't think there were any huge PR campaigns or publicity campaigns. It wasn't that kind of company and it still isn't that kind of company"—the suggestion being that Fante's marketing budget couldn't have been seriously affected if he didn't have one in the first place.[17]

Nor could he have been deprived of a mass audience if the material was too far ahead of its time and thus unsuitable to such a readership. John Martin, publisher of Black Sparrow Press—the house that would rerelease Fante's books in the early 1980s—would argue that while the lawsuit certainly didn't improve Fante's chances of success, the results were likely to have been the same without it. "You've got to remember that *Bandini* and *Ask the Dust* were published in the depths of the Great Depression. And both are serious literary works rather than novels written for wide circulation."[18]

In other words, it's just as likely that the American public didn't have the appetite for Fante's prose. Fante himself was in no position to support the books by following up immediately with other novels as he spent a fair part of the war working for the Office of Strategic Services. Hitler, of course, was to blame for this latter circumstance, but Stackpole's publication of *Mein Kampf*, less directly so.

Stephen Cooper, Fante's biographer and longtime champion of his work—and the person who encouraged me to dig deep through Fante's archives at UCLA and to scrutinize the Hitler narrative—raises an inconvenient piece of evidence about Fante's second book. "In contrast to the really consistently positive reviews that *Bandini* got, the response to *Ask the Dust* [at the time] was a mix of negative and positive and neutral," Cooper said.[19] Critics can't blame Hitler for why they missed what later generations recognized.

Charles Bukowski, who brought Fante's books to Black Sparrow Press and once called him, in earnest, his "god," explained in an unusual written interview done in 1977 why he believed Fante had failed to reach readers: "See Mozart, Van Gogh, and so forth. It's the angle of the action, the people aren't ready, it's the weather, it's the diet, it's the shoes they wear and most of the people are almost always out of touch with the best and the most real because they never had a chance to know what it is." Counterintuitively, Bukowski argued that the passage of time may have actually been what allowed Fante's groundbreaking work—which featured drugs and sex and wrestled with race—to become more palatable. "The fact that his writing is not of the exact present might remove some of the fear that people have of an outward and direct art-statement."[20]

Yet, each of these explanations has a way of letting everyone off the hook. No author, certainly no artist, who understands the high-wire act of releasing something great into the world, would accept the idea that the books were destined to fail. "You can't say it would have happened anyway. You have to say we don't know. We know for certain it *deserved* to succeed," says Frank Spotnitz, creator of the hit television show *The Man in the High Castle* and producer of a forthcoming documentary about Fante.[21]

Fante was himself asked what he thought happened, almost forty years to the day that Stackpole Sons would first become distracted and delayed in answering his letters. With the benefit of significant distance, but before his resurrection story would become the stuff of myth, Fante explained that just as demand for *Ask the Dust* was picking up, stores began to run out of copies between the first and second printings. He was speaking to a salesman at a bookstore when he finally connected the dots. Hitler. *Mein Kampf*. Stackpole. Copyright law.

"To me, that didn't seem like anything because how could Hitler sue and win a case in the United States?" Fante said in a 1978 interview: "But sue he did and win he did and so they kept pushing this cause célèbre right up through to the Supreme Court and it took over a year and all of the publisher's money, all of the exploitation [promotion] money for their whole season that year, was absorbed by this litigation. And not a word was said about *Ask the Dust*. So it was just canceled out because there were other, more important books to fight for."[22]

Does this hold up? Or is this the wishful thinking of an author whose book was simply ahead of its time? Thanks to Fante's wife, Joyce, we have a definitive answer. Joyce, a meticulous organizer and supporter of her husband's work, kept Fante's royalty statements from Stackpole Sons. Fante's royalty statement from January 21, 1941, shows that as of October 15, 1940, less than a year after the release of *Ask the Dust*, he had earned back nearly half of his $800 advance. At the 20 cents royalty he was paid per copy, this means that in less than 12 months, his book sold roughly 1,600 copies of a 2,200-copy run.

Not only does this confirm Fante's claim that his book was selling well at release, but the numbers contrast starkly with the next two royalty periods, which show *Ask the Dust* selling just fifteen and nineteen copies. Authors simply don't go from selling out the majority of their first printing to selling *no* copies, barring some serious intervening event.

Like a lawsuit from Hitler.

The Gods Taketh, But Also Giveth

It was unquestionably a stroke of bad luck for John Fante to release his novels when he did. "It would almost be funny if it weren't Adolf Hitler,"

Spotnitz said. "And it's so random because John Fante had absolutely nothing to do with the decision. It's a tragic twist of fate that his publisher did this and John Fante was victim."

However, Fante's profound bad luck was counterbalanced by unlikely good luck. His story is not that of Sixto Rodriguez of *Searching for Sugarman* fame, where the unappreciated genius toils away in poverty. In some ways the postwar years were quite good to Fante. True, he didn't write many more novels but his day job as an in-demand screenwriter paid the bills. Fante's earnings allowed him to provide for his family and a large estate in Malibu. In 1952, he wrote a novel called *Full of Life*—which he later would classify as a continuation of the Bandini series—about a struggling writer in Los Angeles with a pregnant wife, a wine-tippling father, and a crumbling house he cannot afford. It was not a very good book, he would come to feel, in part because he had written it for money. But in that, he succeeded: book sales, film rights (the movie adaptation for *Full of Life* starred Judy Holliday and Richard Conte), and serial rights netted him more than $150,000 at a time when the average house in Los Angeles cost $12,000. Between the 1930 and the 1970s Fante worked for such studios as Fox, RKO, MGM, and Warner Brothers, as well as on projects with directors Orson Welles and Dino De Laurentiis. He also sold many short stories to *American Mercury, Atlantic Monthly, Harper's Bazaar,* and *Scribner's*.

According to biographer Stephen Cooper, if Fante held a grudge about anything, it was Hollywood, not publishing. "He had way more bitterness about his Hollywood career," Cooper said. Other novelists, William Faulkner being one, had been tempted by Hollywood and grown to hate it, too—a fact that he and Fante were known to commiserate over at the bar of Musso and Frank's. Fante's novels might not have sold well, but they were published, and the critics were usually kind to them. The vast majority of Fante's screenwriting, as is true for many well-paid hacks, never saw the light of day. In Hollywood, Fante was never in control and despite his large salaries, he was just another writer employed by the studios. Interchangeable. Disposable.

The only difference between Fante and the rest of his now mostly forgotten peers is that the wheel was coming back around on *Ask the Dust*. The copy stocked by the Los Angeles Public Library in downtown Los Angeles appears to have possessed singularly magical powers. Charles Bukowski checked it out and fell in love with it. So did *Los Angeles Times* contributor and poet Ben Pleasants. The screenwriter Robert Towne found Fante while researching at the library for the movie *Chinatown*.

Together, these three men independently recognized the beauty of the prose and each contributed significantly to its rediscovery. Bukowski wrote about Fante in his 1978 novel *Women*. Ben Pleasants interviewed Fante for a number of outlets and interested several publishing houses in the titles. Towne acknowledged the influence of *Ask the Dust* on his screenwriting.

On February 28, 1968, Fante received a letter releasing him from his contractual obligations to Stackpole, the publisher that had discovered him as a novelist but that had also, in tangling with Hitler, complicated his career and set it back by perhaps as much as several decades. In 1977, Fante published his first novel in twenty-five years, *The Brotherhood of the Grape*, which received excellent reviews in the *New York Times* and the *Washington Post*. Robert Towne optioned the movie rights and Francis Ford Coppola liked it enough to publish a large excerpt in his *City* magazine.

Most interesting was the publisher that Fante chose for the book: Houghton Mifflin. Clearly not holding a grudge against the company that may have submarined *Ask the Dust*, Fante's main complaint was that he and his editor didn't become closer while collaborating on the book. It wasn't like the old days, he said, when the publisher and writer actually talked to each other. No correspondence with the General, as there had been at Stackpole. Despite high critical praise, however, the book was not a notable success—though by then, Fante had been let down enough that it didn't seem to get to him.

"I think the one thing that a writer must avoid is bitterness," John Fante told Ben Pleasants in an interview in 1979. "I think it's the one fault that can destroy him. It can shrivel him up. . . . I've fought it all my life." His son, James Fante, looks back on his father's complicated journey with regret and pride: "I'm not naive enough to think good work always wins out in the end. There are plenty of painters who died in Auschwitz. I don't necessarily think there is justice in the world, it's that he had the strength of character not to let it break him."[23] (If only Fante, who often saw his own life happening to him as if across the page in a typewriter, could have turned this part of his own heartbreaking and unbelievable story into fiction!)

In 1980, Fante was again in the hands of a small independent publisher, this time one that would deliver on the dreams William Soskin had promised in 1938. John Martin of Black Sparrow Press had been given Fante's novels by Bukowski and Pleasants, and Martin immediately loved them. In 1980 he republished *Ask the Dust*, quickly following up with Fante's other books. In 1982, he published Fante's last book, *Dreams from Bunker Hill*, which Fante, now blind and without legs, dictated to his wife, Joyce, to conclude the Arturo Bandini series.

Since their rediscovery, Fante's books have sold hundreds of thousands of copies in the United States and even more internationally. In France, he has sold more than a half million copies. *Ask the Dust* was turned into a Hollywood movie (sadly, some say) starring Colin Farrell and Salma Hayek. Italy hosts the John Fante Festival in Abruzzo each year. In 2018 alone, BookScan shows Fante moving more copies of *Ask the Dust* than that entire first Stackpole printing. In 2019, the book will celebrate its 80th anniversary and his status as the patron saint of Los Angeles, his adopted city, is indisputable.

If Fante's work had not been preserved in the ash of Hitler's explosion onto the world, if Fante had instead continued to publish novel after novel, who can say whether his books would have survived as such timeless artifacts of the city he loved and the time he inhabited?

In *Ask the Dust*, Fante wrote: "Los Angeles, give me some of you! Los Angeles come to me the way I came to you, my feet over your streets, you pretty town I loved you so much, you sad flower in the sand, you pretty town." In 2010, the City of Los Angeles officially named the intersection of Fifth Street and Grand Avenue "John Fante Square." Twenty-seven years after his death, in a downtown Los Angeles transformed by condos and new businesses and a renaissance of young writers and artists, Fante was given the love he had cried out for so earnestly in 1939.

Mein Kampf, *Backlist Bestseller*

In December 1941, when the United States finally declared war on Nazi Germany, the Trading with the Enemy Act of 1917 came back into effect, ending Houghton Mifflin's relationship with Hitler and his agents. Up until then Houghton Mifflin had been deducting from the firm's taxable revenues its share of the costs of the legal battles to protect the book—including an additional case involving future US Senator Alan Cranston (California), who had published an anti-Nazi tabloid version of *Mein Kampf* said to have sold more than a half million copies. In 1942, the year in which the *New Republic* published some of the first serious reporting on Nazi concentration camps, the US government seized roughly $30,000 in royalties from Houghton Mifflin that would have otherwise made its way overseas to the coffers of the dictator the Allies were now attempting to destroy.[24]

The news was not as upsetting to Houghton Mifflin as one might suspect. Not only had they already sold hundreds of thousands of copies of *Mein Kampf* by 1942, they were now free from the shackles of their former murderous business partner. No longer limited by any editorial constraints from Germany, Houghton Mifflin began work on a third edition to be translated by Ralph Manheim. Released in October 1943, the *New York Times* observed that the edition was a public service which, for the first time, rendered "Hitler's prose almost as unreadable in English as it is in German."[25]

The book was again a cash cow for both Houghton Mifflin and the US government during the war, and later became so for the Justice Department which, after closing the Office of Alien Property Custodian, continued to seize the author's royalties amounting to some $139,393. The relationship between Houghton Mifflin, the US government, and *Mein Kampf* continued until 1979 when, after some negotiation in October of that year, Houghton Mifflin purchased the rights fully from the Justice Department for less than $40,000. Between 1979 and 2000, Houghton Mifflin continued to sell *Mein Kampf* while retaining all net revenues, which a bombshell report from *U.S. News and World Report* estimated to be between $300,000 and $700,000.[26]

Only after public fallout from the revelation of quietly profiting from perhaps the most toxic book ever published—and aggressively defending its right to do so—did Houghton Mifflin finally announce in 2000 the donation of any post-1979 profits from *Mein Kampf* to Holocaust-related charities.

With the recent rise in the United States of the alt-right and its assorted provocateurs, the concept of #NoPlatform has become popular with progressive activists and critics. Inside the publishing industry, there has been debate over whether to #NoPlatform incendiary figures like Milo Yiannopoulos. Yiannopoulos's autobiography was ultimately cancelled by Simon and Schuster, though not before authors such as Roxane Gay returned advances and moved to other publishers. (Yiannopoulos's self-published book still reportedly sold over 100,000 copies on Amazon.) Despite this, there has not been much reflection about publishing's past, or even current, enabling of such figures.

It's an urgent but impossible-to-answer question to ponder: Could World War II have been prevented had more Americans seen in advance the full evil of Hitler's blueprint for destruction and domination? Reflecting on *Mein Kampf*, Winston Churchhill would call it a "new Koran of faith and war: turgid, verbose, shapeless, but pregnant with its message."[27] Could the Stackpole Sons edition have helped enable Americans to realize earlier that the book was a dangerous work of propaganda, and that every cent made off of its evil words—whether it went into Hitler's pocket or not—was stained with blood?

Should Hitler have been #NoPlatformed? Or could *more* platform—as Houghton Mifflin continues to provide for future generations—have alerted the world to his plans before it was too late? That is the question.

Nearly all publishers involved in the dispute over *Mein Kampf* tried, in one form or another, to argue that their interest in the book was motivated by the desire to increase public awareness, rather than by profits. Even today, the Houghton Mifflin edition—currently ranked on Amazon at 11,000 and listing for $23.99—comes with the following publisher's statement: "We cannot permit ourselves the luxury of forgetting the tragedy of World War II or the man who, more than any other, fostered it. *Mein Kampf* must be read and constantly remembered as a specimen of evil demagoguery." It took a number of requests before Houghton Mifflin offered me a statement for this story—understandably so, given that there can be few inquiries less desirable than those regarding your company's working relationship with the Nazis. Declining to answer specific questions, even those relating to John Fante's books, they responded as follows:

> Houghton Mifflin Harcourt's decision to continue printing and disseminating *Mein Kampf* has not been without deep consideration. As a learning company first and foremost, HMH remains steadfast in the belief that, while difficult, the value in making *Mein Kampf* accessible lies in its potential for ongoing education and awareness. By studying the work as a historical artifact, our hope is that we can learn from the atrocities of the past to help create a brighter future. All proceeds from the book are donated to Jewish Family & Children's Services of Greater Boston for direct support of the health and human services needs of Holocaust survivors and their families.

I asked Andrew Wylie—one of the world's leading literary agents with a long track record of selling and securing lucrative foreign rights deals—whether publishers today would dare publish the propagandist memoirs of such strongmen as Vladimir Putin, Kim Jong-un, or Rodrigo Duterte. He replied via e-mail, "They probably would, I'm afraid." When asked the same question, Stephen Cooper told me, "Of course they would, they wouldn't hesitate." And would they move to protect their copyright if another publisher attempted to produce its own edition? Judith Schnell, still helming the ninety-year-old Stackpole Books—which continues to publish books about military history and occasionally even German military history—finds little fault with Houghton Mifflin's 1939 decision. "If that happened today and we had the license and another publisher published a version and didn't have the license to publish…," she said, leaving the hypothetical hanging. "If you have a contract with an author, you're obligated to uphold the terms of the contract."

In 2016, Dr. Christian Hartmann published the first new edition of *Mein Kampf* in Germany since Hitler's death. His scholarly edition, unfortunately available only in German, presents *Mein Kampf* in two volumes with critical commentary on nearly every page—the only ethical way to present a book this toxically dishonest and dangerous, he contends. However, this development has once again turned the book into a bestseller that has gone through at least nine editions. Meanwhile, Houghton Mifflin continues to donate its royalties from the sales of their book—the same unabridged translation they produced in 1943 after being freed of Hitler's editorial input—to Jewish and Holocaust-related charities. In 2017, the company would post revenues of $1.41 billion.

As for John Fante and Stackpole Sons, no reparations were ever made.

A Legacy Lost and Found

"Either the work of John Fante is unknown to you or it is unforgettable. He was not the kind of writer to leave room in between," the *New York Times* critic Janet Maslin wrote in 2002.[28]

I grew up near Roseville, California, where Fante spent a chunk of his life, and I lived in downtown Los Angeles before they named the square after him. I walked the same streets, dreaming the same dreams of becoming a writer and leaving my mark.

At the time Fante was unknown to me. Yet, from the first page I read in *Ask the Dust*, I was hooked and forever changed. It stuns me now to realize how I was nearly deprived of this experience because of, well, Adolf Hitler. To think that Houghton Mifflin, a wonderful publisher of books and textbooks, played a role in that is still to me unbelievable.

"The quality of [*Ask the Dust*] has outlasted all the bullshit and that makes me feel good and that makes my dad feel good," Fante's son, James Fante told me. "Whether he got the recognition while he was alive, I'm not hung up on that and I'm not sure he was either. He had a tremendous amount of confidence about that book. He's not surprised, wherever he is."[29]

Yes, the books did find their audience while Hitler died by his own hand in a concrete bunker, above which now sits an anonymous parking lot. Still, the decision to give a platform to Adolf Hitler nearly came to #NoPlatform one of America's greatest writers, and nearly permanently so. There is a lesson in that, somewhere, I am sure.

It's his biographer, Stephen Cooper, who points out that Fante's is the type of story that sticks with us because it runs from the minutely personal to the sheerly global, from the writer's war to get his novel read to a literal World War: "John Fante was writing this little personal novel about his alter ego who wants to write stories and be in love, and meanwhile the world is about to explode and nations are waiting to invade their neighbors and it's all going to end with the Atom Bomb. It's a spectacularly enigmatic layering of story." It is indeed. One that deserves to be known, so that it is not repeated.

Notes

A slightly different version of this essay was originally published on Medium.com, December 21, 2018, gen.medium.com/how-hitler-nearly-destroyed-the-great-american-novel-ed5f7bb77aeb.

1. Gordon, "Shanghaied in Tinseltown."
2. Quoted in Lankiewicz, "*Mein Kampf*," 15.
3. Lankiewicz, 14.
4. Lankiewicz, 15.

5. *Mein Kampf* (New York: Houghton Mifflin, 1937), dust jacket blurb by *New York Tribune* columnist Dorothy Thompson.
6. Lankiewicz, 18.
7. William Soskin to John Fante, December 20, 1938. John Fante Papers, UCLA Library Special Collections, box 27, folder 7.
8. Fante, *Ask the Dust*, 13.
9. Lankiewicz, 20
10. Katharine Theobald to John Fante, January 16, 1939. John Fante Papers, box 27, file 7.
11. William Soskin to John Fante, February 1, 1939. John Fante Papers, box 27, file 7.
12. Worthington, "Mein Royalties."
13. White and Gibbs, "The Talk of the Town," 15.
14. Judge Charles Edward Clark, "Houghton Mifflin Co. v. Stackpole Sons, Inc., et al. No. 358. Circuit Court of Appeals, Second Circuit, June 9, 1939," Courtlistener.com/opinion/1492918/Houghton-mifflin-co-v-stackpole-sons-inc/.
15. Clark, "Houghton Mifflin."
16. Gordon, "Realization and Recognition."
17. Judith Schnell, interview by author.
18. John Martin, interview by author.
19. Stephen Cooper, interview by author.
20. Pleasants, "When *Ask the Dust* Was Forgotten."
21. Frank Spotnitz, interview by author.
22. Pleasants, "Dust and Fog."
23. James Fante, interview by author
24. Fry, "Massacre of the Jews."
25. Schlamm, "German Best Seller," BR3.
26. Whitman, "Money from a Madman," 55.
27. Churchill, *Second World War*, 1:50.
28. Maslin, "A Truly Famous Unknown Writer," in her review of *The John Fante Reader*, edited by Stephen Cooper.

Works Cited

Churchill, Winston S. *The Second World War*. Boston, MA: Houghton Mifflin Company, 1951.
Fante, John. *Ask the Dust*. Santa Barbara, CA: Black Sparrow Press, 1980.
Fry, Varian. "The Massacre of the Jews." *New Republic*. December 21, 1942, 816–819.

Gordon, Neil, "Realization and Recognition: The Art and Life of John Fante." *Boston Review*. October/November 1993. Reprinted May 23, 2017. bostonreview.net/archives/BR18.5/realandrecog/html.

———. "Shanghaied in Tinseltown." Salon.com, May 12, 2000. www.salon.com/2000/05/12/fante/.

Lankiewicz, Donald. "*Mein Kampf* in America: How Adolf Hitler Came to Be Published in the United States." *Printing History* 20 (July 2016): 3–28.

Maslin, Janet. "A Truly Famous Unknown Writer." *New York Times*, February 28, 2002.

Pleasants, Ben. "The Dust and Fog of LA's Streets: The John Fante Tapes (One)." Interview with John Fante. 3:00 AM Magazine, March 29, 2010. www.3ammagazine.com/3am/the-dust-fog-of-las-streets-the-john-fante-tapes-one/.

———. "When *Ask the Dust* Was Forgotten." *Hollywood Investigator*, March 13, 2006. http://www.hollywoodinvestigator.com/2006/askthedust.htm.

Schlamm, William S. "German Best Seller; *Mein Kampf*. By Adolf Hitler. Translated by Ralph Manheim. 694 pp. Boston: Houghton Mifflin Company. $3.50." *New York Times*, October 17, 1943.

White, E. B., and Wolcott Gibbs, "The Talk of the Town," *New Yorker*, March 11, 1939.

Whitman, David. "Money from a Madman: Houghton Mifflin's *Mein Kampf* Profits." *U.S. News and World Report*, October 16, 2000.

Worthington, Jay. "Mein Royalties," *Cabinet Magazine* 10 (Spring 2003). http://cabinet-magazine.org/issues/10/mein_royalties.es.php.

4. *Ask the Dust* and Its Due: Two Filmmakers and Bukowski Pay Tribute

Interview with Robert Towne

Nathan Rabin

AV CLUB—Can you discuss your relationship with John Fante and his work?
ROBERT TOWNE—Well, it goes back 35 years. It started when I was young and unknown. I hadn't written anything, and nobody had ever heard of me. I think I'd maybe done some rewrite work on *Bonnie and Clyde*. It started because I had written *The Last Detail*, and Jack [Nicholson] and I could not get it made because of the language. People would say that the characters were using language like sailors. 'Cause, you know, they were sailors. That was the whole point, wasn't it? I remember talking to an executive who told me "Bob, wouldn't 20 motherfuckers be more dramatic than 40 motherfuckers?" And I said, "No, they wouldn't." The whole point of the swearing in *The Last Detail* is that it's an expression of powerlessness. It's not Clark Gable cracking wise. These are lifers, and what they do is paradigmatic of all us lifers.

These are people who are struggling to hold onto their jobs, people who do their jobs no matter how distasteful they find them. And they'll

FIGURE 17. The Bunker Hill rooming house where John Fante lived in the early 1930s, basis of Arturo Bandini's beloved Alta Loma Hotel. (From the Arnold Hylen Photograph Collection, courtesy of the California History Room, California State Library, Sacramento, California.)

swear about it and swear about it, but then they'll go ahead and do it. In time we'd get to make the movie, but in the meantime, I saw an article in the *Los Angeles Times* called "Raymond Chandler's L.A." The thing that was really interesting about it was that it was accompanied by these photographs that were taken in the 1970s, but they looked like they could have been taken decades earlier, in the Depression-era '30s and '40s, when Fante's *Ask the Dust* was written. They were of a side of Los Angeles that was rapidly disappearing. I was fascinated by this milieu, and for a variety of reasons, I wanted to use it to tell a detective story. So I was looking for a book or anything that might have been written at the time, or was redolent of that era.

And in my research for it, I stumbled across *Ask the Dust*. And I was amazed, affected deeply by it. It jogged my memory about my own experiences. I know the streets. I know what the fishermen are like. I worked as a commercial fisherman. I knew the little brown brothers who emigrated from Mexico. I knew there were memories that had all been lost, and now the book itself was making me remember these things I didn't even know I knew. And add to that a young writer in Los Angeles coming here to make his fame and fortune, and he's obsessed and narcissistic, self-absorbed, manic-depressive, insecure, like all of us who write, sitting in a room alone, feeling like the world was going by him and along with it all of its experiences. He's thinking that what he's doing is kind of crazy. So I related to it right there and then. There's his obsession with this Mexican waitress. There were all of these things that just made the book seem so much more personal to me than I had any idea it could. So I determined, before I even wrote to Jack [Nicholson], "I'm gonna try and go meet this guy [John Fante] and see if he's alive and still writing." I think my agent or somebody ran into him, and he was living with his family in kind of a curmudgeonly retirement.

He was a very angry little man who felt that he had been roundly ignored by life. He was pissed-off and not very happy to see me. When I told him I wanted to make a movie out of his book, he said to me, "What the hell have you written? Can you even write a screenplay? What are your credits? I've written screenplays. Worst fucking job in the world." And that was what his attitude was: "How would you know how good my book is?" It made me laugh, because he was just like Bandini. His wife was a lovely woman, slender, blue-eyed, blond and beautiful, and he had his teenage kids there. When I told him I liked the book, she told him, "John, he's just saying he liked your book. Why don't you try to be a little nicer to him?" You know how in the movie, I have Camilla [Salma Hayek's character] say, "Arturo, why can't you just try to be nicer to people?" I had his wife in mind, and I had John in mind, when I wrote that.

So we met again, and he was really on his best behavior. He was in his sixties, and I'd started to get a reputation, that might have been part of it. And we started talking about the book, and I asked him about what happened with it. The book had been pretty much buried. His publisher had published *Mein Kampf* without permission, and Hitler sued them, and they went bankrupt and stopped distributing his book, and it nearly ruined his life. So Hitler had ruined John's life along with everybody else's. He was really bitter about it. It was just really fucked. We struck up a friendship, and he gave me the rights to the book for nothing because I had nothing, and he even gave me a first edition and signed it to me. So I went back and I wrote *Chinatown*. I'd already written *The Last Detail* and was working on drafts of *Shampoo*. So at this time I was going a little crazy too, because I had these three scripts. And then somehow they all came together and then came out all at once, and I had a reputation. And that wasn't lost on John: He knew that this kid actually had written stuff.

We remained friends over the years and talked about it. He was encouraged to begin writing again. He was working on a new book and he would call me to talk about it, and that was the first time in my life that I was able to treat a grown man in his 70s like a little kid. He'd say, "Jesus Christ, Bob, I'm writing about my father's death, and I just can't get through this chapter." I said, "John. Just go ahead and write the fucking thing. Your father's already dead. You're not going to kill him by writing about it." And he did. And then Francis Ford Coppola and I were able to get the book published by swearing that we'd make a movie out of it after it came out. And time went by, and I got caught up in the '70s, and he got very sick with diabetes and had to go to the Motion Picture Home. And then suddenly he died, and his wife called me, and I felt so incredibly guilty that I hadn't gotten the film made. But I still loved the book and kept in touch with it.

I ran into some problems of my own in the '80s. By 1993, I was in a position where I could afford to set aside some time and write the script. But there were some problems with the rights. Somebody else had them by that point. I wrote the script really quickly, and his widow was very happy with it, but then there was the problem of getting it financed, which ended up taking 10 years.

AVC—What was the biggest holdup in terms of getting it funded?
RT—Getting money. The studios didn't want to make the movie. It was set in the Depression. It's about two characters who are mean to each other. They thought they were unsympathetic characters, and that it was racist, no matter how many times I explained to them that it was the opposite of racist. They didn't want to hear it. They said, "Look at what names they call each other." Johnny Depp wanted to star back in 1992, but he wasn't a big enough movie star at the time to get it made. So another ten years went by, it's 2002, and while studios didn't want to make it, talent was very responsive.

So I had this agent call me up and say, "I've got this kid. Nobody knows who he is, but he's damned good and he's right for the picture. Colin Farrell." So we had a party, and this kid shows up at the door wearing a cowboy hat and walks in and says, "Ya got a fucking beer?" and I say, "Yeah, come in," and the minute he walked in, the atmosphere became charged. Nobody knew who he was, but there was something magnetic about him. A friend of my wife's said to me, "I don't know who he is, but whatever he wants, give it to him!" He just had that effect. He was supposed to stay for just a half hour, but he ended up staying all day and all night. We drank, we talked, he hung out with me and my family. It was one of those things where a member of the family that you didn't know you had came to the house. I said, "Look I'm not gonna ask you to read for this. Do you want to do it?" He looked Italian. He reminded me of early shots of John [Fante], who was very handsome when he was younger. He said, "Yeah." And I said, "Okay, that's it. If I get this fucker made, you'll do it." And I still couldn't get money for it.

But then this Irish kid, Colin Farrell, became a movie star. Suddenly, we began to get the financing for it, but the budget was constrained. We all had to do it pretty much for nothing. Then there was the business of Camilla. When I showed the script to Salma, she read it and said, "What are you trying to do to me?" I said, "What are you telling me?" She said, "It's so hard for me. I came here from Mexican soap operas, and I'm trying to get a job in gringo-land, and now all I need is to get typecast as a Mexican waitress."

It's hard, you know? There was a story about her trying to get a role in a science-fiction film and getting turned down and told that they didn't have Mexicans in outer space. She was having the same problems that Camilla had, in a different way but no less bad. I understood it. But the years went by, and by the time Colin became a movie star, Salma had done *Frida* and had gotten recognition and acknowledgment. I asked her to look at it again and she read it, and she really embraced it this time.

AVC—Ask the Dust deals a lot with race. How much do you think racial attitudes have evolved or not evolved since the period Fante was writing about?
RT—The difference is that it's less out in the open today. I remember when the cop in the O. J. Simpson trial said racist, derogatory things even off the record, he lost his job, he lost everything. It has evolved to the extent that it is so politically incorrect that people are scandalized by it. But I think the same attitudes are just underneath the surface. Then, it was right out in the open, and there was something bracing about that, and even funny, like a Lenny Bruce routine. You see these two people wildly attracted to each other, and both of them are angry in that way that you can be angry about being attracted to someone, and you don't know if they'll be attracted to you, but you're dependent upon them. You see these people whose feelings are enslaving them in that they can't control their attraction to the last fucking person in the world they want to be attracted to. It's like Camilla says to Bandini late in the movie, "The truth of the matter is, you're too ashamed of being an Italian to want to marry a Mexican." She brings that up. You know, it's like, "Why can't you have a last name like White?" They both wanted to trade up for blondes and live the WASP life. It's a love story as well, because people have to overcome their respective prejudices.

AVC—It seems like the American dream is still to be a blue-eyed blonde, in spite of how multicultural the country has become.
RT—But it was more of an uncomplicated reaction [in the past]. The dream was more "If you can be similar in that way, you can be American and have equal opportunities." Whereas today it's, how can I put it?

It's kind of Balkanized: Black pride. Gay pride. White Anglo-Saxon Protestant pride. All of these things, you know, they're more polarized, aren't they? The red and blue states. Christians, that's the most insidious aspect of it, giving into this great Christian image of America. That's the most frightening thing of all. Whereas [in the past] they're trying to find things that unite us, to minimize the differences, today there's this belief in empowerment and entitlement by maximizing differences. I'm not so sure that that's healthy. I don't mean that it's not healthy to want to hang onto your culture. But I think it's unhealthy to set it up against somebody else's and say, "Ours is better." Then there's the Christian Right saying that this is a Christian country when it's not. When I was a kid, when we pledged allegiance to the flag, there was no "under God." Tom Paine, Ben Franklin, they were Deists. This was not started as a Christian country.

AVC—In the press notes, you talk about how in Ask the Dust, *Los Angeles is still an adolescent city. Do you think L.A. has grown up yet?*
RT—I think it certainly grew out and grew up, but I don't think it matured. It lost the appeal and the hunger and the beauty of its adolescence and went straight to a middle-aged ugly, overfed monster seeking mindless pleasure and being obsessively acquisitive. It's so materialistic. It grew up, but it didn't mature.

AVC—What are some of your favorite books and movies about Los Angeles?
RT—Raymond Chandler: his descriptions of the city had some of the same effect on me that John did with *Ask the Dust*. There were Billy Wilder's seminal noir films—*Double Indemnity* and others—and James M. Cain. I like, to a lesser degree Nathanael West's *Day of the Locust*. I find *The Last Tycoon* interesting, but not as interesting as a lot of other people do.

AVC—What's the most surprising thing you learned about Los Angeles when you were preparing for Chinatown?
RT—Well, how much I knew. I didn't realize that I just knew the city much better than even I thought I did. And that was kind of a revelation to me. I used to drive around the city at night trying to find pieces of its past that would be similar to things that I remembered even if the things that I remembered were gone.

AVC—How has the business changed since you began?

RT—It's very schizophrenic. There are the big tent-pole movies and the struggling independents. All these movies that we've spoken about, like *Chinatown* and *Last Detail*, would probably not be financed in the normal course of things today. And that's unhealthy. The amount of ancillary effort unrelated to what goes up onscreen by filmmakers, all of us, having to beg, borrow, and steal to finance, to go out there with hat in hand, the struggle we have to do in preparation just for the movies to happen, is a drain. It's like I was saying to George Clooney at a film festival recently, it's a drain on you, it's time consuming, it's energy consuming. You get to the point where you're so fucking tired you feel like you've already done the movie, just trying to get enough money to make it. In the old days, the amount of time it took to make *Ask the Dust*, I could have made three movies and not been so tired and thought, "God, I never want to do this again."

Note

A longer version of this interview was published originally in *AV Club*, March 14, 2006, http://www.avclub.com/article/robert-towne-13978. Courtesy Nathan Rabin, proprietor, Nathan Rabin's Happy Place.

Letters from Los Angeles

Jan Louter

Editors' note: One of Dutch director Jan Louter's biggest dreams was to make a documentary film about John Fante and *Ask the Dust*. In 2006, after years of work, *A Sad Flower in the Sand* aired nationally on the PBS program *Independent Lens*.[1] During his 2000 stay in Los Angeles while shooting the film, Jan wrote a series of letters to his friend Jasper Henderson, editor of the Dutch literary journal *Bunker Hill*.

Dear Jasper,

When I'm traveling, I always bring CDs and a portable player with me. That way, when I hear the same music years later, images appear that otherwise would have never been awakened. Like the madeleine biscuit in Proust's *À la recherche du temps perdu*. Here in Los Angeles I always play Handel's *Messiah*. I started doing this in 1989, when I was in Los Angeles the second time. There was an interview in *L.A. Weekly* with the painter David Hockney where he talked about why he loved LA so much and about a passion of his:

driving through the Mojave Desert in the afternoon sun, windows down, blasting the *Messiah*. If you're ever in LA, you must do this. It's an ecstatic experience. The music, the lyrics, the dust from the desert that gets picked up in gusts of wind to descend on the streets of LA. The dust that whispers, that knows about the magical things of life. The dust that plays such an important part in Fante's novel: "Ask the dust on the Road! Ask the Joshua trees standing alone where the Mojave Desert begins. Ask them about Camilla Lopez, and they will whisper her name."

Do you recognize the quote? It's from *Prologue to 'Ask the Dust,'* which I sent to you several months ago. When I visited Joyce [John Fante's widow] again last year, she gave me a copy as a gift. The book is important to me. In it Fante writes about the title of his masterpiece. *Ask the Dust* is such a meaningful title, you have no idea! Fante's biographer Steve Cooper told me a few days ago in an interview that the Norwegian author Knut Hamsun (1859–1952) was Fante's favorite author. (Do you know Hamsun's novel *Hunger*? You absolutely must read it.) In *Pan*, another novel by Hamsun, he writes: "Ask the dust of the road and the leaves that fall, ask the mysterious God of Life; for none other knows these things." In addition to many other meanings, the title of *Ask the Dust* is an homage to Knut Hamsun. And then of course there is the biblical connection, *ashes to ashes, dust to dust*, the lifeless dust in which nothing can grow, especially all those people who come to Los Angeles to realize their dreams, only to be left behind. Let me cite a passage from *Ask the Dust* that I will certainly use in the film:

> I went up to my room, up the dusty stairs of Bunker Hill. . . . Dust and old buildings and old people sitting at windows. . . . The old folk from Indiana and Iowa and Illinois, from Boston and Kansas City and Des Moines, . . . they came here by train and by automobile to the land of sunshine, to die in the sun. . . . And when they got here they found out that other and greater thieves had already taken possession, that even the sun belonged to the others: Smith and Jones and Parker. . . . You'll eat hamburgers year after year and live in dusty, vermin-infested apartments and hotels, but every morning you'll see the mighty sun, the eternal blue of the sky, and the streets will be full of sleek women you never will possess, and the hot semitropical nights will reek of romance you'll never have, but you are still in paradise, in the land of sunshine.
>
> As for the folks back home, you can lie to them, because they hate the truth anyway, because soon or late they want to come to paradise, too.

That's quite something, isn't it? And yet Lost Angeles was built on the sand of the desert, the factory of dreams that still has a magical pull, where dreamers still seek refuge and the hopeless nurse their hopes. Los Angeles breathes, lives. Some she embraces, some she doesn't. Why? I have no idea. But I am convinced that the City of Angels nourished Fante like a mother, comforted him in difficult times, whispered sentences we can read in *Ask the Dust*.

In response to your question about the title of my film: *A Sad Flower in the Sand* is a line from *Ask the Dust* where Fante describes his love for the city: "Los Angeles give me some of you! Los Angeles come to me the way I came to you, my feet over your streets, you pretty town I loved you so much, you sad flower in the sand, you pretty town." Beautiful. When I was downtown for the first time in 1989 with Fante's son Jim looking for locations from the novel, I cited that passage. We were on Bunker Hill, near where the Alta Vista hotel stood when Fante lived there, only to be torn down in 1968 to make way for giant skyscrapers. Tears streamed down Jim's face as he recounted how in 1969 his father had taken him downtown. Jim said that Bunker Hill's metamorphosis had hurt his father, that what little remained from the past now saddened him. I remember saying I could understand that pain, which had to do with time's ever-growing intangibility. Something like that...

Jasper, I don't know what it is but when you're driving in the Mojave Desert with the *Messiah* reverberating from the speakers, you can feel the fragility of time in your bones. A pleasant sort of melancholy will course through your veins, but it won't drag you down, it will redeem you. Jesus, I hope what I'm writing doesn't sound too pompous. Before going to sleep I'll have another shot of tequila, just as you should be waking up...

Dear Jasper,

It's 6:30 in the morning, a lovely time. The city is still fresh and smells special. At the end of Beverly Boulevard, the red of the rising sun colors the buildings and the empty street. Next to my hotel there's a trendy cafe where the girls who wait on you all wear the same extremely short blue skirts with boots up to their knees. As if that's not enough, some wear white panties frilled with lace just visible underneath. By the way, I don't have a bad word to say about the service here...

As for *A Sad Flower in the Sand*: yesterday we recorded some beautiful shots in an abandoned room of the Barclay Hotel on the corner of Fifth Street and Main. The view out the window was of a gigantic billboard showing a seductive woman in sexy lingerie. These shots will represent Bandini's desires to be rich and to possess such beautiful women. Because, as you know, these desires are unattainable for Bandini, who is just scraping by, while women won't grant him a second glance. Do you remember the scene on page 12?

> I was passing the doorman of the Biltmore hotel, and I hated him at once, with his yellow braids and six feet of height and all that dignity, and now a black automobile drove to the curb, and a man got out. He looked rich; and then a woman got out, and she was beautiful, her fur and silver fox, and she was a song across the sidewalk and inside the swinging doors, and I thought oh boy for a little of that, just a day and a night of that, and she was a dream as I walked along, her perfume still in the wet morning air.

What a beautiful sentence, right? The Biltmore still exists, maybe even more lavish than in Fante's days. I went into the lobby a few days ago. Unlike in the thirties the entrance is no longer on Pershing Square. Maybe the hotel bosses were bothered by all the homeless people who sleep on the benches in the square and piss against the wall of the impressive building at night.

You asked why *Ask the Dust* is such a special book, and why John Fante was ahead of his time. In my opinion it has to do with the fact that Fante was a born writer motivated by a quivering wound from his youth. He wrote from his heart, in a style that was unheard of in 1939. And *Ask the Dust* has lost none of its power—it still seems like it was written yesterday. Again and again new generations are able to identify with Arturo Bandini, not unlike the Dutch novel *De avonden* by Gerard Reve, or *Catcher in the Rye* by J. D. Salinger.

While I'm writing this to you, I remember it took me seven years to convince the [Dutch broadcasting company] VPRO of the importance of making a film about John Fante. Was I ahead of my time? And before that, a similar ordeal, with the radio people. "Who in God's name is John Fante?" That was their reaction. A meager budget of 1,500 guilders for at least six weeks of work: that was all an audio documentary was worth to them. So, using my own money for travel and lodging expenses, I flew to LA—and never regretted it. That's when I first met Joyce, John's wife, and we spent unforgettable hours talking in the kitchen of her Malibu ranch house. I also met Robert Towne in his office on Second Street in Santa Monica, with a view of the Pacific Ocean. He's untouchable in Hollywood. He won an Oscar for writing *Chinatown*, you know, that unforgettable Roman Polanski film with Jack Nicholson and Faye Dunaway. Robert told me he'd bought the rights to adapt *Ask the Dust* into a film. Together with Francis Ford Coppola he'd also bought the rights to *The Brotherhood of the Grape*. Peter Falk, better known as detective Columbo, owned the rights to *My Dog Stupid*. Martin Sheen had *Dreams from Bunker Hill*. The money was flowing in, Joyce could live comfortably from the film rights: the pay is quite something here! Maybe now you understand why I named my radio doc *John Fante: The Hottest Dead Writer in Hollywood*.

Jasper, I'll have to finish here. Erik and Bert are coming. We're going out to get some shots of the palm trees on Bedford Drive in Beverly Hills. We'll record them from a convertible, so Erik can keep the camera vertical, with the car driving slowly. The images are going to be slightly surreal. You'll see what I'm trying to accomplish when the film is finished. Now that I'm talking about palm trees, I can't help thinking of the lines from *Ask the Dust* when Bandini recounts his first attempt to write in his hotel room in downtown LA. I know them by heart:

> Arturo Bandini in front of his typewriter two full days in succession . . . not one line done, only two words written over and over across the page, up and down, the same words: palm tree, palm tree, palm tree, a battle to the death between the palm tree and me, and the palm tree won.

Dear Jasper,

A Sad Flower in the Sand isn't going to be a biographical portrait, no. It's going to be a visual film. A confrontation between past and present, dream and reality. A film in the spirit of Arturo Bandini, *lover of man and beast alike*! A passionate film. While I often doubt it's going to turn out well while we're shooting, I'm also convinced that it will be one of my best films. Contradictory, but the truth. To focus on the contents of the film a bit more, it will also be about dreaming—and Los Angeles, the city of dreamers—and hate, love, poverty, racism, which will play a part in the film like a little snake in the grass. This afternoon I met with Steve Cooper, the biographer of John Fante and editor of the recently published collection of his stories, *The Big Hunger*. (There's Knut Hamsun peeking around the corner again.) Steve told me something odd during our interview. Because of her health, about a year ago Joyce had to leave the house on Cliffside Drive where she'd lived with John since 1956. While she was hospitalized, she allowed Steve to come and go at the house to continue his research. And during this time, he found several unpublished stories by Fante. One or two of these stories contained elements that caused John Martin, the publisher of Black Sparrow Press, to fear they might be misinterpreted as racist and so harm Fante's reputation. That, in sum, is the reason they weren't included in *The Big Hunger*. (Maybe it's a nice idea to publish them in *Bunker Hill* sometime. I'll talk about it with Joyce.) Though I haven't read the stories I can understand their decision. But it's interesting, you come across a lot of racism and discrimination in Fante's works. Just look at *Ask the Dust*; it's filled with it. As the son of an Italian immigrant, Fante experienced racism firsthand:

> When I was a kid back home in Colorado it was Smith and Parker and Jones who hurt me with their hideous names, called me Wop and Dago and Greaser, and their children hurt me. . . . They hurt me so much I could never become one of them, drove me to books, drove me within myself, drove me away from that Colorado town, and sometimes, Camilla, when I see their faces I feel the hurt all over again . . . and sometimes I am glad they are here, dying in the sun, uprooted, tricked by their heartlessness . . . fulfilling the emptiness of their lives under a blazing sun.

Can't put it plainer than that. And of course, there is the key scene of the novel, at least in my opinion. The one about white people who move to Los Angeles and whose dreams turn to nightmares, white people who despise everyone else, Mexicans, Filipinos, Italians:

> I have vomited at their newspapers, read their literature, observed their customs, eaten their food, desired their women, gasped at their art. But I am poor, and my name ends with a soft vowel, and they hate me and my father and my father's father, and they would have my blood and put me down, but they are old now, dying in the sun and in the hot dust of the road, and I am young and full of hope and love for my country and my times, and when I say Greaser to you, [Camilla,] it is not my heart that speaks, but the quivering of an old wound.

An old wound, that's what it's all about. I believe that is the source of Fante's authorship. If you ask me if he was a racist, I believe that a racist hides in every man. Which of course doesn't mean you can allow yourself to act or behave in a racist manner. I am convinced that Fante wanted to explore this centuries-old phenomenon in his unfinished novel *The Little Brown Brothers*, which he worked on for years after *Ask the Dust*. In the end I think he got lost in the complexities. His publisher at the time, to whom he'd sent a few chapters, thought it was a *depressing, racist story*, not worth publishing. As you may know, Fante was deeply hurt and for years afterwards barely wrote anything. Now that I'm writing this, I remember something Robert Towne said when I visited him last year and he gave me a copy of his *Ask the Dust* script. He told me how the Hollywood studios reacted, calling it *a depressing, racist story*. In 1993 he almost got the go-ahead to start filming, with Sean Penn starring as Bandini. Why the process was eventually stopped is still unclear. He mumbled something about money, that it was a period piece and therefore expensive. The positions of the world's decisionmakers are almost always filled by the wrong people, that's become clear to me. They have the power, they're the important ones, and they walk away with the cash. Now that you have a steady job as editor at *De Bezige Bij*, Jasper, you might feel you're being attacked. But that's not my intention. Or maybe it is. Once again, it's late. I don't sleep more than four or five hours every night...

Dear Jasper,
Is it true you're going to be publishing *Chump Change* by Dan Fante? A few hours ago, I interviewed Dan in his home. He lives in Santa Monica, in a "clean and sober" apartment. A living room with an open kitchen, and a bedroom. When Erik and Bert were setting up the lights, Dan and I lay down next to each other on his bed. Three walls of his bedroom are covered in photos of Marilyn Monroe. Interesting, though I don't think it works for him. Dan told me he had just returned from his promotional tour through Italy where *Chump Change* was very well received. I understand that you two are in touch by e-mail. I told him that you're very friendly, obsessed with literature (and thus a bad businessman), and absolutely trustworthy. To which he replied that publishers can never be trusted. Is that true?
I met Dan last year in Junior's Deli, a lunchroom for *the white middle class* between Santa Monica and Beverly Hills. I'm still not sure why he wanted

to meet there; he is the complete opposite to the other patrons. He's kind of like a slightly older punk. Short gray hair, a gold ring in his left nostril. He wore a dark T-shirt and wide American camouflage pants. He has the same stocky posture as his father. His expression is permanently like a volcano about to erupt. When I spoke to him, he was excited. *Chump Change* had just been published in the United States, and a play that he'd written was receiving a lot of praise from critics. I discovered later that he's like his father in many more ways: he's short-tempered and passionate, has issues with alcohol, and he's a natural writer. (Did you know that John's eldest son, Nick, passed away a few years ago from the effects of drinking?) And just as John's father had a love-hate relationship with *his* father—it's all in *The Brotherhood of the Grape*—so does Dan with John. History repeats itself. By the way, Joyce isn't happy with Dan's book. She told me she thinks it's too vulgar. She's afraid that Dan is abusing his father's reputation, something like that. For a while they were out of touch but now it's back to how it should be between a mother and a son. If you meet Dan, you'll notice that he speaks quickly, without hesitations. Nice, short sentences that fit with his temper. I recorded a really great interview with him. Very candid. He told me that *Chump Change* is an ode to his father and that he understands his dad's feelings about being an outsider much better now. According to Dan his father was 99 percent author and 1 percent dad. Dan also told me about the meaning of the friendship between his dad and Robert Towne. The last few weeks before his death John wasn't conscious very often. One afternoon Robert visited to say goodbye. Fante was delirious. Dan whispered in his father's ear that Robert was there. Suddenly, John was completely lucid for about five minutes, a miracle. Besides the friendship, Robert represented money, fame, and recognition.

After our interview Dan wrapped his arm around my shoulder; he's very demonstrative, probably because of the Italian blood. A moment later he pressed one of his father's pipes in my hand, the scratches from his teeth etched in the mouthpiece. It's one of the pipes John smoked during the last few years of his life. Dear God, Jasper, for a moment I didn't know what to say. A moment later he gave me a sheet of yellow paper, saying that John Fante had written *The Brotherhood of the Grape* on paper like that. Dan had gotten the leftover paper from his father before he, Dan, ever published anything. Dan went on to write *Chump Change* on it. Now that I am writing you this, I realize the significance of the gesture. Think about it. If I ever write a novel, I'll start it on this empty yellow page. Maybe I'll pick up some of his talent. Who knows?

Dear Jasper,

The last four times that I've visited LA. I've stayed in the Beverly Laurel Hotel. All the rooms look the same: the familiarity is comforting. It's like coming home rather than arriving. The TV is on while I'm writing this, the deciding game of the NBA finals between the Indiana Pacers and the LA Lakers. It's a really big deal here, like the final of the Champions League back home.

Today we recorded the opening shot of the film and we got it exactly as I had hoped. Amazing! I discovered the spot last year when I was here doing research for the script. It's a dirt road in the Mojave Desert, about sixty kilometers outside of the city, a junction of the Pearblossom Highway just past Little Rock. To give you an idea of the shot I'll describe the beginning of the film. First, the familiar words "*Los Angeles give me some of you! Los Angeles come to me the way I came to you*" appear onscreen. You'll hear music as well, of course. (Paul M. van Brugge will be our composer.) Below that, in a smaller font, it will say "John Fante, *Ask the Dust*, 1939." Then the opening shot. It's magic hour, the moment when day changes into night. You see the desert, rocks, cactuses—a desolate landscape cut in two by the sloping road. In the far background, the mountains that hide LA. Everything is suffused in an orange-blue light. (Getting this kind of a shot is extremely difficult and exciting, because you have only about half an hour.) After about ten seconds you see a cloud of dust rising slowly in the distance, extremely mysterious. You have no idea what it could be. Slowly the front of a Greyhound bus appears from behind a hill; only when the bus has reached the top of the hill can you see the glow of the headlights. (Initially Greyhound was going to loan us a bus but because of insurance issues they pulled out. Our local producer Christina Berio tracked down our bus at Hollywood Film Rental just in time. Christina is my hero.) The bus floats down the road getting slowly closer, leaving clouds of dust in its wake. When the bus isn't too far away the lighted panel up front comes into focus with the destination "Los Angeles." The bus passes the camera and a giant cloud of dust fills the screen, clearing up again after about twenty seconds. Very special. On top of this image will appear the film's title. The sequence is a minute and a half! After the title you hear Bandini speak. (Sean Penn, who was a good friend of Bukowski, will probably narrate selections from *Ask the Dust*.[2]) Bandini's first words in the film are: "It was five months ago, the day I got to town by bus from Boulder, Colorado, with a hundred and fifty dollars in my pocket, a typewriter and big plans in my head." The images we'll then show will have their own unique style, a suggestion of the director of photography, my good friend Erick van Empel. Erik records all these shots from his shoulder or his hip. Very dynamic. They're being made "ugly" on purpose, the framing always a little odd. I want it to feel like you're looking through Arturo Bandini's eyes, walking with him down Broadway, Main, Third Street or Bunker Hill. These shots have all been recorded at twenty frames per second instead of twenty-four, which will make them a little jerky, like an 8mm film. In postproduction we'll make the image grainier, and the colors will be significantly altered. This letter will get too wordy if I go into greater detail, but elements of these images will return in other moments of the film suggesting that what Bandini/John Fante saw long ago can still be seen today, if only you look carefully enough (fig. 18).

Jasper, it's midnight now, and I stopped writing for an hour to watch the news. The victory of the LA Lakers is being celebrated, but there are also riots. Teenagers have set cars on fire and looted stores. None of them are white, all are probably extremely poor and without dreams. To stop everything from getting out of hand (after all, a few years ago half the city was on fire) the star of the team, a multimillionaire, appeared on TV. A bald black guy with giant earrings. We'll find out tomorrow if his words have had any effect. Yesterday evening we were filming in the neighborhood where the riots are right now. (The Lakers' stadium is downtown.) When we're down there, Ray, our security guard, is always circling us. He is like a giant. Without him we would've been robbed ages ago. Downtown is quite a heavy neighborhood. Especially at night you have to be careful. During the day it's not as bad, but it is extremely busy: the sidewalks are filled with people from all over, especially Mexico. There is loud music coming out of every shop selling cheap clothes, shoes, and electronics. During lunch break you see a lot of office workers as downtown is an important business district. The odd thing though about downtown is that it's nothing like what you'd expect Los Angeles to be like. There are no palm trees, no beautiful neon signs, no expensive convertibles, Mercedes, or Porsches. No streets lined with shops where famous fashion brands display their newest designs in the windows. Nothing like that! Even the amazing California light is different—it hurts

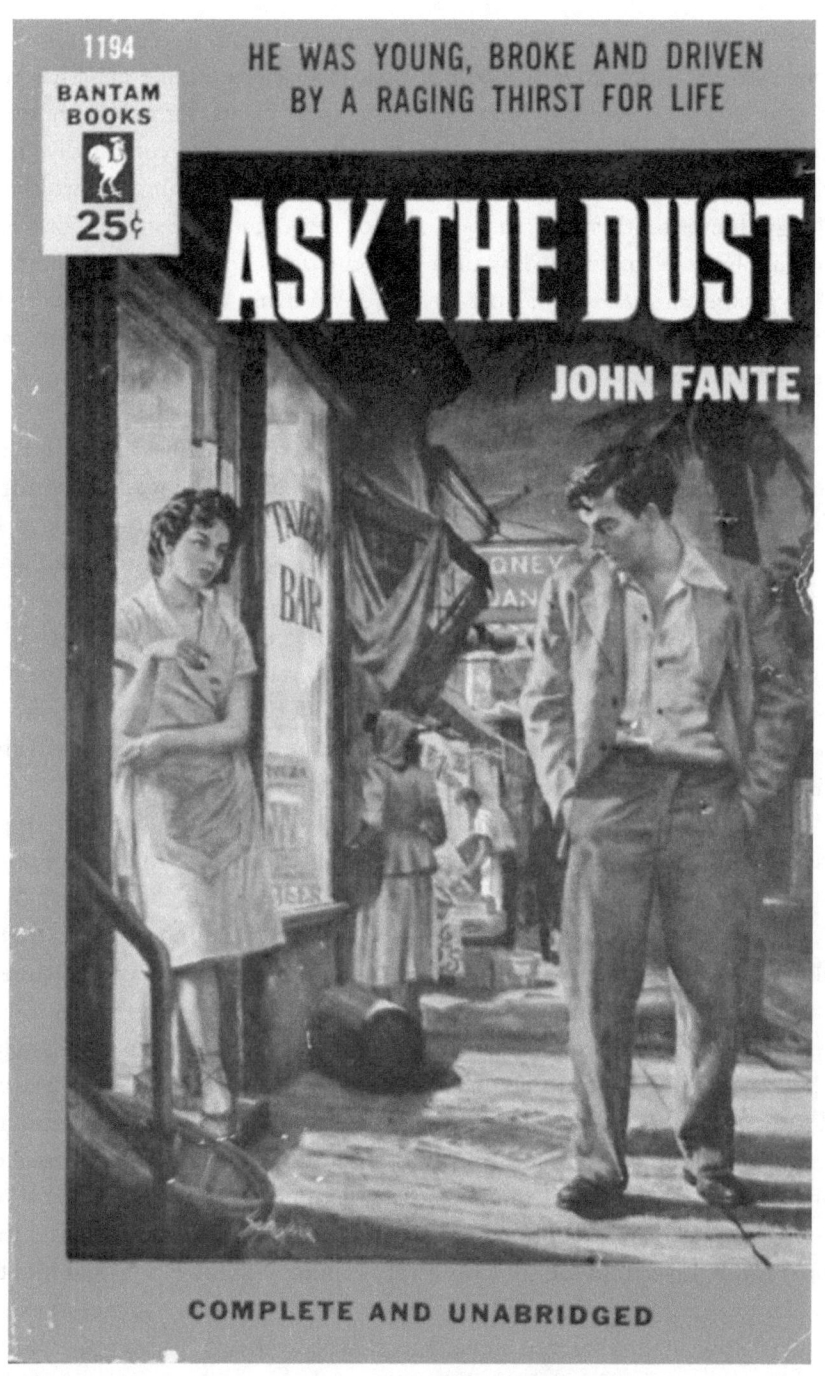

FIGURE 18. Cover of the 1954 Bantam paperback edition of *Ask the Dust*. (Courtesy of John Fante Literary Group LLC. Photo by Charles Hood.)

your eyes. An hour after the offices close, the white middle class has retreated to their gated neighborhoods, the shop fronts with steel shutters feel like impregnable fortresses, and downtown changes completely. You wouldn't believe what you see. Roisterous drunks, begging for whiskey. Dodgy thieves on their way to a job. Hollow-eyed junkies yearning for a fix. Wailing lunatics, tormented by their hallucinations. It's an unparalleled mix of *les paumés du petit matin*.[3] Just a block down from Main Street hundreds of homeless people lie on cardboard boxes on the sidewalk. Another block further and you're almost certain to become the victim of a gang. Dear God, what misery![4]

And just think, our hero sat behind his typewriter writing stories in that neighborhood, surviving on two oranges a day because he was so poor. It's also where he wrote his letters to H. L. Mencken and met Camilla Lopez. If you walk around there now it becomes difficult to imagine all that. But also not. Right now, I don't have the words to express it. In Fante's time downtown must have been dazzling. Amazing Art Deco buildings, gigantic, ornate cinemas. At the same time there was poverty; after all, it was the end of the Great Depression, though I think it was a different type of poverty from now. Back then everyone was poor. The buildings still have an overwhelming beauty, by the way, except it's the beauty of decay.

Thinking of Camilla Lopez, I remembered something that will interest you. I've got some files from the fifties in which the Columbia Buffet from *Ask the Dust* appears, you know, the bar where Camilla worked. She was a beautiful girl, I know, because Joyce showed me a photo. When we're filming downtown, I sometimes think I see her walking down the street. Or she's suddenly behind the cash register at one of the cheap shops. Dear God, Jasper, some Mexican women have a beauty I thought was impossible, a beauty that reveals pride, if you know what I mean. Joyce told me in March (I recorded all her interviews back then) that the love affair between Bandini and Camilla happened basically as John described it. Camilla really existed. She was a beautiful Mexican girl and she disappeared into the desert. The photo of Camilla is the only thing Joyce didn't share with Steve Cooper, the biographer. Joyce told me she's been very candid with Steve, allowed him to look into everything. But she knew that if she showed him the picture, he'd want to publish it.[5] I still remember Joyce's words—she said that some things are simply too painful. John still met up with Camilla a few times in the first years of their marriage. When I asked whatever happened to Camilla afterwards, Joyce answered with a small smile and her flair for the dramatic: "Ask the dust."

Dear Jasper,

For 250 dollars we were allowed to film for two hours in the lobby of the Baltimore Hotel in downtown LA, on the corner of Fifth and Los Angeles. Many people live there permanently, they'll rent a room for a year, or longer. This is quite normal in LA. In the thirties Fante lived in cheap hotels for long periods of time. You often see *"Daily, weekly and monthly rates"* painted on the walls of the gigantic old hotels. The decrepit Million Dollar Hotel has over a thousand rooms, all too disgusting to step into. A few days ago, with Christina I went to see if it might be a suitable location. It's not. The residents of the Baltimore are almost all aging white guys whose dreams didn't come true, who were never embraced by the city. Now they're in their sixties, or older. Glazed eyes, pale faces, hollow unshaved cheeks. A few of them sit in the lobby staring in the direction of the TV, others are playing cards. Some are sleeping in dilapidated armchairs. The loneliness in these people makes me shudder. They're waiting for their deaths. Do you know what a hot meal consists of for them? A tiny heated can of Campbell's Soup, which you can buy for one dollar from a machine. There's a choice of three types of mashed potatoes with vegetables—bon appétit! Just reading the label makes me almost throw up. And yet they can still afford food and a room, since the room is only twenty-five dollars per week. You don't need much of an imagination to get a shiver from the thought alone. But most of the black people who roam downtown have absolutely nothing. Unless you think of a cardboard box to sleep in as property.

My room is clean, my bed is soft. I am tired. It's the middle of the night. When you write you forget the time...

Dear Jasper,

I'd promised to write you about Robert Towne. Though I'm very tired, I'll make an attempt. Robert is an imposing man with longish grey hair and a grey beard. He's sixty-five years old. He's written the scripts for *Shampoo, The Last Detail, Chinatown, The Godfather, Reds, The Firm, Mission Impossible,* and more. The last several, if I remember correctly, he wrote together with other people. Robert has a great reputation in Hollywood. He lives in a fantastic house in Pacific Palisades, close to the ocean. There's no smog and always a cool breeze. I met Robert for the first time in 1989. In the years since then I've visited him a few times. We get along well. I'm not sure why I'm always welcome. I say this because he very rarely replies to requests for interviews. He lives out of the public eye as much as possible, together with his wife Luisa, of Italian descent, and their eight-year-old daughter Chiara. It's lovely to sit on the terrace next to the pool with a glass of wine, talking to Robert. Especially about John Fante, of course. Over time Robert has brought up a lot of Fante anecdotes. A few of those he recalled in the interview that we shot this afternoon. Masterful, the way Robert expresses himself, thoughtfully smoking his Davidoff cigar. When I asked if John Fante ever talked about Camilla Lopez he started to chuckle. "You know what John said? 'Bob, she was a dyke!'" Hilarious. That's how you learn who you're dealing with.

Yesterday we went to visit Fante's grave with Robert. Like a pilgrimage. John Fante is buried in a big Catholic cemetery, Holy Cross, on Slauson Avenue. It's a nice scene, Robert driving his car, a black Infiniti, telling how he discovered *Ask the Dust* while doing research for *Chinatown*. (That movie is set in the thirties, just like *Ask the Dust*.) When Robert read *Ask the Dust* for the first time he was blown away by the novel's descriptions of the city of his own youth, the Los Angeles that's just come into existence, only to disappear under a thin layer of dust. On every page he saw Fante's love for the city reflected back at him. It was the beginning of one man's passionate love for a novel. It was also the beginning of a friendship that continued until John's death in 1983.

Jasper, I've written this to you before: the film is about having a dream, about John Fante's dream of becoming a writer. But to make a dream come true, you have to work hard and long. It's a bit of a sidetrack but I just remembered a passage from *John Fante and H. L. Mencken: A Personal Correspondence 1930–1952*. They wrote each other for twenty-two years and yet they never met.

> Dear Mr. Mencken,
>
> Will you answer a question for me? In the past thirty days I have written 150,000 words. I know a writer with a reputation does not do that many, but is a man just starting supposed to do that much? I certainly feel the effects, for,

being broke throughout, I ate very little and lost a pound a day, which is thirty pounds now...

Now that is passion. Maybe you should show that to the young writers in your foundation. Do you know why I like Robert so much? He still has dreams. Even though he has a beautiful house, and millions in his bank account. Make sure you always have a dream, that's what life is all about. Robert's dream is to make *Ask the Dust* into a movie. And he's going to do it. A few weeks ago, he spoke to the actor Colin Farrell. He's a rising star, twenty-three years old. Every studio wants to offer him a contract. And he'd love to play Bandini. Happy as a child, Robert said, "I got my man!" I hope that Joyce will still be here to see it happen, so that her last dream will have come true as well.

Dear Jasper,

Tomorrow I leave for Amsterdam, a twelve-hour flight. And the next day twelve more hours in the car to my home in France, where I've been living for the past three years. LA will be behind me; I'll be surrounded by nature once again, and silence, and the solitude that I love. I can't live without it anymore. Now that we're done filming—we're bringing back fifty-six rolls of film, beautiful material—I suddenly really miss my wife and our son. If I look at his picture, I get tears in my eyes. (I don't care if you think that's sentimental.) All I have then is the desire to hold them close to me and stop time. Do you have someone who waits for you when you're traveling, who looks forward to your coming home? That's really the only important thing in life. Everything else is just details.

Jasper, in September, October, and November I'll be busy finishing the film: editing, sound, color corrections, etc. I'll keep you up to date, brother. I think I can call you that; we're both a part of the Fante family, after all. In December I won't be reachable, I already know I'll be having withdrawal symptoms. I'll have to say goodbye to John Fante. For over a year I've felt his breath on my neck, for over a year he's sat on my shoulder. I'll miss him!

Regards,
Jan

Translated by Leonoor Kemperman

Notes

1. See "A Sad Flower in the Sand," *Independent Lens*, http://www.pbs.org/independentlens/sadflowerinthesand/film.html.
2. As it turned out, Sean Penn did not narrate the film.
3. Title of a song by Belgian singer Jacques Brel, in English, "The misfits of the early morning."
4. The scene that Louter paints here of downtown Los Angeles has been transformed in the last decade by gentrification. But go east from Main a block or two on Fifth or Sixth Streets and you will still see the living nightmare.
5. [Editors' note] When Cooper saw the photograph of Fante's lover Marie Baray, on whom the character of Camilla Lopez was largely based, he asked Joyce for permission to publish it. Her response was succinct: "If you publish that picture, I'll cut your throat." Only after some long and sensitive negotiations was Joyce finally persuaded that the world deserved to see the image, which did in fact appear in Cooper's biography.

"My Dear Bukowski," "Hello John Fante":
Preface to *Ask the Dust*

John Fante and Charles Bukowski

"The finest novel written in all time."[1]

That's how Charles Bukowski felt about *Ask the Dust* in his advancing age. To be sure, he had felt that way for decades, all the way back to his wayward youth when he stalked the streets of Bunker Hill drunk on wine and the desire to write, seeking the room where the young John Fante had written and starved so that he, Bukowski, could imagine himself as Arturo Bandini, the self-proclaimed greatest writer who ever lived.

In his first published story, Bukowski paid homage to Fante and to Fante's own strongest influence, Knut Hamsun. Like Hamsun's *Hunger* and Fante's *Ask the Dust*, Bukowski's "Aftermath of a Lengthy Rejection Letter" offers up his version of the hapless young writer lost in the dream of literary greatness—a dream that for all three authors came true.[2]

In granting permission for the use of her late husband's writings in this volume, Linda Bukowski urged us to "reiterate how important, beautiful, and timely it was for John . . . and Hank to meet up and get to know one

FIGURE 19. Bukowski and Fante (right) in good company (Woody Guthrie and Tom Waits), Werdin Place or "Indian Alley," downtown Los Angeles. (Photo by Charles Hood.)

another. Hank wrote and spoke about John . . . throughout our life together . . . with true tenderness and empathy. . . . He loved John and always kept him close in his heart."[3]

The following pages offer a glimpse into the bond that was key to both men, born out of *Ask the Dust* (figs. 19 and 20) as well as the original typewritten pages of Bukowski's preface to the 1980 Black Sparrow edition of *Ask the Dust* (fig. 21).

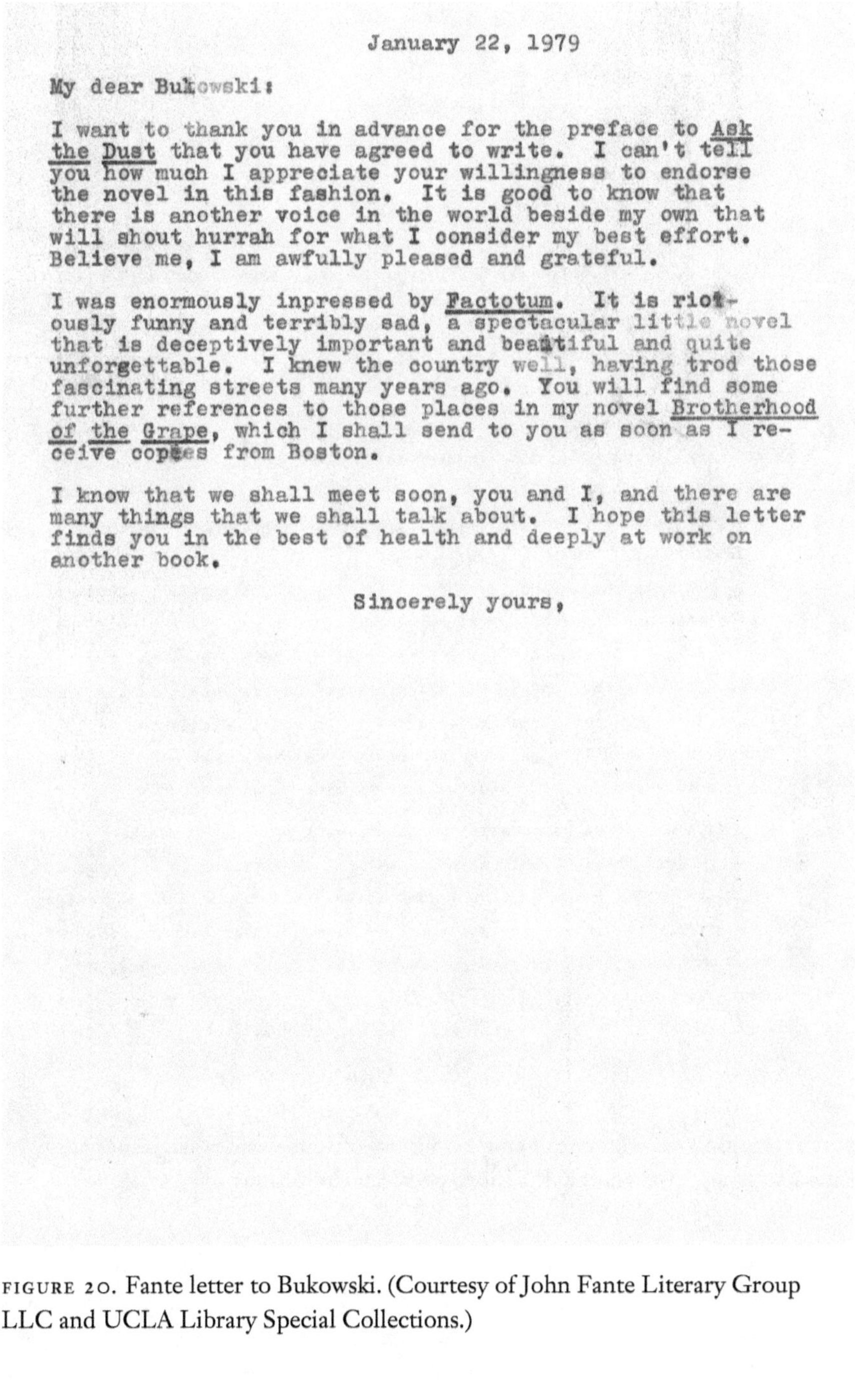

January 22, 1979

My dear Bukowski:

I want to thank you in advance for the preface to <u>Ask the Dust</u> that you have agreed to write. I can't tell you how much I appreciate your willingness to endorse the novel in this fashion. It is good to know that there is another voice in the world beside my own that will shout hurrah for what I consider my best effort. Believe me, I am awfully pleased and grateful.

I was enormously impressed by <u>Factotum</u>. It is riotously funny and terribly sad, a spectacular little novel that is deceptively important and beautiful and quite unforgettable. I knew the country well, having trod those fascinating streets many years ago. You will find some further references to those places in my novel <u>Brotherhood of the Grape</u>, which I shall send to you as soon as I receive copies from Boston.

I know that we shall meet soon, you and I, and there are many things that we shall talk about. I hope this letter finds you in the best of health and deeply at work on another book.

                    Sincerely yours,

FIGURE 20. Fante letter to Bukowski. (Courtesy of John Fante Literary Group LLC and UCLA Library Special Collections.)

Feb. 2, 1979

Hello John Fante:

    In my last letter I meant to ask you:
    In what year or years was ASK THE DUST WRITTEN?
    What year was it published?
    Did you write it in Los Angeles?
    Were you living in Los Angeles when it came out (was published)?
    Did you actually live in that place along ######Angel's Flight?

    To me, of course, it doesn't matter whether things are fiction or fact, or an admixture--as long as the writing is live, and Christ knows, it's plenty live in ## ASK THE DUST. But I'd like it if you would answer the above questions. No salesman will call at your door, and it will help with the foreword and/or preface; I hope to keep it fairly short so as not to detract from the novel but I'm by nature a windy bastard (#in writing only; I don't talk very much in person unless drunk).

    I'm into the screenplay about a bar fly in Los Angeles, and there is this French director and he says, "Hank, each page is a minute and we only have 90 minutes." It's a new media to me. I have the guy just sitting around and taking off his shoes and the movie is one third over. I don't think it's for me but since I have taken some money in advance I'll go ahead and do it. Oh, yeah, won $102 at the track yesterday. I know you want to hear about that.

    Anyhow, if you can answer the questions I will get into the preface soon, well, fairly soon. I never like anything to be <u>work</u>, so it must jump on me. It will jump on me. ASK THE DUST reads better than ever. You can really put the line down, full of butter and sunlight and agony. This ########novel deserves a roaring ######## rebirth.

                          yes, yes, yes, (HANK)
                                 Charles Bukowski

[Handwritten margin notes: "BAUDINI STREET. IT'S out" / "I LIVE RIGHT OFF Block EAST...." / "P.S.—"]

FIGURE 21. Bukowski letter to Fante. (Courtesy of Linda Bukowski, John Fante Literary Group LLC and UCLA Library Special Collections.)

preface

I was a young man, starving and drinking and trying to be a writer. I did most of my reading at the downtown L.A. Public Library, and nothing that I read related to me or to the streets or the people about me. It seemed as if everybody were playing word-tricks, it seemed as if those who said almost nothing at all were considered excellent writers. Their writing was an admixture of subtlety, craft and form, and it was read and it was taught and it was ingested and it was passed on. It was a comfortable contrivance, it was a very slick and careful Word-Culture. One had to go back to the pre-revolution writers of Russia to find any gamble, any passion. There were exceptions but those exceptions were so few that the reading w of ~~them~~ THOSE was quickly done with and you were left staring at rows and rows of exceedingly dull books. With all the centuries to look back upon, with all their advantages, the moderns just weren't very good.

I pulled book after book from the shelves. Why didn't anybody say anything? Why didn't anybody scream out?

I tried other rooms in the library. The section on Religions was just a vast bog--to me. I got into philosophy. I found a couple of bitter Germans who cheered me for a while, then that was over. I tried mathematics but upper math was just like religion: it slid right off of me. What I needed seemed to be absent from everywhere.

I tried geology and found it curious but, finally, non-sustaining.

I found some books on surgery and I liked the books on surgery: the words were new and the illustrations were wonderful. I particularly memorized the operation on the mesocolon.

Then I dropped out of surgery and I was back in the big room with the novelists and short story writers, but whenever I had enough cheap wine to drink I never went to the library. A library was a good place to be when you had nothing to drink or to eat, and the landlady was looking for you AND the back rent money. In the library at least you had the use of the toilet facilities. I saw quite a number of other bums in there, most of them asleep on top of their books.

I kept on walking around the big room, pulling the books out of their shelves, reading a few lines, a few pages, then putting them back.

Then one day I pulled a book down and opened it, and there it was. I stood for a moment, reading. Then like a man who had found gold in the city dump, I carried the book to a table. The lines rolled across the page, there was a flowing ease. Each line had its own energy and was followed by another like that. The very substance of each line gave the page a form, a feeling of something carved into it. And here, at last, was a man who was not afraid of emotion. And the humour and the pain were intermixed with a superb simplicity. Getting into the beginning of that book was a wild and enormous miracle to me.

I had a library card. I checked the book out, took it to my room, climbed into my bed and read it, and I knew long before I had finished that here was a man who had EVOLVED a DISTINCT way of writing. The book was ASK THE DUST and the author was John Fante. He was to be a lifetime influence on my writing. I finished ASK THE DUST and looked for other books of Fante's in the library. I found two: DAGO RED and WAIT UNTIL SPRING, BANDINI. They were of the same order, written of and from the gut and the heart.

Yes, Fante had a mighty effect upon me. Not long after reading these books I got into living with a woman. She was a worse drunk than I was and we had some violent arguments, and often I would scream at her: "Don't call me a son of a bitch! I am Bandini, Arturo Bandini!"

Fante was my god and I knew that the gods should be left alone, one didn't bang at their doors. Yet I liked to guess about where he had lived along ANGEL'S FLIGHT and I imagined it possible that he still lived there. And almost every day I walked by and I thought, is that the window Camilla crawled through? And, is that the hotel door? Is that the lobby? I never knew.

39 years later I reread ASK THE DUST. That is to say, I reread it this year and it still stands, as do Fante's other works, but this one is my favorite because it was my first discovery of the magic. There are other books beside DAGO RED and WAIT UNTIL SPRING, BANDINI. They are BRAVO BURRO (a collaberation with Rudolph Berchet); MY DOG, STUPID; FULL OF LIFE; and THE BROTHERHOOD OF THE GRAPE. And, at the moment, Fante has a work in progress: HOW TO WRITE A SCREENPLAY.

> 4-preface　　　　　　　　　　　　　　　　　　　　　　　　　4-buk
>
> Through circumstance, I finally met the author this year. There is much more to the story of John Fante; it is a story of terrible luck and a terrible fate and of a rare and natural courage. Some day it will be told but I feel that he doesn't want me to tell it here. But let me say that the way of his words and the way of his way are similar: strong and good and warm.
>
> That's enough. Now this book is yours.
>
> *Charles Bukowski*
> Charles Bukowski
> 5-6-79

FIGURE 22. Bukowski's typewritten preface to the 1980 Black Sparrow edition of *Ask the Dust*. (Courtesy of Linda Bukowski, John Fante Literary Group LLC, and UCLA Library Special Collections.)

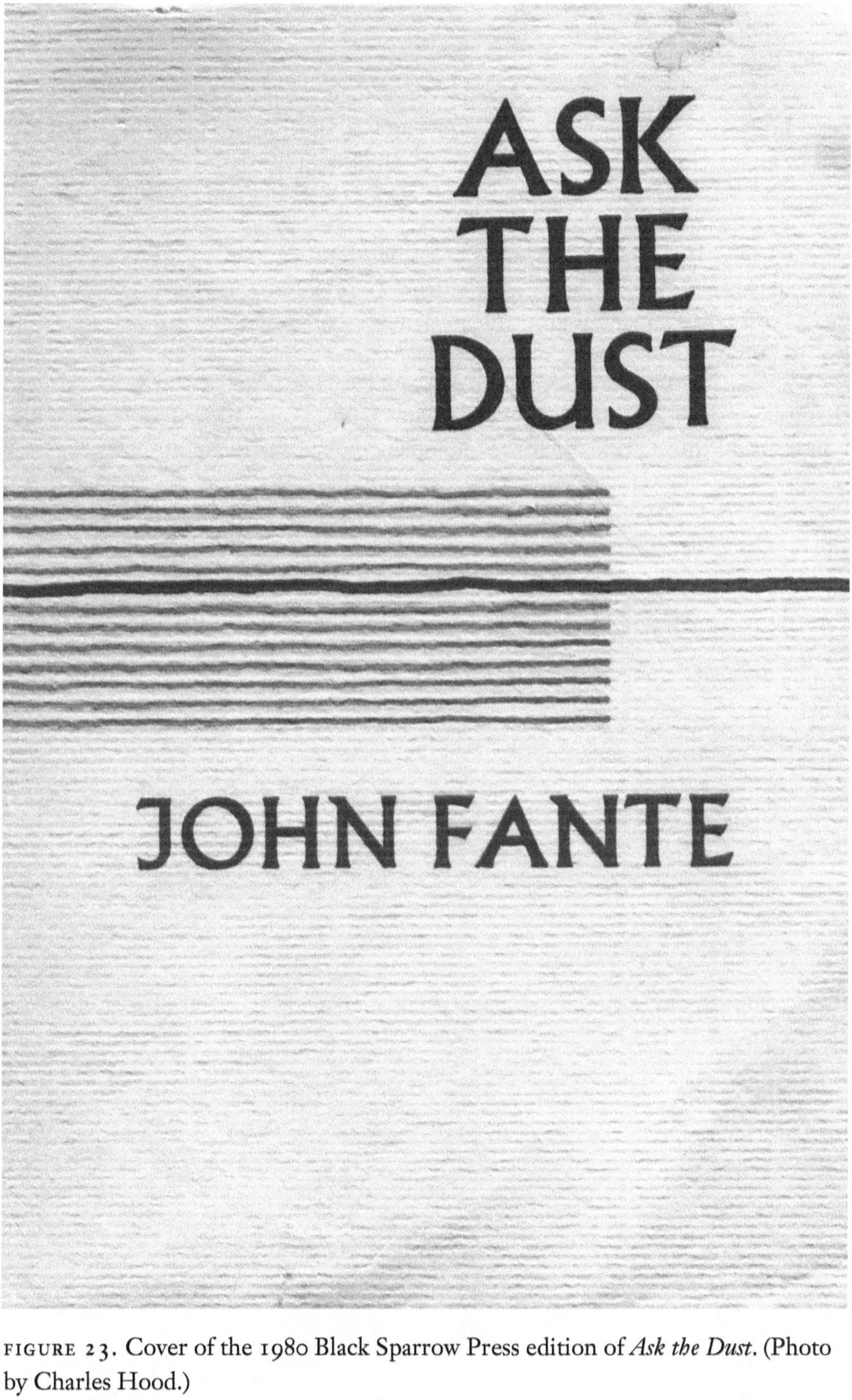

FIGURE 23. Cover of the 1980 Black Sparrow Press edition of *Ask the Dust*. (Photo by Charles Hood.)

Notes

1. In a letter to Joyce Fante dated December 18, 1985—a letter in which he was openly critical of other Fante works—Bukowski offered this full-throated tribute to *Ask the Dust*. See John Fante Papers, UCLA Library Special Collections, box 28, file 2.

2. Charles Bukowski, "Aftermath of a Lengthy Rejection Letter." *Story* 24, no. 106 (March–April 1944): 2, 4–5, 97–99. See also Stephen Cooper, "Madness and Writing in Hamsun, Fante and Bukowski," *genre: Madness and Literature*, no. 19 (1998): 19–27.

3. Linda Lee Bukowski, email to Stephen Cooper, June 19, 2018. The pages that follow are held in the John Fante Papers, box 25, folder 1. Note that in his typescript of the preface, Bukowski misspells the name of Rudolph Borchert.

5. The Attic, the Archive, and Beyond

From Family to Institutional Memory:
A Conversation with Stephen Cooper

Teresa Fiore

Two thousand and nine marked the 100th anniversary of the birth of novelist John Fante. While his success continues to grow in Europe, and in particular in Italy—his father's country of origin—sustained recognition of his work in the publishing world and among readers in the United States has yet to come. The story of Fante's papers somewhat reflects the fate of this niche author whose legacy is profoundly linked to Los Angeles, but also speaks to a large spectrum of geographical and cultural locales. For years, his papers were kept in private storage by his family members in California until finding a permanent home at UCLA Library Special Collections in 2009. The transfer of papers from a partially accessible place to an institutional one such as an official archive can be seen as the entry into that world of immortality that Fante himself had unabashedly pined for along with his literary alter egos Arturo Bandini and Henry Molise. For a writer who wrote incessantly about writing, the careful physical preservation of his papers and the wider access provided to interested and qualified individuals for research purposes is an even more profound pact with eternity, especially if regular cultural events based on the special collection will attract the attention of publishers and readers alike. This 2009 conversation with Fante's biographer, Stephen Cooper of California State University, Long Beach, contributes to the debate on the relationship between archives, memory, and cultural awareness, with specific reference to the Italian American community's efforts to preserve and disseminate its history. The conversation specifically revolves around the acquisition trajectory of Fante's collection by a university archive and analyzes the implications of this move for the academic field and for literature at large across time and space.

TERESA FIORE—*The website of the Archives of Irish America at New York University—a space comparable to what Italian America has at other institutions*[1]*—opens with a quote by Pete Hamill, journalist of Irish descent and Sinatra biographer: "One of the great arguments for an archive, for a place, a repository, is to be certain that the accidents and vagaries of life don't affect the valuable things." What is the definition of an archive that you find relevant as an experienced researcher and as a biographer, in particular?*

STEPHEN COOPER—The Greek root of *archive* puts us in mind of beginnings, rule, (right) government. Literally, an archive is a place where historical documents are protected from the often-harmful vagaries of life and thus preserved for the good of posterity. Those vagaries run the gamut from the elemental to the political to the subconscious and neurological. The natural forces of fire, water, earth and air can all be destructive to such documents; so can the manmade forces of this ideology or that regime; so can our mere forgetfulness. The archive stands against all such destruction and for the creative exercise of our ability to understand the past as it informs and influences both the present and the future. By identifying, collecting, preserving and making available documentary traces of the past as resources for research, the archive helps to uphold fundamental democratic values and to maintain lines of cultural continuity.

Sound high minded? Well, it is—and it all depends on the commitment to safeguarding, in perpetuity, even the lowliest scraps of smudged typewriting. Fante's wife, Joyce, was no trained archivist, but the four large steel file cabinets that she tended to for decades on the service porch of the Fante home in Malibu, filling each drawer with every kind of evidence of John Fante's life and career, proved to be the perfect biographical archive.

TF—Your critical work on Fante's writings, but in particular your important biography of Fante, would have been impossible without the special permission to access his papers. How did you find them and how did they become available to you?

SC—I first approached Joyce in the mid-1990s by sending her a letter. In this letter I introduced myself as a writer, a teacher, and a longtime admirer of John Fante's works. I mentioned that twenty years earlier, after reading a long-out-of-print copy of *Ask the Dust*, I had written an unabashed fan letter to John, and that he had responded with an encouraging note. All this was preamble to my main point, namely, the unsolicited proposal that she consider my offer to undertake the first biography of her late husband.

To tell the truth, I was flying blind. Up to this time I had never written a biography and I had no idea about John Fante's papers, what they might be, or if any such archive even existed.

Months passed. When a reply finally came it was not from Joyce but rather from her agent. Yes, her agent, a character straight out of Hollywood. You see, Joyce was as emotionally devoted to nourishing John Fante's memory as she was determined to foster his legacy. There followed a number of meetings, first on the patio of the Fante home, then at the dining room table over countless cups of coffee. In fact, these meetings were interviews, with Joyce the interviewer probing my motivations and testing my intentions, until one day she asked point blank, "What do you want to do?"

The question was an important one, I could tell, but I had no prepared answer. I responded simply, "I want to tell the truth about John Fante." It was enough. Leading me through the kitchen and onto the service porch, Joyce showed me those four large file cabinets and invited me to open the nearest drawer. Soon we had drawn up an agreement outlining our respective obligations, but from that day forward I was free to use the files as I saw fit. Joyce had granted me her permission.

TF—What do the papers contain? Is there some uncharted section of the papers that could potentially become the core of another work by you or another researcher?

SC—The collection holds over 50 boxes totaling 23.5 linear feet of materials. Included are all known original short story and novel manuscripts, many heavily annotated; dozens of screenplays, teleplays, and treatments; over 240 letters; family photographs and memorabilia, including audio recordings of John Fante speaking; business records and professional awards; Fante's high school scrapbook; one of his favorite typewriters; even a lock of his hair.

There is much still to be learned from these papers, and from a variety of angles. The novel and short story manuscripts offer a rich opportunity to continue the study of Fante's creative process and his development as a writer. Scholars of film history will find the screenplays of interest if not for any intrinsic literary merit then for the light they shed on diverse industrial exigencies, from changing audience tastes for escapist entertainment to the real-world pressures of Cold War politics. Certainly, the letters contain more raw biographical information than I was able to fit into my book; I can easily imagine their yielding future studies of Fante's life and career.

One way great writers come to be known is by the number of biographies they inspire. Few developments could be more fulfilling to me as Fante's first biographer than to see others using the collection to research, write, and publish new lives of John Fante.

TF—What is the current state of the papers?
SC—Following Joyce's death in 2005, the papers sat out of reach and unused in a private storage facility in Thousand Oaks, California, while the three surviving Fante children debated their options. They knew that certain elements of the collection could fetch a price on the international private market; interest in Italy was especially strong. In the end they decided that their father's legacy as an important American writer would be best served by keeping the papers together as an integral collection that would be accessible to scholars at a top university library in Los Angeles, the city where John Fante came of age as a writer.

On the day before the April 8, 2009, centenary of Fante's birth, a press release went out announcing that the papers had been acquired by the Department of Special Collections at UCLA's Charles E. Young Research Library. The many materials took nearly two years to process.

Working under the auspices of the Center for Primary Research and Training, a PhD student in UCLA's Department of English by the name of Daniel Garner did a great job of organizing everything. On March 10, 2011, at the Department of Special Collections, I gave a talk entitled "The Road to John Fante's Los Angeles." This was in fact the latest in the university's Bonnie Cashin Endowed Lecture series, and it marked the opening of a wonderful exhibit of the Fante Collection that will be open to the public until September 2011. Anyone interested in getting a taste of the collection can visit *John Fante: A Life in the Works*, the permanent virtual exhibit maintained by UCLA Special Collections (fig. 24).[2]

TF—How do you think private and public interests intersect in the transfer of a writer's papers? What's at stake in moving memory from the family to the institution, especially when we talk about Italian American families whose culture has not always been necessarily identified with or channeled into books vs. *music, cinema, etc.*

SC—I worked closely with Joyce for several years. During that time I came to see how the same impulse that led her to collect and keep safe her personal John Fante archive also prevented her from parting with it. Note that Joyce herself was neither Italian American nor book deprived. Rather, she was the daughter of white Anglo-Saxon protestant privilege, a highly educated alumna of Stanford University who was at home in the world of literature, art, and culture. Nonetheless, try as I did, I never succeeded in persuading her to relinquish control of the papers to a university library so that they could benefit other researchers. She was "keeper of the flame," as she proudly identified herself, and though she gave me a free hand and her fullest support in writing my biography, she could not or would not allow herself to be separated from the physical evidence of her memories of John Fante so that they could be, so to speak, institutionalized.

One point we can draw from this seeming contradiction is that family memories are extremely sensitive. It's a broad point, to be sure, but I wonder if it might apply with special force to those families referenced in the question, Italian Americans "whose culture has not always been necessarily identified with or channeled into books." It's difficult to overstate the deeply visceral *and* spiritual significance that palpable

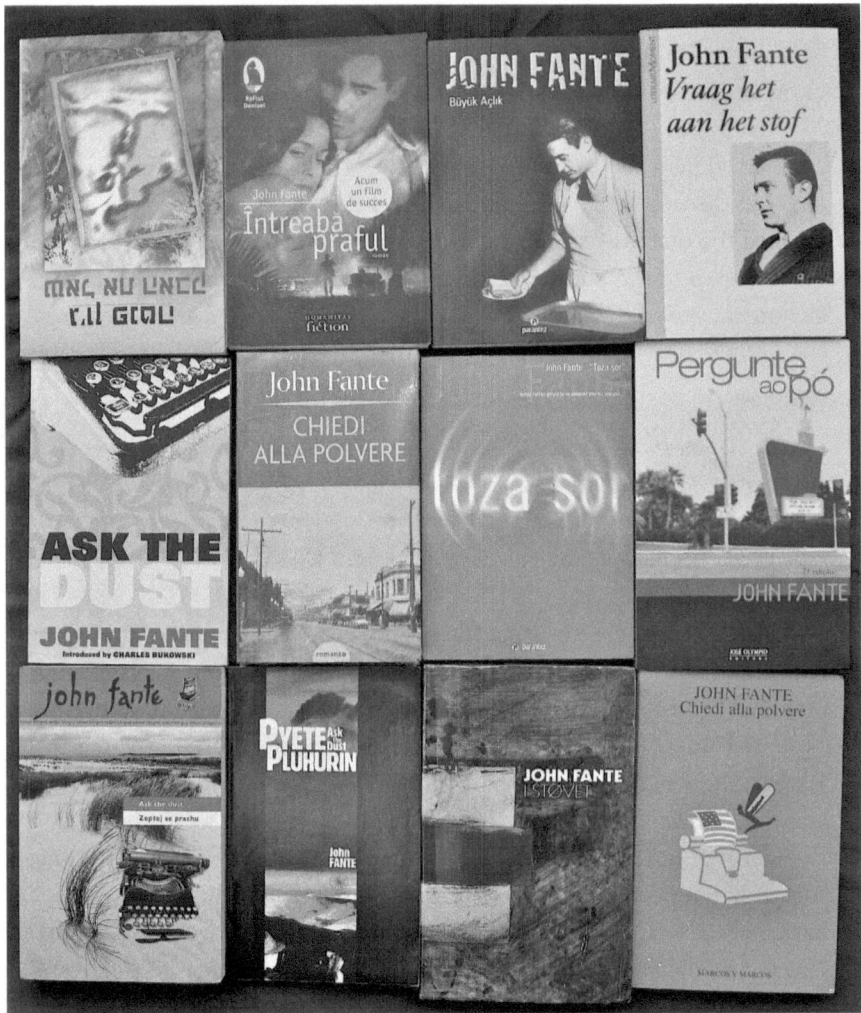

FIGURE 24. Covers of international editions of *Ask the Dust*. (Courtesy of John Fante Literary Group LLC. Photo by Charles Hood.)

mementos of deceased family members hold for their survivors: witness the role of religious relics in traditional Italian Catholicism.

I have not studied these matters in any systematic way so I hesitate to generalize from my experience. What I can say is that the conversation about the ultimate disposition of the Fante papers was always a delicate one. Even after Joyce had died and her children inherited the conversation, it elicited strong feelings, not the least of which was ambivalence. Anyone entering into such a conversation from the outside should realize that the balancing act between a family's private interest and those of the larger literary world will likely be a central challenge.

TF—What can a community of scholars like the one focusing on the Italian American experience do to ease such acquisitions? Is it a question of promoting a different culture around private papers or is there a financial aspect involved in relinquishing a private collection to a public institution that should be seriously considered?

SC—The financial aspect cannot be overlooked. For one thing, a professional appraisal of the collection's value is required, the expense of which usually falls to the collection's owner. These evaluations are not cheap, especially if, as is recommended, more than one appraisal is conducted in order to make comparisons. Even when the collection is donated as a write-off, an appraisal is needed for tax purposes.

Unfortunately, there is a popular misconception about the kind of money that can be made by selling off collections of papers. People assume that because what they own has great personal value to them, they should be paid accordingly. The fact is that money is scarce, and yet exceptions to the rule are all the public hears about. So, for example, news persists about the famously well-endowed Ransom Center at the University of Texas, Austin, paying $2.5 million for the Norman Mailer collection. But Mailer was both a bestselling author and an international celebrity, and his archive amounts to over 1,000 boxes of materials that, if lined up side by side, would stretch longer than a football field. Few collections can compete at that level. (Gay Talese, anyone?)

To ease the acquisition of materials focusing on the Italian American experience, I would hazard to say that interested scholars should work to educate the potential sources of such collections. Families need to be reassured that what matters to them also matters to the larger community, and that memory is best served when it extends and expands into the future. I can think of no better way of ensuring the long-term life of precious family memories than by sharing them as a whole with others who in turn will learn about the past in order to teach the generations of tomorrow.

Notes

This is an edited version of an interview that was published originally in *Italian Americana* 31, no. 1 (Winter 2013): 17–23.

1. Such archives include the Immigration History Research Center at the University of Minnesota, for example. Archives for Italian American literature are available in more circumscribed forms in individual libraries. For instance, Pietro Di Donato's papers can be found at the State University of New York Stony Brook Library, Jerre Mangione's at the University of Rochester River Campus Libraries, and Helen Barolini's at Syracuse University.

2. *John Fante: A Life in the Works*, http://jfiala.bol.ucla.edu/fante/index.htm. To browse the contents of the entire collection, go to the Online Archive of California at http://www.oac.cdlib.org/ and search "John Fante."

Prelude to "Prologue to *Ask the Dust*"

Stephen Cooper

In fall 1938 John Fante wrote an astonishing letter from his Los Angeles apartment to William Soskin, his editor at the small independent firm of Stackpole Sons publishers, based in Harrisburg, Pennsylvania. Fante was twenty-nine years old, a seasoned screenwriter, and the author of several published stories as well as a well-received first novel, *Wait Until Spring, Bandini*. Now he was burning to plunge into his second. In a fever of creativity, he sat down and wrote a dense and lyrical seventeen-page synopsis of the new novel that was forming inside him. Delivered by turns in his own hardheaded, professional voice and the voice of his emotionally volatile alter ego protagonist Arturo Bandini, these seventeen pages encapsulated the whole plot of the novel: Arturo's comic dreams of becoming a great writer amidst all the other lost souls in Depression-era Los Angeles; his racially charged affair with the beautiful Mexican waitress Camilla Lopez; Arturo's war of guilt and pride over the Catholic faith of his Italian American heritage; Camilla's self-destructive love for the sadistic bartender Sammy;

Arturo's grotesque sexual charade with the mysteriously scarred Vera Rivkin; the calamitous Long Beach Earthquake of 1933; Camilla's slide into drugs and madness; and Arturo's desperate attempt to prevent her from vanishing into the desolation of the Mojave Desert (fig. 25).

The letter succeeded. In January 1939 Fante signed a contract to write the book. Over the next several months he worked in a white heat to produce the novel we now consider one of the most seminal works of fiction ever written about Los Angeles. He wrote it fast, in a state of pure creative abstraction, with little need to revise. "It was an easy book to write," Fante later marveled. "It just poured out of me."[1]

In 1990, seven years after John Fante died, that 1938 letter was published by Black Sparrow Press as "Prologue to *Ask the Dust*." Upon reading it I recall my amazement at Fante's seemingly effortless clairvoyance in foretelling not only the novel's intricate mesh of events but also its intense, indeed, manic emotional complexity.

That effortlessness becomes something of a mystery when we pause to consider that the novel's protagonist Arturo Bandini, unlike its author John Fante, has to struggle, suffer, and agonize in order to write almost anything— and then for the most part only to fail. The hilarious, painful scene in *Ask the Dust* comes to mind of Arturo's two-day battle pounding away at the typewriter, and in the end only two repeated words filling the page, "palm tree palm tree palm tree." Or later when Arturo has an idea and it floats "harmlessly through the room ... like a small white bird.... It only wanted to help me.[2] But I would strike at it, hammer it out across the keyboard, and it would die." Or yet again, "I was scared and worried [as] I sat before my typewriter and the great awful void descended.... I beat my head with my fists [but it] was useless."[3]

These are but three of many such scenes throughout Fante's works dramatizing the frustrations, often the impossibility, of writing. As Janet Maslin observed in her *New York Times* review of *The John Fante Reader*, "Of all the subjects [Fante] tackled, none brought out the best [in him] more than writer's block—[he] was paradoxically eloquent and effusive about wordlessness, making it a haunting symbol of any artist's isolation."[4]

So then: what's up with that paradox? How could Fante sail so smoothly through the writing of his great American novel when that novel is all about a writer who can hardly sit down at the typewriter without enduring the

Ask the dust on the road! Ask the Joshua trees standing alone where the Mojave begins. Ask them about Camila Lopez, and they will whisper her name. Yes, ~~Soskin~~ for, the last anyone ever saw of my girl Camila Lopez was an old tubercular living on the edge of the Mojave, and she was heading East with a dog I gave her, and the dog was named Pancho, and nobody has ever seen Pancho again either. You will not believe that. You will not believe that a girl would start across the Mojave desert in October with no companion save a young police dog named Pancho, but it happened. I saw the dog prints in the sand, and I saw the footprints of Camila's alongside the dog's, and she has never come back to Los Angeles, her mother has never seen her again, and unless a miracle happened she is dead out there on the Mojave tonight, and so is Pancho. I do not have to weave a plot for this my second ~~second~~ book. It happened to me. The girl is gone, I was in love with her and she hated me, and that is my story.

Ask the dust on the road. Ask old Junipero Sierra down on the Plaza, his statue is there, and so are the streaks across it where I lit matches, smoked cigarettes, and watched humanity pass by, Arturo Bandini, friend of man and beast alike. Those were the days! I wandered these streets and sucked them up and the people in them like a man made of blotter Biber. Arturo Bandini, with one short story sold, great writer dreaming big plans. I can still see that guy, that Bandini guy, with a green covered magazine under his arm, perpetually under his arm, walking this town with gentle tolerance for man and beast alike, a philosopher he was, a young one, the plain tale of a writer who fell in love with a bar girl and was told to go.

FIGURE 25. Page one of Fante's seventeen-page letter to Stackpole editor William Soskin. (Courtesy of John Fante Literary Group LLC and UCLA Library Special Collections.)

torments of the damned? Well, five years before writing the letter now known as the Prologue, Fante had written another letter that I think helps answer that question—a letter that for over 80 years remained unread.

You see, not long ago an e-mail appeared in my inbox with the subject line "Jo Pagano." I knew the name. More than a mere contemporary of Fante, Pagano was for a time one of his closest friends, a fellow Italian American who, like Fante, had moved from Colorado to Los Angeles to become a writer. By late 1932, when Fante rolled into town broke and friendless, Jo and his big brother Ernest had already established themselves as working screenwriters in Hollywood's old studio system, and Jo would go on to write several well-regarded novels, including *Golden Wedding* and *The Condemned*, the latter of which he would adapt into the award-winning 1950 thriller *The Sound of Fury*. From other letters by John I knew that the Pagano brothers had made him a guest of honor his first November in Los Angeles at their traditional Italian family Thanksgiving, and that after a night of hard drinking in the Brass Rail saloon at the corner of Hollywood and Vine, John and Jo had spent the night sleeping it off in jail before coughing up a fine of six bucks apiece. So, John Fante and Jo Pagano. Common backgrounds. Shared experiences. Parallel ambitions. Paisans.

But back to my inbox. Who might be writing me about Jo Pagano? I opened the e-mail and read:

Dear Stephen Cooper,
My name is Danny Shain. My grandfather [was] Jo Pagano.
While my grandfather was intimate friends with John Fante, I only discovered [Fante] a few years ago. His writing had an immediate and lasting impression upon me, as I know it has had on you.... I learned a great deal from your book, Full of Life, including some things about my grandfather...

[M]y Aunt... has... custody of all my grandfather's papers. There are some interesting things in there. I had a chance to visit her yesterday and in just a superficial glance through one of the boxes we found letters from William Saroyan, Dalton Trumbo, and John Fante. The letter from Fante... dated... 1933 [is] an intimate and frank correspondence that John asked to remain confidential.

My aunt and I would like these papers to be taken care of and made available to students and researchers. We admire the fine job you did with John Fante's work. I hope you would consider doing the same for Jo Pagano.

Thank you,
Danny

An intimate and frank letter from 1933, and confidential to boot? Well, the biographer in me could hardly wait to drive out to Pasadena and meet Danny Shain in his home. When I arrived, over a cup of strong Italian coffee Danny reiterated that his Aunt JoJean Pagano Meek, daughter of Jo Pagano, was eager to do the right thing with her father's papers. Danny had laid out on a table several manuscripts, screenplays, and yellowed news clippings for me to peruse, but it was the old steamer trunk off to one side that kept drawing my eye. When Danny asked if I would like to have a look inside, I said yes. He bent over the trunk, unfastened the lid, and I inhaled the aroma of old newsprint and onionskin. From deep inside Danny pulled out a letter—three dense pages of single-spaced typing (fig. 26)—that provides the solution to our paradox. John Fante could effectively whistle while he worked filling *Ask the Dust* with Arturo's crippling insecurities because he, John Fante, had survived the same insecurities himself; and five years later, after the necessary gestation, he would be able to soar on angel wings through the writing of his best novel. Without reducing the art of *Ask the Dust* to mere psychology, and recalling that every masterpiece is a gift never to be repeated, I like to think of the voice crying in the wilderness of his 1933 letter as that of a young writer-prophet as yet unaware of how far he will be able to see when he finally trusts his innermost vision and nourishes it until its time is come.

Of course, this is no guarantee that following Fante's example will have the same results for everyone, and I would refrain from recommending his more extreme character quirks—all those manic highs and lows, the penchant for bloody fights, an inherited weakness when it came to wine. What I do believe though—and here I'm speaking as a writer and a teacher of young writers—is that writers today, both young and old, should take courage from Fante's letter, recognizing that their own doubts place them in the best of company, if only they can be brave enough to overcome their isolation, seek out the right guidance, and keep writing.

Thank you.

June 30, 1933

Dear Jo,

Make way for some astounding news. Give this letter your utmost thought, if you please; it means a lot to me that you understand, and I'm going to be very candid.

I have temporarily thrown up the spongue about the novel. I am stuck. I know what the matter is, and that's where I make bold to thrust myself upon you. I am coming South in a couple of days. I'll talk the matter over with you more thoroughly then, but for the present I wish you'd formulate some sort of a judgement and let me have it when I see you in a few days.

Here's the trouble. Not in the writing. No; not there. I can write a novel a week if it comes to the mere fact of putting down words. It isn't the writing. It's something bigger. It's a self-consciousness, a thinking about critics, a fear of what people will say, a totally disintegrating, almost morbid panicky feeling that I am not doing a good piece. This has never happened to me before, this feeling. I can't account for it. There are various causes which I suggest to myself, but most of them seem rather insipid and full of holes. In the first place, I feel that I am going through a mental crisis. I feel that I'm growing up, as it were, and that the approach and method of my earlier short stories is not adequate for the novel. Not that I am writing the novel in that meter. Nope. I am writing it on a better and maturer style. But I write screeeeeecy-----screeeechy writing. I hammer away with a lot of terrific exclamation points cluttering my prose. There's something wrong in that kind of writing. It shows affectation. It shows a desire to attrack attention by the artificial devise of the mechanics of writing, by grammatical tricks. To hell with it. I don't want that kind of a book. I want a good, solid book, a sincere book. A piece of artistry. I don't know how I'm going to get it, but I've got it inside me. I feel this way: I can—I will. What I mean is, I got feeling. It won't come out of me. It's stuck somewhere in my head or in my gut, or wherever feelings get stuck. I know this, though: I must open a spout somewhere. Once I do so, the book will pour forth. I mean good stuff. Stuff that will make me proud. I would rather croak than turn in a mediocre novel, and I'm no fool. I know when my writing is up to snuff. It isn't now. Every now and then I get a flash. A swell dab of real literature into the story. But it doesn't happen often enough. I want a hundr3d thousand words of this flash.

Here is where I force myself on you. Here's where you come into the picture. I figure that I will take you on the way Maupassant took on Flaubert. If I have a solid, good mind, a sympathetic fellow like yourself to show me that my stuff is not so lousy, I can go ahead with the writing. You see, I think every line, with few exceptions is lousy. Now this can't be true. I have that feeling about it: that I am underestimating myself. Yet I do so anyway. I seem to get a pleasure out of persecuting myself, and it wears me out.

At the moment I am just completing a short piece which Lieber returned for revision. He says he can sell it to Mencken, so I am cutting it down from the too-lengthy 10,000 words to about 5000. After I finish it, I am coming South.

It isn't going to take very much to set me aright. I trust you so implicitly and think so highly of your intelligence that it won't take much more than a few talks with you to put me on the right road. You see, I realize certain defects. I know, for exmaple, that I am chaotically tempermental. It won't do to be that way, and I am that way here at home. I run things to suit myself. I make a big fuss and go around raising a lot of unnescoearry hell with both the organic and inorganic environment, and it does me a lot of harm. I'm a sonofabitch, Jo. I like to be babied, and if I am babied, I raise hell. I want sympathy. I get it. Then I hate it. What the hell's the matter with me, anyway? My mother and father and brothers and my sister annoy me. Yet they stay out of my way. They steer clear. It infuriates me. I want them to come around. So they do come around. Then I raise hell. I think they are deliberately annoying me. I tell them to go away. When they are gone I wonder why they have left. I then say that they are selfish and unsympathetic. Ah me! I can't understand why I amthis way. I hate it. I get sick thinking of it. It's my own fault, and it isn't. I got to have somebody I respect talk to me. Someone I won't take a punch at; someone I can look upon as a person who won't tolerate my pukey eccentircities; for you see, I'm selfish. If I think I am going to lose a friendship (for example, with you) I listen to reason. And when I reason, I reason with the best of them. I'm not a fool altogehter, I can think and think well when I am forced to it, but I have a goddamn fucking streak of dirty lowdown meanness in me and it comes out whenever I feel that way, and God help anyone who gets in my way. Specially those nearest me——the ones I love most. My own people. I hope you try to understand what I am trying to say, Jo. I did something tonight which horrifies me. My mother came into the kitchen, and I was drinking coffee. She said, simply, sweetly, delightfully, "If the coffee isn't strong enough for you Johnnie, I can make a new potful." What did I do? I got on my high horse. "Jesus Christ!" I said. "Leave me alone. How you people love to torture me!" Now was that the thing for a sane man to say? Ten minutes later I wanted to kill myself. I was heartbroken. That's the way it goes. I go to these stupid emotional heights a hundred times a day. I hate myself abomnibally one minute and love myself idiotically the next.

    I'm going to put myself in your hands, and you've got to accept me for what I am and make something out of me. I don't give a damn whether you'll like the job or not. You have <u>got to</u>, Jo. You <u>must</u>. Otherwise I'm lost. I pick you as the best bet first because of our friendship and second because you're a sage with a hell of a lot of brains. I can't say what good it's going to do you, but you'll have no regrets. I can at least dedicate my book to you. (I'm talking nonsense now) But I know you won't regret anything. I want someone who is my intellectual superior so that I won't get smart. You're the man. You're sent right out of heaven, and I'm a voice crying in the nostalgic wilderness. You take the place of Helen Purcell on an intellectual plane. She did a lot of damage to me, that Helen, that cloud of a woman who went right through me with her edible sweetnesses.

I am coming South with enough money to live comfortably for three months, but I must make certain sacrafices which will do me good. I will talk this over with you too. You may not realize it, or be prepared for it, or take any pleasure in it, but the importance with which I esteem you, and the way you loom up at this moment is really astonishing. I should have had aman like you around me all the time. I might have —I would have written better stories. I will write a great story now—in this novel—with you to give me the intelligent advise I need. Oh, I'll write the book myself. The idea is that I need a positive and tangible impetus. I'm a lost soul. I don't say this in any melancholy fashion. It is the fact which I have been avoiding for the last three years. I am acceding to it before it is too late.

I write this letter after serious reflection. It is not written impetuously. It is not a flying and gadding about in desperation. These things , this gadding about, does not exist for me. I am a serious person, and what I think now is not an impulsive thought that has come to me after a temporary despair. No. I have known it a long time. I am looking it in the face now.

Let me digress a minute, Jo. I have no doubt of my ability. I am so bulging with a genuine conviction of talent that it might be called foolish, so strong it is. I know though, that what talent I have is in a generative process still. It needs discipline, otherwise it will grow wild. But I am not able to discipline myself. (Say! Don't get me wrong here, Jo. I am not conceited. I am facing what I think are facts.)

    If I can be near you, talk to you, get out of this furious vacuum, get a breath of shrewd and mature advise, get a word of encouragement from a man who recognizes defects and faults and does not moralize about either, then I will be getting the things I need in this business of writing.

    Think it over, will you? On the other hand, I feel that I can be of assistance to you. Here again, I don't mean that I write your book (or you write mine), but of something better. It is the practise, I think, among sophisticated and seasoned novelists to work alone. But name one author, great author, who has produced his initial efforts without assistance? I need yours. I am honest about it. I need help, but not help in the sense of a colloborator. No. I need a better intelligence than my own to stand beside me and tell me to write the book to suit myself. I think you understand.

    I hope you'll think it over, Jo. Naturally, this is confidential, and when I get to LA I hope you'll have something to say with reference to this letter.

                                    best of luck.

                                        johnnie

FIGURE 26. Letter from John Fante to his friend-turned-fellow-Hollywood-writer from Colorado Jo Pagano. (Courtesy of JoJean Pagano Meek, Danny Shain, and the John Fante Literary Group LLC).

Notes

A slightly different version of this paper was presented as a talk during the symposium "John Fante's *Ask the Dust*: 75 Years and Counting" at California State University, Long Beach, November 6, 2014.

1. Pleasants, "Dust and Fog."
2. Fante, *Ask the Dust*, 27.
3. Fante, 78.
4. Maslin, "A Truly Famous Unknown Writer," E9.

Works Cited

Fante, John. *Ask the Dust*. 1939. Santa Barbara, CA: Black Sparrow Press, 1980.
Maslin, Janet. "A Truly Famous Unknown Writer." *New York Times*, February 28, 2002.
Pleasants, Ben. "The Dust and Fog of LA's Streets: The John Fante Tapes (One)." Interview with John Fante. *3:00 AM Magazine*, March 29, 2010. www.3ammagazine.com/3am/the-dust-fog-of-las-streets-the-john-fante-tapes-one/.

Goodbye, Bunker Hill

John Fante

I used to live on Bunker Hill. It was my first home in this incredible city. That was in 1932, a time of dreams for me, and of poverty. I had a typewriter and a stack of white paper, and I had my room in a hotel on Bunker Hill.

It cost me $3 a week, that little room, a fabulous sum in those lean days; but I wish I might do it over again, sit in my little room with its worn green carpet, sit there in the high, old-fashioned rocker, eating an orange, my feet out the window, feasting my eyes on the city below. Such dreams for a man! A whole afternoon with the sun pouring down, a whole evening under white, chunky stars.

"This is the place," I used to gasp. "I shall never leave here."

I never did very much work in those days, never finished more than a short story. It held me, that mysterious little room with its startling view, that lonely Bunker Hill with its ancient buildings, its quiet streets and lonely trees with here and there a bright spot from which came the scent of singing hamburgers, the crooning voice of Bing Crosby, the soft sound of men speaking and laughing.

I remember the cool afternoons, the city below, a film of carbon monoxide choking it, the deep moaning of traffic within the Third Street tunnel, the high frightened squeal of the cable car lurching up Angels Flight.

I was higher than the City Hall, higher than the Biltmore, higher than the Richfield Tower. It was paradise. I couldn't work. I was drugged on dreams, steeped in the fascination of old houses and gentle eucalyptus trees growing out of the green slopes there on the west side of Bunker Hill. Sometimes I went down to the library and got a book, some poetry maybe, some gentle and persuasive book, something to read on the hillside, something to put me to sleep under the eucalyptus trees (fig. 27).

FIGURE 27. "Goodbye, Bunker Hill," by John Fante, *Los Angeles Times*, June 30, 1940. (Copyright © 1940. *Los Angeles Times*. Used by permission. Courtesy of John Fante Literary Group LLC.)

Tetsu Hagamoro, what has happened to him? He isn't there now, but in 1932 that wonderful Tetsu had a grocery store at Third and Flower. He used to see me coming, his black eyes laughing as he reached for a big paper sack. Lean days for me: sometimes only a nickel a day for food. The old man understood, nodding his head: in Tokyo he had an uncle who was a writer, too. Tough town, Tokyo. Tough for writers. So. Chasso. Verrie, verrie tough. Chasso. And Tetsu's bullet-shaped head bent over the fruit stall: always the same five-pound sack, Tetsu filling it with apples, oranges and bananas. Sometimes I had a dime, sometimes 15 cents. No matter to Tetsu, he always filled the sack. Once he saw me circle his little store on the other side of the street. Not even a nickel that day. Tetsu called me. "Chasso," said Tetsu. "Uncle in Tokyo. Him stahve, too. Not gottem nickel. So. Chasso. Takem fruit. So. Takem. Pay rater. So. Thank you so much."

And the day was saved.

Fruit, fruit, fruit. Apples for breakfast. Oranges for lunch. Bananas for dinner. I used to sit with my feet out the window, watching the city's lights bursting in the green twilight, my lap piled with banana skins and orange peels. But I liked it, waiting for the darkness, waiting for the night and a prowl through the dismal effulgence of Main Street and lower Fifth Street. Down the eternal stairs of Angels Flight to Hill Street and the blazing inferno below. Down to the Plaza. Down to Chinatown and Olvera Street. Down to the jungled bitterness of lower Fifth Street, drinking it down, gulping it down, the wild, beautiful, terrible city. Then midnight and the slow pull of the steep stairs of Angels Flight, counting the stairs just for the fun of it, always getting mixed up after a hundred, happy to reach my hotel, grateful for the hard bed in my little room, its sheets so worn and thin you saw the striped mattress beneath. And there to lie and watch the neon lights jumping red and blue across the foot of the bed, my head whirling with a jumble of panting sensations. Gala days, those. Old Bunker Hill, I loved you then!

Strange people in that hotel. Strangers from Ohio, from New York, from Indiana. Suspicious folk, lonely folk, hating their suspicion, eager to quench their loneliness, but afraid, afraid. Of what? They didn't now. They had been warned: Los Angeles, bad, be very careful of strangers.

I used to sit on the porch and watch them in the evenings as they returned from the roaring city below. Their eyes were startled, their mouths open, their breaths coming hard after the steep climb. Gratefully they threw themselves into porch rockers and gazed in confusion at the mysterious sky. The quiet hill relaxed them, the swishing, grease-stained palms told them they had returned to their earth again, back from the crazy whirl below. Their limbs sang with gratitude for Bunker Hill, the softness of children filled their harried eyes.

I knew a few of them. Mr. H. lived next door. "H.," retired from the Army with a meager pension, had scarcely enough money to pay his liquor bills. Often poor H. had to abstain from gin three and four days a month. He was so miserable there in his room, always naked under a gray bathrobe that showed hair and bones beneath, stumbling barefoot through a litter of empty gin bottles, forced to survive on cheap wine until the next check arrived. At night I could hear him in bed, tossing and groaning, smoking cigarettes and scratching matches savagely against the wall, denouncing his life, the government, the earth, mankind and particularly the lousy wine which clucked in his throat like a hen.

On the other side was Mrs. C., a widow, tall, gaunt, ferocious, uncommunicative, not even a nod when you met her in the hall and said hello. She had come from Battle Creek, Michigan, and she was the oldest guest in the hotel, having lived in the same room for 22 years.

Occasionally I saw the inside of Mrs. C.'s room, especially in the hot afternoons, when she opened the door for the cooling cross draft. It made you gasp.

To the very ceiling it was piled with boxes and trunks and old newspapers. What one saw of the walls was covered by fly-specked daguerreotypes in heavy gold frames, pictures of men and women long dead, their grim faces defying complete obliteration.

Mrs. C.'s key box was beside mine behind the clerk's desk. In all the months I lived there I never saw Mrs. C. get a letter. But every afternoon her mailbox contained a new piece of mail: The Battle Creek News. Half of her room was piled to the ceiling with back numbers.

And there was the lad named Cross, who washed dishes at Bernstein's, and dreamed of the day when there would be money enough to return to Sydney, Australia. He had to have a stake. He had to return home with the appearance of a rich young man. It was his plan for vindication, for he had run away from home three years before and had got himself into serious trouble with his folks, writing them that he was a big executive in the lumber business.

And Julio, the Filipino, a bellhop at the Biltmore who wrote novels in his spare time, wrote novels with the facility of a boy scrawling his name on a back fence. Julio, the pest, who wrote a couple of novels a month and brought them to me for criticism. And Elaine, the shady, lovely Elaine, who arrived quietly at night and for two weeks had the hotel humming like a beehive with gossip; Elaine, who did a grand business around there, until the landlady found out and ordered her to leave.

And Leon from San Francisco, always shouting in the lobby, denouncing Los Angeles endlessly, praising San Francisco with such fury no one dared dispute him. And Miss L., always draped in black, her small, white lips perpetually smiling, so that the smile gradually became somewhat sinister: Miss L., always scurrying to the library and returning with an armload of theosophic books. Miss L. was a student of palmistry and card reading. She claimed a great knowledge of dogs and pets, but one day the landlady's wirehaired terrier came down with distemper and Miss L. went screaming down the halls, shouting, "Run for your lives! Run for your lives!" She believed distemper brought influenza and tuberculosis to humans, and they had a hard time quieting her. She locked herself in her room and sprinkled the walls and carpets with Lysol. For weeks we held our noses as we passed her door.

The dream of Miss L.'s life was to set up a little parlor where, for small sums, she could read palms, coffee cups, tea leaves and head bumps. The loafers in the lobby had some curious interpretations of Miss L.'s strange machinations, but they are unprintable.

But they are gone now, these people, scattered like dust. Everything changes, and for better or worse the change came for me, and the years have trickled away, and Bunker Hill is only a memory. But it lives on. It gave my thought food and drink, it sated my hunger for life, despite the harsh rigors of straight fruit diet during those heroic months.

Everything changes, and now Bunker Hill faces change. It seemed timeless, and now they are putting it away. The papers carry the story: the old Bunker Hill must go. The old hotels, the brave palms, the quiet streets—away with all of them! They are going to tear Bunker Hill down, or build it up, or wipe it out, or something. It hurts me. I wet my lips and inhale my cigarette and smile. Those precious months! Those tender nights! How shall I mark them? Where shall I go to find their souvenirs?

They are changing Bunker Hill, yes, but in my heart the palms still sigh, the little plots of grass on the slopes remain forever green, and a boy's kite lies helplessly entangled in the branches of a brave eucalyptus tree.

Note

This essay was first published in the *Los Angeles Times*, June 30, 1940, H6.

The Road to John Fante's Los Angeles

Stephen Cooper

Thank you, Tom. Thank you, Genie. And so many of you! Family, friends, colleagues, students, the children of John Fante: Jim, Vickie, and families, including filmmaker Giovanna DiLello, all the way from Italy—thank you all very much for coming. I'm honored to be at UCLA this afternoon to share a few reflections about John Fante and my work. Like John Fante and Bonnie Cashin, the visionary fashion designer whose legacy this lecture series commemorates, the people at UCLA Library and Special Collections understand the importance of creativity. Thanks to them—to University Librarian Gary Strong, former Head of Special Collections Vicki Steele, her successor and now Director of Library Special Collections Tom Hyry, Manuscripts Librarian Genie Guerard, Daniel Gardner of the Center for Primary Research and Training, Visual Arts Specialist Octavio Olvera, Cindy Newsome, Annie Watanabe-Rocco, Dawn Setzer, and everyone else on staff—thanks to them UCLA is not only host to our gathering today but also home to all fifty-some boxfuls of John Fante's papers. Starting now and for all posterity, this collection will be an invaluable resource for scholars of many subjects, from twentieth-century American literature, to the Hollywood film industry, to, in my view, the most compelling, contradictory, emblematic, exasperating, and inspiring creative writer in the history of Los Angeles: yes, John Fante (fig. 28).

I'm also happy to be here. You see, forty years ago this year I graduated from UCLA with a BA in English. Heading out into the great world I took with me a powerful sense of how literature mattered, how, through reading and writing, I might find a life. That sense was at the heart of my response when, at age twenty-four, I bought a second-hand copy of an obscure old novel. The title was strange, *Ask the Dust*, and the author, John Fante, unknown to me. But that book changed my life. From the first page it possessed me with the voice of its hero, Arturo Bandini, and with the way his Los Angeles of the early 1930s felt just like mine, a city filled with soaring desires and crushing defeats and the crazy-making search for love as Arturo writes and dreams and pursues the beautiful Camilla Lopez to the book's haunting climax in the desert. I read that book and knew *I* had to write. But write what? A review, that's what. A book review—brilliant! Of a book that had been out of print for decades, and me a no-name wannabe scribbler. The odds were long, but the world needed to know. And so, brimming with a young man's certainties, I mailed my review to the *Los Angeles Times*, assuring then book editor Digby Diehl that here was a masterpiece, a forgotten tragicomedy for the ages—all as if I knew what I was saying.

Well, turns out I did; which didn't prevent my review from bouncing back, rejected. Not to be deterred, albeit twenty years later, I tried again. This time, after a six-year adventure of research and writing, the book being reviewed was mine.

Who was John Fante, and why does he matter to us in Los Angeles and to others around the world? What provokes people to call Fante "the father" of the Los Angeles novel and "the patron saint" of LA writing?[1] What made quintessential LA poet Charles Bukowski go so far as to say, "Fante was my god"?[2] These are a few of the questions I'll try to answer today, keeping in mind the Cashin Lecture's stated purpose, namely, to celebrate the creative process. I'll start our celebration with a brief summary of Fante's life and works. Then I'll take up a few of the creative challenges I faced in writing my book and the ways I overcame them—or failed to. By the time

FIGURE 28. Poster for the *John Fante: A Life in Works* exhibit at UCLA, February–June 2011 (Courtesy of UCLA Library Special Collections. Photo by Charles Hood.)

we adjourn, my hope is that you can enjoy all the more the story that our exhibit tells.

John Fante was born April 8, 1909, in Denver, Colorado, into a poor Italian American family. In 1901 his father, Nick Fante, had left the mountains of Italy's impoverished Abruzzi province to work in the Mile High City. No matter how blue a state Colorado might be today, in the early twentieth century it seethed with anti-immigrant and anti-Catholic sentiment. The mayor of Denver belonged to the Ku Klux Klan, and racist suspicions of catlicker dagoes and papist wops prevailed. Growing up, the young John Fante thus learned firsthand the dark, sometimes violent lessons of American xenophobia. His formal education came from Sisters of the Blessed Virgin Mary at Boulder's Sacred Heart of Jesus parish, where he served as an altar boy, and later from the Jesuits at Denver's Regis High. There, a fleeting call to the priesthood was lost to a mania for sports, a predilection for fistfights, and telltale plummeting grades. The cause of this adolescent turmoil could be traced to home. Although Nick Fante was an expert stonemason whose skills were in demand, his diehard drinking, gambling, and womanizing led to poverty for the family and a troubled relationship with eldest son John. Over time, these formative experiences left their marks on Fante, becoming central themes in his writing.

As the country sank into the Depression, Nick Fante deserted his family and disappeared with another woman. Soon John fled Colorado, hitchhiking and hopping freights to California. In blue-collar Wilmington he began to write and starve under a merciless regimen; in one month, he claimed, he lost thirty pounds while writing 150,000 words and devouring great stacks of Hemingway, Dos Passos, and DeMaupassant. He eked out a living at menial jobs around the harbor: ditchdigger, dishwasher, loading-dock grunt. Through it all he stuck to his writing and in 1932 he broke into print when H. L. Mencken published "Altar Boy" in *The American Mercury*; a book contract with publisher Alfred A. Knopf ensued. When the resulting novel was rejected, Fante plunged into another, calling it *The Road to Los Angeles*. Here he fictionalized his experiences at a Terminal Island cannery through an archly named alter ego protagonist, the fire-breathing Arturo Bandini. Written under the spell of Mencken's iconoclasm and the nihilist dithyrambs of Nietzsche, Fante's searing satire of politics, religion, and sex was too much for its time, and this novel too was rejected. Against these setbacks, Fante found support for his outsized literary aspirations from Mencken. In return, Fante idolized the so-called Sage of Baltimore in equally outsized ways, revering him as "a better ideal than ten thousand Jesus Christs, twelve thousand popes, ninety thousand St. Johns, ninety-eight thousand St. Teresas, and . . . sixty-nine million Jesuits."[3] Defiantly lapsed as he might be, Fante's *Baltimore Catechism* was showing.

By now Fante had moved to the faded Bunker Hill district of downtown Los Angeles. There he met another Mencken protégé, Carey McWilliams. Despite all their differences—Fante the hot-blooded writer of autobiographical fiction, McWilliams a cool intellectual radical-activist lawyer whose nonfiction writings on Los Angeles and California today are hailed as classics—despite these differences, the two formed a lifelong bond. Via McWilliams, Fante met people in Hollywood. Soon he was a contract scenarist at Warner Bros. alongside such other writers of note as James Hilton, W. H. Burnett, Dalton Trumbo, and William Faulkner. Thus began the split in Fante's career between serious fiction and the piffle he wrote holding his nose for a studio paycheck. But then as now the industry was fickle, and paydays were at best sporadic.

So went the 1930s, a constant shuffle between studio stints churning out B-movie undercards, and far less lucrative bouts writing short stories and the first three of the four novels that would make up the Saga of Arturo Bandini. In 1937 Fante eloped with Joyce Smart. Joyce was a beautiful blue-eyed poet and Stanford alumna, but she was also the daughter of a wealthy WASP family that frowned on Fante for all he was, an Italian, a Catholic, and a writer. The marriage was volatile, veering from verbal fisticuffs to passionate reconciliations, on the carpet, in the shower, often several times a day. But owing in no small part to Joyce's gifted editorial eye, Fante's literary star was rising. His first published novel, *Wait Until Spring, Bandini*, featuring Arturo as a boy amidst family turbulence in Boulder, appeared in 1938 to glowing reviews. *Ask the Dust* followed in 1939, one in that remarkable year's list of stand-out releases, including Raymond Chandler's *The Big Sleep*, Nathanael West's *The Day of the Locust*, and John Steinbeck's *The Grapes of Wrath*. True, the reviews were not as strong and sales of *Ask the Dust* suffered when a lawsuit brought on behalf of Adolf Hitler against Fante's publisher for releasing an unlicensed edition of *Mein Kampf* stole the wind from the firm's promotional efforts; but with two widely noted novels out and a forthcoming story collection, *Dago Red*, Fante's reputation was blossoming.

And yet, because of the money, movie work always beckoned. This time it was at RKO under the genius of *Citizen Kane*, Orson Welles. Welles's new film, however, the now legendary *It's All True*, collapsed early on in production, and as the war years darkened so did Fante's literary outlook. His brief service in the San Francisco branch of the Office of War Information ended under a cloud, even as he was failing to finish *The Little Brown Brothers*, a long-planned California epic about Filipino migrant workers. Before the decade ended Fante found himself hostage to family life, having fathered three of his four children. More to the point, he had wasted most of that time golfing, drinking, losing at cards, and in general raging against the world. But when Joyce, fed up, challenged him to write or get out, he at last fell back to work.

The result was his one critical and popular hit, 1952's *Full of Life*, a sunny novel about suburban parenthood and reawakening faith which was also a 1956 smash film. But examine the manuscript page in the display case right behind me and you'll see how an editor's red pencil deprived us of a fifth Bandini novel, changing the narrator's name from Arturo Bandini to John Fante. Fante was disappearing into his own fictional alter ego, hiding in plain sight behind the mask of doting and devout husband and father. If this wasn't exactly an act of vanguard political engagement, maybe it wasn't such a bad idea in an age of growing political savagery, when writers were being blacklisted for the charge now aimed at Fante, namely, of being a communist. In fact, Fante's mood had never been blacker than at the height of the Red Scare, but gone now was the wild-eyed young Arturo of yesteryear, replaced by the domesticated middle-aged "John Fante."

Still, for a time the money poured in and soon the family moved to a remote ranch house on Malibu's Point Dume. There Fante would lie low, working when he could as a writer-for-hire, by turns well paid and broke, of mostly unproduced film and television scripts that he hated. In the late 1950s and early 1960s three writing jobs took him to Naples, Rome, and Paris, but these too were largely disappointments. Interviewed about his Naples experience, Fante put on a brave face. "Failure is good," he said. "Not the kind that crushes you, but the kind that . . . drives you on. Failure is a challenge. It is healthy. In a field where all you need is a paper and pencil, what have you got to lose? I like to fail."[4] Brave face notwithstanding, with his books out of print and his focus breaking up in the endless hunt for movie gimmicks, Fante struggled to recapture the magic of youth when the stream of his prose had flowed. Nor could he find anyone to publish the fiction he labored over during the long dry era through the mid-1970s, including "The Orgy," "The First Time I Saw Paris," *My Dog Stupid*, and *1933 Was a Bad Year*. In the end though and against all obstacles he managed to survive the drought.

After searching for over twenty years, Fante finally found the key to writing about his vexed relationship with his father. In 1977 *The Brotherhood of the Grape* was serialized in Francis Ford Coppola's short-lived *City* magazine, with an admiring note by screenwriter Robert Towne. To have two young Oscar winners trumpeting his work—three if we count then future awardee Larry McMurtry, who in reviewing the novel compared it favorably to both *The Brothers Karamazov* and *King Lear*—this late turn was a welcome boon to Fante, whose health was by now badly failing.

And then came Charles Bukowski. In the outlaw author's 1978 novel *Women* the narrator is asked to name his favorite writer. Fante, he answers. And why? "Total emotion. A very brave man."[5] Instincts aroused, Bukowski's publisher, John Martin of Black Sparrow Press, inquired if this John Fante were real or not. Assured that he was real and a great writer, Martin read *Ask the Dust* and at once began planning a reprint. Fante was now blind, legless, and intermittently deranged from the ravages of diabetes, but the news so buoyed him that he had Joyce wheel him out onto the patio with a pen and a yellow legal pad. Over the next two months, his creative energies reborn, he dictated to Joyce his final novel, *Dreams from Bunker Hill*. Nearly half a century after starting, he was completing the Bandini Saga with Arturo now a headstrong studio hack in the madcap Hollywood of 1934, still longing to write great fiction. Close your eyes and imagine writing a page or even a paragraph, much less an entire novel, in an elegiac voice that sums up a time and a place, not to mention a character, as well as your lifelong dreams, and you'll see what a triumph this was—and what a perfect end to a career.

John Fante died in 1983 at the Motion Picture Hospital in Woodland Hills, but his afterlife was only beginning. Black Sparrow Press continued releasing his books to an ardent American readership even as they were being widely embraced in many other languages. Ironically, given Fante's contempt for Hollywood, his life and writings continue to attract filmmakers, both documentary and feature. And though he has yet to be canonized by the *Norton Anthology of Literature*, who's to say what may happen as critical recognition forges ahead and his influence on young writers endures? Meanwhile, the City of Los Angeles has come through with its 2009 dedica-

FIGURE 29. Corner of Fifth Street and Grand Avenue, downtown Los Angeles, with Central Library in background. (Photo by Charles Hood.)

tion of John Fante Square at the historic foot of Bunker Hill, in front of our beautiful public library. On his way to that library in *Ask the Dust*, Arturo sings, "Los Angeles, come to me the way I came to you."[6] Well, our prodigal city *has* come back to John Fante, and will keep coming back as long as it remains built on dreams and desires and in need of its own special guardian spirits (fig. 29).

Which brings us back, with added urgency, to the question of Fante's provocations. How is it that the story of his life and the life of his stories can push some of us into a mode verging frankly on the hagiographic, all that patron-saint stuff, if not outright blasphemy, Fante-was-my-god and so forth? Well, for one thing, if I'm reading it right, there's the outsider effect, the way that being marginalized, beyond settled lines, can lead to overcompensation. The cultishness of cults, we might say, with the extra fervor that results from the us-versus-them dichotomy where the *us* constitutes an initiated if not quite anointed minority. I suppose this is related to the hipness factor, the grooving on the object of this or that relatively private enthusiasm that others live in ignorance of, or, worse, just don't get. We get it, we can point to the lyrics where Sheryl Crow or the Red Hot Chili Peppers sing Fante's praises, or we can pop in for a beer at the skid-row dive bar the King Eddie Saloon at the corner of Fifth and Los Angeles, where in *Ask the Dust* Arturo gets hustled by the tubercular bottle blond—*we* get it. And so taste shades into virtue and virtue is, well, virtuous. And who more virtuous than the saints in whatever heaven we may project to whom we can turn with our need to identify and our desire to be like them, to have a life of our own that paradoxically someone else has already lived, but lived better, more deeply and fully, and who thus can now stand as our model in life and, yes, imperfections aside, as our very own uncanonized patron saint?

And you don't even have to be Catholic. The guy who first called John Fante the patron saint of LA writing was Jewish novelist and screenwriter Michael Tolkin, author of *The Player*, *The Rapture*, and so on. Which is to say that just as there's a patron saint for pretty much everybody—alcoholics, acrobats, spelunkers, sleepwalkers—so too can everybody who wants a patron saint have one. And so, a patron saint for LA writers? Indeed—and why not for readers too?

To be clear and more serious, I'm not saying that the intensely positive and personal reactions inspired by Fante's work result only from overcompensation or the need to belong to a secret society of Those Who Know. Far from. I witness these reactions every time I teach *Ask the Dust* to undergraduates in introductory writing classes, or when I spend entire semesters on Fante's complete works in specialized senior and graduate seminars. I know that the shocked expressions on these young readers' faces—of astonishment, recognition, and sheer delight—are genuine, and that their motivations are pure.

Earlier I mentioned that pure sense I acquired as an undergrad here at UCLA of how through reading and writing I might find a life. While working on the book I had the good fortune of joining a writers' group of local biographers. Actually, the LA BioGroup's motto was "Get a life!" It was a fine group to belong to, filled with professionals as savvy about the craft as they were generous in sharing all it had taught them.[7] More than ten years after finishing my life of John Fante, however, I have to admit I'm not quite so professional any longer. Why? Because I can hardly imagine ever finding another biographical subject to engross me as thoroughly as Fante has, to get *another* life, then the next one, and yet the next. No, not a professional, but an amateur again, as I was when I started out, an amateur in the root sense of the word, from the Latin *amare*, to love, one whose primary motivation is not money or duty or even pride in doing a good job—but love. From the age of twenty-four I loved *Ask the Dust* in a way I had never loved any other book, and when I came to write the life of its author, I loved the strange, sometimes frightening journey I had to make into the experiences, the perspectives, and the spirit of someone who was not myself.

Richard Holmes, the eminent Romantics biographer of Shelley and Coleridge, has spoken of biography as both a pilgrimage and a haunting, "an act of deliberate psychological trespass, an invasion or encroachment of the present upon the past, and . . . the past upon the present, [and] a continuous living dialogue" between biographer and subject.[8] I know now what he means, for the time I spent living and breathing John Fante amounted to a kind of haunting. I haunted him and he haunted me, never more so than when in the middle of my research Joyce Fante fell seriously ill. From the time of John's death in 1983 Joyce had stayed on by herself in the sprawling ranch house on Point Dume's Cliffside Drive. This house was both a curiosity and a sight. Shaped like a giant Y, with two multiroomed wings flying away from each other into the walled and overgrown estate, Rancho Fante was filled with every vestige of John Fante's life, lovingly saved by Joyce through nearly fifty years of marriage and fiercely guarded in her widowhood. But now, in the late 1990s, Joyce was ill and had to be hospitalized; an extended stay in a Santa Monica convalescent home would follow. I should say that in the year or so after winning her permission to do the biography, I had been driving out to visit her in the Cliffside house as often as I could, sharing endless cups of coffee and tape-recording our talks; so that when, before the ambulance drove away, she pressed a key to the front door of the house into my hand and said I was free to continue my researches, I knew what I had to do.

For the next several weeks I spent virtually every day at that house. I rented a big fast Xerox machine, had it delivered, and went to work copying every page of manuscript, every screenplay, every letter, and every other shred of everything else that was crammed into those four black file cabinets on the service porch; and then I began to arrange thousands and thousands of pages on the green felt of the pool table in the library, trying to conjure up the outlines of a life. Did I say it was a wet winter, often storming, with the row of pines outside the windows swaying dark in the ocean wind? Or that a plague of ravens had once infested those trees, driving John to distraction? Joyce told me how she had hired a sharpshooter veteran of the Vietnam War to solve that problem. Now the ravens were gone and the house was empty except for their echoes and a million reminders of the man whose life I was haunting, and whose life was haunting mine.

So I copied and arranged and conjured. Few better ways exist for understanding any writer than by knowing the books that he or she treasured. Cataloguing Fante's books, I learned not only the range of his interests, from literature and history to human anatomy, but also the depth of his absorptions. No mere coincidence that he had reserved a place of honor for the massive four-volume set of *Butler's Lives of the Saints*; or that he had saved the Jesuit prayer manual that failed to govern him in high school. Joyce's books told a different story. While her general reading too was varied it was more strictly literary, leaning toward poetry, biography, and murder mysteries. Her deepest, most serious interest, however, was in the occult. Shelf after shelf groaned with treatises on Wicca, astrological almanacs, and handbooks of incantations and spells. Joyce had been, in fact, a practicing member of a coven, leading the skeptical Carey McWilliams to dub her the Witch of Malibu. Likewise, Joyce had told me how little stock John put in her trafficking in magic; but when, one night, unbeknownst to him, she had recited the ceremonial invocation summoning Anubis, the Egyptian dog god of the dead, Fante reported feeling a looming canine presence in his room, as if the ghost of his beloved bull terrier Rocco had returned.

And now there I was, day after day, alone in that drafty, rambling house, working often long past dark. *Haunting*: that's the word.

Maybe this is what led David Kipen to observe in the *San Francisco Chronicle* that my book was written "with a degree of identification bordering on demonic possession."[9] David meant that in a nice way, I think, and of course the demon trope is apt given all the saints and spirits and gods and monsters that animate the thing. Less spookily, a candid biographer will admit to a couple of the art's dirty little secrets, one, that any biography is also in some degree *auto*biographical, and, two, that biography is the novel that dare not speak its name. Just as Flaubert declared of *Madame Bovary*, "C'est moi," and John Fante said of Arturo's creation, "It's myself," so too does the biographer transmute the thought and the time and the passion of his or her life into the imagined life of someone else, all the while honoring the discipline of fact.[10] There's nothing paranormal about this exchange of selves, as we might call it; rather, it's a process that's thoroughly existential, a scholarly mode of production that takes certain raw materials—documents, interviews, photographs, etc.—and through the sweat of the biographer's brow and a willingness to sympathize turns them into something new: a book. At the same time, it's also an aesthetically creative process inasmuch as shape and tone and rhythm and pulse are as important to biography as they are to the novel. It's a process, in short, both scholarly and creative, its nonidentical twin aspects inseparable.

But, so, there I was, in that haunted, haunting house, sifting through reams of paper, searching for the narrative line of a life. I remembered how in his preface to the Black Sparrow reprint of *Ask the Dust*, Charles Bukowski had described discovering the novel in the downtown Los Angeles Library as a moment when he felt like a man finding gold in the city dump. Surrounded by John Fante's writings, the original pages that had passed through his hands, *I* now felt as if I had stumbled into the lost gold mine itself as I discovered nugget after nugget, unpublished manuscripts that for all I knew were being read now for the first time, by me. And as if I weren't already haunted enough, among these manuscripts I found a ghost story, "The Case of the Haunted Writer" (fig. 3).

In this story the narrating writer of the title buys a house where the previous resident has died, a man by the lugubrious name of Coffin. No sooner does the writer move into the Coffin house and try to start writing, however, than he discovers he can no longer find the words. While his wife redecorates, he slides into deepening paranoia. He purchases a handgun for protection against the noises at night, but even then he cannot escape into sleep. "I lay in the bed of a dead man," he tells us, "felt the curvature of the mattress that had once pressed against his body, and stared at the very ceiling which had been his last view of this world."[11] One of the strangest stories Fante ever wrote, "The Case of the Haunted Writer" reads like unwitting but disturbingly accurate self-psychoanalysis, all the more so when we note that at about the same time he was writing it, the late 1940s, he was also working on a melodramatic movie treatment about a magician's doomed search for the secret of raising the dead, a murder mystery called "The Long Nightmare."[12]

For a writer like Fante, famous for the exuberance of his prose and the fullness of his characters' emotional lives, all this emphasis not only on the dead, and nightmarish efforts to raise them, but also on writers who can't seem to write, may strike us as odd if not perverse. But ponder this. Reviewing *The John Fante Reader* in the *New York Times*, Janet Maslin has suggested that "of all the subjects [Fante] tackled, none brought out the best [in him] more than writer's block." Maslin continues: Fante "was paradoxically eloquent and effusive about wordlessness, making it a haunting"—there's that word again—"a haunting symbol of any artist's isolation." And it's true. From the earliest to the latest his writings trace this darkly comic theme, the writer's lifelong struggle with writing.

Usually the struggle is right there in front of us, as in *Ask the Dust* when for two full days Arturo squares off with his typewriter in "the longest siege of hard work . . . in his life, and not one line done, only two words written over and over across the page: palm tree, palm tree, palm tree" (17). Or later when Arturo has an idea, and it floats "harmlessly through the room . . . like a small white bird. It meant no ill-will. It only wanted to help me. . . . But I would strike at it, hammer it out across the keyboard, and it would die" (27). Or then again, in the short story "The Dreamer": "After three days all I had to show for the ferment of my brain was wads of crushed paper. . . . I pounded my head, rolled on the bed . . . trying to salvage a few sentences."[13]

At other times the writer's anxiety is displaced. In "Altar Boy," for example, Fante's first published story, young Jimmy Toscana accepts the gift of a stolen fountain pen, then tries to brazen out his reaction. "[A] fountain pen does not scare me," Jimmy claims, "but I wanted to run away. . . . Fountain pens are nothing. It is nuts to be scared of them [but] I was scared about something."[14] No amount of denial prevents the fear of fountain pens, or typewriters, which is to say the fear of writing, from returning to the surface, as it does on the last page of the last novel Fante would ever write, *Dreams from Bunker Hill*. For the *n*th and last time, Arturo sits down at his typewriter hoping to write only a single sentence. "But suppose I failed?" he thinks. "Suppose I had lost all my beautiful talent? Suppose it had burned up [and was] dead forever? What would happen to me?"[15]

This is the fear that haunts writers. It's a major reason, I suspect, why Fante is held in such high esteem by so many writers, for he tells the truth about how we can feel—and makes us laugh at ourselves. By the same token, he also tells the truth about the joy that overtakes us when the block dissolves: that's when Arturo's voice soars highest.

> Six weeks, a few sweet hours every day, three and four and sometimes five delicious hours, with the pages piling up and all other desires asleep. I felt like a ghost walking the earth, a lover of man and beast alike, and wonderful waves of tenderness flooded me when I talked to people and mingled with them in the streets. God Almighty, dear God, good to me, gave me a sweet tongue, and these sad and lonely folk will hear me and they shall be happy. Thus the days passed. Dreamy, luminous days, and sometimes such great quiet joy came to me that I would turn out my lights and cry, and a strange desire to die would come to me. Thus Bandini, writing a novel. (*Ask the Dust* 113)

In 1938 Fante had sent his editor at Stackpole Books a long, extraordinary letter, written we can surmise in that same fugue-like state of oneness with his writing. In this letter Fante projected the passage that I've just quoted even as he outlined the whole plot of *Ask the Dust*. In 1990 Black Sparrow Press published that letter as "Prologue to *Ask the Dust*." At the time, when I read it, I was amazed by the prophetic clarity of its vision. At the same time, the ending felt abrupt, even truncated; so that when, years later, alone in the Fante house amid mountains of paper I came upon a brittle brown sheet of typescript that seemed to fit nowhere, it dawned on me: I had discovered the missing last page of the *Prologue*. The complete "Prologue to *Ask the Dust*" can now be found in Fante's final posthumous book, *The Big Hunger*, along with other previously unread stories I found buried in those cavernous file cabinets.

And yet one thing was missing, and I never noticed until it was too late to ask the one person, Joyce Fante, who might have told me where it was or where it had gone. You see, the original manuscript of *Ask the Dust* was not in those file cabinets, nor is it in the John Fante Papers at UCLA. In all the time I spent talking with Joyce, listening to her recall the early days of her marriage and the incandescent time when John was writing the novel, it never occurred to me to wonder about that manuscript. Joyce's memories were so vivid, and they agreed so thoroughly with John's written testimony about how the book had gushed out of him—like a boil "that had to be bled and cleansed"[16]—that I took their words at face value rather than asking to see the manuscript. The result of that oversight is that I now have to believe with no primary documentary evidence to support my belief, that Fante wrote *Ask the Dust* in much the same state of lucid dreaming that he wrote the seventeen-page letter/outline/prologue that he sent proposing the novel to his editor, Bill Soskin. Certainly nothing in Soskin's letters to Fante suggests that the installments he submitted through the early months of 1939 required any serious editorial intervention. And yet how I wish I could hold and read and study the pages that Fante typed, like so many others in the Fante Papers. But no.

When after Joyce's death the extremity of my distraction finally dawned on me, I tried my best to track down the manuscript. John and Joyce's daughter, Victoria Fante Cohen, graciously agreed to my request to accompany her to the family bank, where she unlocked several safe deposit boxes; but the manuscript was not there. I flew to Boston and drove a rental car to the suburbs of Worcester to meet with the widow of John and Joyce's eldest son, Nick, for she was certain that the manuscript had been in Nick's possession at some point before he died. But when she opened the briefcase where she expected it should be, it wasn't there either, no.

Today I am baffled by the blind spot that kept me from questioning such an obvious, such a glaring absence. But there it is, like a gaping hole in the midst of all the other manuscripts I did find, among others "The Criminal," "To Be a Monstrous Clever Fellow," "I Am a Writer of Truth."

A writer of the truth: and suddenly, there it is, the line of a life, John Fante's life, rich, winding, inevitable, from confused juvenile criminality, to early- and mid-adult monstrosity, to the truth and yes timeless and haunting beauty that comes only with age: that's the line I endeavored to trace in my biography of John Fante. And why? Because as Richard Holmes puts it, gazing into "the intensely burning point of a single life [provides the biographer] with an instrument of moral precision and analysis, a way of making sense of [his] own world."[17]

FIGURE 30. From a Fante family album. (Courtesy of John Fante Literary Group LLC. Photo by Charles Hood.)

But what was it Fante said about literary biographers in a 1972 letter to Carey McWilliams? Ah, yes, now I remember: "A curious fact about biographers of writers is their stubborn resistance to reality."[18] Talk about a glass of ice water in the face. But Carey himself was an accomplished literary biographer, of none other than the arch-ironist Ambrose Bierce, who in *The Devil's Dictionary* defined biography as "The literary tribute that a little man pays to a big one."[19] But Fante knew who he was writing to when he wrote to his lifelong friend, and how to write with his tongue in his cheek. I like to think that the ironic severity of Fante's pronouncement prodded me on in my efforts to convey the realities of his life and to weigh the real value of his works. Ultimately, it's for others to judge how well I did or didn't do, and I take responsibility for all my failures. If I have any regrets, and I do, chief among them might be that I didn't go far enough, as far for example as my former student now friend novelist and journalist Alan Rifkin has gone in assessing Fante's importance. In an expansive cover story in the *Los Angeles Times Magazine* entitled "Writing in the Dust," Alan has shown why *Ask the Dust* deserves to be recognized as the wellspring of much if not all contemporary Los Angeles writing, a rich and varied school that rightly could be called Southern California Dream Realism. As failures go that's one I can live with—and in any event, what a strange thing failure can be.

Written decades after *Ask the Dust* and published only posthumously, *My Dog Stupid* is about a washed-up writer consumed with guilt for his failures as a writer, a husband, a father, and a man. "No wonder I couldn't finish a novel anymore," he confesses. "To write one must love, and to love one must understand."[20] In November 1960 John and Joyce's son Nick disappeared, leaving behind a note imbued with a gnawing sense of failure. A brilliant young man, Nick had been operating the mechanical horse-race attraction on the pier at Pacific Ocean Park, a textbook case of underachievement. Now he was imploring his parents not to try to discover his plans or his whereabouts. Hoping to signal a father's concern, and yes, a father's understanding, and love, Fante wrote to a friend of the family who he thought might know something of Nick's flight: "We . . . want to tell him that whether he fails or not in this world is not important to us. Success is too vague a challenge. Maybe even failure is better; certainly, it is more beautiful."[21]

We should all fail half so beautifully as John Fante.

Thank you.

Notes

A slightly different version of this talk was given March 10, 2011, as that year's Bonnie Cashin Endowed Lecture to mark the opening of the exhibit *John Fante: A Life in the Works* at UCLA Library Special Collections, http://jfiala.bol.ucla.edu/fante/index.htm.

1. The "father" of the Los Angeles novel: Tom Christie, "Fante's Inferno." *Buzz*, October 1995, 60. "the patron saint of . . . L.A. writing": Michael Tolkin, quoted in "L.A. Lit (Does It Exist?): A Symposium." *Los Angeles Times Book Review*, April 25, 1999, 8.

2. Bukowski, preface to *Ask the Dust*, 6.

3. Moreau and Fane, *Fante/Mencken*, 36.

4. Jacobson, "Writer John Fante," n.d., c. 1957–1958.

5. Bukowski, *Women*, 200.

6. Fante, *Ask the Dust* (Black Sparrow), 13.

7. Members of the moveable feast that was the LA Biogroup included such Los Angeles-based biographers as Tom Nolan, Noël Riley Fitch, James Curtis, Ann Rowe Seaman, Ed Cray, Kay Mills, Bernice Kert, Carole Easton, Bill

Boyarsky, Margaret Leslie Davis, Beverly Gray, Peter Levinson, Cari Beauchamp, and Jon Krampner.

    8. Holmes, *Footsteps*, 66.
    9. Kipen, "Writer Fante's Life," E7.
    10. Fante, "Prologue, n.p.
    11. Fante, *Big Hunger*, 241.
    12. John Fante Papers, UCLA Library Special Collections, box 13, folder 10.
    13. Fante, *Wine of Youth*, 239.
    14. Fante, *Wine of Youth*, 48–49.
    15. Fante, *Dreams from Bunker Hill*, 147.
    16. Cooney, *Selected Letters*, 294
    17. Holmes, *Footsteps*, 83.
    18. Cooney, *Selected Letters*, 294.
    19. Bierce, *Devil's Dictionary*, 26.
    20. Fante, *My Dog Stupid*, 109.
    21. John Fante in a letter to Teddy Wilcox, November 17, 1960. John Fante Papers, UCLA Library Special Collections, box 27, folder 8.

Works Cited

Bierce, Ambrose. *The Unabridged Devil's Dictionary*. Edited by David E. Schultz and S. T. Toshi. Athens: University of Georgia Press, 2000.
Bukowski, Charles. Preface to *Ask the Dust*, by John Fante. Santa Barbara, CA: Black Sparrow Press, 1980, 5–7.
———. *Women*. Santa Barbara, CA: Black Sparrow Press, 1978.
Christie, Tom. "Fante's Inferno." *Buzz* (October 1995): 60.
Cooney, Seamus, ed. *Fante, John: Selected Letters 1932–1981*. Santa Rosa, CA: Black Sparrow Press, 1991.
Fante, John. *Ask the Dust*. 1939. Santa Barbara, CA: Black Sparrow Press, 1980.
———. *The Big Hunger*. Santa Rosa, CA: Black Sparrow Press, 2000.
———. *Dreams from Bunker Hill*. Santa Barbara, CA: Black Sparrow Press, 1982.
———. "My Dog Stupid." *West of Rome*. Santa Rosa, CA: Black Sparrow Press, 1985.
———. *Prologue to* Ask the Dust. Santa Rosa, CA: Black Sparrow Press, 1990.
———. *The Wine of Youth*. Santa Rosa, CA: Black Sparrow Press, 1985.
Moreau, Michael, and Joyce Fante. *Fante/Mencken: John Fante and H. L. Mencken: A Personal Correspondence 1930–1952*. Santa Rosa, CA: Black Sparrow Press, 1989.
Holmes, Richard. *Footsteps: Adventures of a Romantic Biographer*. New York: Viking, 1985.

Jacobson, Denise. "Writer John Fante Says He Never 'Felt Famous' until He Went to Italy for 'The Roses.'" *Malibu Times*, n.d. (ca. 1957–1958).

Kipen, David. "Writer Fante's Life as Pulp Nonfiction." *San Francisco Chronicle*, March 30, 2000, E7.

Maslin, Janet Maslin. "A Truly Famous Unknown Writer." *New York Times*, February 28, 2002, E9.

Rifkin, Alan. "Writing in the Dust." *Los Angeles Times Magazine*, November 13, 2005.

Tolkin, Michael, et al. "L.A. Lit (Does It Exist?): A Symposium." *Los Angeles Times Book Review*, April 25, 1999, 8.

Acknowledgments

In 2014 we arranged to gather with a few friends in the Anatol Center at California State University, Long Beach (CSULB) to celebrate the seventy-fifth anniversary of John Fante's *Ask the Dust*. The standing-room-only audience that showed up, most of them students, was at first a pleasant surprise, but the exhilaration that kept building throughout that afternoon stayed with us for a long time. How could we let a new generation's feeling for the 1939 masterpiece end there? Four decades after the novel had gone out of print, Charles Bukowski had contributed a preface to the 1980 reissue of *Ask the Dust* that helped give Fante's forgotten novel new life. Nearly four decades after that, was it time for another rebirth?

The answers came tumbling in as we started casting about for a possible corps of fellow believers. Fante scholars, readers, translators, adaptors and just plain fans came forward with the exciting set of essays that make up this volume. Let us begin, then, by thanking all our contributors, whose eclectic, profound, sometimes quirky but always authentic responses to *Ask the Dust* offer the best testimonial anyone could wish for to John Fante's abiding legacy and future spark.

We are particularly grateful to those writers of different stripes who lent their voices to our anniversary gathering five years ago. Thanks to David Kipen, Anna Mavromati, Daniel Gardner, and Miriam Amico for providing that first impetus to measure the vibe of Fante studies today.

Stephen Cooper also presented that day, reading a letter that Fante had written in 1933 to fellow West Coast Italian American writer Jo Pagano confessing his struggles, doubts, and grandiloquent certainty that he, Fante, was destined to write a great novel. That letter, published here for the first time with the kind permission of Jo Pagano's daughter JoJean Pagano Meek, held the audience rapt as they recognized once again the inimitable voice of John Fante, soaring with confidence, plunging in despair, fully intact after lying for decades in a dusty steamer trunk filled with memorabilia belonging to JoJean, aunt to Danny Shain.

It was Danny who had contacted Stephen out of the blue one day to tell him about the letter and ask if he might like to see it. From that moment a friendship was struck, steeped in mutual Fante appreciation, to be sure, but even more so tempered by their shared creative desire to give the author his due. That is how Danny Shain, an artist and the grandson of Fante's friend Jo Pagano, came to design the cover of this volume, the images of which lock into place the author's looming persona together with the names of those gathered to pay him homage under a sad, brave palm tree in the LA twilight. In fact, look closely and you will see Danny's artful nod to the original 1939 Stackpole Sons book jacket in the dusty desert rose hues of the cover's spine.

Few pleasures could match our long breakfast and lunch meetings with Danny Shain at Scotty's on the Strand in Hermosa Beach to exchange ideas and our synergetic yearnings to do this work together, and do it right. Those meetings were all the livelier when James Bell joined in. If we owe any one young writer and assistant a debt of gratitude for his unwavering editorial expertise and bibliographical acumen, it is James, the MFA graduate of CSULB who worked with us tirelessly from a place of reverence for a great writer's work. We are similarly grateful to Manuel Romero, research assistant and coordinator at CSULB's George L. Graziadio Center for Italian Studies, for his administrative support in keeping the project on track.

We would like to thank the CSULB College of Liberal Arts for supporting us through summer stipends and course releases, as well as the George L. Graziadio Center for its generosity in covering permissions, releases, and commissions for the visual and archival materials that appear in the volume. We are also grateful to the Department of English and the Department of Romance, German, Russian Languages and Literatures, as well as our students in each major, for their enthusiasm for all things Fante and for ongoing moral support.

Victoria Fante Cohen, her husband Michael Cohen, and Vickie's brother Jim Fante and the Fante Literary Group LLC all deserve our heartfelt appreciation for supporting this project with permission to reproduce precious family photos and various other materials.

Charles Hood's enthusiastic photographic expertise and at-the-ready availability warrant special credit for the quality of many of the images included in the volume. Also essential in the search for and reproduction of rare images were Molly Haigh of UCLA Library Special Collections, Ned Comstock of the Cinematic Arts Library at the University of Southern California (USC), and Nathan Masters of the USC Libraries.

Genie Guerard of UCLA Library Special Collections helped lay the foundations for this project through her work several years ago in acquiring and archiving the John Fante Papers, and she remains a constant source of help and support in providing access to the papers. To her and the rest of the UCLA Special Collections staff, including Heather Briston, Octavio Olvera, Annie Watanabe-Rocco and others, we owe a particular debt of gratitude.

We wish to thank the Italian American Studies Association for providing a forum to present a sneak preview of the essays that make up this volume at the association's fall 2017 annual conference, held at CSULB under the auspices of the Graziadio Center.

Special recognition is also in order to volume contributor Giovanna Di Lello, artistic director of the annual John Fante Festival held every summer in Torricella Peligna, hometown of John's father. Tiziano Teti, the mayor of Torricella Peligna, as well as the entire organizing committee are to be commended for their concerted efforts in keeping the Fante ties alive between Italy, the United States, and the rest of the world.

Finally, we are grateful to Fordham University Press and the people who have built its prestigious Critical Studies in Italian America series. We extend sincere thanks to series editors Nancy C. Carnevale and Laura E. Ruberto, managing editor Eric Newman, editor Will Cerbone, copyeditor Michael Koch, and Fordham University Press director Fredric Nachbaur, not least for selecting two such astute and constructively critical external reviewers for our book's manuscript as Donatella Izzo of the University of Naples L'Orientale and Fred Gardaphé of the John D. Calandra Italian American Institute at Queens College, City University of New York. Your collective stewardship of our volume has been the best that our profession has to offer.

In closing, as coeditors of this volume we wish to acknowledge our debt of gratitude to one another, in Steve's case for Clorinda's insistence that he return to Fante and finish what he had started, in Clorinda's case for Steve's unveiling of Fante's Los Angeles and helping her understand the city as a unique site of Italian Americana, one whose time has finally come.

Stephen Cooper and Clorinda Donato
California State University, Long Beach

CONTRIBUTORS

MIRIAM AMICO was born and raised in Sicily, where she received a master's degree in Modern Euro-American literature and languages at the University of Palermo with a thesis on John Fante. She now lives in Los Angeles working as a library assistant at the Getty Research Institute. She also conducts research on a variety of subjects, and has cowritten, with professor Clorinda Donato, the interview essay "In Her Own Words: Caterina Salemi's Sicilian-American Journey" published in the journal *VIA: Voices in Italian Americana*.

CHARLES BUKOWSKI, one of America's best-known writers of poetry and prose, was born in Andernach, Germany in 1920 to an American soldier father and a German mother. Bukowski lived in Los Angeles for fifty years. He died in San Pedro, California, in 1994, shortly after completing his last novel, *Pulp*.

STEPHEN COOPER is the author of *Full of Life: A Biography of John Fante*, editor of Fante's *The Big Hunger: Stories 1932–1959* and *The John Fante Reader*, and with David Fine coeditor of *John Fante: A Critical Gathering*. In 1995, he organized "John Fante: The First Conference," a three-day international gathering of scholars, writers, filmmakers, journalists, and Fante family members at California State University, Long Beach, where he is a member of the Creative Writing faculty. His short stories have appeared widely along with essays on literature and film. He developed and coproduced the 2018 Netflix Original documentary *Struggle: The Life and Lost Art of Szukalski*.

GIOVANNA DILELLO, journalist (*L'Espresso, Il Centro*) and cultural events organizer, was born in Hamilton, Canada, to an Italian emigrant family and raised in Vevey, Switzerland. She graduated with a degree in foreign languages and literature from D'Annunzio University in Pescara, and has a master's degree in cultural economy from Tor Vergata University, Rome. In addition to working for the secretariat of the Committee for Italians Abroad in the Senate of the Republic of Italy, chaired by Senator Claudio Micheloni, she has directed many film documentaries including *John Fante: Profilo di scrittore* (2003). Since its founding fourteen years ago, she has been artistic director of the annual John Fante Festival "Il dio di mio padre" in Torricella Peligna, Abruzzo, Italy.

CLORINDA DONATO is the George L. Graziadio Chair of Italian Studies at California State University, Long Beach, and professor of French and Italian. She is an eighteenth-century specialist who has published extensively on encyclopedism, gender, the Protestant enlightenment, and Fortunato Bartolomeo De Felice, an eighteenth-century Italian diaspora intellectual. Recent publications include *The Life and Legend of Catterina Vizzani: Sexual Identity, Science and Sensationalism in Eighteenth-Century Italy and England*, Oxford University Studies in the Enlightenment, Liverpool University Press, 2020. She directs the Clorinda Donato Center for Global Romance Languages and Translation Studies.

JOHN FANTE (1909–1983) was the author of many novels, short stories, and screenplays. Born into a poor Italian American family in Colorado, he made his way west to Los Angeles at the start of the Depression. His experiences there would inform his best-known novel *Ask the Dust* (1939).

VALERIO FERME (PhD, comparative literature, UC Berkeley) is Dean of the McMicken College of Arts and Sciences at the University of Cincinnati. His books include *Tradurre è tradire: La traduzione come sovversione culturale sotto il fascismo* (Longo, 2002); *Women, Enjoyment, and the Defense of Virtue in Boccaccio's Decameron* (Palgrave, 2015); and, with coauthor Norma Bouchard, *Italy and the Mediterranean in the Post-Cold War Era* (Palgrave, 2013). He is also coeditor of *From Otium to Occupatio in Italian Culture, Annali d'Italianistica* (2014) and *Mediterranean Encounters in the City* (2015), and cotranslator of *Southern Thought and Other Essays on the Mediterranean* (Fordham University Press, 2012). He has published over fifty articles and reviews.

TERESA FIORE is the Inserra Endowed Chair in Italian American Studies at Montclair State University. She is the author of *Preoccupied Spaces: Remap-*

ping Italy's Transnational Migrations and Colonial Legacies (Fordham University Press, 2017) and editor of the 2006 issue of *Quaderni del '900*, devoted to John Fante. Her numerous articles on migration to and from Italy linked to twentieth- and twenty-first-century Italian literature and cinema have appeared in Italian, English, and Spanish in both journals and edited collections. Two articles by her on new migration flows from Italy were recently published by Routledge and the University of Illinois Press in volumes about Italians in the United States.

DANIEL GARDNER is an assistant professor of English at Cerritos College where he teaches composition and literature. He earned his PhD in English from the University of California, Los Angeles, in 2014 with a dissertation examining the interplay between popular cultural representations of the mythic American West and early twentieth-century ethnic American fiction. As a member of the UCLA Library Special Collections' Center for Primary Research and Training, Daniel processed the John Fante Papers. He and Stephen Cooper cocurated a 2011 exhibit of items from the collection titled *John Fante: A Life in the Works*.

PHILIPPE GARNIER was born in Le Havre, France, in 1949. For twenty-nine years he worked for the French daily *Libération* as a cultural journalist. As a translator he has introduced many American authors in France, including Charles Bukowski, John Fante, James Ross, and James Salter. He has also interviewed many literary figures and film personalities on French public television. Among his seven books published in France are *Honni soit qui Malibu* (1996), about writers in Hollywood in the 1930s and 1940s; *Caractères* (2006), about classic Hollywood character actors; and *Freelance* (2009), about magazine writer Grover Lewis. His biography of paperback writer David Goodis, *Goodis: A Life in Black and White* was published in 2015.

ROBERT GUFFEY is a lecturer in the Department of English at California State University, Long Beach. His most recent book, cowritten with Gary D. Rhodes, is *Bela Lugosi and the Monogram Nine*. His previous books include the novel *Until the Last Dog Dies* (Night Shade/Skyhorse, 2017), *Chameleo: A Strange but True Story of Invisible Spies, Heroin Addiction, and Homeland Security* (OR Books, 2015), a collection of novellas entitled *Spies and Saucers* (PS Publishing, 2014), and *Cryptoscatology: Conspiracy Theory as Art Form* (TrineDay, 2012). He has also published short stories in the *Mailer Review*, *Pearl*, *Postscripts*, and the *Third Alternative*.

RYAN HOLIDAY is the bestselling author of *The Obstacle Is the Way*, *Ego Is the Enemy*, *The Daily Stoic*, and other books about marketing, culture, and the human condition. His work has been translated into thirty languages and has appeared widely, from the *New York Times* to *Fast Company*. His company, Brass Check, has advised companies such as Google, TASER, and Complex, as well as multiplatinum musicians and some of the most popular authors in the world. He lives in Austin, Texas.

JAN LOUTER (1954) is an independent director of documentaries that are visually and conceptually both imaginative and challenging. He has portrayed writers and artists but is equally interested in social issues transcending local importance. His more than thirty films have all been broadcast in the Netherlands and most of them have screened at national and international film festivals in Europe, the United States, Asia, and Australia. His documentary *A Sad Flower in the Sand* about John Fante had its US premiere in 2001 at the AFI Fest in Los Angeles and was awarded with a Jury Special Mention. It aired nationally on the PBS series *Independent Lens* in 2006.

CHIARA MAZZUCCHELLI is associate professor of Italian studies at the University of Central Florida. She is the author of *The Heart and the Island: A Critical Study of Sicilian American Literature* (SUNY Press, 2015). Her articles have appeared in *Nuova Prosa*, *Forum Italicum*, the *Journal of Modern Italian Studies*, the *Journal of Lesbian Studies*, and *Italian Americana*. Since 2009, she has been editor-in-chief of the semiannual peer-reviewed journal *VIA: Voices in Italian Americana*.

MEAGAN MEYLOR graduated summa cum laude from California State University, Long Beach, in 2016 with a double BA in English literature and English rhetoric and composition. An earlier draft of her essay on Camilla Lopez was submitted as her senior Honors Program thesis. She is currently a PhD student in the Literature program at the University of Southern California, where she is studying nineteenth- and twentieth-century American literature, with a focus on the literary history of Los Angeles.

J'AIME MORRISON is a professor in the Department of Theatre at California State University Northridge where she teaches theatre movement and creates interdisciplinary performances. She was a Fulbright Scholar to Lisbon, Portugal, in theatre movement. Her dance-theatre work and choreography have been performed in Los Angeles, New York, Shanghai,

Dublin, Belfast, and Lisbon. She is currently working on a new dance-theatre piece titled, *When at Last...*, inspired by Ionesco's *The Chairs*.

NATHAN RABIN is a columnist at the *A.V. Club*, *Rotten Tomatoes*, *TCM Backlot*, and *Splitsider*. He is working on a book about the video game and movie *Postal* and Donald Trump. He lives in Decatur, Georgia, with his family.

ALAN RIFKIN is a former *Details* and *LA Weekly* contributing editor who has also written for *Premiere*, the *San Francisco Bay Guardian*, *Los Angeles Times Magazine*, *Black Clock*, and the *Quarterly*. A finalist for both the PEN Center-USA Award in Journalism and the Southern California Booksellers' Award in Fiction, he has led workshops in magazine writing, the short story and creative nonfiction at UCLA Extension, Santa Monica College, Chapman University, and California State University, Long Beach. He is active in the homeless ministry at Saint Luke's Episcopal Church in Long Beach and is the father of three children.

SUZANNE MANIZZA ROSZAK is assistant professor of English at East Carolina University. Her articles on transnational American literature have appeared in *Studies in the Novel*, *Arizona Quarterly*, and *Children's Literature*. Her book *Intersecting Diasporas: Italian Americans and Allyship in US Fiction* is forthcoming from SUNY Press.

DANNY SHAIN, who designed the cover art for *John Fante's* Ask the Dust: *A Joining of Voices and Views*, is a native Angeleno and the grandson of John Fante's friend and fellow Italian American writer Jo Pagano. Danny's paintings and collages have been exhibited internationally and are in several public and private collections, including the Long Beach Museum of Art, close to the setting of his favorite line in *Ask the Dust*: "But, I have to smile, for the salt of the sea is in my blood, and there may be ten thousand roads over the land, but they shall never confuse me, for my heart's blood will ever return to its beautiful source."

ROBERT TOWNE won the Best Screenplay Academy Award for *Chinatown* (1974), Roman Polanski's classic detective neo-noir set in 1930s Los Angeles. Inspired by the dialogue in John Fante's *Ask the Dust* and a chapter in Fante's friend Carey McWilliams's *Southern California Country: An Island on the Land* (1946), Towne's script is now hailed as one of the greatest in film history. His many screen credits include *The Last Detail*, *Shampoo*, *The Firm*, *Mission Impossible*, and *Ask the Dust* (2006), which he wrote and directed. With director David Fincher, he is developing a *Chinatown* prequel series for Netflix.

JOEL WILLIAMS is a fifty-five-year-old Shoshone-Paiute Native American who was raised in Southern California. Incarcerated in a series of California maximum-security prisons for most of his adult life, he began reading extensively, then writing short stories. Those stories have appeared in various literary magazines, chapbooks, a collection in French translation titled *Du sang dans les plumes* (13E Note Editions, 2012), and in two e-books from Amazon Kindle, *A House Burning* and *13 Pieces!* Granted parole after serving twenty-eight years, he is now pursuing a bachelor's degree in agriculture.

BIBLIOGRAPHY

A. O. G. "Rough Romance." Review of *Ask the Dust*, by John Fante. *Cincinnati Enquirer*, December 30, 1939, 5.
Anonymous. "*Ask the Dust* by John Fante." *American Mercury*, January 1940, 114.
Anonymous. "New Novel Written by Ex-student." *Long Beach Press Telegram*, November 10, 1939.
Barry, Iris. "Behind the Orange Blossoms." *New York Herald Tribune*, November 12, 1939, IX9.
Becker, Sharon. "Angels of Destruction: Masculinity, Modernity, and the Fiction of 1930s Los Angeles." PhD diss., Claremont Graduate University, 2008. ProQuest (304673994).
Berry, Lee. "This World of Books: Writer." *Pittsburgh Post-Gazette*, November 18, 1939, 6.
Bessie, Alvah. "An Italian American Who Could Have Been Another Dostoevsky." *San Francisco Chronicle Review* (Sunday edition magazine supplement), September 5, 1982, 7.
Binsse, Harry Lorin. "Ask the Dust, by John Fante." *Commonweal* 31, no. 6 (December 1939): 140–141.
Boddy, Kasia. "Fante's Inferno." *Guardian*, June 9, 2000. https://www.theguardian.com/books/2000/jun/10/fiction.reviews.
Boyd, Malcolm. Review of *Ask the Dust*, by John Fante. *Los Angeles Times*, February 17, 1980, M12.
Brookhouser, Frank. "The Modern American Novel: 2 Realists, One Romanticist." *Philadelphia Inquirer*, November 8, 1939, 29.
Bukowski, Charles. "I Meet the Master." *OUI, For the Man of the Eighties* 13, no. 12 (December 1984): 75.
Caltabellota, Simone, and Marco Vichi, eds. *John Fante*. Rome: Fazi Editore, 2003.
Champlin, Josh. Review of *Ask the Dust*, by John Fante. *Mesa Press*, February 5, 2014. http://www.mesapress.com/top-stories/2014/02/05/book-review-ask-the-dust/.

Christie, Tom. "Finding Fante." *LA Weekly*, December 11, 2003. http://www.laweekly.com/supplement/finding-fante-2137402.
———. "The Great Los Angeles Novel." *LA Weekly*, December 28, 1979.
Clark, Tom. "California Letters: The Luck of John Fante." *Los Angeles Times*, April 9, 1989, M4.
Collins, Richard. *John Fante: A Literary Portrait*. Toronto: Guernica, 2000.
Cooney, Seamus, ed. *Fante, John: Selected Letters 1932–1981*. Santa Rosa, CA: Black Sparrow Press, 1991.
Cooper, Stephen. *Full of Life: A Biography of John Fante*. New York: North Point Press, 2000.
———. "John Fante in the Library." *Italian Americana*, 30, no. 1 (Winter 2012): 97–101.
———. "John Fante's Eternal City." In *Los Angeles in Fiction: A Collection of Essays*, edited by David Fine. Albuquerque: University of New Mexico Press, 1995, 83-99.
———. "John Fante's Great Gift to Los Angeles." *Los Angeles Times*, April 8, 2009. http://www.latimes.com/entertainment/la-etw-fante-appreciation8-2009apro8-story.html.
———. "Madness and Writing in the Works of Hamsun, Fante, and Bukowski." genre: *Madness and Literature*, no. 19 (1998): 19–27.
Cooper, Stephen, and David Fine, eds. *John Fante: A Critical Gathering*. Madison, NJ: Fairleigh Dickinson University Press, 1999.
Crowder, Joan. "Book Gets New Life from Devoted Fans." *Santa Barbara News-Press*, February 2, 1980.
Elliott, Matthew. "Erasure and Reform: Los Angeles Literature and the Reconstruction of the Past." PhD diss., University of Maryland, College Park, 2004. https://drum.lib.umd.edu/handle/1903/2075?show=full.
———. "John Fante's *Ask the Dust* and Fictions of Whiteness." *Twentieth Century Literature* 56, no. 4 (2010): 530–544. ProQuest (1014266830).
Fiore, Teresa, ed. *Quaderni del '900: The Road to Italy and the United States: La creazione e diffusione delle opere di John Fante*. Vol. 6. Rome: Istituti Editoriali e Poligrafici Internazionali, 2006.
Garside, E. B. "John Fante vs. John Selby." *Atlantic Monthly*, December 1939, 716.
Gordon, Neil. "Realization and Recognition: The Art and Life of John Fante." *Boston Review* 18, no. 5 (October/November 1993): 24.
Gosnell, Beverly. "Local Author's Work Focuses on the City." *Malibu Surfside News*, April 10, 1980.
Hansen, Harry. "The First Reader: *Ask the Dust*." *Pittsburgh Press*, November 20, 1939, 35.
Hassett, William L. "She Wasn't What the Doc Ordered." *Des Moines Register*, November 12, 1939, 42.

Hinek, Arjay. "John Fante: Father of the Los Angeles School, Neglected Son of the Lost Generation." PhD diss., Fayetteville State University, 1996. https://digitalcommons.uncfsu.edu/dissertations/AAI1390614/.

Hylen, Arnold. *Bunker Hill: A Los Angeles Landmark*. Los Angeles: Dawson's Book Shop, 1976.

Jack, Peter Monro. "A Brash Young Man in Love with Fame." *New York Times*, November 19, 1939, 7.

Jackson, Joseph Henry. "Mr. Fante Produces an Apt Sequel to the Bandini Story." *San Francisco Chronicle*, November 14, 1939, 15.

Kellogg, Carolyn. "John Fante's 'Ask the Dust' Grows with Time." *Los Angeles Times*, April 7, 2009. http://articles.latimes.com/2009/apr/07/entertainment/et-john-fante7.

Kordich, Catherine J. "John Fante's *Ask the Dust*: A Border Reading." *MELUS* 20, no. 4 (1995): 17–27.

Kordich, Catherine J. *John Fante: His Novels and Novellas*. New York: Twayne Publishers, 2000.

Lankiewicz, Donald. "*Mein Kampf* in America: How Adolf Hitler Came to Be Published in the United States," *Printing History*, no. 20 (July 2016): 3–28.

Lazar, Jerry. "Fante Fever." *California* 14, no. 4 (April 1989): 122–124.

Lee, Patrick W. *Fante, Bandini, and Franklin's American Dream*. MA thesis, California State University, Long Beach, 1997.

Lowe, Katherine Rice. "Two Differing, Enjoyable Novels: Salten's Forest Creatures and Fante's Westerners." *Nashville Tennessean*, December 10, 1939, 8B.

Margaretto, Eduardo. *Non chiarmarmi bastardo, io sono John Fante*. Soveria Mannelli: Rubbettino Editore, 2017.

McCormack, Christopher P. "Cracking the Codes: A Textual and Editorial Examination of John Fante's Literature." PhD diss., McGill University, 2002.

Moreau, Michael. "My Mentor, Mr. Mencken: L.A. Writer John Fante Carried on a 20-Year Correspondence with the Sage of Baltimore." *Los Angeles Times*, April 26, 1987, 22.

Moreau, Michael, and Joyce Fante, eds. *Fante/Mencken: John Fante and H. L. Mencken, a Personal Correspondence 1930–1952*. Santa Rosa: Black Sparrow Press, 1989.

N. L. R. "Review of *Ask the Dust*, by John Fante." *Saturday Review of Literature*, November 25, 1939, 20.

Needham, Ida. "Reviews of Latest Books: Author's Love Remains Despite Complications." *Los Angeles Times*, November 26, 1939, C7.

Noble, Johnny. "Slim Reason for New Tale with Old Hero." *Oakland Tribune*, December 17, 1939, 6B.

Nordine, Michael. "Best L.A. Novel Ever: *Ask the Dust* vs. *Less Than Zero*,

Round 2." *LA Weekly*, March 29, 2013. http://www.laweekly.com/arts/best-la-novel-ever-ask-the-dust-vs-less-than-zero-round-2-4180173.

———. "Best L.A. Novel Ever: John Fante's *Ask the Dust* vs. Charles Bukowski's *Post Office*, Round 1." *LA Weekly*, November 2, 2012. http://www.laweekly.com/arts/best-la-novel-ever-john-fantes-ask-the-dust-vs-charles-bukowskis-post-office-round-1-2370106.

O'Grady, Carrie. Review of *Ask the Dust*, by John Fante. *Guardian*, November 6, 1999.

Pettener, Emanuele. *Nel nome, del padre, del figlio, e dell'umorismo: I romanzi di John Fante*. Florence: Franco Cesati Editore, 2010.

Pleasants, Ben. "The Last Interview of John Fante." *Los Angeles Times Magazine* 39, no. 2 (February 1994): 90–95.

———. "Stories of Irony from the Hand of John Fante." *Los Angeles Times*, July 8, 1979, K3.

Poener, Arthur R. "Able John Fante's Second Novel." *Democrat and Chronicle*, December 17, 1939, 10.

Rifkin, Alan. "Writing in the Dust; the Fabulist Literature that's Peculiar to Los Angeles is the Only American Fiction that's really Worth Reading." *Los Angeles Times*, November 13, 2005, MAG.12.

Ritchie, Ryan. "Unburying Fante." *LA Weekly*, May 13, 2010. http://www.laweekly.com/news/unburying-john-fante-2165004.

Romaine, Paul. "Do not ask the dust, Bandini—act!" *Record Weekly*, December 2, 1939.

Roszak, Suzanne. "Diaspora, Social Protest, and the Unreliable Narrator: Challenging Hierarchies of Race and Class in John Fante's *Ask the Dust*." *Studies in the Novel* 48, no. 2 (2016): 186–204. Project MUSE, doi:10.1353/sdn.2016.0022.

Ryan, Melissa. "At Home in America: John Fante and the Imaginative American Self." *Studies in American Fiction* 3, no. 2 (2004): 185–212. Project MUSE, doi:10.1353/saf.2004.0005.

Scambray, Kenneth. *Queen Calafia's Paradise: California and the Italian American Novel*. Madison, New Jersey: Fairleigh Dickinson University Press, 2006.

Scruggs, Charles. "'Oh for a Mexican Girl!': The Limits of Literature in John Fante's 'Ask the Dust.'" *Western American Literature* 38, no. 3 (2003): 228–245. *JSTOR*, www.jstor.org/stable/43022257.

Sekhon, Sharon E. "Exposing Sin City: Southern California Sense of Place and the Los Angeles Anti-Myth," PhD diss., University of Southern California, 2002.

Sternberg, Ron. "Rereading John Fante's 'Ask the Dust.'" *Los Angeles Review of Books*, December 22, 2016. https://lareviewofbooks.org/article/rereading-john-fantes-ask-dust/.

Svoboda, Alva. "The Consummate LA Novel." *Santa Barbara News and Review*, February 7, 1980.

Thompson, Ralph. "Books of the Times: Bandini." *New York Times*, November 9, 1939, 21.
Tobar, Hector. "Dusting Off A Gritty, Glamorous California Classic." *All Things Considered*, December 28, 2011.
———. "Honoring L.A.'s Lost History." *Los Angeles Times*, May 7, 2009, A2.
Ulin, David L. "Back from the Dust: Scholars Seek to Burnish the Reputation of John Fante, the Legendary Los Angeles Writer." *Los Angeles Times Book Review*, May 14, 1995, 9. ProQuest (293047269).
Vichi, Marco. *John Fante: Fuori dalla polvere*. Florence: Edizioni Clichy, 2005.
Volpe, Gerald. "*Ask the Dust*." *MELUS* 7, no. 2, 1980, 93–95. *JSTOR*, www.jstor.org/stable/467091.
Warga, Wayne. "A Reclamation of Bunker Hill." *Los Angeles Times*, March 5, 1980, F3.

INDEX

Note: Images are indicated by page numbers in *italics*. Fictional characters are alphabetized by first name.

Abruzzo, Italy, 131, 142n22, 177–178, 228
Abruzzo, Ray, 185
acceptance: diasporic communities and, 46–47
"Accolita dei rancorosi, L'" (Capossela), 133, 181–182
"Album of the Year" (The Good Life), 133
Alfred A. Knopf (publisher), 299
Alianò, Sebastian, 19
alienation, 43–49, 52, 54n5, 59, 61, 97, 173–174
Almamegretta (dub group), 138
"Altar Boy" (Fante), 299, 308–309
Amelio, Gianni, 130
American Dream, 47, 128, 135, 142n22, 242–243
American Mercury, The (magazine), 38n21, 129, 141n7, 226, 299
Americana (Vittorini, ed.), 15–16, 23–25, 31, 35n2, 37n14, 38nn32–33, 130, 180
Amidon, Stephen, 188
Ammaniti, Niccolò, 130
Angels Flight (railway), 114–116, 148, 158, 291–292
Apache dance, 120–121
Articolo 31 (hip-hop group), 137
Arturo Bandini: alienation of, 61; Americanism of, 6–7, 32–33, 135; Apache dance and, 120–121; Camilla Lopez as reflection of, 59; and censorship of translations, 25–26; diaspora and, 44–48; Fante *vs.*, 40n46; identity and, 70, 73–76, 91–94, 135–136; insecurity of, 135–136; origin of name, 90, 104n18; as racist, 40n46; religiosity of, 53–54; as representative of modern man, 23; as victim of racism, 91; as white, 90–91; whiteness and, 66, 73–76, 88, 90, 93–96
Ask the Dust (Fante), 208, 255, 269, 278; as object of translation, 25–26; pitching of, 281–282, 283; preface for, 265–268; prologue to, 309. *See also* Arturo Bandini
Ask the Dust (film), 162, 228, 239, 241–242
Aspetta primavera, Bandini! (Ammaniti), 130
assimilation, 47–48, 94, 96, 104n24, 105n26, 114, 122, 135, 178
Auster, Paul, 205
Aznavour, Charles, 160

Babel, Isaac, 198
Badnjevic, Dunja, 187
Balanchine, George, 121
Baldelli, Simona, 187
ballet, sung, 121
Balzac, Honoré de, 160
Bancroft, Anne, 162

331

Bancroft, Hubert Howe, 90
Bandini (publishing house), 189
Bandini, Don Arturo, 90
Bandini, Helen Elliott, 90
Baray, Marie, *63*, 260n5
Baricco, Alessandro, 130
Barolini, Helen, 280n1
Barthes, Roland, 7, 111
baseball, 28–29, 88–90. *See also* DiMaggio, Joe
Baum, L. Frank, 148
Baxter, Warner, *89*
Bear (American Indian prisoner), 193–194
Beauchamp, Cari, 313n7
Beckett, Samuel, 112
Benni, Stefano, 189
Berio, Christina, 253, 257
Bhabha, Homi, 103n2, 104n15
Bible, The, 131
Bierce, Ambrose, 311
Big Hunger, The (Fante), 250, 309
Big Sleep, The (Chandler), 300
Biltmore Hotel, 115, 248, 257, 294
biography, as genre, 305
Black City (film), 172, 180
Black Skins, White Masks (Fanon), 105n28
Black Sparrow Press, 3, 130, 159, 162, 223–224, 227–228, 302
Blaylock, James, 205
Block, Francesca Lia, 202–203, 206, 210
Bompiani, Valentino, 16, 38n33
Borgnine, Ernest, 180
Borchert, Rudolph, 267
Borzage, Frank, 24
Bourgois, Christian, 159–160, 163
Boyarsky, Bill, 312n7
Bozzi, Tonino, 188
Bradfield, Scott, 205
Brambilla, Andrea, 190
Brancaccio, Luisa, 187
Braverman, Kate, 206
Bravo Burro (Fante), 187
Brecht, Bertolt, 121
Brel, Jacques, 260n3
Brontë, Emily, 127

Brooks, Mel, 162
Bruce, Lenny, 242
Brotherhood of the Grape, The (Fante), 133, 167, 172, 181–182, 227, 249, 252, 302
Buck, Pearl S., 36n5
Bukowski, Charles, 3, 9, 133, 137, 145, 151–152, 157–158, 169–170, 175n3, 190, 194, 199, 224, 226, 228, 253, 261, 263-264, *268*, 270, 297, 302, 307; on Fante's early reception, 224; Italian readers and, 182–183; letters between, and Fante, 169–171, 175n3; 186; letter to, from Fante, 262; preface by, 264–267; in Van Sciver, 149, 151–154; *Women*, 130
Bukowski, Linda, 261
Bunker Hill, 68, 115–116, 148, *238*, 290–295, *291*
Burnett, W. H., 300
Bunker Hill (journal), 245, 250
Burroughs, William, 149, 205
Bush, Kate, 127
Butler, Octavia, 205

Cabell, James Branch, 149–151
Cain, James M., 243
Caldwell, Erskine, 19–20, 23, 36n5
Caltabellonta, Simone, 183
Camilla Lopez (character), 58–77, *63*, 86-87, 94-99, 105n31, *116*, 118–120, *124*; Apache dance and, 120–121; basis of, 256–257, 260n5; as colonial subject, 96–97; as dancer, 120–121; in film adaptation, 239–240; in music, 132–133
Camino nella polvere, Il (Vittorini), 15, 17–18, 24–34, 37n14
"Can't Stop" (Red Hot Chili Peppers), 132
Capossela, Vinicio, 133–134, 141n17, 181–182, 185, 191
Carroll, Lewis, 127
"Case of the Haunted Writer, The" (Fante), 307–308
Cashin Lecture, 10, 277, 296–312
Cassano, Franco, 143n32

Catholicism, 49–54
Céline, Louis-Ferdinand, 180
censorship, 16, 19, 24–28, 27, 30–31, 34, 38n33
Chandler, Raymond, 154, 198, 238, 243, 300
Cheever, John, 206
Chiedi alla polvere (Baricco), 130
"Chiedi alla polvere" (Citizen Kane), 134
"Chiedi alla polvere" (Marracash), 137
"Chiedo alla polvere" (Perturbazione), 134
Chinasky, Vincenzo Costantino, 181–182
Chinatown (film), 243, 249
Chump Change (Fante, Dan), 179, 251–253
Christie, Tom, 312n1
Churchill, Winston, 230
Ciarcelluti, Monica, 189
Cimini, Mario, 187
Citizen Kane (rock band), 134
Cixous, Hélène, 73
Clark, Charles Edward, 222
Clifford, James, 43–45
Clooney, George, 244
Cogo, Flavio, 37n13
Coletti, Duillio, 172, 180
Collins, Richard, 141n7, 142n23
colonialism, 83, 96–97, 103n10
Condemned, The (Pagano), 284
Conte, Richard, 226
Conversazione in Sicilia (Vittorini), 17, 24
Cooder, Ry, 122, 206
Cooper, Stephen, 36nn6,8, 40n46, 59, 67, 78n19, 104n18, 117, 141n13, 168, 171, 199, 207, 209, 224, 226, 231–232, 246, 250, 260n5; conversation with, 273–279; on Fante's politics, 67; *John Fante, Profilo di scrittore* film and, 179; John Fante literary festival and, 188; talk by, 296–312
Coppola, Francis Ford, 172, 227, 240, 249, 302
Cranston, Alan, 228–229
Cray, Ed, 312n7
Crenshaw, Kimberlé, 55n17
Criminal Novel (De Cataldo), 189

Crosby, Bing, 115, 290
Crow, Sheryl, 132, 304
Cruciani, Federico, 190
Curtis, James, 312n7

Dago Red (Fante), 38n21, 300
D'Agostino, Peter R., 55n19
dance, 120–121. *See also DUST* (dance theatre)
dance halls, 104n24
Davis, Margaret Leslie, 313n7
Day of the Locust, The (West), 203, 210, 243, 300
Days Between Stations (Erickson), 145–146
De Carlo, Andrea, 188
De Cataldo, Giancarlo, 189
de Certeau, Michel, 112
Defoe, Daniel, 17
De Gregori, Francesco, 133–134, 186
De Laurentiis, Dino, 172, 180, 226
Delgadillo, Efren, Jr., 115
Del Rio, Dolores, 89, 103n9
Depp, Johnny, 241
DeRosa, Tina, 172
Deruddere, Dominique, 163n3
desert, 6, 26, 35, 77, 87, 98, 100, 111–113, 116–118, 121, 123, 147, 206, 246
Deverell, William, 71
diasporic communities: acceptance and, 46–47; alienation in, 43–44; collective history in, 45; defining, 44–48, 54n5; displacement and, 45–46; music and, 134–140; religion and accommodation of host culture by, 49–50; religious ambivalence and, 53–54; selective accommodation and, 43–44, 47–48, 52; spirituality as tie in, 51. *See also* Italian Americans
Dick, Philip K., 205
Dickens, Charles, 205
Didion, Joan, 202–203, 207
Di Donato, Pietro, 19, 190, 280n1
Diehl, Digby, 297
Dillard, Annie, 204
DiMaggio, Joe, 28–29, 46–47, 88–89, 135

Dinesen, Isak, 154
Di Pietrantonio, Donatella, 187
Di Renzo, Gianluca, 188
Di Terlizzi, Elisabetta, 189
Dire Straits, 127
"Dirty Old Man" (column, Bukowski), 157
displacement: of Arturo Bandini, 34; of Camilla Lopez, 72; diaspora and, 45–46; *DUST* and, 112
Divine Comedy, The, 131
Djian, Philippe, 163
Doe, John, 202
Dogo Gang (rap group), 137
Dog Soldiers (Stone), 203
Donato, Clorinda, 191
Donne donne (Women women) (Varchi), 183
Dos Passos, John, 299
Dostoevsky, Fyodor, 6, 199
Double Indemnity (film), 243
Dowd, Maureen, 119
Dowson, Ernest, 71–72
"Dreamer, The" (Fante), 308
Dreams from Bunker Hill (Fante), 3, 141n13, 151, 168, 228, 249, 302, 309. *See also* Arturo Bandini
Drew, Roland, 89
Dreiser, Theodore, 23
Du Bois, W. E. B., 66
Dunaway, Faye, 249
Durante, Francesco, 130, 180, 187
DUST (dance theatre), 111–125, *116*, *124*
Dust of Via Bellini, The (Bozzi), 188
Duterte, Rodrigo, 231
Dylan, Bob, 186

Easton, Carole, 312n7
Editrice Tespi (publishing house), 189
Eher-Verlag (publishing house), 214
E il cagnolino rise (And the little dog laughed) (collection), 189
Einaudi (publishing house), 130
Elliott, Matthew, 54n1, 64, 75, 135
Emerson, Ralph Waldo, 221

Enemy Alien Act of 1940 (US), 38n33
Erickson, Steve, 145–146, 203–204, 207, 209, 211n3
Essex, Harry, 2
Exene (punk musician), 202

fabulist fiction, 202, 206, 211n3
Falk, Peter, 249
Falqui, Enrico, 37n15
Fanon, Frantz, 105n28
Fante, Dan, 179, 185, 188, 251–253
Fante, Dorina, 177
Fante, Jim, 188, 227, 232, 247
Fante, John, *195*, *262*, *298*, *264*, *311*; background of, 299; death of, 302; letters between, and Bukowski, 169–171
Fante, Joyce, 141n13, 159, 162, 179–180, 225, 228, 249–250, 252, 256–257, 259, 260n5, 269n1, 274–277, 279, 300–302, 305–306, 309–310
Fante, Nick (father), 134, 142n22, 177, 178–179, 182, 184, 299
Fante, Nick (son), 252, 310, 312
Fante, Victoria, 179–180, 188, 310
Fante, Vincenzo, 182
Fante Bukowski (Van Sciver), 149, *150*, 151–155
Farinaccio, Luigi, 187
Farrell, Colin, 228, 241, 259
Farrell, James, 128, 142n21
Fascism, 6, 15–17, 25–26, 27, 38n33, 66
Faulkner, William, 19, 36n5, 37n17, 78n18, 80n40, 154, 211n3, 226, 300
Federal Housing Administration, 80n42
festival, literary, 177, 184–191, *186*
film adaptations, 2, 226, 228, 239–242
films, American, in Fascist Italy, 38n33
Fiore, Teresa, 141n17
"First Time I Saw Paris, The" (Fante), 302
Fitch, Noël Riley, 312n7
Fitzgerald, F. Scott, 154
Flaubert, Gustave, *286*, 307
Florio, Fabio, 188
Flynn, Gillian, 119
Foster, Norman, 2

France, 157, 159–160, *161*, 162–163, 185, 190, 222, 228
Franklin, Benjamin, 243
Frascella, Cristian, 187
Freud, Sigmund, 146–147
Full of Life (Cooper), 36n8, 188, 207, 226, 284
Full of Life (Fante), 162, 167, 301
Full of Life (film), 226
Full of Life (Rava), 187

Gable, Clark, 237
Gadda, Carlo Emilio, 17
Gaiman, Neil, 151
Galasso, Domenico, 185
Gallione, Giorgio, 190
Galsworthy, William, 17
Gandolfo, Simon, 190
Garcia Lorca, Federico, 112
Gardaphé, Fred, 190
Gardner, Daniel, 277, 296
Garnier, Philippe, 190, 209
Garofano rosso, Il (Vittorini), 17–19, 23
Gay, Roxane, 229
gender, 5; and "bisexual spaces," 78n18; in Crenshaw, 55n17
gender politics, 94–95
gender roles, 75
gendered dynamics, 75
gendered spaces, 60
Gilbert, Sandra M., 76
Golden Days (See), 203
Golden Wedding (Pagano), 284
Good Life, The (musical group), 133
"Goodbye, Bunker Hill" (Fante), 290–295, *291*
Goodis, David, 160
Gordon, Neil, 223
Graham, Martha, 120
Grande fame, La (Mazzucco), 130
Grapes of Wrath, The (Steinbeck), 300
Gray, Beverly, 313n7
Gray, Zane, 152
Great Depression, 2, 26, 34, 46, 61, 77, 88, 215, 256

Grey, Zane, 36n5
Gubar, Susan, 76
Guerard, Genie, 296
Guidelli, Giovanni, 190
Guitiérez, David G., 68
Guns N' Roses, 127
Guthrie, Woody, 262

Hackmuth, J. C., 129, 131, 141n7, 152
Hagamoro, Tetsu, 292
Hamill, Pete, 274
Hamsun, Knut, 6, 26, 160, 163, 194, 199, 246, 250, 261
Handel, George Frideric, 245
Handley, William, 85
Hannibal, 138
Hartmann, Christian, 231
Hayek, Salma, 162, 228, 239, 241–242
Hayworth, Rita, 207, 211
Heinlein, Robert, 151
Hemingway, Ernest, 36n5, 154, 198, 299
Henderson, Jasper, 189, 245–259
Hilton, James, 300
historicity, 67–69, *69*
Hitler, Adolf, 1–2, 9, 214–219, 220, 221, 222–232, 240, 300
Hockney, David, 245–246
Hoffmann, E. T. A., 146–147
Holliday, Judy, 226
Hollinger, David A., 55n19
Holmes, Richard, 305, 310
"Home Is the Hunter" (Fante and McWilliams), 99
Hotel del Coronado, 148
Houdini, Harry, 112
Houghton Mifflin (publishing house), 214–222, 228–230
Hunger (Hamsun), 160, 163, 246
Hurston, Zora Neal, 154
Huxley, Aldous, 154
Hyry, Tom, 296

Ianniello, Enrico, 187
Immigration Acts of 1921 and 1924, 67
Intuitionist, The (Whitehead), 205

336 Index

Italian Americans: assimilation of, 49; mementos and, 277–278; music and, 134–140; prejudice against, 46; religiosity of, 55n20; in *The Road to Los Angeles*, 40n46; whiteness and, 88. *See also* diasporic communities
Italian Unification, 142n24
Italianità, 3, 174
Italoamericana (anthology), 180
It's All True (film), 301

Jackson, Helen Hunt, 7, 61, 83
J-Ax (hip-hop artist), 137
jail, 193–200
Jewish diaspora, 44
"JJ Leaves LA" (Lanois), 121–122
John Fante, Profilo di scrittore (film), 178–183
John Fante First Book Prize, 187
John Fante Square (Los Angeles), 302–303, *303*
Joyce, James, 112
"Julius Knipl, Real Estate Photographer" (Katchor), 205–206
Jurgen: A Comedy of Justice (Cabell), 151
Justine, or Good Conduct Well Chastised (Sade), 171

Katchor, Ben, 205–206
Kazan, Lainie, 207
Kemperman, Leonoor, 259
Kent, Ira Rich, 216
Kerouac, Jack, 180
Kert, Bernice, 312n7
Kim Jong-un, 231
Kipen, David, 307
Klein, Norman M., 61, 78n14, 205
Kordich, Catherine, 54n1, 59, 72, 142n21
Krampner, Jon, 313n7
Kropp, Phoebe, 94, 103n2
Kundera, Milan, 153

LA Biogroup, 312n7
Lady Esther (radio show), 2
Laing, R. D., 202

Lance (American Indian prisoner), 194, 198
Lange, Dorothea, 160
Lankiewicz, Donald, 218-219
Lanois, Daniel, 121–122
Last Tycoon, The (Fitzgerald), 210, 243
Laughlin, Henry, 219
Laughlin, James, 37
Laurila, Mark, 79n33
Lawrence, D. H., 17
Leiber, Fritz, 151
Lennon, Garry, 118
Leonardo (publishing house), 130
LeRoy, Mervyn, 220
Levinson, Peter, 313n7
Lewis, Jerry, 160
Lewis, Nathaniel, 85
Lewis, Sinclair, 23, 36n5
Ligabue, Luciano, 134
literary festival, 177, 184–191, *186*
Little Brown Brothers, The (Fante), 209, 301
"Little Dog Laughed, The" (Fante), 131
Lolita (Nabokov), 127–128
London, Jack, 36nn4–5
Los Angeles, 168–169, 201–211, 243, 245–246, *303*
Louter, Jan, 245–259, 260n4
Lovecraft, H. P., 154
Lummis, Charles Fletcher, 88
lynchings, 46–47
Lyons, Charles, 118

Mack, Lulu, *116*, 119
Mailer, Norman, 279
Malamud, Bernard, 205
Mandelli, Francesco, 189
Mangione, Jerre, 280n1
Manheim, Ralph, 229
Mansfield, Jayne, 207
Marazzi, Martino, 130
Marcos y Marcos (publishing house), 130
Margaretto, Eduardo, 188
Marracash (rapper), 136–138
Marroni, Francesco, 190
Martin, Jay, 212n5
Martin, John, 3, 159, 223, 228, 250, 302

Martone, Maria, 20
Maslin, Janet, 231, 282, 308
Maupassant, Guy de, 160, *286*, 299
Mazzucco, Melania, 130, 189
McMurty, Larry, 302
McNamara, Kevin, 79n33
McWilliams, Carey, 2, 60, 66–67, 78n20, 84–86, 97, 99, 220, 300, 306, 311
Meek, JoJean Pagano, 285
Mein Kampf (Hitler), 1–2, 214–219, 221, 221–231, 240
Mencken, H. L., 103n9, 128–129, 152, 162, 191n4, 256, 258–259, 299–300
Mexican repatriation, 67–69, *69*, 79n27, 98–99, *286*
Mills, Kay, 312n7
mirage, 117
Mondadori (publishing house), 27, 130
Monicelli, Giorgio, 16
Montale, Eugenio, 17
Montefoschi, Paola, 25–26, 36n7
Mossino, Alberto, 187
Mozart, Wolfgang Amadeus, 180, 224
Mule Creek State Prison, 193
music: Fante in panorama of American and Italian, 132–134; Italian American ethnic experience in, 134–140; at Torricella Peligna literary festival, 186–187
musicality, 112
Mussolini, Benito, 6, 30, 38n33
Muzzatti, Andrea, 37n14
My Dog Stupid (Fante), 162, 249, 302
"My Father's God" (literary festival), 177, 184–191, *186*
My Last Movie Star (Sherrill), 203

Nabokov, Vladimir, 127
Native Americans, 97–98
Nduccio (cabaret artist), 190
Newsome, Cindy, 296
Nicholson, Jack, 237, 239, 249
Nicholson, Joy, 204, 206
Nietzsche, Friedrich, 49–50, 203, 299
1933 Was a Bad Year (Fante), 178, 302
Nolan, Tom, 312n7

Norm (American prisoner), 194
Norris, Frank, 23
Norton Anthology of Literature, 302
Notes of a Dirty Old Man (Bukowski), 157
Nunn, Kem, 205
Nussbaum, Felix, 214

O'Connor, Flannery, 198
"Odyssey of a Wop, The" (Fante), 104n19, 178
Olvera, Octavio, 296
Open City (weekly), 157
"Orgy, The" (Fante), 302
originality, 149–151
Otis, Harrison Gray, 87
Our Ecstatic Days (Erickson), 204, 207
Our Lady of Guadalupe, 117, 122
Our Lady Queen of Angels (mission chapel), 50
Oz book series (Baum), 148

Pagano, Ernest, 284
Pagano, Jo, 284–285, *286–288*
Paine, Tom, 243
Pan (Hamsun), 26
Paoletti, Gianni, 188
Paris, Texas (film), 122
Pascal, Blaise, 202
Pavese, Cesare, 16
Pavolini, Alessandro, 38n33
Pelú, Piero, 134
Penn, Sean, 253, 260n2
Pensiero meridiano, Il, 143n32
Perturbazione (rock band), 134
Pessoa, Fernando, 112
Picolla borghesia (Vittorini), 23
Plascencia, Salvador, 206, 211
Play It as It Lays (Didion), 203, 207
Pleasants, Ben, 227–228
Polanski, Roman, 249
Police, The (rock band), 127
Post Office (Bukowski), 157
Powers, Tim, 151, 205
Praz, Mario, 17
Prezzolini, Giuseppe, 171

prison, 193–200
"Prologue to *Ask the Dust*" (Fante), 309
Proust, Marcel, 200n1, 245
Pulp (Bukowski), 154
Purcell, Helen, 287
Putin, Vladimir, 231
Puzo, Mario, 4
Pylon (Faulkner), 37n17

Rabi, Dustin, 121
Rabinowitz, Paula, 77, 80n46
race: American Dream and, 242–243; in Fante's time, 242; gender and, 55n17; in *The Intuitionist*, 205; Mussolini and, 30; in Raiz, 139; and Vittorini translations, 29, 31; whiteness and, 66, 70, 75–76, 88, 90–91, 93–96
racism, 7, 30–31, 40n46, 47, 55n17, 59, 62, 65–67, 70–71, 74, 85, 91–93, 98, 100, 155, 209, 241–242, 250–251
Raiz (dub artist), 136, 138–140, 142n31, 186
Ramona (film), 103nn9,10, 104n18
Ramona (Jackson), 7, 61, 83–88, 89, 97–98, 102, 103n5
Rava, Enrico, 187
Realism. *See* Southern California Dream Realism
Red Hot Chili Peppers, 128, 132, 304
redlining, 75, 80n42
religion: in *Ask the Dust*, 48–53; and diasporic accommodation of host culture, 49–50; Italian diaspora and, 53–54, 174
restrictive covenants, 80n42
Reve, Gerard, 248
Ricci, Nino, 188
Riders of the Purple Sage (Grey), 152
Rifkin, Alan, 311–312
Rivera, José, 206
Roach, Joseph, 115
Road to Esmeralda, The (Nicholson), 204
Road to Los Angeles, The (Fante), 40n46, 99, 141n13, 151, 167, 299–300. *See also* Arturo Bandini

Robinson, Kim Stanley, 205
Rodocanachi, Lucia, 17–18
Rodriguez, Sixto, 226
Rodondi, Raffaella, 16
Romano, Alessio, 189
Roosevelt, Franklin Delano, 215
Rossi, Luigi, 188
Roth, Henry, 142n21
Ruiz, Vicki L., 69
Rusca, Luigi, 15–16, 20, 24
Russo, Richard, 204
Ryan, Melissa, 54n1

Sad Flower in the Sand, A (documentary), 245–248, 253–254
Sade, Marquis de, 171
Safran, William, 43, 54n5
Salinger, J. D., 248
Sam (American Indian prisoner), 198
Sánchez, George J., 68–69
sand, 146–147. *See also* desert
"Sandman, The" (Hoffmann), 146–147
Santaolalla, Gustavo, 122
Saroyan, William, 19–20, 22–23, 34, 36n5, 137, 223, 284
Sarri, Maurizio, 191
Sbarbaro, Camillo, 17
Scaife, Roger, 215
Scarpelli, Furio, 180–181
Schnell, Judith, 223, 231
Scholten, Jaap, 189
Scruggs, Charles, 54n1
Seaman, Ann Rowe, 312n7
secularization, 54n2
See, Carolyn, 202–204
selective accommodation, 43–44, 47–48, 52
Seth, Vikram, 204
Setzer, Dawn, 296
Seven Deadly Sins, The (sung ballet), 121
sexual identity, 51
Shain, Danny, 284
Sheen, Martin, 249
Sherrill, Martha, 203, 207, 211
Simpson, O.J., 242

Sinatra, Frank, 274
Smart, Joyce, 300. *See also* Fante, Joyce
Smart, Justine, 171
Sogni di Bunker Hill (Amelio), 130
Solo sigari quando è festa (Only cigars when it's a party) (Romano), 189
Soskin, Bill, 2, 217–219, 220, 227–228, 281, 310
Southern California Country: An Island on the Land (McWilliams), 84–85
Southern California Dream Realism, 207, 210, 312
Spanish past, 65, 70, 84–88, 92–96, 104n25
Spotnitz, Frank, 224–226
Stackpole, Edward, Jr., 217, 219–220
Stackpole Sons (publishing house), 1–2, 58, 217–225, 227, 231, 281, 309
Steele, Victoria, 296
Steinbeck, John, 19, 142n21, 154, 206, 300
Sterling, Christine, 88, 93
Stone, Robert, 203, 210
Strada per Los Angeles, La (Veronesi), 130
Strong, Gary, 296
sung ballet, 121
"Superstar" (Crow), 132
"Swimmer, The" (Cheever), 206

Talese, Gay, 279
Teatro de Esperanza (theater collective), 79n37
Teele, Arthur, 216
Teti, Tiziano, 185
Theobald, Katharine, 219
Thompson, Dorothy, 216
Thoreau, Henry, 221
"To Be a Monstrous Clever Fellow" (Fante), 149, 151, 310
Tolkin, Michael, 304, 312n1
Tondelli, Pier Vittorio, 130
Torricella Peligna, Italy, 179, 184–186
Towne, Chiara, 258
Towne, Luisa, 258
Towne, Robert, 2, 9, 162, 227, 237–244, 249, 252, 257–258, 302
Trading with the Enemy Act, 228–229

"True Story of John Fante in Torricella, The" (Di Renzo), 188
Trumbo, Dalton, 284, 300
Turpin, Waters Edward, 37n17
Tuzi, Federica, 187

UCLA Library Special Collections, 273, 275–277, 279, 296–297, 298
Unbearable Lightness of Being, The (Kundera), 153

Vandehei, Peter, 116
Van Empel, Erick, 254
Van Gogh, Vincent, 224
Van Sciver, Noah, 149, 150, 151–155
Van Straten, Henk, 189
Varchi (novelist), 183
Vargas, Alberto, 205
Venegas Yolanda, 96
Vera Rivken (character), 29, 72, 95–96, 99–102
Verga, Giovanni, 143n29
Veronesi, Sandro, 130, 182–183, 185–186, 189
Vichi, Marco, 183–184, 191
Vigne, Daniel, 162
Vincenzoni, Luciano, 180–181
Vittorini, Elio, 15–34, 130
Vittorini, Rosa, 17–18, 37n13

Wagner, Bruce, 205
Wait Until Spring, Bandini (Fante), 1, 141n13, 151, 157–158, 182, 218, 300; censorship and, 26–28, 27; critical success of, 36n6; Italian translation of, 16; Nick Fante in, 142n22; Vittorini and, 15–16, 19–20, 24–25, 37n14. *See also* Arturo Bandini
Waits, Tom, 262
Warner Bros., 3–4
Watanabe-Rocco, Annie, 296
Waugh, Evelyn, 201–202, 210
Webb, Clive, 46
Weill, Kurt, 121
Welles, Orson, 2, 226, 301

West, Nathanael, 154, 202–203, 243, 300
Whitehead, Colson, 205
whiteness, 66, 70, 75–76, 88, 90–91, 93–96. *See also* race
Whitewashed Adobe (Deverell), 71
whitewashing, 71
Wilcox, Teddy, 313n21
Wilder, Billy, 243
Women (Bukowski), 130, 183, 302
writer's block, 282–284

Wyatt, David, 59, 105n31
Wylie, Andrew, 231

Yamamoto, Paul, 162
Yiannopoulos, Milo, 229
Young, Loretta, 103n9

Zacchigna, Graziano, 184
Zola, Émile, 23, 143n23, 160
Zweig, Stefan, 214

Critical Studies in Italian America

Nancy C. Carnevale and Laura E. Ruberto, *series editors*

Joseph Sciorra, ed., *Italian Folk: Vernacular Culture in Italian-American Lives*

Loretta Baldassar and Donna R. Gabaccia, eds., *Intimacy and Italian Migration: Gender and Domestic Lives in a Mobile World*

Simone Cinotto, ed., *Making Italian America: Consumer Culture and the Production of Ethnic Identities*

Luisa Del Giudice, ed., *Sabato Rodia's Towers in Watts: Art, Migrations, Development*

Nancy Caronia and Edvige Giunta, eds., *Personal Effects: Essays on Memoir, Teaching, and Culture in the Work of Louise DeSalvo*

Teresa Fiore, *Pre-Occupied Spaces: Remapping Italy's Emigration, Immigration, and (Post-)Colonialism*

Giuliana Muscio, *Napoli/New York/Hollywood: Film between Italy and the United States*

Danielle Battisti, *Whom We Shall Welcome: Italian Americans and Immigration Reform, 1945–1965*

Stephen Cooper and Clorinda Donato, eds., *John Fante's* Ask the Dust*: A Joining of Voices and Views*

www.ingramcontent.com/pod-product-compliance
Lightning Source LLC
Chambersburg PA
CBHW030432300426
44112CB00009B/958